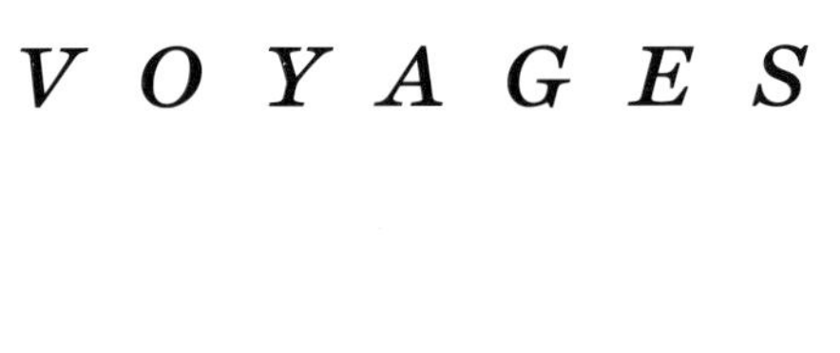

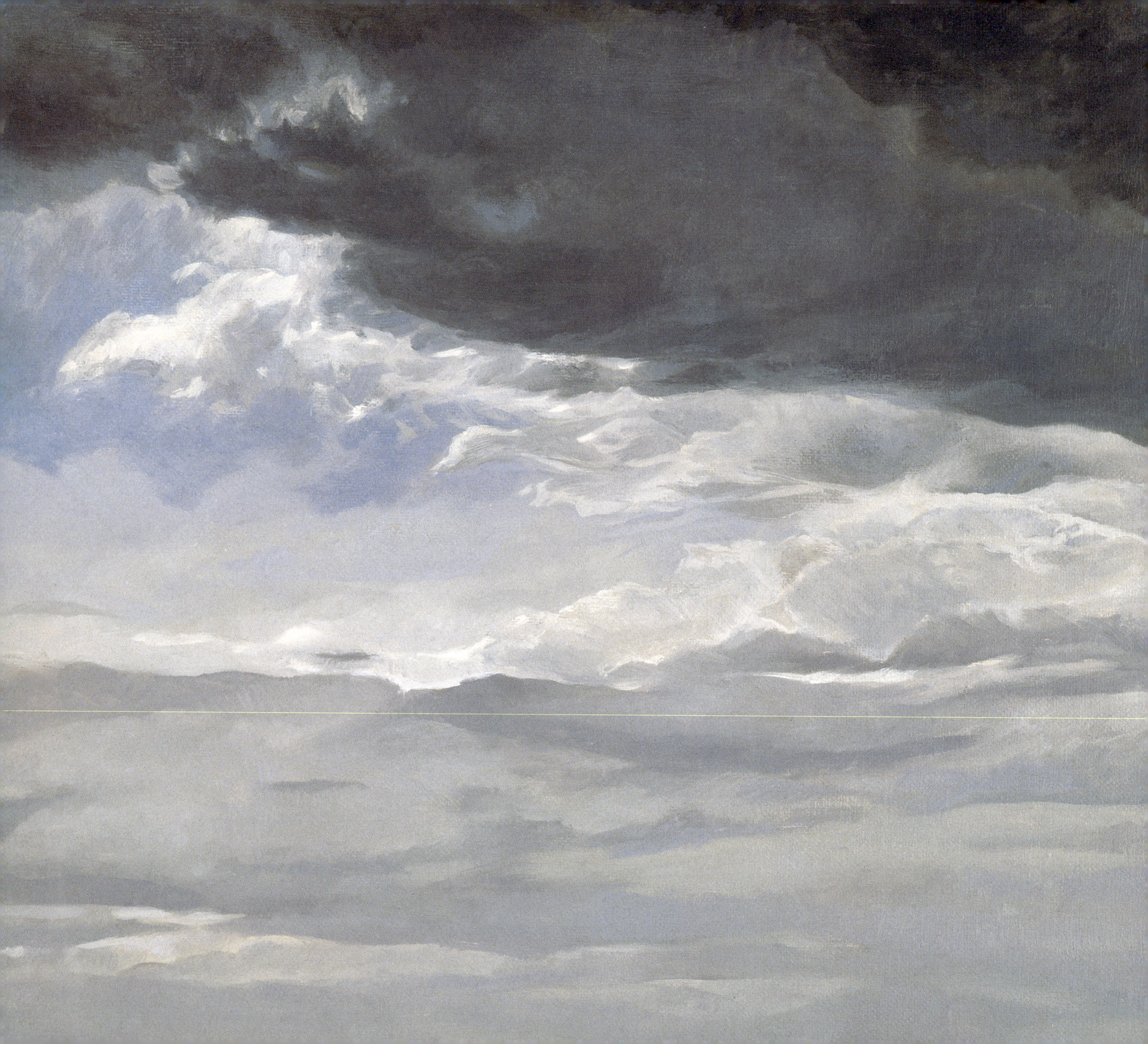

GORDON MILLER

VOYAGES

TO THE NEW WORLD AND BEYOND

Douglas & McIntyre
D&M PUBLISHERS INC.
Vancouver / Toronto

University of Washington Press
Seattle

For my wife, Dale, my constant reminder of what is truly important in life.

11 12 13 14 15   5 4 3 2 1

Douglas & McIntyre
An imprint of D&M Publishers Inc.
2323 Quebec Street, Suite 201
Vancouver BC Canada V5T 4S7
www.douglas-mcintyre.com

Cataloguing data available from Library and Archives Canada
ISBN 978-1-55365-573-2 (cloth)
ISBN 978-1-55365-289-2 (ebook)

Published simultaneously in the United States of America by University of Washington Press
PO Box 50096
Seattle, WA 98145-5096
www.washington.edu/uwpress

Library of Congress Cataloging-in-Publication Data
Miller, Gordon.
Voyages : to the new world and beyond / Gordon Miller.
p. cm.
ISBN 978-0-295-99115-3 (hardcover : alk. paper)
1. Discoveries in geography—History. 2. Voyages and travels—History.
3. Ships—History. 4. Explorers—History. I. Title.
G80.M575 2011
910.9—dc22   2011010707

Editing by John Eerkes-Medrano and Ruth Wilson
Jacket and text design by Jessica Sullivan
Jacket paintings by Gordon Miller
Maps by Gordon Miller
Printed and bound in China by C&C Offset Printing Co., Ltd.
Text printed on acid-free paper

Douglas & McIntyre gratefully acknowledges the financial support of the Canada Council for the Arts, the British Columbia Arts Council, the Province of British Columbia through the Book Publishing Tax Credit and the Government of Canada through the Canada Book Fund for our publishing activities.

Key to captions: WC = watercolor. Dimensions are paper size, in inches; images are slightly smaller. Oil sizes are canvas or panel sizes, in inches. Height precedes width.

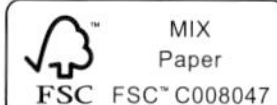

CONTENTS

INTRODUCTION

IN THE MID-EIGHTEENTH century sailing ships began appearing on the northwest coast of America, the last temperate coast in the world to be discovered by Europeans. These ships were in the final years of a journey that had begun four centuries earlier and thousands of miles away. Lured by the riches and mystique of the Orient, the men who sailed them had explored most of the world's oceans and coastlines and had helped to define the size and grandeur of the planet.

My home for many years has been on Canada's west coast, in a city named after George Vancouver, the great British navigator who slept only one night on the shores of the inlet where the city is situated. The coastal charts of British Columbia and Alaska are liberally sprinkled with British and Spanish names. Commemorating monarchs, benefactors, captains, mates, ships and battles, they are the endowment of the first literate visitors to these waters. Occasional native names survive—oddly spelled interpretations of the languages of the Haida, Salish, Kwagiuth and Nuu-chah-nulth peoples—but for the most part the names are a celebration of faraway people and places, the legacy of the first European explorers and the settlers who followed them.

This book and the paintings in it arose from my desire to know more about the maritime history of this coast and about the men and ships that first ventured here. This remote corner of the world could only be reached by ship, and then only after months at sea traveling thousands of leagues of uncharted oceans and rounding at least one of the world's great southern capes. The ships that made these voyages were the product of many centuries of evolution, and their navigators were the beneficiaries of decades of accumulated experience. The ventures that began with the Norse in the first millennium ended in the eighteenth century with the arrival of the first sailors off these misty, magical shores.

This book offers a Eurocentric version of history: medieval Arabs were great seafarers, with centuries of trading experience in the Mediterranean Sea and the Indian Ocean, and the Chinese were master shipbuilders who also made trading voyages to the Indian Ocean and East Africa; but the Arab traders did not venture farther, and the Chinese eventually restricted their sailing to their home waters. It was seamen from the Iberian peninsula, Italy, France, the Netherlands, Britain and Scandinavia who ventured into the unknown and defined the true dimensions of the oceans and coastlines of the world.

The rich fishing grounds of northern seas and oceans drew Europeans offshore, but the driving force behind their world exploration was their passion for the luxuries of life. First it was the spices and other exotic products of the Orient, followed by gold and ivory from Africa. Then it was gold, silver, beaver pelts and coffee from the Americas, and finally the rich pelts of sea otters on the northwest coast of North America. We know the shape of the world today because ships, driven only by wind and human muscle, were navigated into every last bay and estuary on Earth, searching for wealth and glory.

I live four short blocks from the beaches of Burrard Inlet, and it has always been a comfort to think that the waters lapping these shores are connected to the seas sailed by Leif Ericsson and Christopher Columbus, and that any small vessel sailing southwest from here would eventually cross the paths of the great navigators Ferdinand Magellan, Francis Drake, James Cook, William Bligh and even Joshua Slocum.

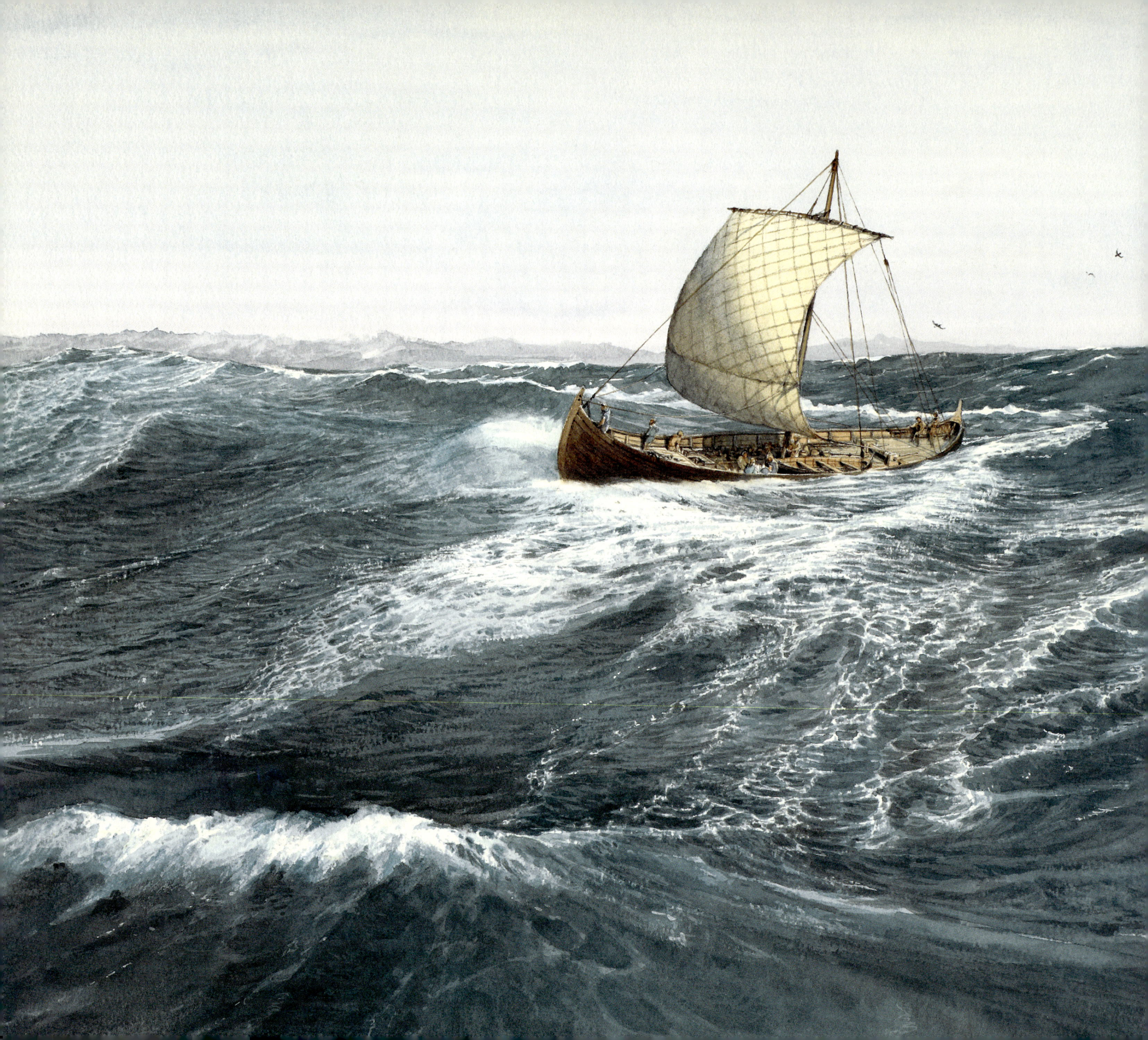

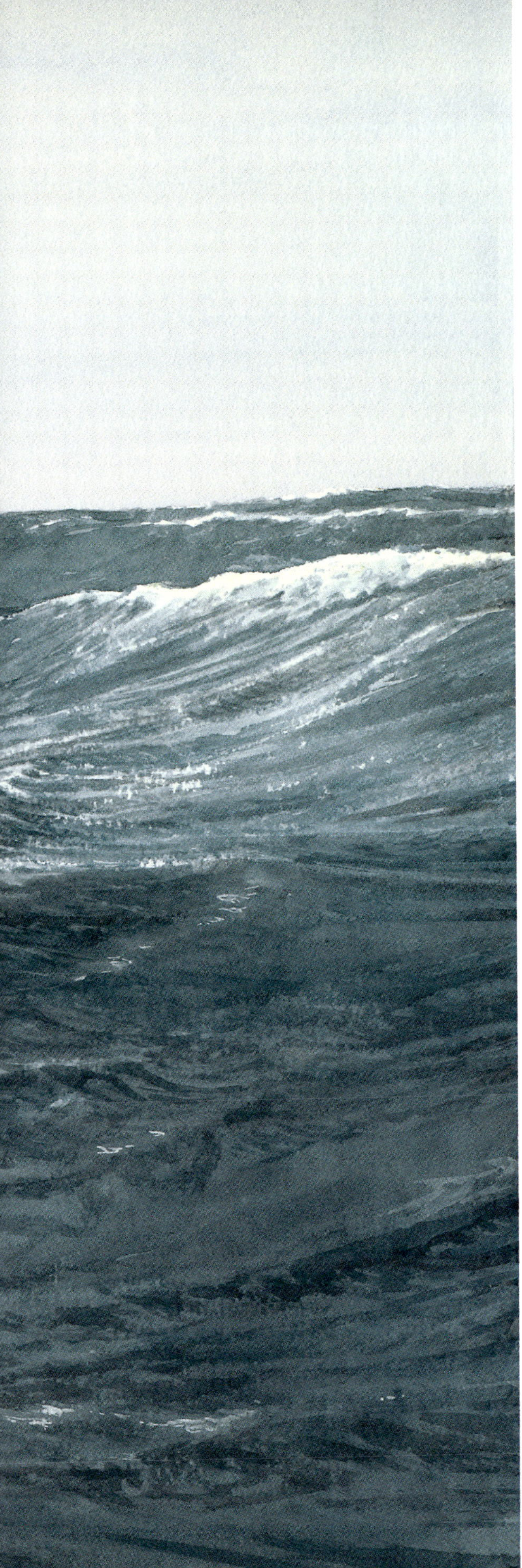

Leif Ericsson west of Greenland (WC, 15″ × 22″)
Almost five hundred years before Christopher Columbus "discovered" America, Leif Ericsson set off to explore the land seen earlier by Biarni Heriulfson. After a landfall on Baffin Island, Ericsson and his crew explored coastal areas of Labrador and northern Newfoundland. They stayed one winter, most likely at L'Anse aux Meadows, before returning to Greenland.

1

ANCIENT SHIPS AND EARLY NAVIGATION

For as long as humans have been standing upright, they have been on the move. About 150,000 years ago our ancestors, only a few thousand in number, lived in East Africa, exploited the same environment, presumably shared similar beliefs and spoke the same language. From this small population emerged the world's first explorers, who gradually spread across the globe until all but the polar extremes were inhabited. They adapted to a variety of new environments, developed into many diverse cultures having innumerable languages and, over time, largely lost touch with one another.

In the environments these people adapted to, they developed new techniques for survival. High among their achievements was the creation of practical and beautiful

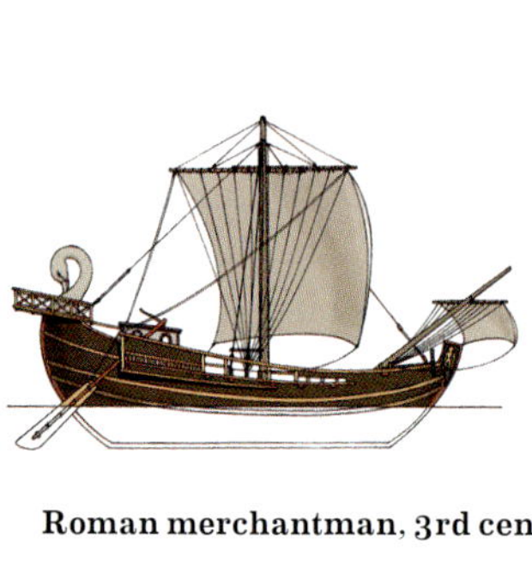
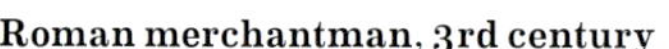
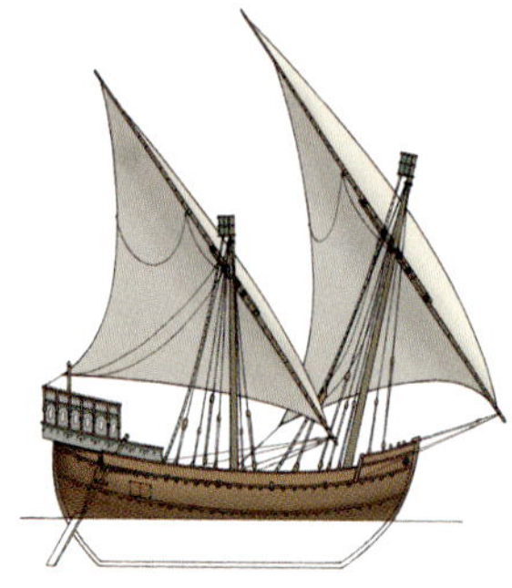

MEDITERRANEAN TRADITION

Roman merchantman, 3rd century

Venetian ship, 13th century

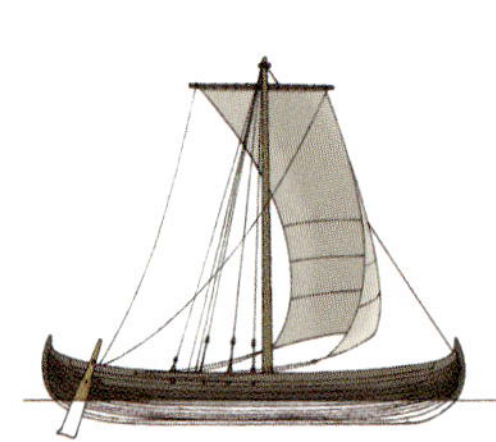
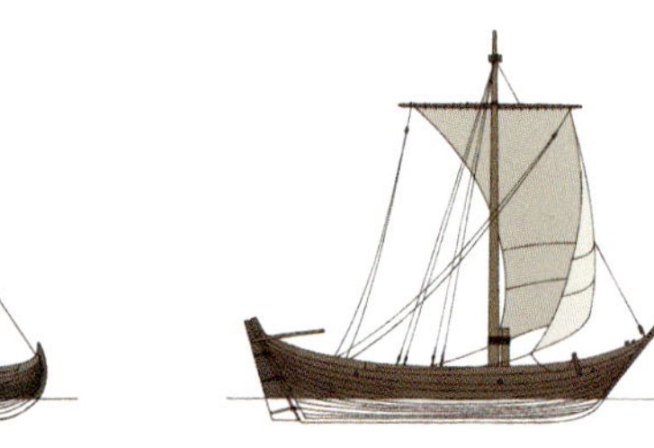
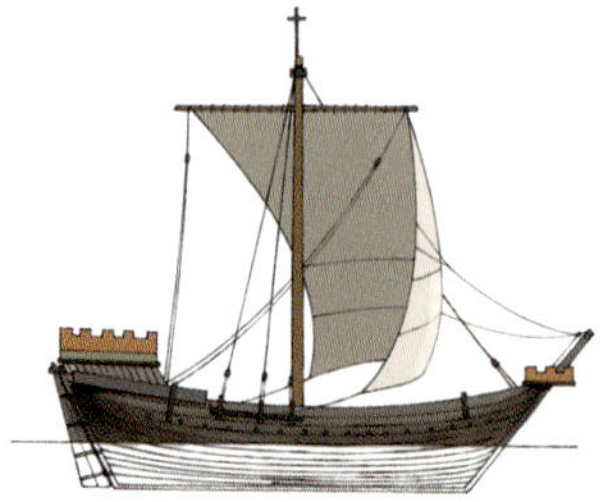

NORTHERN TRADITION

Norse *knarr*, 10th century

Gotland ship, 12th century

Hanseatic cog, 13th century

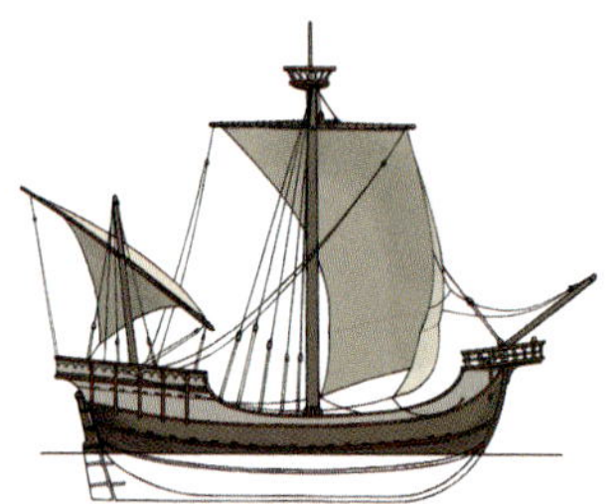
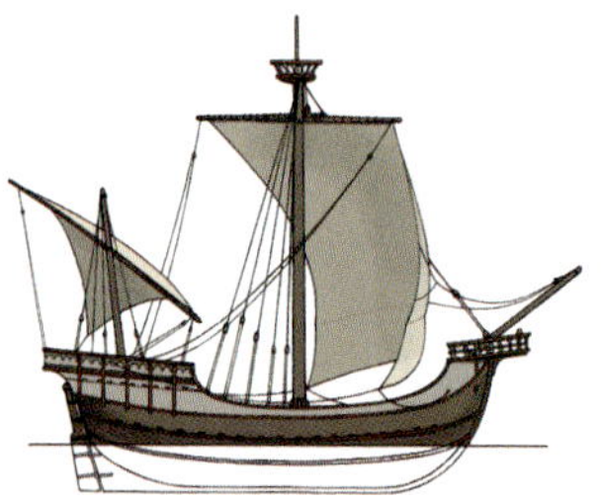
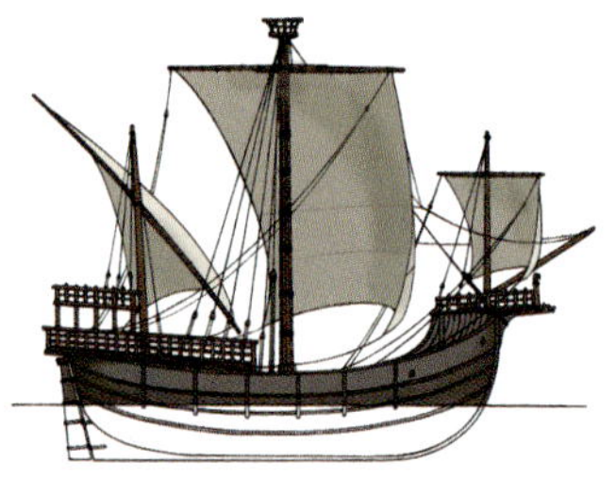
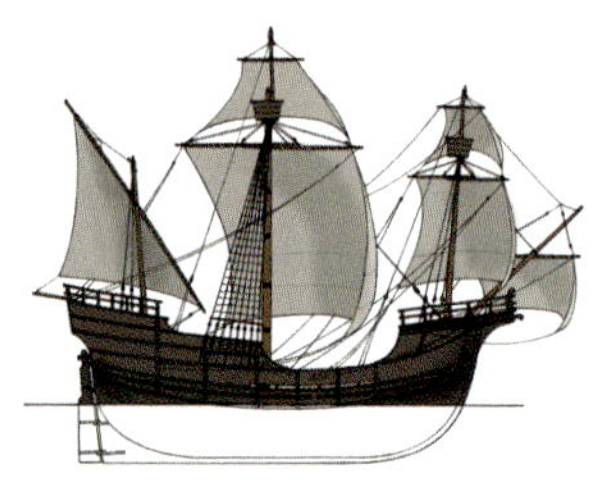
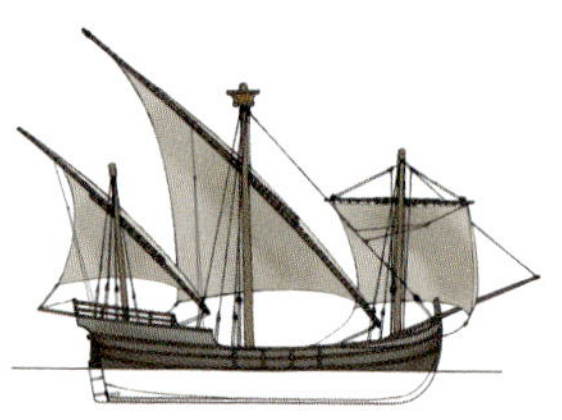

COMBINED MEDITERRANEAN AND NORTHERN TRADITIONS

Carrack, 14th century

Carrack, 1450

Nao, 1490

Caravel, 1490

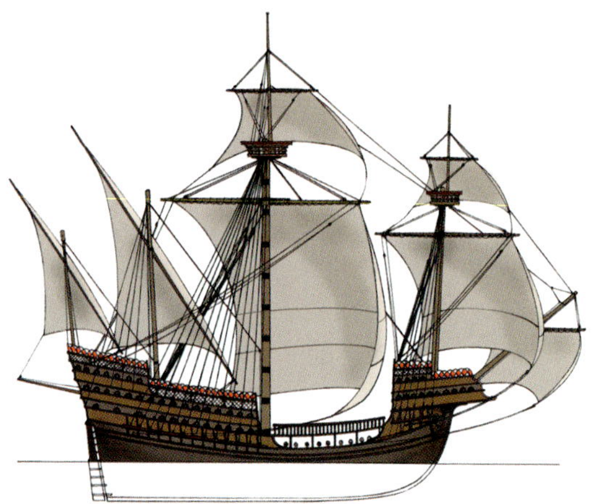

Carrack, 1520

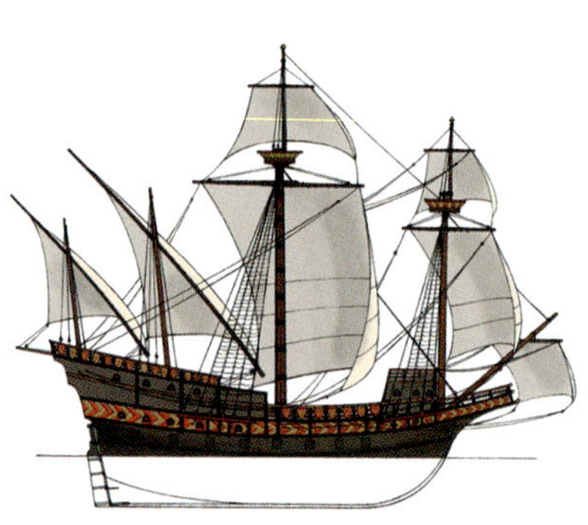

Spanish galleon, 1540

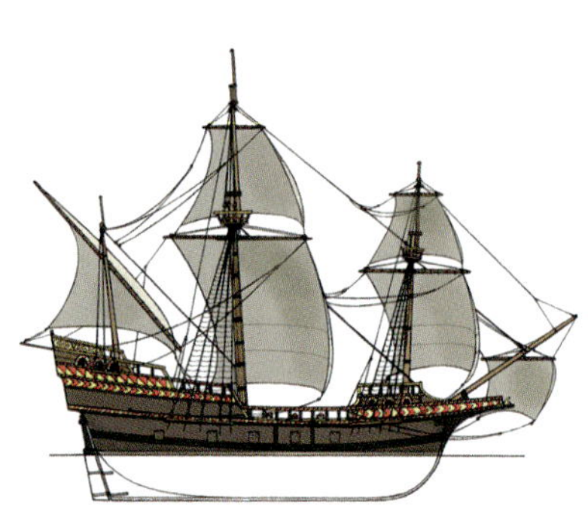

English galleon, 1570

watercraft. In the past ten thousand years or so, these vessels have been improved and enlarged, reaching a state of refinement capable of taking people safely around the world. The sailing ship was the instrument that finally reconnected the many cultures and societies that had scattered around the globe.

Adding planks to the top edges of a dugout log was the first step in the development of wooden boats. Over many centuries of trial and error, and in response to local needs and conditions, these dugouts evolved into distinct and functional watercraft. Adding a sail was a natural next step. From the first simple rig, sailing ships have been evolving for more than four thousand years. They have a longer history than any other human technology, and at the height of their refinement they were the most advanced and elegant form of technology developed. By the fifteenth century, they had evolved to the point where they could sustain themselves and their crews for long periods at sea and return safely to their starting points.

The Origins of Seafaring Ships

Seaborne trade flourished at the height of the Roman Empire, and Mediterranean ships moved unmolested from the Caspian Sea to the British Isles, but after the Roman withdrawal from northern and western Europe in the fifth century, these regions descended into a bleak, chaotic period. Coastal trade was still active in spite of the disorder, but little is known about European ships from this period.

From early town seals and from a growing number of illustrations, it is possible to follow the evolution of European ships. From simple, open and undecked boats, they progressed to become two- and three-masted ships with permanent structures at the bow and stern. Almost all medieval merchant ships were broad in relation to their length and were obviously meant to be sailed, not rowed.

Mediterranean ships were always "carvel-built"—their internal frames were set up first and the planking was applied over, with the edges butted and caulked. Early Atlantic coastal traders were small, sailed short distances and carried few goods. They were "clinker-built"—their planks overlapped and were clenched together at the edges, the internal framework of ribs and beams installed afterwards to stiffen the hull—and had a single mast and a square sail. All early ships were steered with an oar or side rudder, but as the size and height of their hulls increased, steering oars became impractical, and eventually a rudder was fixed permanently to the stern.

Square sails, which had predominated in the Mediterranean until the fourth century, were by the ninth century replaced by the triangular "lateen" rig introduced by the Arabs. The lateen rig provided better windward ability, but as ship sizes increased the enormous yards needed to support the sails became extremely heavy and cumbersome. The square sail of Atlantic and Baltic tradition, although not able to sail as close to the wind, could be managed by a much smaller crew. Increasing trade

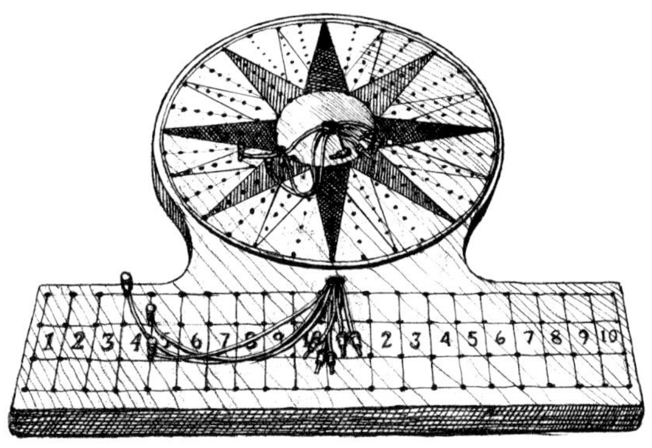
Traverse Board

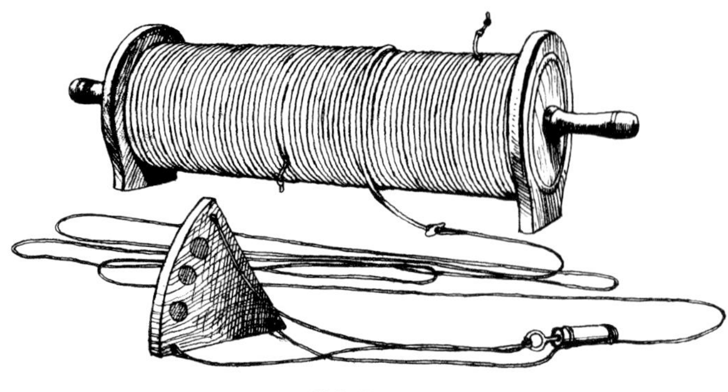
Chip Log

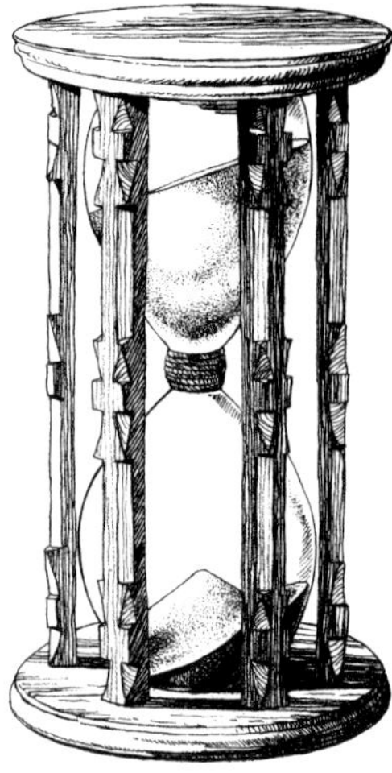
Sandglass

^ left to right *The* TRAVERSE BOARD *was used by illiterate sailors to keep track of a ship's speed and direction on each four-hour watch. Every thirty minutes, pegs were inserted in a hole that marked the compass heading, and the speed was measured by the log.*

The CHIP LOG, *by measuring the length of line that paid out in a measured period, was used to estimate a ship's speed. The line was divided in fifty-seven-foot, four-inch sections, each marked with a knot—thus, a ship's speed was measured in knots.*

A half-hour SANDGLASS *would be turned, and a bell rung, every thirty minutes. If each watch was four hours long, the glass would be turned eight times; thus the watch would be eight bells long.*

made both the Mediterranean and the Atlantic/Baltic sail traditions familiar to all European shipbuilders. Sometime in the fifteenth century these shipbuilders began to combine the best features of each tradition—carvel plank-on-frame hulls, with a rig that combined both lateen and square sails. This, in various combinations of rig, was the form of ship that first ventured offshore from the Iberian peninsula at the close of the fifteenth century.

With few exceptions medieval ships were merchant or fishing vessels that could do double duty during times of war. Early warfare at sea was conducted much as it was on land, at close quarters with bows and lances. High stages at bow and stern and fighting tops on the masts allowed seamen to fire down on an enemy deck. The objective was to disable enough of the enemy to board their ship. The introduction of small firearms did not alter the procedure, but eventually the use of cannons led to gunnery from a distance. This was a major influence on the design of ships after the sixteenth century, when they were beginning to be built specifically as warships and ship types began to be more specialized.

Early Navigation and Life at Sea

Early sailors who left their familiar shores for a voyage into the unknown undoubtedly hoped to return safely home. They rarely ventured out of sight of land, reaching their destinations by keeping the land visible on one side outbound and on the opposite side going home.

A requirement for making successful passages into the open sea was the ability to fix a position on the surface of the globe when no known landmarks were in sight. The earliest instrument for determining latitude by measuring sun angles was probably the Greek *scaphe*, a vertical pin in the center of a series of concentric circles, whose shadow length at noon would indicate the sun's elevation above the horizon. The Norse voyagers to the west used a

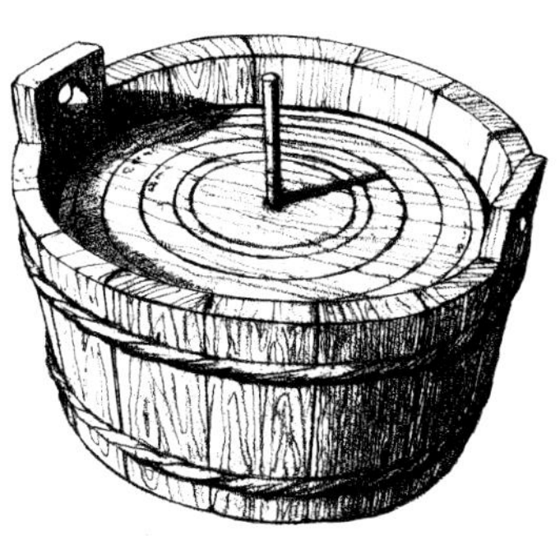

Solskuggafjol

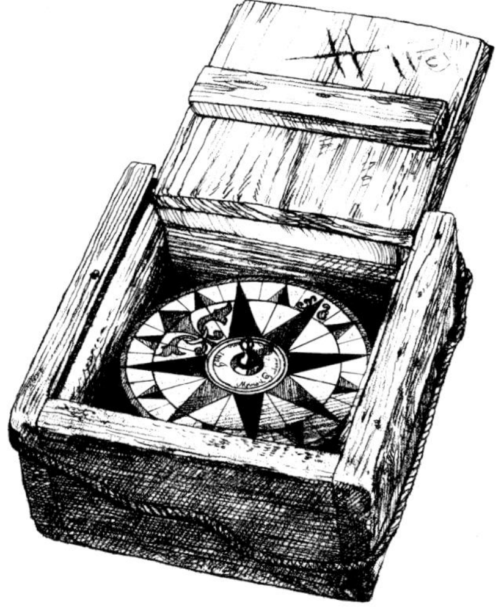

Compass

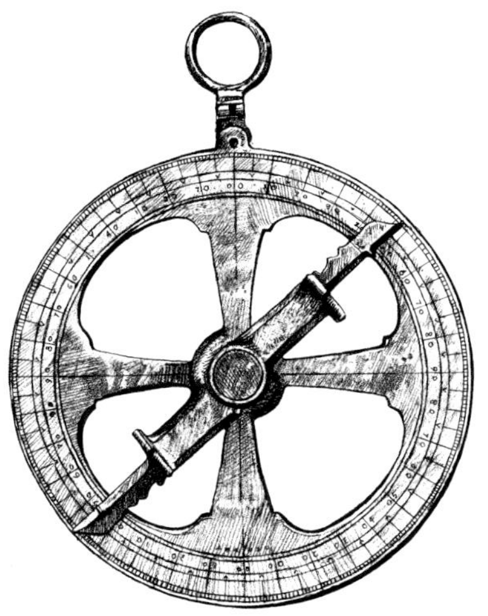

Astrolabe

similar instrument called a *solskuggafjol*, a wooden disk with a center pin floating in a tub of water. The shadow of the pin fell across concentric circles that had been calibrated to known latitudes. As the sun's angle changed gradually through the seasons, the pin was calibrated vertically to correspond to the time of year. With this simple device, and the accumulation of knowledge over time, the Norse made many successful voyages to Iceland, Greenland, Newfoundland and the east coast of North America.

The astronomical astrolabe and the steering compass were both available in Europe by the end of the thirteenth century. Latitude was easily calculated on land by measuring the angles of the sun and the stars above the horizon, and pilots always knew the latitude of their point of departure. To reach another known port, the ship was sailed to that latitude and then stayed on it until the destination was reached. Later European explorers had more sophisticated instruments, such as quadrants, for measuring sun and star angles. Although not perfect, these instruments enabled explorers to make long voyages and find their way back to their starting points. This was the practice until late in the eighteenth century, when accurate timepieces made it possible to determine longitude with certainty. The sextant with which eighteenth-century sailors charted the globe was the refined culmination of these earlier instruments.

Before electric lights polluted night skies and dimmed the stars, the shape and movement of the constellations were as familiar to navigators as the paths and byways around their homes. By the nineteenth century, as navigation instruments improved and tables were developed, an accurate position anywhere on Earth could be determined by star sights alone. To sailors at sea, the heavens provided a dependable instrument to guide them and a comforting aid to fixing their position on the oceans. A star ahead could be used by a helmsman as a point to steer

▲ left to right *The* SOLSKUGGAFJOL *was a Norse device for identifying latitude by marking the end of the center pin's shadow on a floating disk at noon.*

The mariner's COMPASS *had a magnet attached to a circular card, which kept it oriented to magnetic north. The card was divided into thirty-two equal parts with four cardinal points: north, south, east and west.*

The ASTROLABE *was an instrument for measuring the altitude of the sun and stars. It consisted of a graduated brass ring with a sighting rule pivoted in the center.*

towards, and the height of the pole star above the horizon was an easy and dependable check for latitude.

Right to the end of the age of sail, seamen lived uncomfortable, brutal and dangerous lives. The little *naos* and caravels of the early explorers had no accommodation for the crew. Men lived on open decks, slept wherever they could find shelter from the wind and were warm and dry only when the weather was fair. The first voyages from Spain and Portugal were made in temperate or subtropical zones, but as these passages lengthened the men had to endure first tropical and eventually subarctic conditions without any form of shelter. Hot meals were prepared on open fires on deck on a bed of sand, but only when conditions were right and firewood lasted. When the ships became large enough to have forecastles they were still unheated, crowded, damp and unventilated spaces in the bow, where the motion was constant and most violent.

Because they could be called out at any time, the crew was often sleep-deprived and overworked. Crewmen were considered expendable and a lower form of life. They were, nevertheless, essential, so ships often left home with twice the crew needed, in the hope that enough would survive to get the ship home. Food, except for the first days out, was never fresh, seldom adequate and often barely edible. Unless the men were lucky enough to work a ship that took prizes, chances were that after a voyage of several years their pay would cover only their expenses ashore for a week or two. As a final indignity they were at the mercy of the officers, who had absolute control of every moment of their lives and could even order their deaths. Some of these mates and masters were notorious for their brutality and kept discipline only with corporal punishment and constant fear. Not surprisingly, many sailors deserted at the first opportunity, and mutiny was not uncommon.

The Norse Seafarers and the *Knarr*

It may never be known who the first seaman to leave the familiar coasts of Europe, sail off into the sunset and return to tell about it was. What is known is that the Shetland Islands have been occupied for more than three thousand years, and when the first Norse sailors reached Iceland in AD 870 a community of Irish monks was already living there. The monks had probably arrived in skin-covered wicker boats called curraghs. Propelled by a square sail, curraghs were tough enough to carry a small crew with adequate stores but were still light enough to be beached and carried ashore.

From the ninth to the twelfth centuries, the Scandinavians were the most aggressive seafarers in Europe. While sailors from southern Europe timidly kept within sight of land, seamen from Norway, Denmark and Sweden were boldly venturing into uncharted waters. These remarkable Norsemen were not the Viking freebooters who terrorized Russia, Ireland, England and Normandy and who invaded Sicily in the eleventh century; they were traders and farmers who intended to establish colonies in newly discovered lands, sometimes to escape punishment for indiscretions at home. Whatever their reasons for these brave voyages, the Norse had reached the Faeroe Islands before AD 800 and Greenland by the late 900s. Since the longest passage between landfalls in the far northern Atlantic is only 350 miles, a navigator skilled enough to find the Shetland Islands, the Faeroes and Iceland, and who had favorable winds, was never more than three or four days from land.

One of the Norse traders, Biarni Heriulfson, was probably the first European to sight North America. Sailing westward from Iceland, he missed Greenland and fetched up off what he described as a level, wooded land. Back in Greenland his discovery excited Leif Ericsson, who procured Heriulfson's boat and set off to explore the land that Heriulfson had seen. In AD 1001 Ericsson made landfall somewhere on the Baffin Island coast, then sailed southward for several days. Ericsson and his crew explored the area around southern Labrador and northern Newfoundland and then returned to Greenland, 491 years before Columbus made his "discovery" of America.

Those ocean voyages were not made in the graceful and familiar longships of the Viking raiders. Instead the vessels used were *knarrs*—"beamy" (wide), clinker-built, double-ended vessels with a single woolen square sail on a mast set amidships, and managed by a single steering oar. *Knarrs* were open and provided no protection for up to forty crew, but they were partly decked in the ends and could carry cargo and cattle amidships.

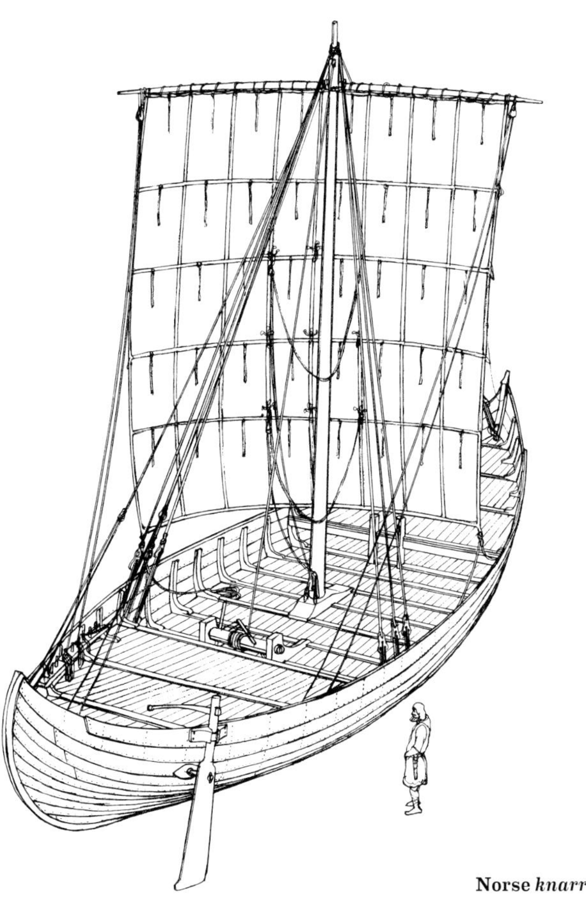

Norse *knarr*

Although *knarrs* provided the connection between distant settlements and the home countries for several hundred years, the settlements were gradually ignored and left to die. Sometime in the late fifteenth century the last Norse Greenlanders passed away, and the memory of their existence faded from European consciousness. There are the remains of a Norse settlement at L'Anse aux Meadows, on the northern tip of Newfoundland, likely the first and oldest non-native settlement in the Americas.

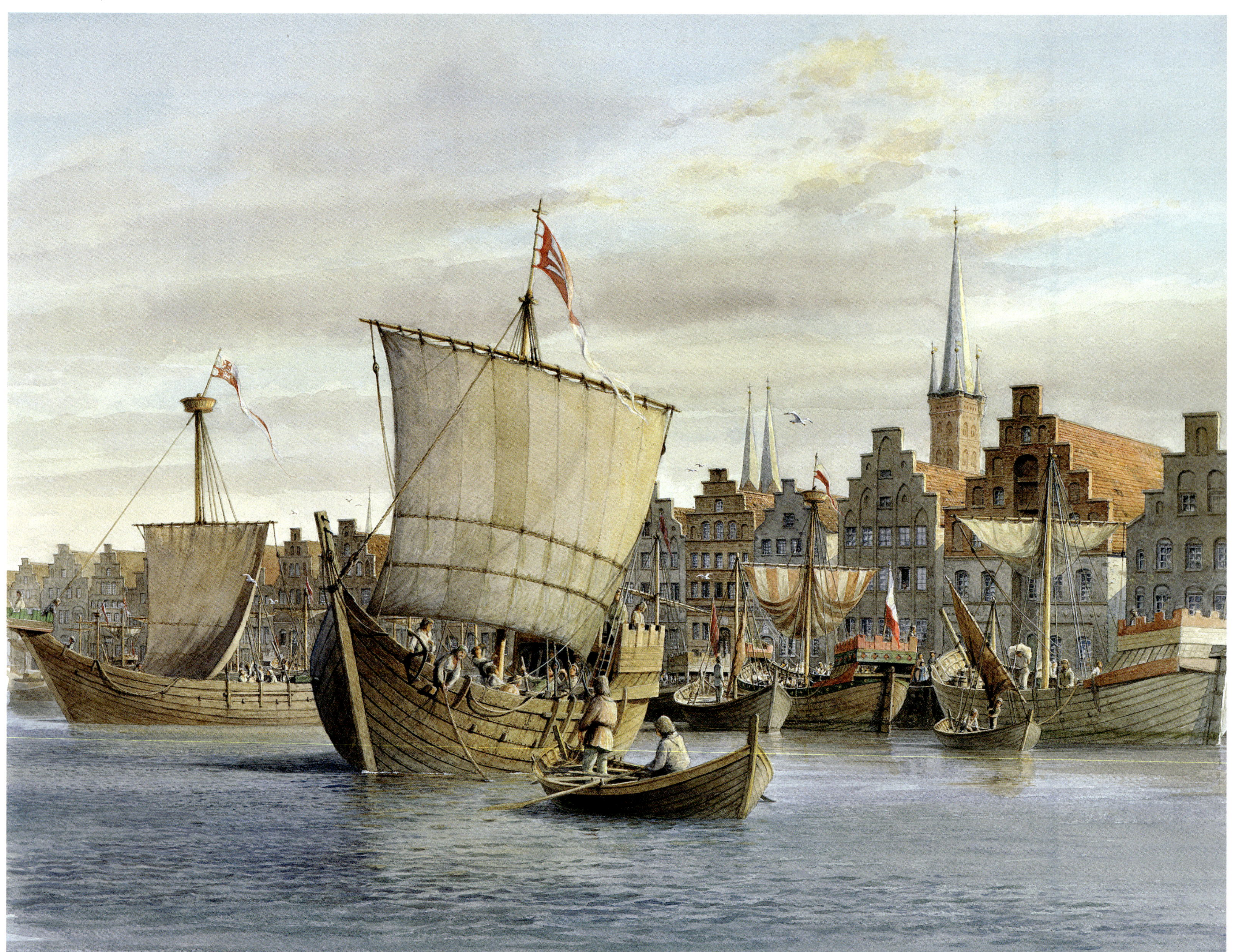

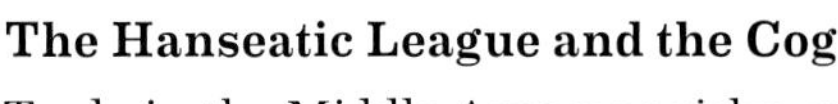

The Hanseatic League and the Cog

Trade in the Middle Ages was risky: roads were dangerous, and piracy at sea was common. Merchants found it advantageous to share the risks by sailing in company and by distributing goods among several vessels to lessen potential losses, and towards the end of the twelfth century North German merchants began to join together for mutual protection. This trading alliance, known as the Hanseatic League, grew to include more than sixty cities and over one hundred affiliated towns, which dominated trade in northwestern Europe for the next four centuries. This loose but effective alliance negotiated trading privileges, regulated prices, collected tariffs, maintained navigational aids and provided protection for its members. Its trading centers became wealthy with ever-increasing trade in furs, lumber, cloth, grain, honey, beer, salt, herring and cod.

Central to the success of the Hanseatic League was a vessel known as the cog. Although the Norse had elegant and seaworthy vessels, their carrying capacity was too small to satisfy the ambitious Hanseatic merchants. Cogs were simple, rugged, double-ended and clinker-built, with a single mast amidships, setting a single square sail on a yard. What distinguished the cog from its Nordic predecessors were its high-sided, flat-bottomed hull and straight stem and stern. The most important innovation was a rudder hung from the stern post, a necessary development for controlling a vessel of this size and weight, and an important milestone in the evolution of the ship. At first, castles were temporarily added to the ends for defense, but eventually they became permanently incorporated into the design of the hull, especially in the larger cogs. This was a distinct vessel type, and its importance is evidenced by the number of cogs displayed in the official seals and coins of the Hanseatic towns.

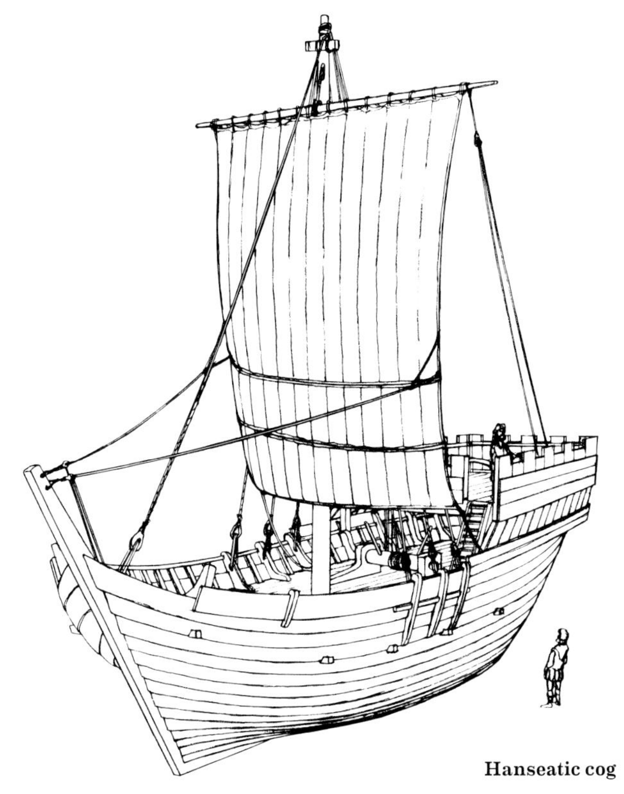

Hanseatic cog

Because cogs were square rigged and poor sailers, their voyages were planned to sail with the prevailing winds, which tended to blow seasonally in opposite directions. These boats seldom sailed alone, preferring to be in convoy for mutual protection, following the seasonal winds to make a trading circuit in a year's time.

‹ **Cogs preparing to sail, Lübeck, circa 1350**
(wc, 15″ × 22″)
Almost all the Baltic Sea trade went through Lübeck, Germany, in the fourteenth century. The port's "factories" were the three- to five-story headquarters of the merchants' operations lining the waterfront. Retail space was on the first floor, warehouse space was on the second and living quarters and offices occupied the upper floors.

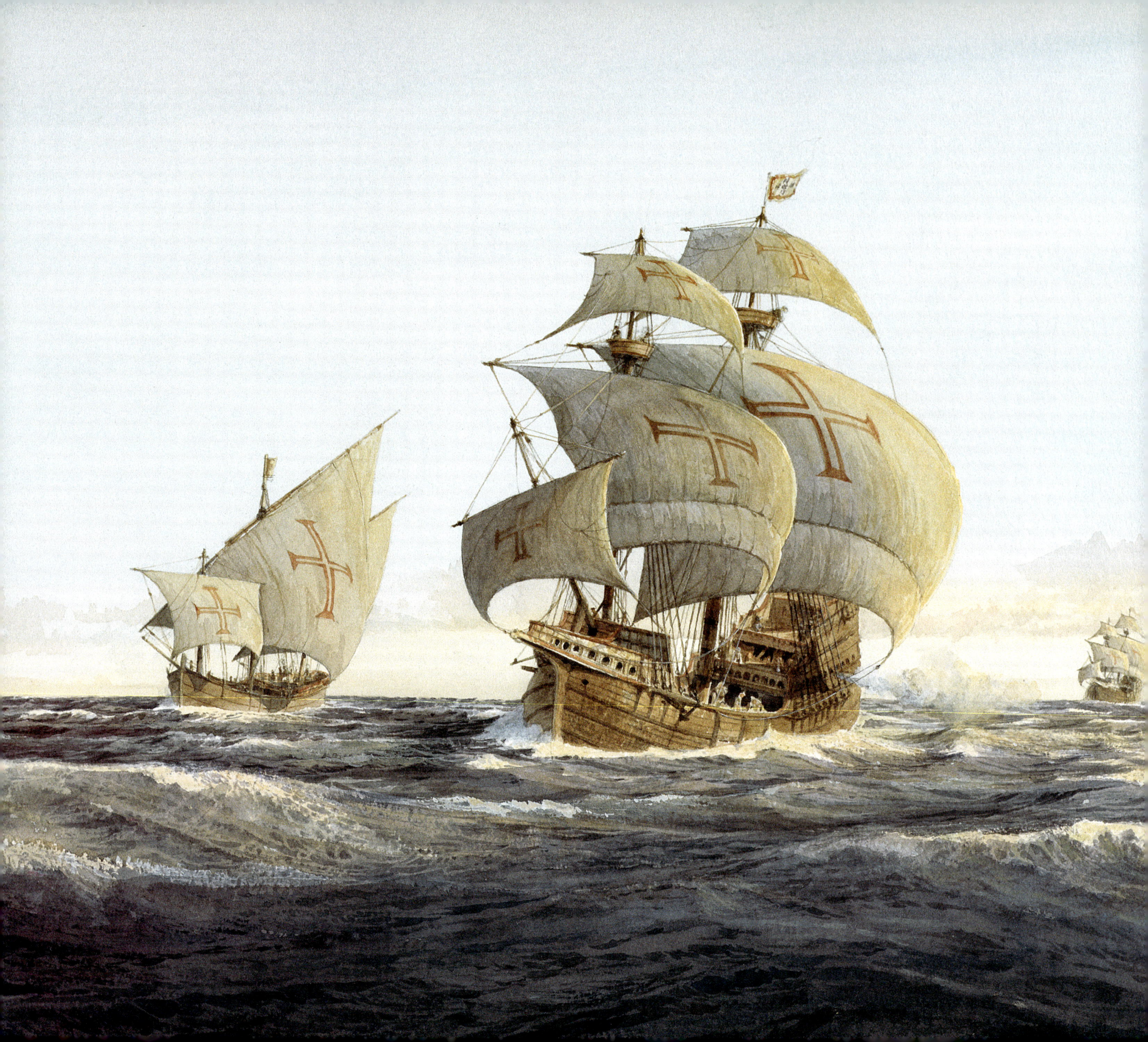

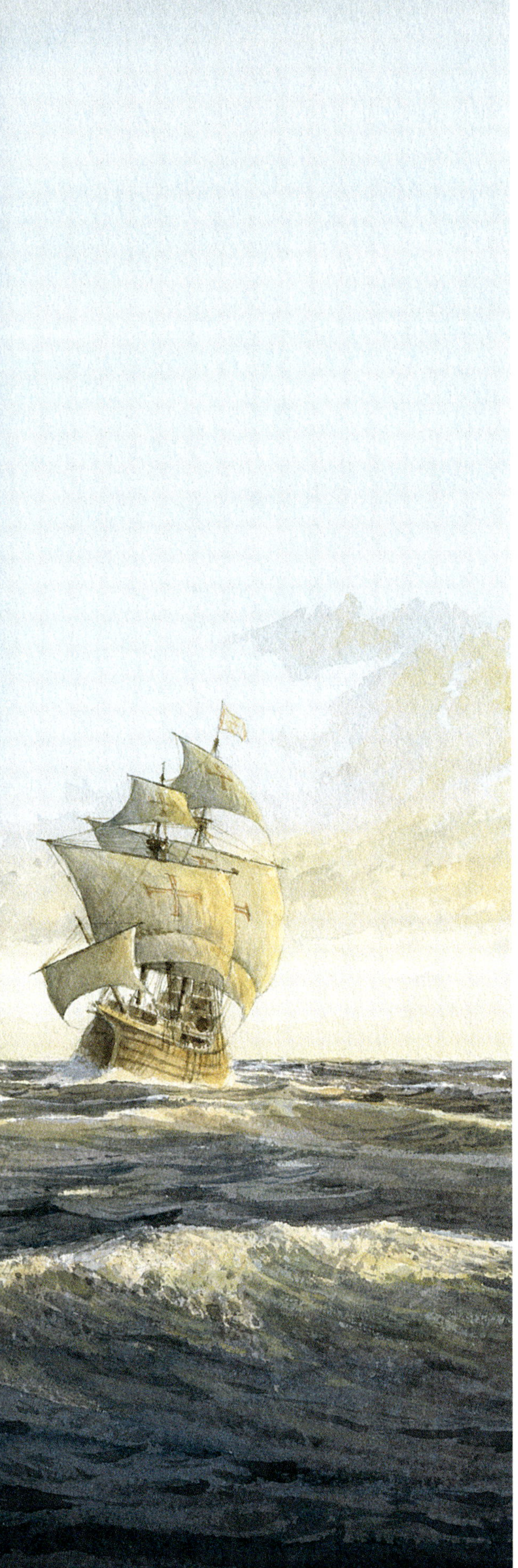

Vasco da Gama approaching the Cape of Good Hope, 1497 (WC, 15″ × 22″)
Da Gama took his four-ship fleet well west and south into the Atlantic Ocean before turning east to run down to the Cape of Good Hope. On the morning of November 22, 1497, he signaled the sighting of land at the cape by firing a cannon from the ship São Gabriel.

2

THE AGE OF EXPLORATION

To FIFTEENTH-CENTURY Europeans the unknown world beyond their shores was filled with frightening beasts and inhospitable climates—fears that were fueled by ancient myths and Christian orthodoxy. Voyagers knew well the lands around the Mediterranean, the western coasts of Europe and parts of northern Africa. But as they gradually ventured beyond their familiar horizons, they began to imagine places of exotic cultures, great riches and unimagined beauty.

Only the superstitious still believed the world was flat. Geographers of the time generally agreed that the world was round, but they badly underestimated its size. Early Greek and Egyptian astronomers and mathematicians had estimated it correctly, but later Europeans, in their dreams of easy wealth and glory, had optimistically shrunk the globe by 25 per cent. Their world contained no American continents and no Pacific Ocean.

Medieval Europeans were meat eaters by preference, but having few ways to keep their herds alive over winter they slaughtered most of their animals in the fall. Salted meat kept for a while, but spices, many of them imported from the Far East, made it more palatable. Spices were also believed to contain medicinal properties, and as a result they became the most highly valued and expensive luxuries of the time.

Europeans had enjoyed the fruits of trade with the Orient since Roman times, but the caravan routes that connected the Christian world to China and India were long and dangerous. Making matters even more difficult, these routes were controlled by Mongol and Muslim traders who kept their sources secret and extracted fees at every opportunity. Silks, cotton, precious stones and spices from the eastern lands passed through many hands, and by the time they reached European consumers the markup might be as much as 5,000 per cent. Western traders, who had long dreamed of the riches to be won by dealing directly with the producers of spices, began to consider the possibility of traveling directly to India by sailing around the African continent.

The World of the Portuguese

The medieval Portuguese, cut off from the world by a Muslim empire on one side and by the wild and mysterious Atlantic Ocean on the other, were beginning to stir restlessly inside their borders. Prince Henry of Portugal (1394–1460), known as "Henry the Navigator" because of his keen interest in exploration, gathered a community of scholars at the southwestern tip of Portugal to promote the sciences of astronomy and navigation. There he welcomed mathematicians, astronomers, mariners and cartographers to share their knowledge. Under Prince Henry's direction, nautical charts were improved, astronomical tables were compiled, instruments were refined and improvements to ship design were encouraged. At that time the caravel, combining both the square and lateen rig, evolved to become the leading vessel of Portuguese and Spanish maritime exploration.

However, before Prince Henry's navigators could begin exploring, they had to overcome their fear of the unknown. Their breakthrough may have been accidental. In 1420, blown offshore by a storm, a Portuguese expedition was driven onto the island of Madeira, and Portugal inadvertently gained its first offshore possession. Henry sent some colonists and a few grapevines to the island, and in time Madeira wines became renowned for their ability to survive long passages at sea without deteriorating.

Gaining experience and courage, the hardy Portuguese seafarers gradually extended their voyages down the West African coast and farther offshore. In 1427 an expedition reached the Azores, eight hundred miles out in the Atlantic, and by the 1440s Portuguese navigators had ranged as far south as Senegal. Each expedition took their ships farther south, and with every voyage pilots gained valuable knowledge of the ocean winds and currents.

In 1453 the Turkish capture of Constantinople, a center of the overland spice trade, added more vigor to Portugal's exploratory endeavors. A Papal Bull in 1454 granted the kingdom exclusive rights to exploration and conquest on the "south and east route to the Indies," and thereafter Portugal claimed the legal right to bar its rivals' access to the Indian Ocean around Africa.

Towards the end of August 1487 the Portuguese navigator Bartolomeu Dias sailed on what was to be the final push to round the tip of Africa. With two fifty-ton caravels and a smaller store ship, he made directly for the Congo to resupply. At Angra dos Alde, Dias left the store ship. As the two caravels neared the tip of Africa, they encountered fierce storms and headwinds. When the weather finally moderated, they had lost sight of land. Dias turned east to pick up the coast, but after many days of sailing he realized his ships had passed south of the continent. Without even seeing the southern tip of Africa, they had rounded the cape.

In 1497 Portugal's King Manuel I, confident that Dias had discovered the route to India, gave the navigator Vasco da Gama four ships to complete the exploration and to establish trading and diplomatic relationships with the merchants of Calicut. Da Gama rounded the Cape of Good Hope, sailed up the east coast of Africa and was guided to India by a Muslim pilot following ancient and well-established sea routes. Subsequent expeditions took Portuguese ships all the way to the Spice Islands (the Moluccas), an archipelago in present-day Indonesia, where in 1511 the voyagers seized the city of Malacca. In

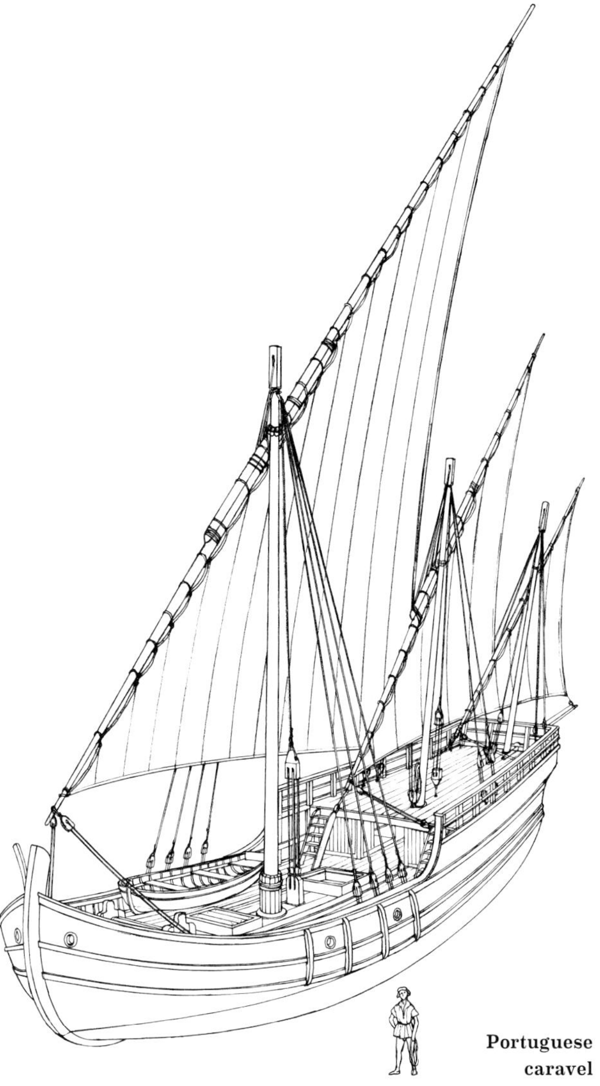

Portuguese caravel

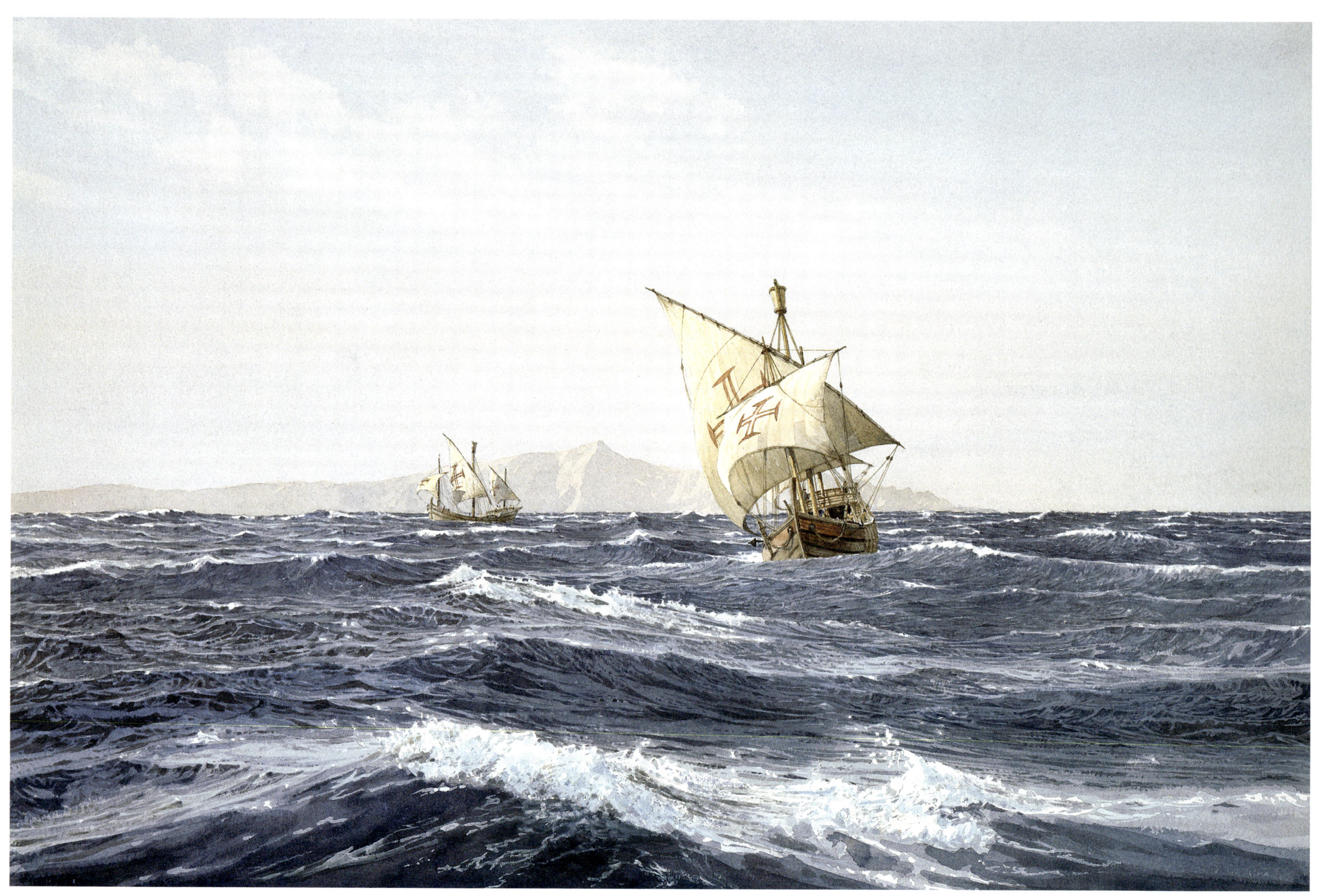

the Moluccas, Portugal established the first known European presence in the region—and a monopoly that was barely challenged for the rest of the century.

The Voyages of Christopher Columbus

Christopher Columbus was born into a family of wool merchants and weavers in Genoa in 1451. Little is known of his early years, but it is likely that he worked in the family business as soon as he was old enough. Genoa was the largest port on the Italian peninsula, and its seamen had a reputation for competence throughout Europe and the Mediterranean. Genoese seamen and pilots had been making regular trading voyages to England and Flanders for more than one and a half centuries. They had, as well, been instrumental in the Portuguese discoveries of the Azores, Madeira and the Canary Islands, and in the probes down the west coast of Africa.

Columbus first went to sea at about age fourteen, and over the next ten years he became a competent seaman. In 1476 he was a foremast hand in a Genoese fleet that was attacked by a Franco-Portuguese fleet off Cape St. Vincent, Portugal. Columbus was wounded and his ship was sunk, but with the aid of an oar he managed to swim the six miles to shore. From there he traveled to Lisbon, where his brother Bartolomé had established himself as a cartographer.

Columbus arrived in Lisbon at the height of Portugal's extraordinary maritime expansion. In the next five years he worked as a mapmaker with Bartolomé and made extensive voyages in Portuguese vessels. In 1478 he was the captain of a ship that made a passage to Madeira, and by 1482 he had traveled as far as was possible in the world that was known to him. He had been to Chios in the Aegean Sea, from which the shores of Asia Minor could be seen. He may have traveled as far north as Iceland, and he had been close to the equator on the tropical coast of Africa. The "Grand Idea"—to reach the rich and mysterious East by sailing west—might have been born during this time.

Columbus's knowledge and experience were expanding rapidly. He had married into a family of minor nobility and had obtained Portuguese citizenship. He had learned to speak Portuguese and later Castilian, and his Latin was good enough to comprehend scholarly works. He had learned navigation and cartography, and had years of experience in ocean passage-making, where he gained extensive knowledge of North Atlantic winds and currents. It appears he never doubted that he could sail to the west and return home again. This idea became his lifelong obsession.

Columbus was able to obtain an audience with the king of Portugal, but his proposal for a fleet to sail west was eventually rejected by the king's advisers. Abandoning his ties to Portugal, he took his ideas to the royal court in Spain, where he arrived in 1485. Ferdinand of Aragon and Isabella of Castile, in the last stages of their campaign to oust the Moors from Spain, had little time to consider

‹ **Bartolomeu Dias off the Cape of Good Hope, 1488** (WC, 15″ × 22″)
After many days of sailing down Africa's west coast, Dias realized that his two caravels had passed the southern end of the continent, so he turned his ships north to find the coast again. They picked up land at present-day Mossel Bay, South Africa. Storms had exhausted and frightened the crew, and with provisions running low they became increasingly reluctant to continue the voyage. Homeward bound, Dias retraced their course to the west, and in the vicinity of the cape the crews went ashore, planted a cross and left to search for their supply ship.

>> ***Pinta*, *Niña* and *Santa Maria*, departure from Spain** (WC, 15″ × 22″)
*On August 3, 1492, Christopher Columbus's three ships—*Pinta, Niña *and* Santa Maria*—sailed down the river from Palos, Spain, and out to sea. Sailing on the same tide was a ship carrying the last Jews expelled from Spain by Ferdinand and Isabella.*

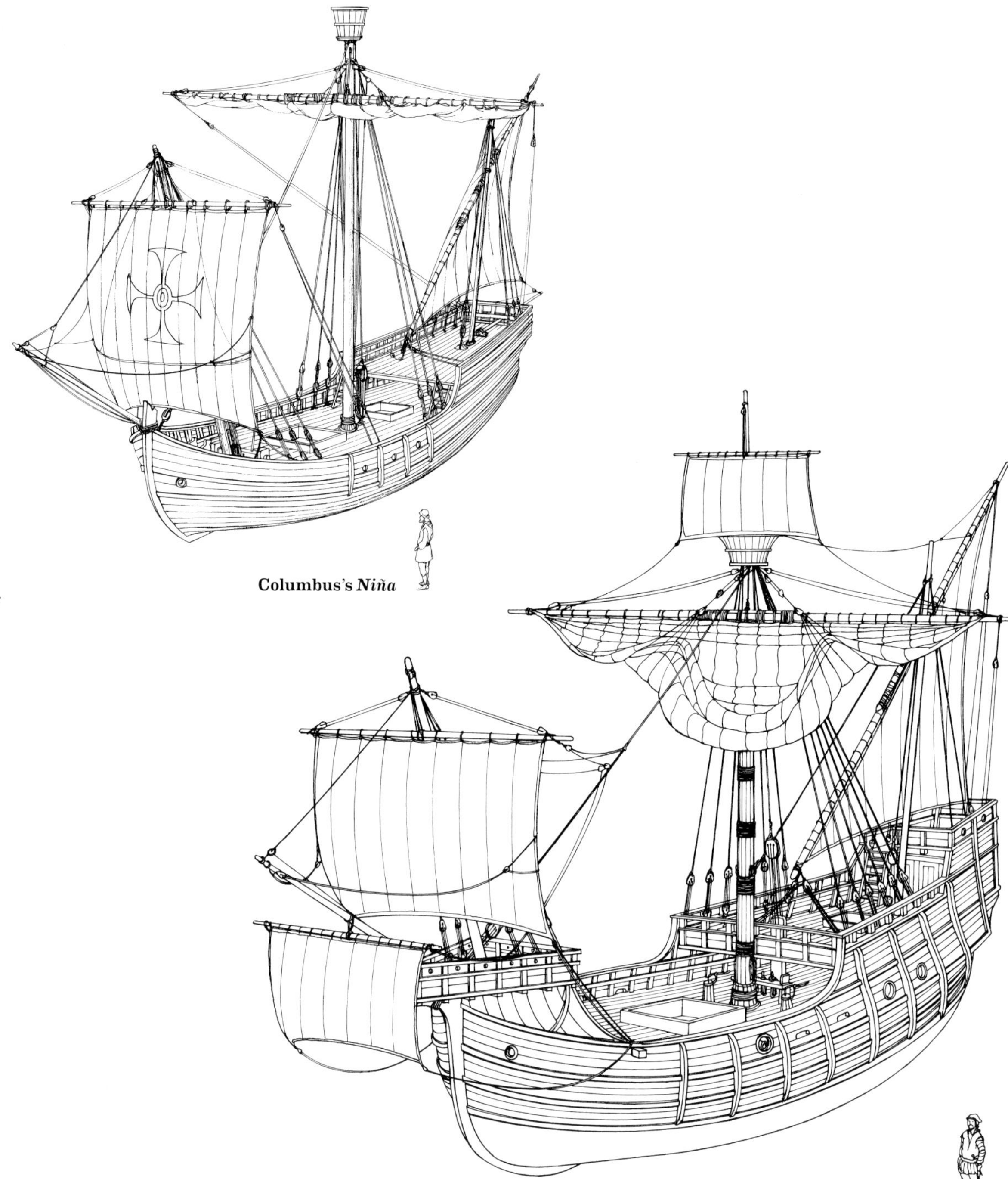

Columbus's *Niña*

Columbus's *Santa Maria*

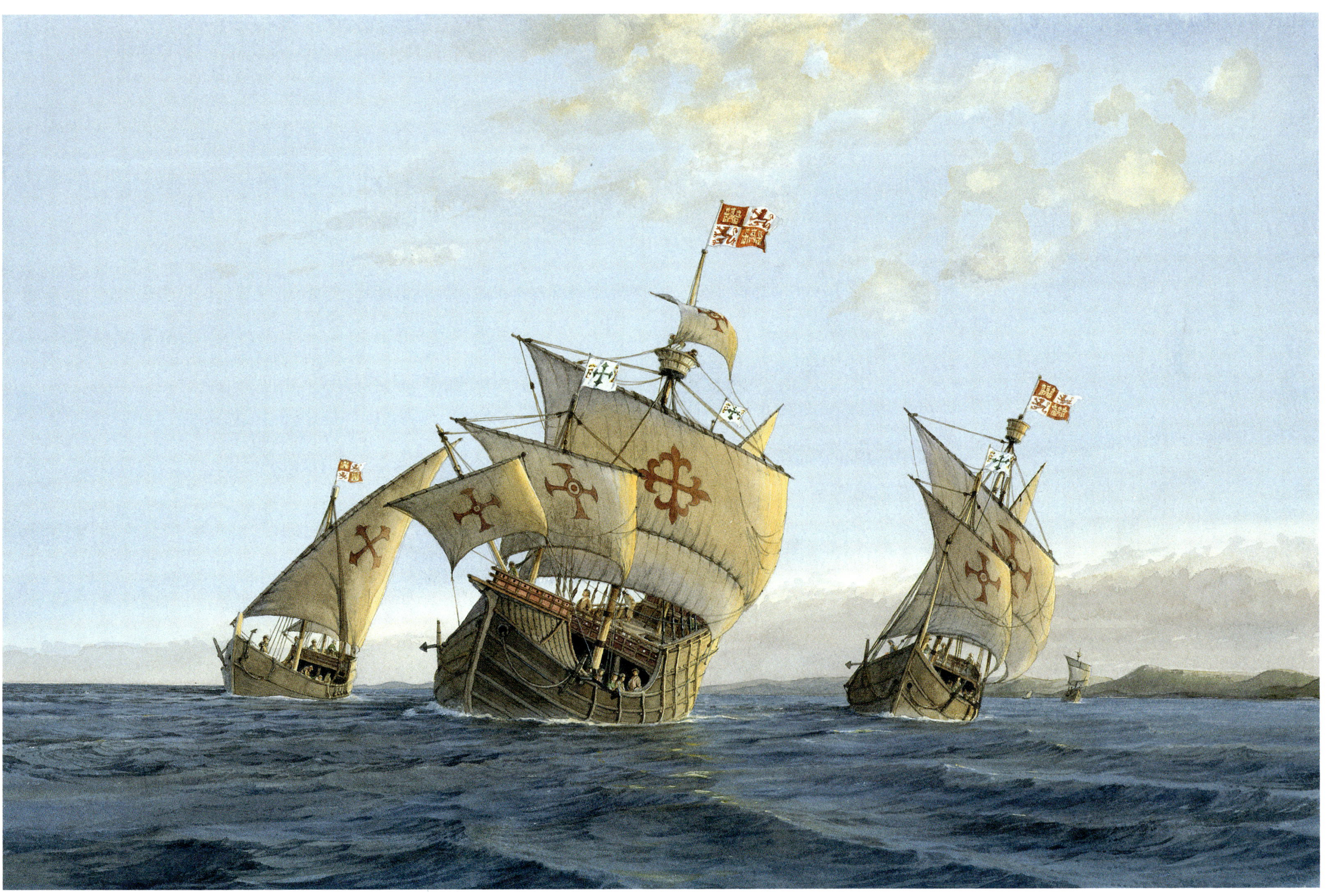

➤ *The voyages of Leif Ericsson, Christopher Columbus, John Cabot, Giovanni da Verrazzano and Jacques Cartier.*

funding a voyage of discovery by an unknown Genoese sailor from Portugal. For seven years Columbus stubbornly petitioned for his cause, barely subsisting on earnings as an itinerant bookseller.

His fortunes finally turned in early 1492, by which time Ferdinand and Isabella had succeeded in defeating the Moors and uniting Spain under their Catholic monarchy. On April 17 Columbus signed a contract granting him what he had requested: the title "Admiral of the Ocean Seas" and viceroy of whatever lands he discovered, two ships (Columbus chartered a third) and the funding to carry out his voyage. On August 3, just before sunrise, *Pinta, Niña* and *Santa Maria* set sail. After provisioning in the Canary Islands, they embarked on the final stage of the voyage that marked their place in history. On October 12, 1492, they made landfall in the Bahamas. Columbus thought he had reached the eastern islands of Asia.

For two weeks the fleet cruised through the Caribbean islands, searching for Cipangu (Japan). Columbus touched at Isabella (Fortune Island), Fernandina (Long Island), Cuba and Hispaniola. Off the northwest coast of Hispaniola, at midnight on an innocently calm Christmas Eve, *Santa Maria* struck a coral reef on a falling tide. In the relentless swells she was a total loss, but with the aid of friendly Tainos natives everything that could be useful was saved. Sensing that God had sent a message to establish a Christian community at this place, Columbus built a fort from *Santa Maria*'s salvaged timbers and named the site La Navidad, the first Spanish settlement in the Americas. He selected thirty-nine men to man the fort, fully expecting to return in the future to find a rich and thriving community.

Columbus returned to Europe aboard *Niña,* arriving in Lisbon on March 1, 1493, and anchoring at Palos on March 15—224 days after setting sail. He was now truly home to honor and glory. His sovereigns summoned him to Seville, from where the now-exalted "Don Cristobal Colon, Admiral of the Ocean Seas and Viceroy and Governor of the islands discovered in the Indies" made a glorious procession across Spain and a triumphant appearance before Ferdinand and Isabella.

Columbus was at the height of his fame, but his triumph was short-lived. On the second voyage, undertaken in late 1493, he returned to find his settlement at La Navidad destroyed and all the settlers murdered. He established a new colony on Hispaniola called La Isabella, but the site was an insect-infested swamp. Disease soon erupted, the natives broke into open revolt and the colony survived for only four years. Columbus's abilities as a navigator and promoter had not prepared him to be an administrator.

On his third voyage west in 1498, on the way to Hispaniola, Columbus landed on the shores of Venezuela's Paria Peninsula, becoming the first European to set foot

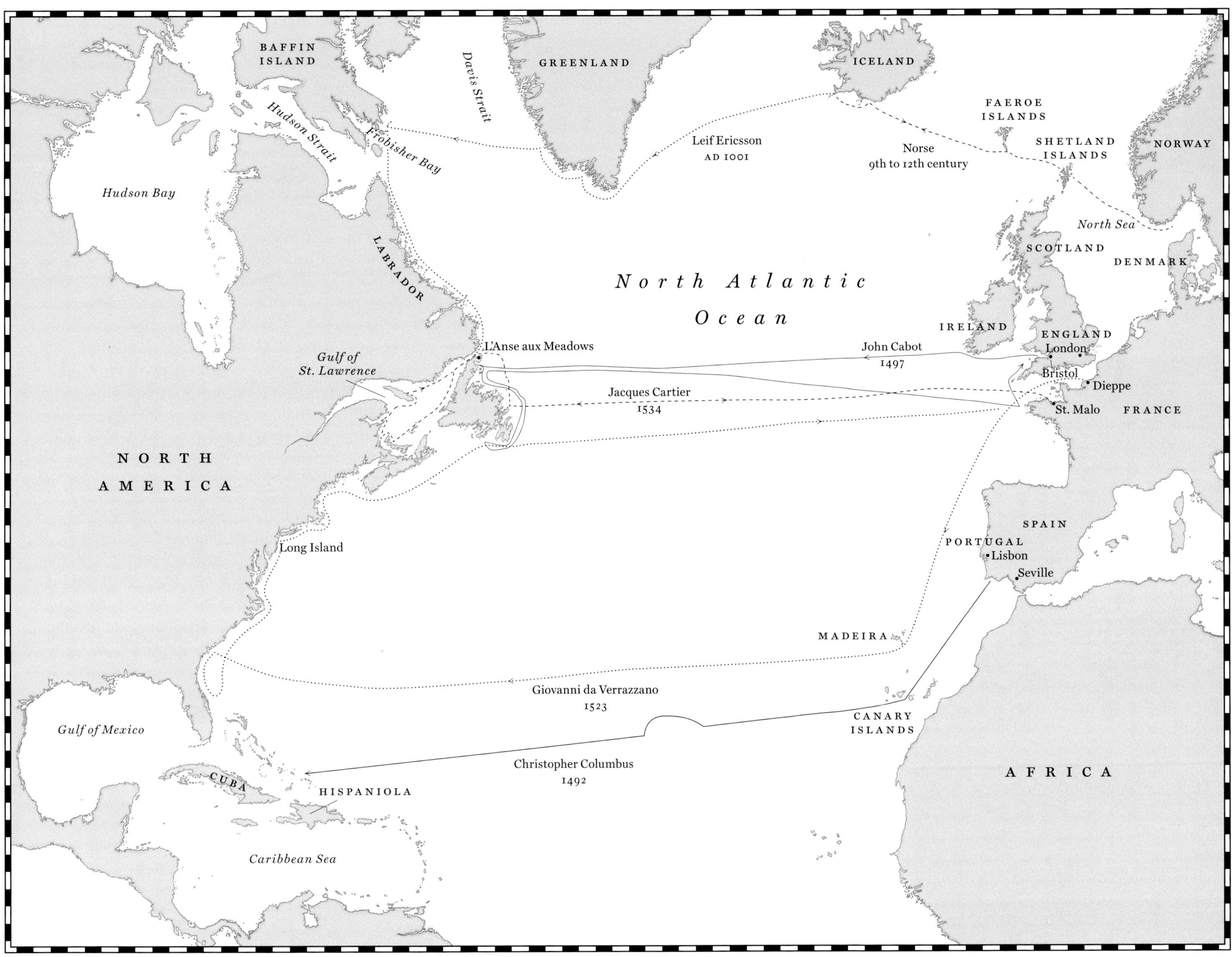
BAFFIN ISLAND
GREENLAND
ICELAND
Davis Strait
FAEROE ISLANDS
Hudson Strait
Frobisher Bay
Leif Ericsson
AD 1001
Norse
9th to 12th century
SHETLAND ISLANDS
NORWAY
Hudson Bay
North Sea
LABRADOR
SCOTLAND
DENMARK
North Atlantic Ocean
IRELAND
ENGLAND
L'Anse aux Meadows
John Cabot
1497
London
Gulf of St. Lawrence
Bristol
Dieppe
Jacques Cartier
1534
St. Malo
FRANCE
NORTH AMERICA
SPAIN
PORTUGAL
Lisbon
Long Island
Seville
MADEIRA
Giovanni da Verrazzano
1523
Gulf of Mexico
CANARY ISLANDS
Christopher Columbus
1492
AFRICA
CUBA
HISPANIOLA
Caribbean Sea

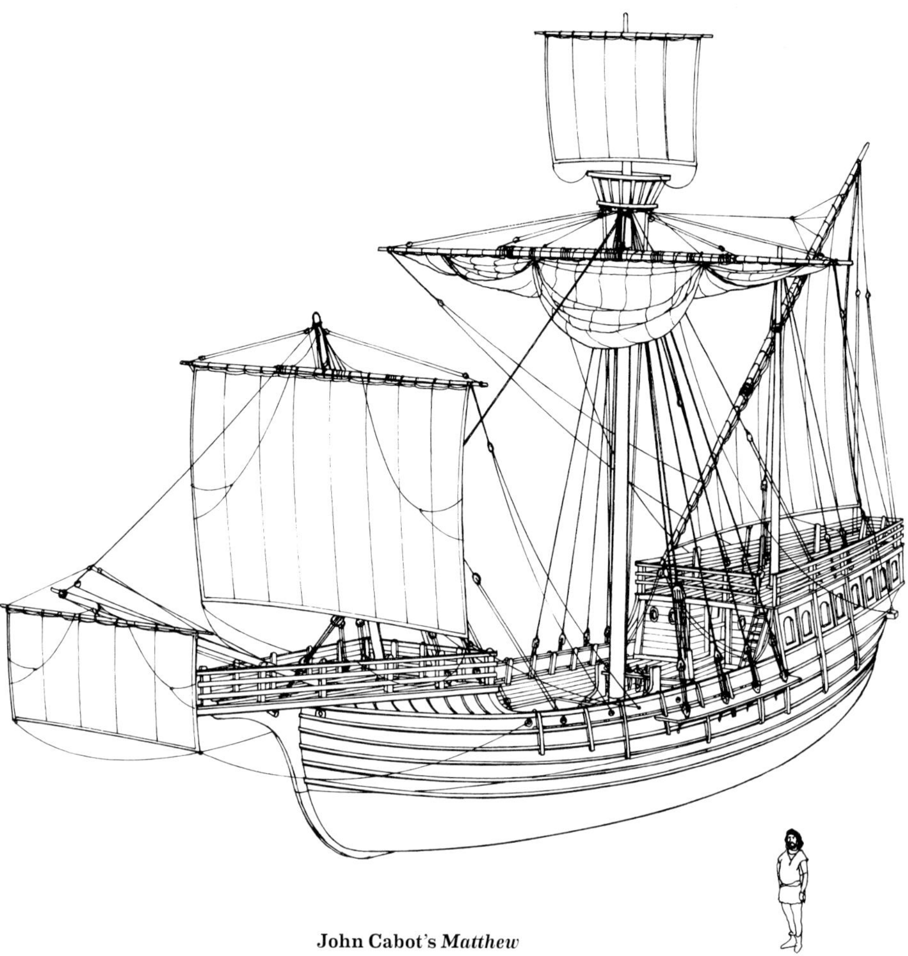

John Cabot's *Matthew*

on the mainland of the Americas since the Norse, five centuries before. Once on Hispaniola he found La Isabella in turmoil. The settlers had little to eat, and they had not found the riches they had been promised. The Spaniards, now disdaining Columbus as a foreigner, rebelled. He returned to Spain in disgrace, and in chains.

Freed by Ferdinand and Isabella, Columbus made a fourth and final voyage to the West Indies in 1502–04. Although he was able to regain some royal favor when the promised revenues began to trickle in from the new colonies, he never again achieved the honors he had enjoyed on his triumphant return from the first voyage.

Columbus died in 1506, still firm in his belief that he had reached the outlying islands of either Cipangu or Cathay (China). In his final years, he suffered from failing health and discouragement at the lack of recognition he felt he deserved. Although he was financially secure, he enjoyed none of the privileges he cherished.

Christopher Columbus was not the first to reach America from Europe, and he never found what he was looking for. Yet he alone was responsible for opening the door to a new age of exploration and a vastly wider world.

John Cabot: The Discovery of Newfoundland

Five years after Columbus made his historic voyage, another Genoese seaman crossed the Atlantic in search of a way to the Orient, this time in the service of the king of England. Giovanni Caboto—John Cabot, as he was known in the English-speaking world—was the first European after Leif Ericsson to set foot in North America. The year was 1497.

Cabot left no notes, logs or journals, and almost everything told about him is conjectural. It appears he was born around 1450 in Italy and spent his early years in Genoa, at the same time Christopher Columbus was there. He apparently became obsessed with the same desire as Columbus—to find a sea route to the Indies. He sought support for a voyage in Seville and Lisbon but was turned down in both cities, so in 1495 he went to England to petition Henry VII for assistance. To avoid the Portuguese and Spaniards, Cabot proposed a voyage north of their territorial claims.

The English king regretted having earlier turned down the same request from Columbus, so he was more favorably inclined towards Cabot's proposal. In 1496 the king granted letters patent to "our well beloved John Gabote, citizen of Venice—full and free authoritie, leave and power, to sayle to all partes, countreys, and seas, of the East, of the West, and of the North, under our banners and ensignes." Cabot took his royal commission to Bristol and began searching for backers for his enterprise.

Although he had been promised five ships, Cabot ended up with only one: *Matthew*, a *navicula* (little ship) of fifty tons. A typical three-masted trader of the period, she sailed from Bristol around May 20, 1497, crewed by one Burgundian, one Castiglione and sixteen Bristol seamen. Cabot's son Sebastian may also have been on board. Their point of departure was Dursey Head, the southwest point of Ireland, at 51°37´ north. Following that latitude to the west, the most likely course Cabot would have taken, would mean that the first land encountered was Cape Dégrat, the northeast point of Newfoundland.

Land appeared at 5 AM on June 24, and *Matthew* followed the coast south searching for a place to land, which she did later in the day. Ashore the crew saw no people but plenty of signs of life, enough that Cabot was reluctant to venture inland with his small band of sailors. In a cove he recorded as being 51°33´ north, he planted his banners and took formal possession of the land for King Henry VII. This was the only place the crew went ashore, and on that one event England based all her later claims to North America. Cabot spent about twenty-six days exploring the newly discovered coast, sailing south before returning north to take his departure for home from the cape where he had made his first landfall. His return across the Atlantic took only fifteen days, ending up off the coast of Brittany. On August 6, *Matthew* was again made fast to the key in the heart of the city of Bristol.

Cabot immediately traveled to London for an audience with the king. His story must have made a good impression, for the king gave him £10 and awarded him a pension of £20 a year for life. He also issued new letters patent for a second Cabot voyage, with the power to impress six English ships of two hundred tons or less to "theym convey and lede to the lande and Isles of late found by the seid John in oure name." This time the king provided one ship, and the merchants of Bristol provided four more. In May 1498 the five ships sailed together, but one put into an Irish port in distress. Cabot and the other four ships sailed on and were never heard from again.

Although he believed otherwise, Cabot had not reached Asia. Nothing of value, no gold or spices, was obtained on the voyage, and the king showed no immediate interest in following up on Cabot's claim.

› ***Matthew* approaching the Newfoundland coast, 1497** (WC, 15″ × 22″)
The only information about John Cabot's voyage in Matthew *is in a letter written by John Day, a Bristol merchant, in the winter of 1497–98. According to Day, Cabot "was en route 35 days before he found land ... the seas were smooth on the outward as on the homeward passage, save one day when there blew up a gale, and that was two or three days before he found land." There was no mention of fog or ice, but they are always a part of the Newfoundland experience at that time of year.*

Amerigo Vespucci: Claiming the Americas

At the dawn of the sixteenth century, the world portrayed on European maps was a wonderfully imaginative and colorful place consisting mainly of land: Europe, Asia and northern Africa, surrounded by a small body of water. In 1507 Martin Waldseemüller, a Swiss cartographer, created a new world map that incorporated all the latest discoveries of contemporary explorers. His map was the first to show the New World as a distinct continent well to the east of Asia. Prophetically, printed over the southern portion of the new land was the word "America." Waldseemüller believed, on the basis of the writings of Amerigo Vespucci, that Vespucci had been the first to set foot on the mainland of the continent in 1499—a year before Columbus—and rightly deserved to have the new lands named for him. Waldseemüller later regretted his decision, but by then the name had stuck. It would later be applied to the entire continent to the north as well.

Amerigo Vespucci was born in Florence on March 9, 1454, into a prominent family of bankers and merchants. In 1471 he entered the commercial house of the influential Lorenzo di Pierfrancesco de' Medici. Vespucci's employer sent him as an agent to Seville, where in 1498 he helped outfit the third voyage of Columbus. But Vespucci proved to be boastful and egocentric, and consequently his reputation suffered when he falsely claimed that he had participated in a 1497 voyage to the Americas. Many New World narratives at that time were attributed to him, but no charts from any of his voyages have been found, and the claims he made about them are confused and unverifiable.

Vespucci did make two (possibly three) passages to the Americas, fulfilling a lifelong dream to participate in voyages of exploration. On the first, in 1499, he joined the Spanish captain Alonso de Hojeda as an investor and self-appointed navigator. They sailed in May and made landfall on what is now the northeast coast of French Guiana, near the mouth of the Oyapoc River. From there Vespucci parted company with Hojeda, taking one of the caravels to explore the coast to the east while Hojeda sailed westward to the Gulf of Paria. Amerigo reached as far as the mouth of the Amazon, then returned to meet Hojeda off Maracaibo, Venezuela, before sailing home to Cadiz, in Spain. Like other explorers of the time, he thought he had been exploring the southerly projection of Asia and concluded that had he proceeded farther south he would have encountered the Ganges.

Early on Vespucci developed a fascination for navigation, which was to interest him all his life. While on the American coast in 1500, he had calculated the longitude of his position with considerable accuracy. In the late spring of 1501, he joined a fleet of three caravels under the command of Gonçalo Coelho. While waiting in Lisbon for the ships to sail, he had researched the technical problem of determining longitude. In the process he calculated the circumference of the earth at the equator to be

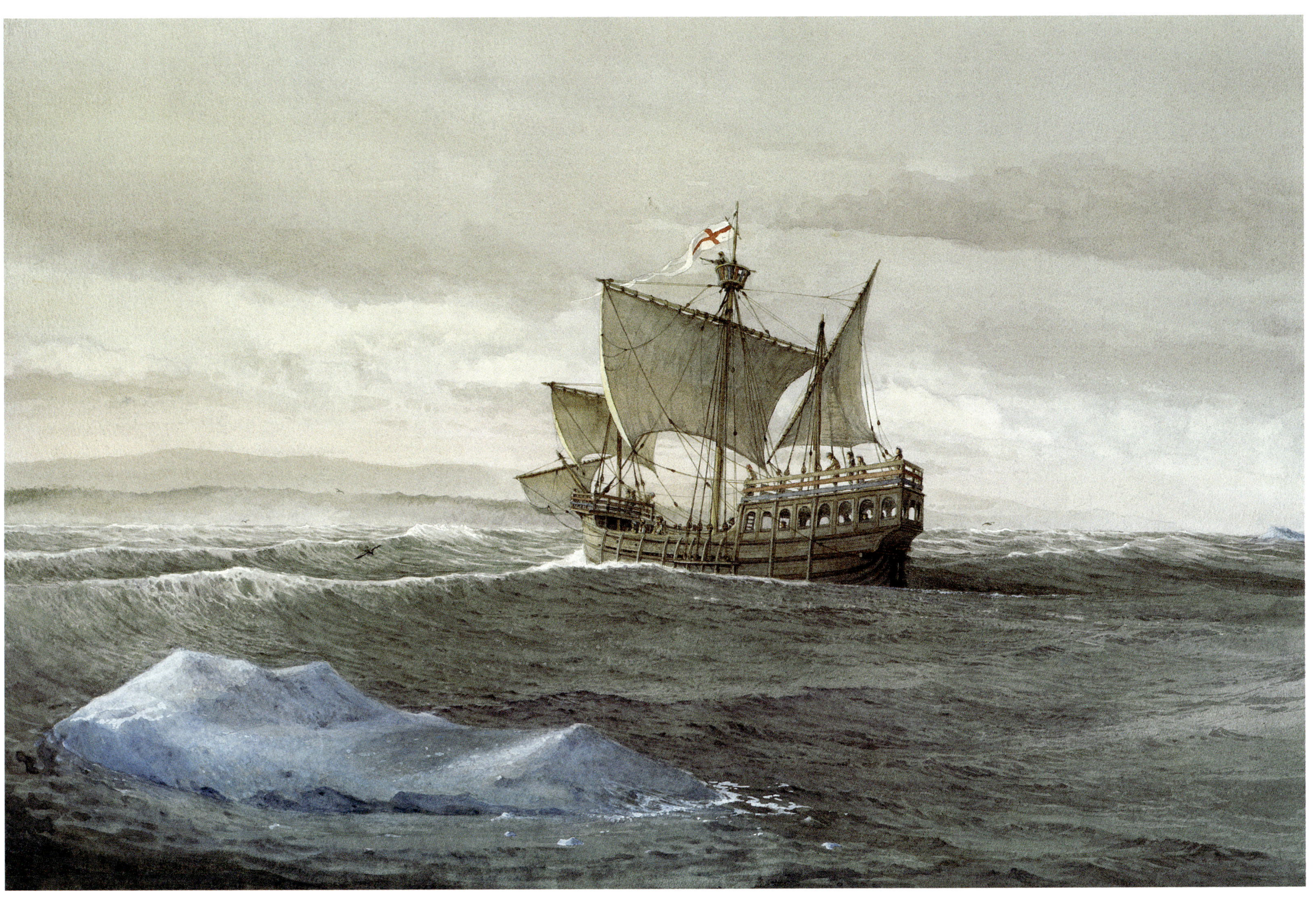

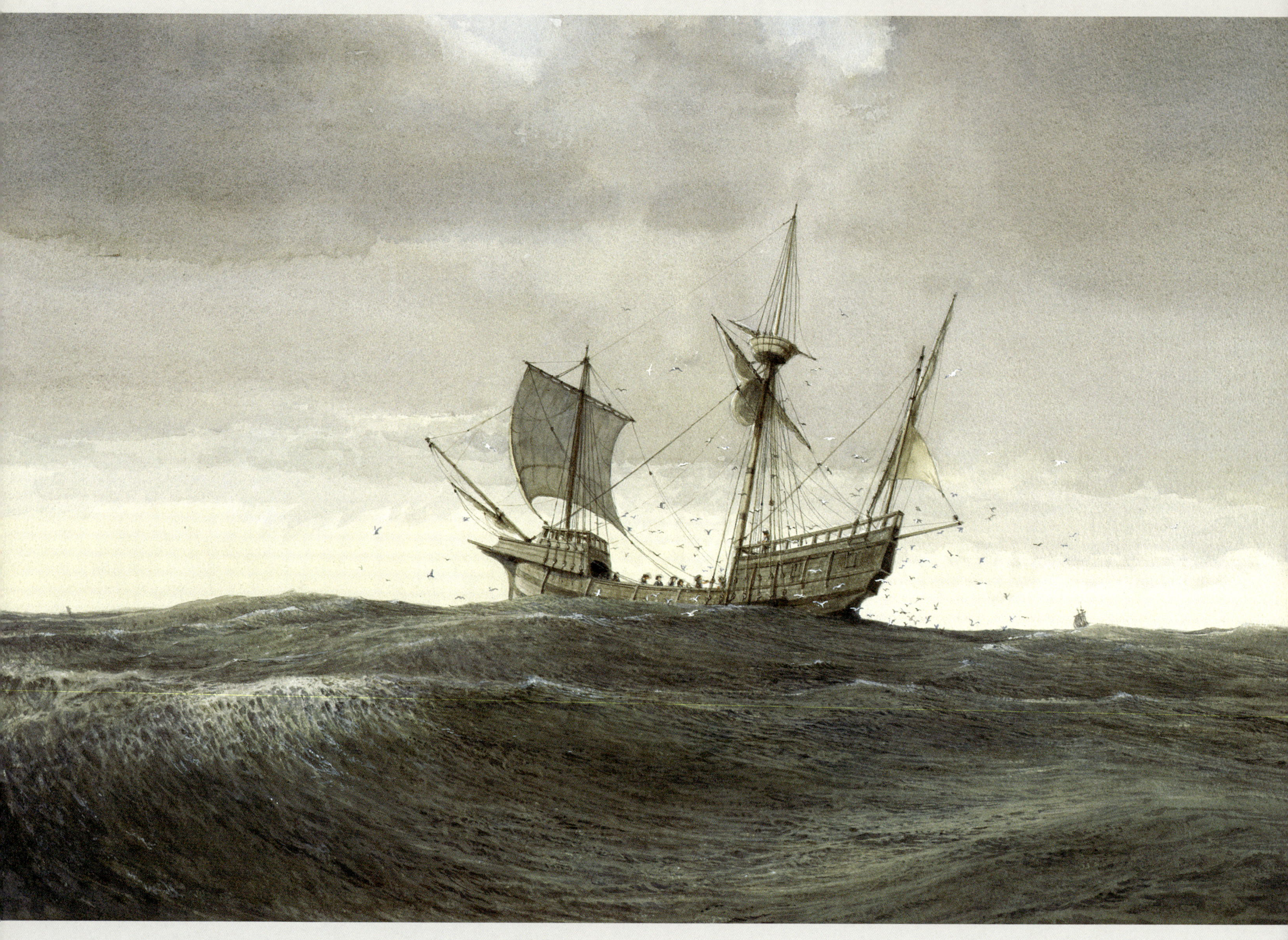

THE GRAND BANKS OF NEWFOUNDLAND

TOWARDS THE END of the medieval era, Europe's periods of peace became longer, its populations increased, its urban centers began to grow and many of its cities outstripped the capacity of local food sources to feed them. Freshwater fish had always been a part of the medieval diet, but eventually pollution in lakes and rivers depleted this resource. The Church proclaimed up to 150 meatless days a year, creating an even greater demand for fish. This large market made it possible for people to fish exclusively for a living, and for fishermen to earn much more than peasants or farmers.

To replace the diminishing freshwater stocks, Europeans began to fish the seas off their coasts. At first the fish in coastal waters were so abundant that all Europe's requirements were met close to shore. But over time these stocks were depleted and the search for fish took the ships on extended voyages farther out to sea. By 1383 English ships were fishing off Norway. They were off Iceland by 1408, and they began establishing settlements there as early as 1425. The French and Iberians fished Irish waters, Basques were taking whales in the Bay of Biscay and the Portuguese were off the Azores and Cape Verdes fishing for tuna.

The offshore fisheries were great training grounds for early seamen and navigators. Their increasing knowledge of ocean winds, currents and distant shores gave confidence to the explorers who followed in their wake. By the fifteenth century medieval ships had developed to the point where they could make extended offshore passages and return safely with a catch. From that time until well into the eighteenth century, the Dutch and English had fleets of large fishing vessels called "busses," square-rigged on three masts, that were capable of spending a long time at sea.

Fifteenth-century ships from Europe were certainly capable of reaching the Grand Banks and may have discovered Newfoundland in the search for new fishing grounds, but there is no proof of such voyages occurring before John Cabot ventured there in 1497. On his return, reports of enormous schools of fish were soon circulating in England. Within in a month the Milanese ambassador in England sent a report of Cabot's claims to the Duke of Milan: "They assert that the sea is swarming with fish, which can be taken not only with the net, but in baskets let down with a stone . . . that they could bring so many fish that this kingdom would have no further need of Iceland."

It was not the English but the Portuguese who were the first to exploit the Grand Banks fishery—as early as 1502. They were soon followed by the French and the Basques. In a very short time, crossing the Atlantic was almost routine. In 1517 it was reported that fifty ships were on the banks fishing for cod; by 1600 there were 150 ships a year. Eventually the banks were visited every season by the offshore fleets, and the practice continued well into the twentieth century.

Fishing on the Grand Banks, 16th century (WC, 15″ × 22″)
Two forms of fishing were employed off the Grand Banks: dry and wet. In the dry fishery, the ships would spend the season laid up in a bay on the Newfoundland or Labrador coast while a fleet of shallops fished close to shore, returning to a temporary camp where the fish were gutted, cleaned, salted and dried. In the fall the ships were loaded with the season's catch and returned home. The wet fishery was conducted entirely at sea, using long lines of baited hooks. The catch was gutted, deboned, cleaned and layered with salt in barrels.

› **Discovery of Rio de Janeiro**
(WC, 15″ × 22″)
On Amerigo Vespucci's second voyage to the Americas the fleet resupplied at Cabo Verde, on the west coast of Africa, and made a stormy two-month passage to the west before making landfall near Cabo São Roque on the coast of Brazil. They then sailed southwest along the coast, naming bays and promontories as they went. On January 1, 1502, the three ships entered Guanabara Bay (Rio de Janeiro). Later they reached at least as far as the Rio de la Plata estuary.

24,852 English miles, only fifty miles short of the actual distance—an error of less than 1 per cent. This was truly remarkable accuracy for the time and an indication of Vespucci's mastery of navigation.

In 1500 Pedro Álvares Cabral, outward bound on a voyage to India, had accidentally fallen in with the coast well south of the bulge of Brazil. There he planted a cross and claimed the land for Portugal. News of this act reached the king of Spain, who placed an embargo against any participation by foreigners, including Vespucci, on future Spanish voyages. As a result, Vespucci's next voyage was in the employ of the Portuguese king, Manuel I.

On his second voyage Vespucci calculated that the Tordesillas line, the arbitrary line that divided the undiscovered lands of the globe between Spain and Portugal, crossed the Brazilian coast at latitude 25° south, 370 leagues west of the Cape Verde Islands. Again he displayed remarkable accuracy: his line was correct within two miles. It was on this voyage that he realized that China must lie much farther to the west than anyone had previously believed, and he deduced that the land he had explored the year before was a distinct land mass separate from Asia.

Vespucci might have made another voyage with a Portuguese fleet in 1503–04, again under the command of Coelho, but almost nothing is known of this event. Back in Lisbon he wrote several letters describing his discoveries, his new theory about the size of the globe and his realization that the land he had explored was an entirely new continent. Versions of the letters received wide circulation, and his ideas were first incorporated by Waldseemüller in his 1507 world map.

Vespucci received no gratitude from King Manuel for his efforts, so he transferred his allegiance back to Spain. In 1505 he returned to Seville, where the court credited him with adding a considerable land mass to Spain's territories in the New World. He was given Spanish citizenship by the monarch, who employed him as official cosmographer, and in 1508 Vespucci was appointed *piloto mayor,* an important position that he held until his death from malaria in 1512.

Ferdinand Magellan and the Spanish Lake

The first navigator to sail around the world—Fernão Magalhães to the Portuguese, Fernando de Magallanes to the Spaniards and Ferdinand Magellan to the English—was born around 1480, in northern Portugal to parents of minor nobility. By all accounts Magellan was an extraordinary man: ambitious, courageous, confident and tough. Orphaned at twelve, he was given a position of page in the Portuguese court during a period of unprecedented discovery and expansion. His real career began in 1505, when he was selected to accompany Dom Francisco de Almeida, the first Portuguese viceroy of India.

It was Almeida's intention to break the Arab trading monopoly in the Indian Ocean, and as a king's soldier Magellan participated in the Portuguese campaign on

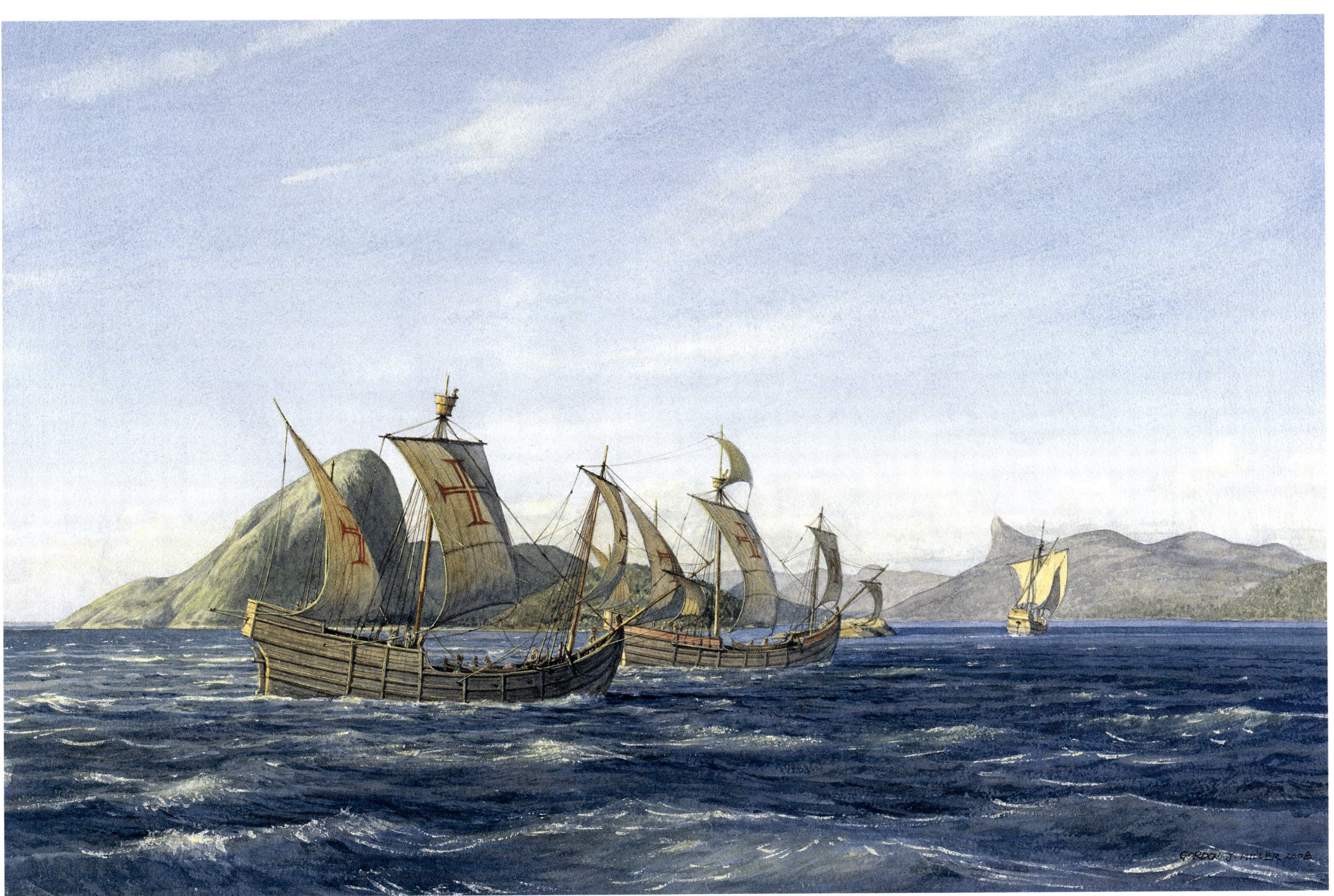
GORDON J. MILLER 2008

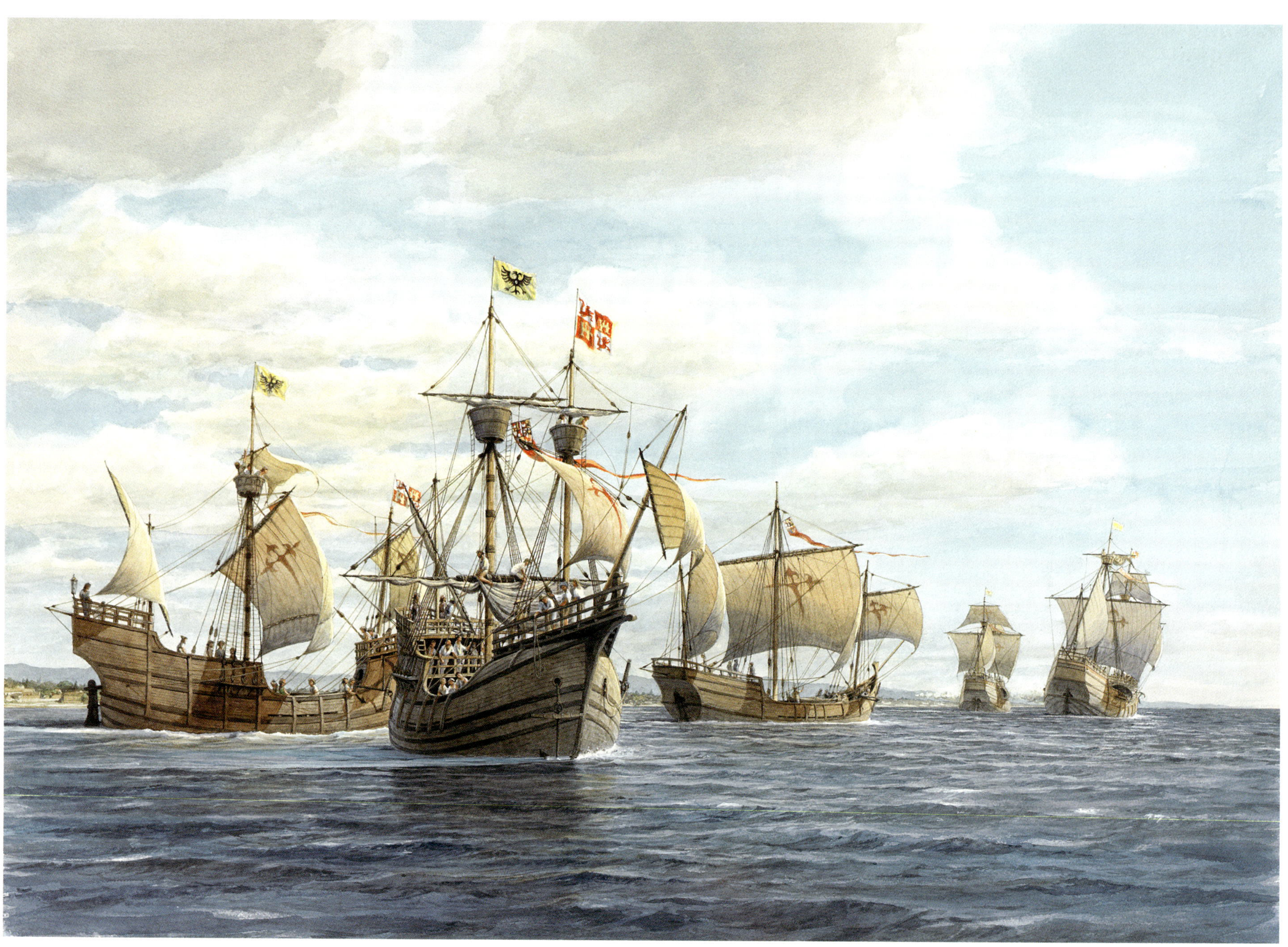

the East African coast, the establishment of the colony of Goa in India and, in 1511, the capture of Malacca, the key to controlling the sea route to the Moluccas, the Spice Islands. Magellan commanded the smallest of three ships to reconnoiter the Moluccas—the first Portuguese ships to sail into the Pacific Ocean.

Magellan returned to Portugal a seasoned soldier and competent navigator, and he began to nurture the idea that the Moluccas could be reached from the east, if a passage could be found through the American continents. Several times he offered his services to King Manuel I to lead an expedition, but he was repeatedly rebuffed. The king had formed a personal dislike of Magellan and eventually told him he was free to sell his services elsewhere. In response Magellan renounced his Portuguese nationality and in 1517 took his proposal to Seville, where he was met with a much warmer reception. In 1518 he was given command of five ships and granted a royal charter to undertake a voyage to the Moluccas in the name of King Charles V of Spain. The preparations took eighteen months, but finally in 1519 he sailed from the Guadalquivir River on Spain's Atlantic coast.

Magellan's officers were a problem right from the start. Appointees of the court, most were young, inexperienced hidalgos, members of the lower nobility. They were arrogant and resentful of their Portuguese captain, and they began making trouble before they were barely out of sight of Spain. The mutinous feelings came to a head in Bay San Julian, on the southern coast of Argentina, where the fleet anchored to wait out the winter. There the Spanish captains and senior officers conspired to seize three of the ships.

Magellan's reaction was swift, brutal and decisive. Two days later, when the mutiny was over, Captain Mendoza, who had had his throat cut by one of Magellan's men, was drawn and quartered. Captain Quesada and five others were condemned to death, but only Quesada was beheaded. The rest were kept at hard labor for the rest of their stay. The corpses of Mendoza and Quesada were hung in gibbets on Gallows Hill, where their remains were still visible when Francis Drake arrived there more than fifty years later.

But Magellan's troubles were far from over. While careening the ships in Bay San Julian, it was discovered that the fleet had been cheated by the chandlers in Spain. Instead of having provisions for a year and a half, they had only enough for six months. *Santiago* was dispatched to look for anything to supplement their meager supplies, but she was caught in a storm and lost. The four remaining ships left Port San Julian in August, and after another stop of two months in Puerto Santa Cruz, Argentina, set sail for the final push to the south. Three days later, on October 21, 1520, at 52° 20′ south, they opened an inlet marked by a high, grass-topped promontory. This point

‹ **Armada de Molucca** (WC, 22″ × 30″) *Ferdinand Magellan's fleet, grandly known as the Armada de Molucca, sailed on September 20, 1519. The five small, old and badly provisioned ships were well armed, but were essentially small merchantmen. Except for* Santiago, *which was a caravel, the ships were probably all* naos*—stubby, three-masted vessels, square-rigged on the fore and main masts and lateen-rigged on the mizzen. The largest measured only 120 tons.*

› **Magellan in the Strait of Magellan**
(WC, 15″ × 22″)
The Strait of Magellan has always been a difficult passage to negotiate. The high mountains create erratic winds, and the narrow, twisting channel is strewn with treacherous currents, hidden rocks and sandbanks. Even in summer the weather can be erratic. It took Magellan thirty-eight days to cover the strait's 360 miles.

they named Cabo Virgenes, the eastern opening to what Magellan later named the Channel of All Saints and was eventually known as the Strait of Magellan.

When Magellan's fleet arrived at the western exit, it had been reduced to three ships. *San Antonio* had been captured by her pilot, Estêvão Gomes, who had been nursing a bitter jealousy towards Magellan. Sent ahead to reconnoiter one of the many passages, *San Antonio* had slipped past the fleet under cover of darkness and scurried back to Spain. When her loss was discovered, many days were wasted in the search to find her; she was the fleet's largest ship, and with her went much of the remaining stores of food: one-third of the biscuits, one-third of the meat and two-thirds of the currants, chickpeas and figs.

On November 28, 1520, *Trinidad*, *Victoria* and *Concepcion* sailed out of the strait into an empty and gentle ocean, and the beginning of what was to be one of the most appalling ocean passages in history. The goal of the little fleet lay six thousand miles to the west. Although the first few weeks were pleasant enough, the ravages of scurvy soon began to take their toll. By some tragic trick of fate, the fleet followed the only path that completely avoided all of the hundreds of islands that lay strewn across that part of the ocean. Except for two tiny islands which provided no place to anchor, they saw no land for ninety-eight days. Long before that, the crew members began to die. Their meager provisions became maggoty and turned to dust, and the water in their casks was soon putrid and stinking. In desperation they ate rats and leather chaffing gear, boiling the latter to make it edible.

Finally, after a passage of nine thousand miles, they found relief. On March 6, 1521, they raised Guam, a high, lush island that offered coconuts, sugar cane, yams and fish. The crew stayed only three days, however, because the island's natives proved to be fearless thieves, and several were killed while Magellan retrieved a stolen boat. After gathering enough fresh food to halt the scurvy, they departed for an easy six days of sailing westward to the Philippines, which the ships reached on March 15. Magellan rested the crew on Homonhon Island for a week before sailing southwest into Surigao Strait.

On March 28 one of the magical moments in history occurred. Ten years earlier, in 1511, Magellan had reached his farthest point east from Portugal at the island of Banda, longitude 130° east. Now, ten years later, he crossed this meridian again while sailing west, thus justifying his claim to be the first man to sail around the world. (While in Malacca in 1511 he had purchased a slave, later christened Enrique, who accompanied him on the historic voyage. While anchored off the island of Limasawa, the ships were approached by eight men in a small boat. Enrique hailed them in his native dialect and was answered immediately in the same tongue. The linguistic circle had been closed by a ship sailing from the east, and Enrique de Malacca thus has an equal claim to the title of "First Around.")

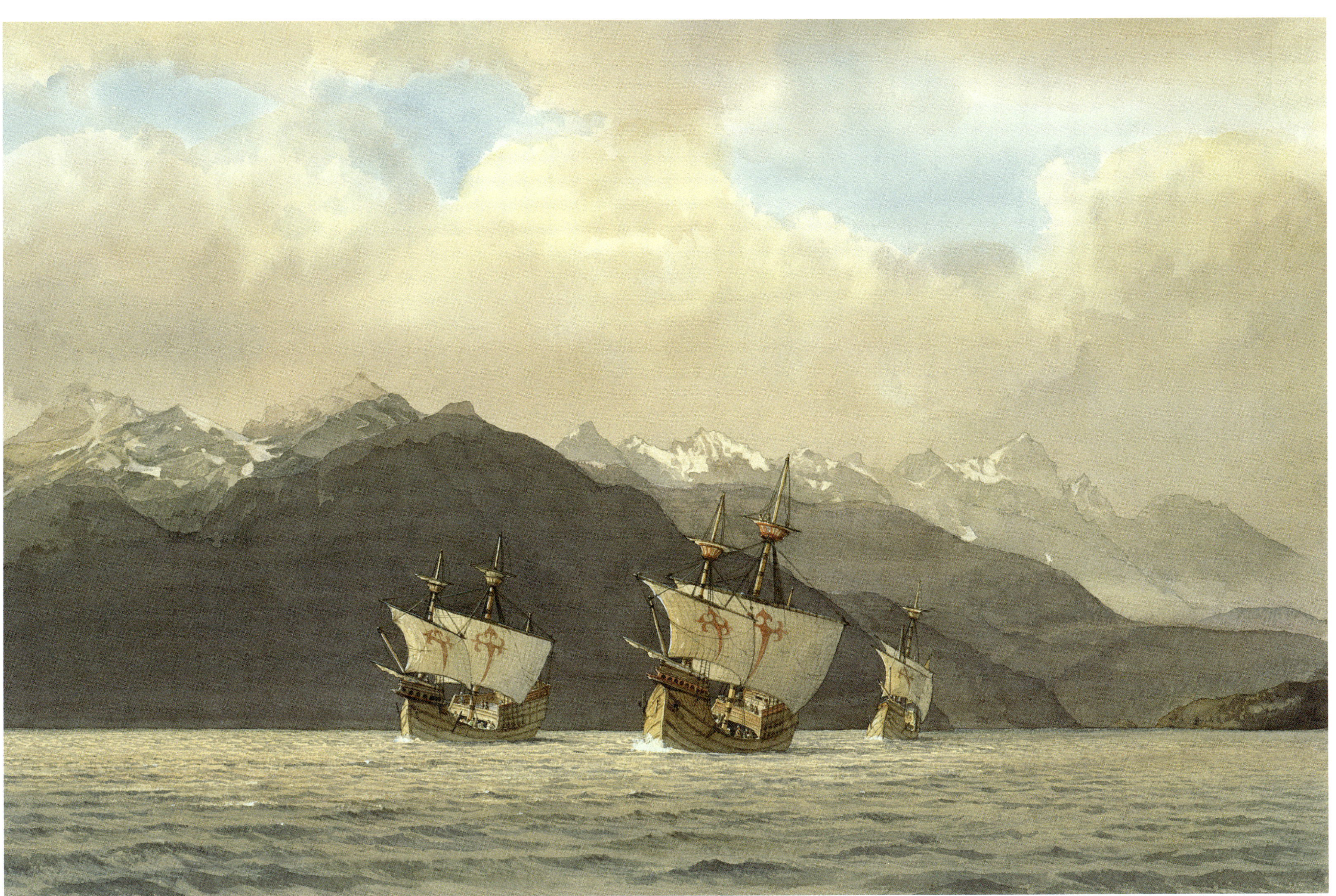

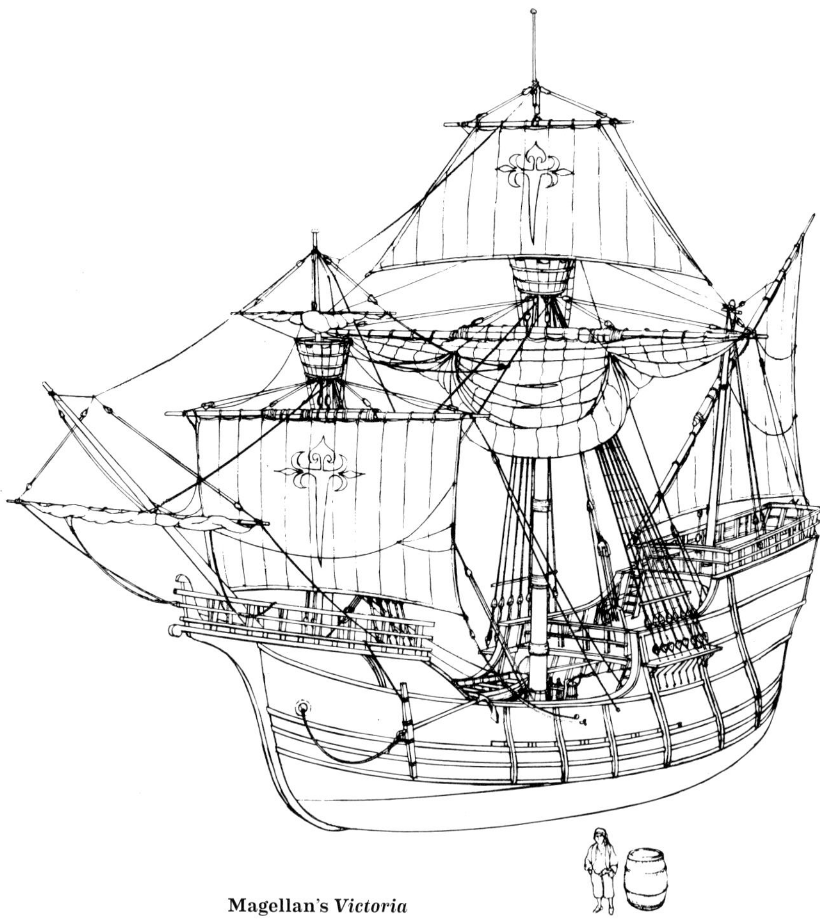

Magellan's *Victoria*

On April 7, 1521, the fleet came to anchor off the village of Cebu, where Magellan established friendly relations with the local rajah. While there he foolishly tried to demonstrate the power of his Christian god and Catholic king over a rebellious minor rajah of the neighboring island of Mactan. At first light on April 27 he led sixty men in three boats into a bay out of range of the ships' cannon. Against a force of 1,500 armed and determined warriors, the outcome was inevitable. Eight Spaniards were killed, many others were wounded and Magellan was hacked to pieces. In the aftermath of this tragedy, the fleet was in disarray. The company was further reduced by disease, starvation and warfare to only 110 men, barely enough to man the ships. The decision was made to abandon *Concepcion,* which was riddled with worms and leaking badly. *Trinidad,* leaking too much to reach Spain, was later captured by the Portuguese while trying to make Panama.

With Magellan dead, the responsibility for getting back to Spain fell on Juan Sebastián de Elcano, the only captain left alive. He faced the prospect of a thirteen-thousand-mile voyage through Portuguese-controlled waters and around the Cape of Good Hope against prevailing westerlies. On December 21 the only remaining ship in the fleet, *Victoria,* weighed anchor for home. The passage took another eight and a half months, with only one stop at the Cape Verde Islands, where the crew was finally forced to stop for provisions.

Victoria limped into Sanlucar de Barrameda, Spain, on September 6, 1522, the only surviving ship of the five that had sailed two years, ten and a half months earlier. Of the original 250 crewmen who sailed with the fleet, only eighteen were aboard when *Victoria* dropped anchor in the river. They were tired and sick. They had been pumping the sinking ship night and day for weeks and had barely the strength to struggle into the nearest chapel to give penitence.

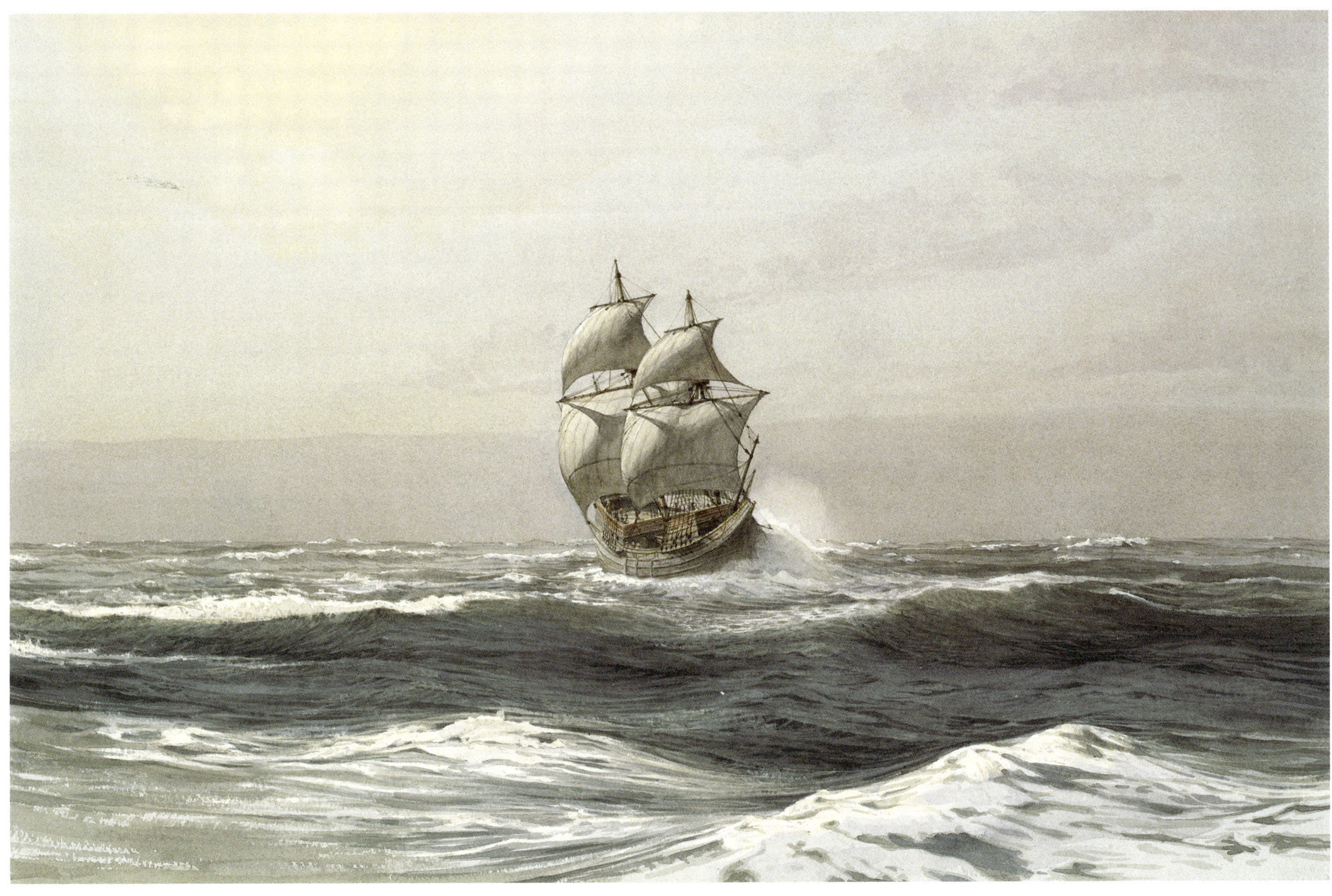

Manila galleon in the North Pacific, 1565
(WC, 15″ × 22″)
In the sixteenth century Manila was a major trading port, patronized regularly by Chinese traders and conveniently close to the Spice Islands. At first the Spanish had no understanding of the wind circulation in the Pacific Ocean, and ships from Manila carried goods home to Spain around the Cape of Good Hope. But in 1565, under the direction of Andres de Urdaneta, the fleet leaving the Philippines sailed north until they came to the latitude of the northwest trades, then rode these strong, steady winds back to Mexico. For the next 250 years the treasure galleons from Manila followed this route, sailing east between latitude 30° and 45° north until they reached North America, then continuing south to Acapulco.

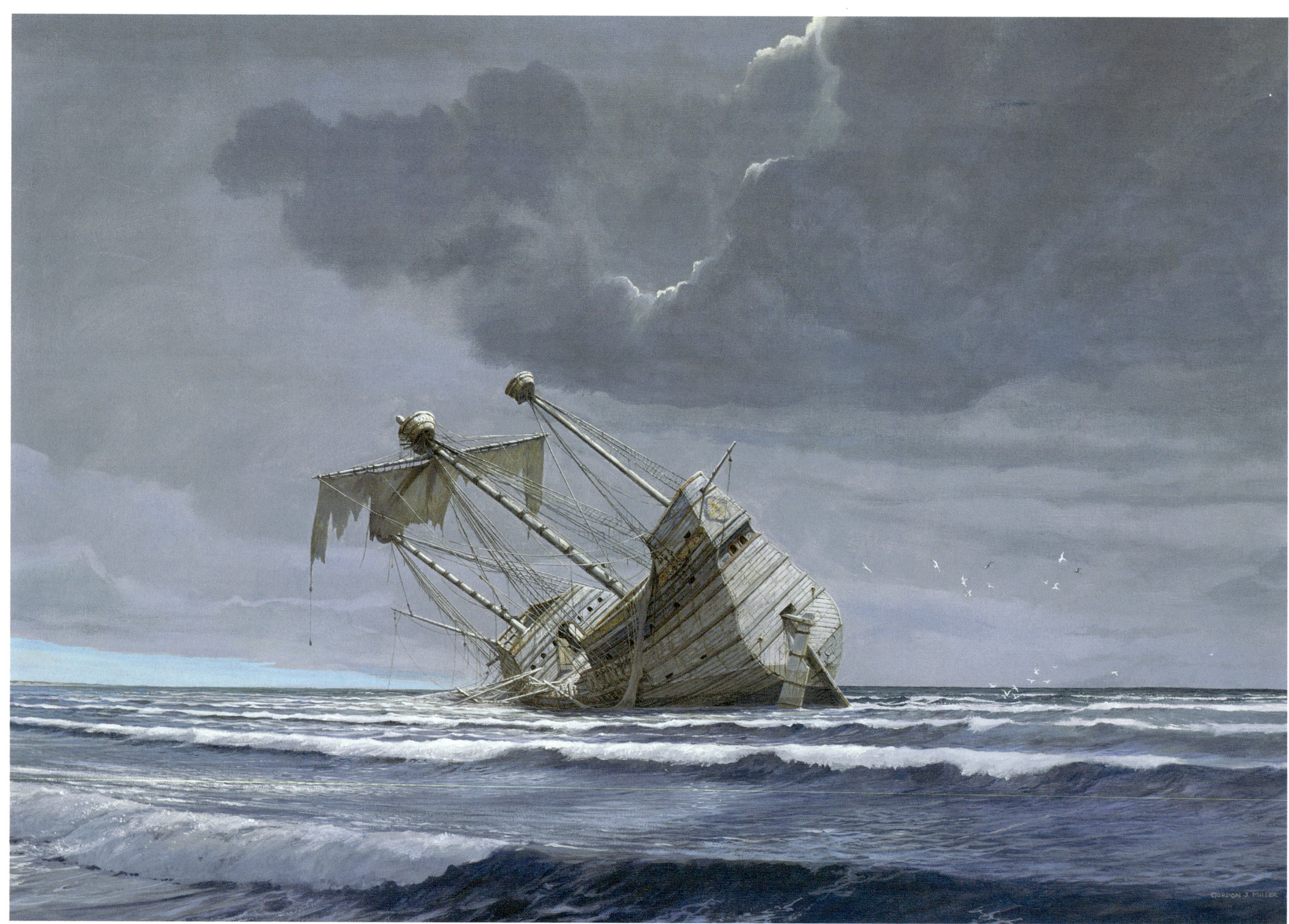
GORDON J. MILLER

The voyage was surely one of the greatest in recorded history, and Elcano and his seventeen crewmen were the first true circumnavigators. They had sailed 14,460 leagues, or more than fifty thousand nautical miles. Although Magellan did not survive to complete the voyage, he had been its inspirational and organizational force, and his accomplishment was of incalculable importance to Spain. When he had finally reached the Philippines, Magellan, believing he was still within the Spanish half of the world, had claimed the islands for the Spanish king. From then on, Spain considered the whole Pacific Ocean to be its own.

In the sixteenth century Spain also quickly took advantage of the sailing tracks pioneered by Columbus, establishing and supplying a growing number of bases in the Caribbean from which conquistadors launched their assault on Central and South America. In 1519 Hernán Cortés, a wealthy merchant, landowner and shipbuilder, landed on the coast of Mexico and, in two years, with only a few hundred men, defeated an Aztec army of thousands. In the following decade, conquistadors overran the native populations of Central America and the west coast of South America. The incredible wealth of the Incas rescued the Spanish crown from bankruptcy and financed its expanding empire for decades. More important for Spain's later expansion into the North Pacific, that wealth allowed Spain to establish several naval bases on the Pacific coast of Mexico, from which treasure galleons made regular voyages to Manila in the Philippines, which Magellan had earlier claimed for Spain.

Early in the sixteenth century the Spaniards in Mexico exhibited little interest in their coasts to the north, but in 1542 Juan Rodríguez Cabrillo was instructed to search for a mythical land of golden cities and fabulous riches. Cabrillo was a conquistador in the service of Cortés and the first to explore the coast of Alta California. On June 27 he sailed from Puerto de Navidad, a harbor near present-day Manzanillo, on *San Salvador,* accompanied by the smaller *Victoria,* with enough provisions for two or three years.

After a landfall near Cabo San Lucas the explorers kept in with the coast, searching for signs of natives and safe harbors, anchored almost every night and described and named many of the geographic features they saw. They performed acts of possession at several locations, the first at a bay they called Puerto de la Posesión, at about 31° north. They met and described for the first time natives at San Diego, Santa Catalina Island and the islands in the Santa Barbara Channel. On September 28, on the way north, *San Salvador* and *Victoria* sailed into a "closed and very good port" and Cabrillo stepped ashore, claimed the land for Spain and named it Bahia de San Miguel. This was the site that would become San Diego.

On Isla de San Miguel in the Channel Islands off the coast, Cabrillo was injured in a fall on a rocky beach. His wounds became gangrenous. On January 3, 1543, he died

‹ **Wreck of *San Felipe*** (Oil, 24″ × 36″)
In 1576 the Spanish galleon San Felipe *sailed from Manila for Acapulco, laden with silk, spices, porcelain and other Oriental luxuries. After six months at sea, weather-beaten and probably with most of her crew dead or dying, she was sailing south off the Baja California coast far to the east of the safe galleon track, likely with no lookouts posted.* San Felipe *ground to a stop on sands hundreds of yards from shore. The coast where she grounded was one of the most inhospitable in the world. No one aboard survived, although the ship rested intact on the beach for at least a year before being destroyed by a storm.* San Felipe*'s fate remained a mystery until 2003, when some of her cargo was found on a remote Baja California beach.*

Cabrillo entering San Diego Bay, 1542 (wc, 15″ × 22″)
Juan Rodríguez Cabrillo was a wealthy conquistador who led the first European voyage of exploration along the north coast of New Spain. On September 28, 1542, his ships San Salvador *and* Victoria *sailed into the port that would later be named San Diego.*

Wreck of *San Agustin* (Oil, 24″ × 36″)
With only dead reckoning to determine position and a passage of up to three months across the open Pacific, Spanish ships sailing from Manila to Mexico would be low on water and provisions, and the crews weak from scurvy and hunger. A safe port on the north coast to provision and rest would have been a great benefit, and San Agustin *was given the task of searching for one. On her return voyage from Manila in 1595, she came to anchor off the beach in Drakes Bay, just north of present-day San Francisco, and all but a skeleton crew went ashore. A sudden storm from the west drove the ship on the beach, where she became a total loss—the first known wreck on the California coast. Everyone but those left on the ship eventually survived and returned to Acapulco in the ship's boats.*

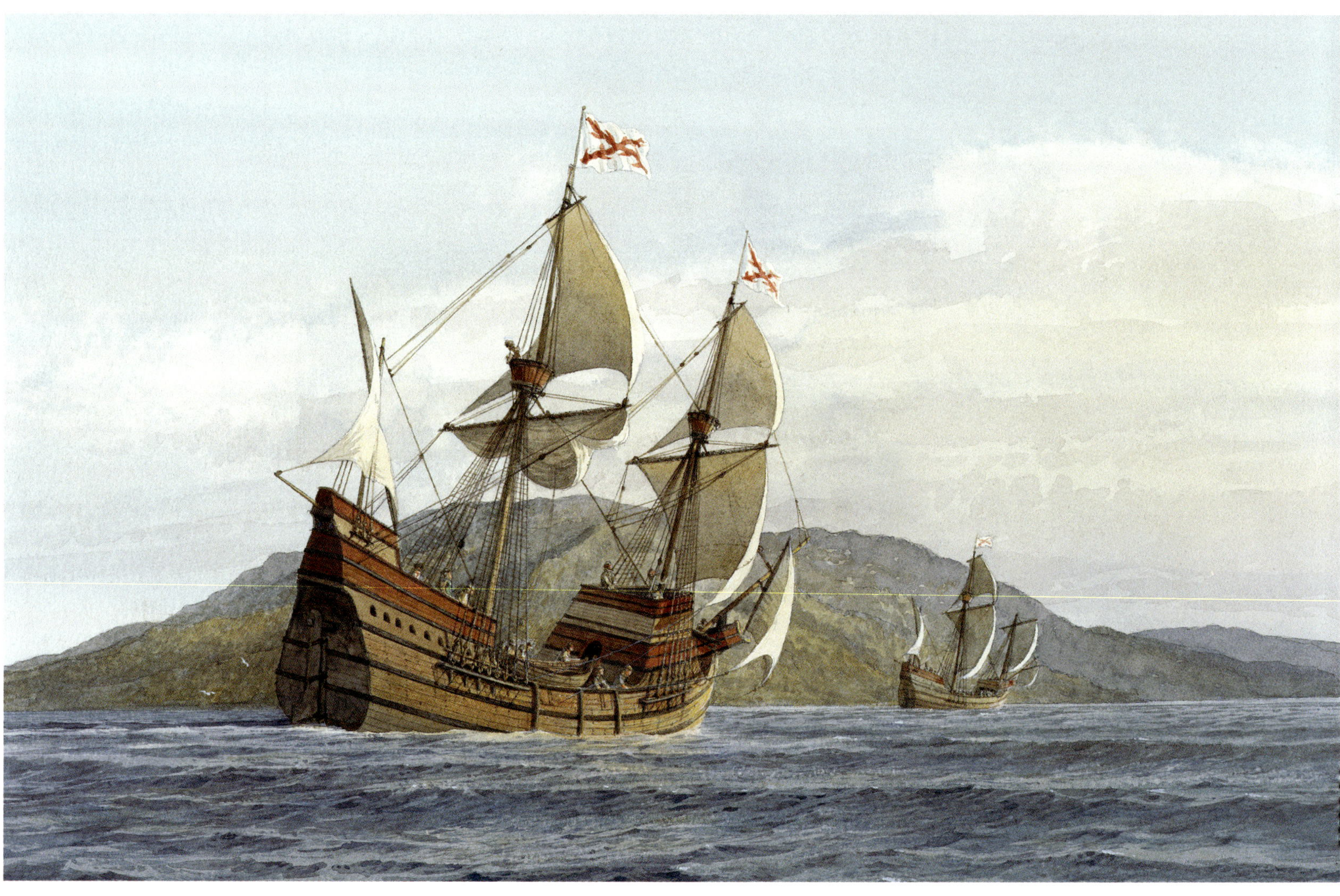

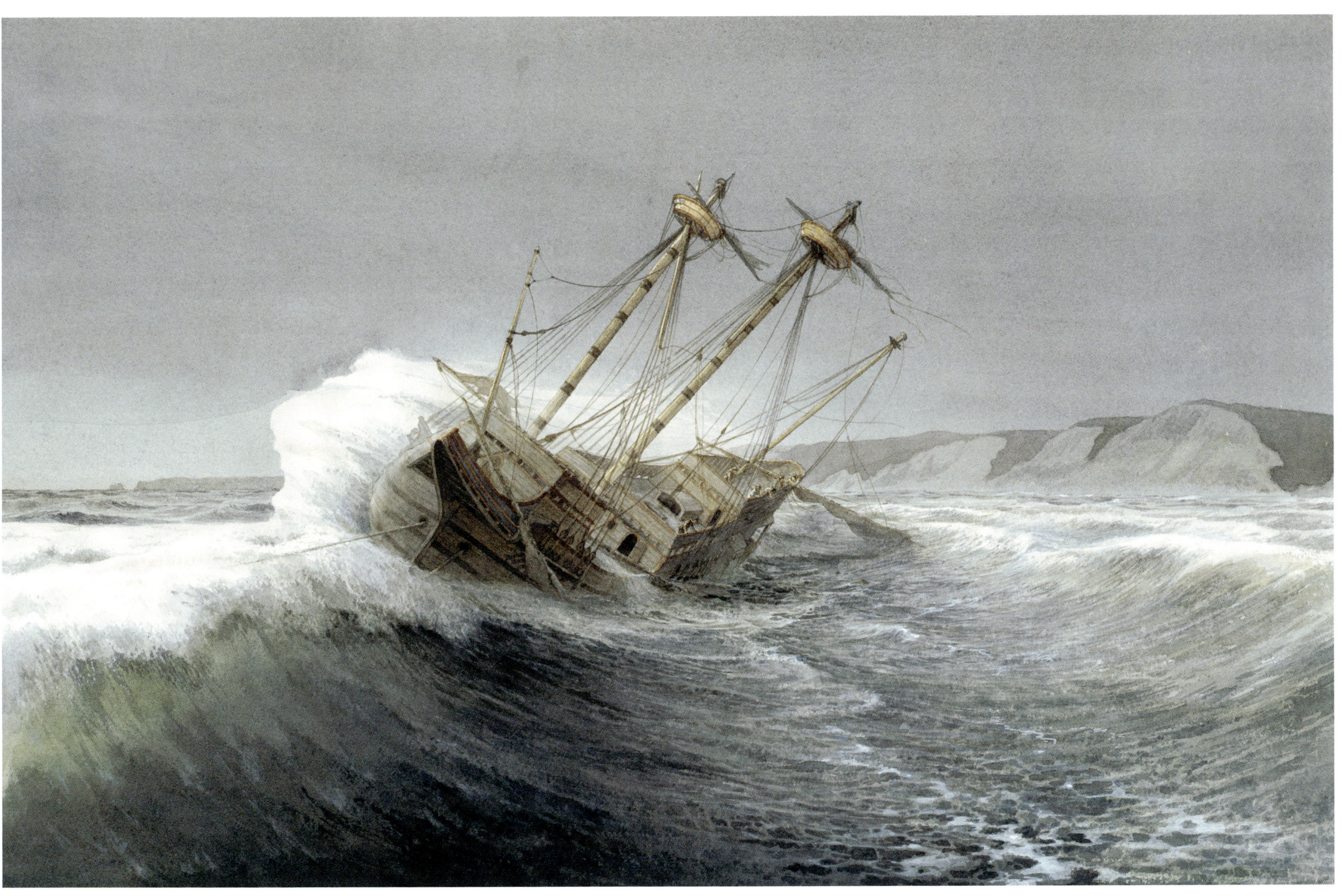

➤ **Verrazzano in the Narrows** (WC, 15″ × 22″) *On April 17, 1524,* La Dauphine *was off the east coast of Staten Island, sailing before an easy southwest wind. Ahead a great bay opened: "We found a very pleasant place, situated amongst certain little steep hills," Giovanni da Verrazzano noted. "From amidst the hills there ran down into the sea a great stream of water, which within the mouth was very deep, and from the sea to the mouth of same, with the tide, which we found the rise 8 foot, any great vessel laden may pass up."* La Dauphine *anchored in what now is called the Verrazzano Narrows, the entrance to the future harbor of New York.*

and was buried on the island they renamed Juan Rodríguez. After this expedition, Spain sent no more vessels north for more than two hundred years—not until the Russian incursions in Alaska ignited their concern.

Giovanni da Verrazzano and Jacques Cartier: Encountering "the New Land"

In 1523 France joined the race to find the Northwest Passage to the Orient. To this end a group of Italian bankers and silk merchants in Lyon, anticipating huge profits from the control of an easy sea route to China, formed a syndicate and financed the provisioning of four ships. Giovanni da Verrazzano was appointed commander of the expedition. Born into a wealthy Tuscan family, Verrazzano was educated in Florence before moving to Dieppe to pursue a career at sea. By the time he took command of the fleet he was an experienced seaman and navigator, with extensive voyages in the Mediterranean and to the Newfoundland fishing grounds.

Loaned the flagship *La Dauphine* by the Royal French Navy, Verrazzano sailed with a commission from the French king, Francis I, to explore the east coast of "the New Land." *La Dauphine* measured one hundred tons and had a crew of fifty, whom Verrazzano called *la turba marittima*—"the maritime mob." Their unruly behavior might be explained by their having almost no opportunity to go ashore during their six months at sea because of Verrazzano's unseamanlike habit of anchoring in open roadsteads off exposed beaches.

On about March 4, 1524, Verrazzano made a landfall near Cape Fear, North Carolina. He kept a daily log, and his description of the American coastline and the natives he encountered is the earliest known to exist: "Pursuing our voyage towards the West, a little northwardly... we reached a new country, which had never before been seen by any one, either in ancient or modern times... many people who were seen coming to the sea-side fled at our approach, but occasionally stopping, they looked back upon us in astonishment... they showed the greatest delight in beholding us, wondering at our dress, countenances, and complexion."

La Dauphine explored briefly to the south, then turned northeast along the coast, admiring the many islands and harbors of Maine, before easterly winds forced her offshore, thus missing the Bay of Fundy, most of what is now Atlantic Canada and the Gulf of St. Lawrence. In late June she was off the coast of Newfoundland. There the crew took on wood and water and headed for home. By July 8, 1524, *La Dauphine* was anchored at Dieppe. On this remarkable voyage Verrazzano had mapped and described the American east coast from Carolina to Maine and confirmed the existence of a completely new land. But he had not found a northwest passage, nor had he returned with riches for his backers.

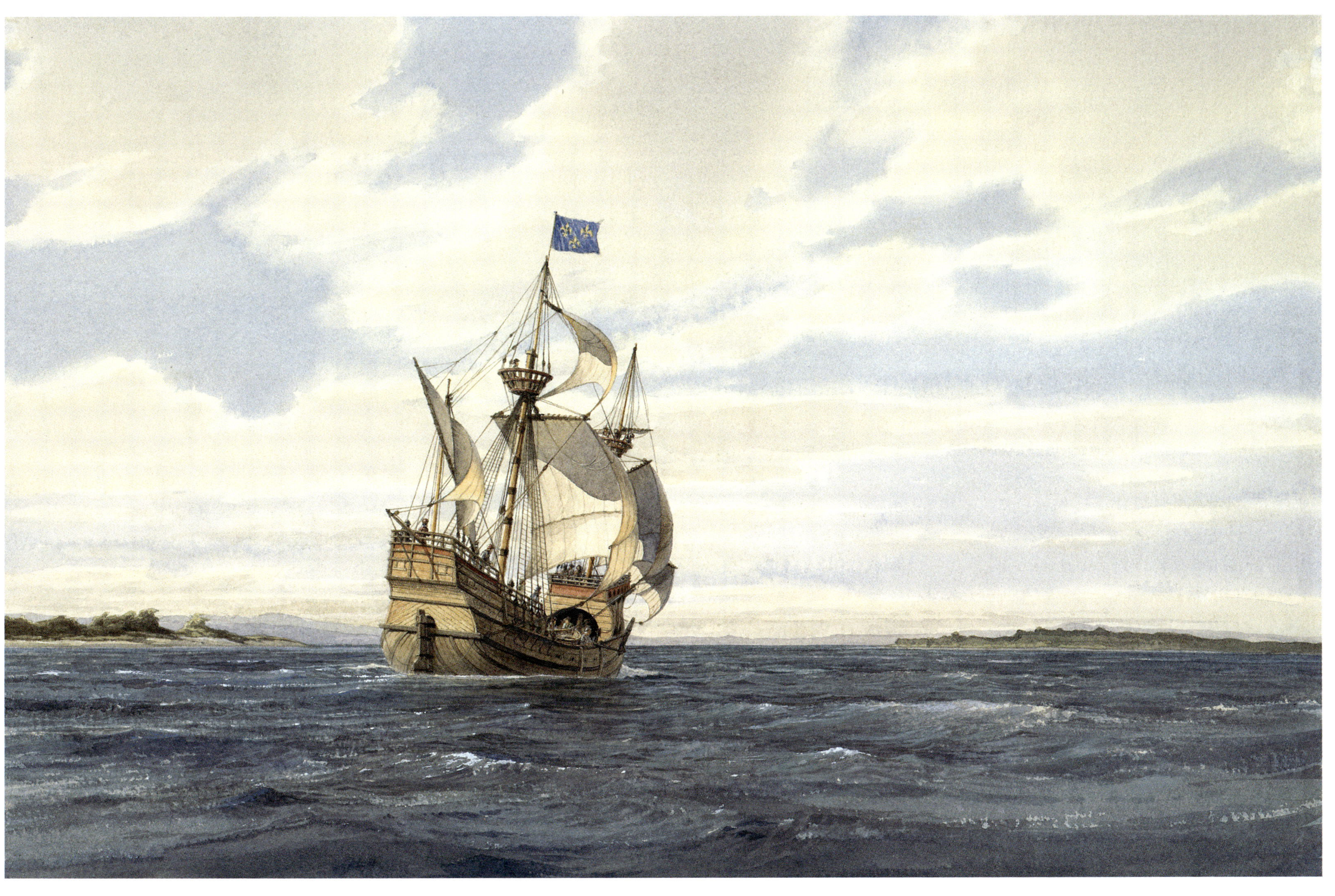

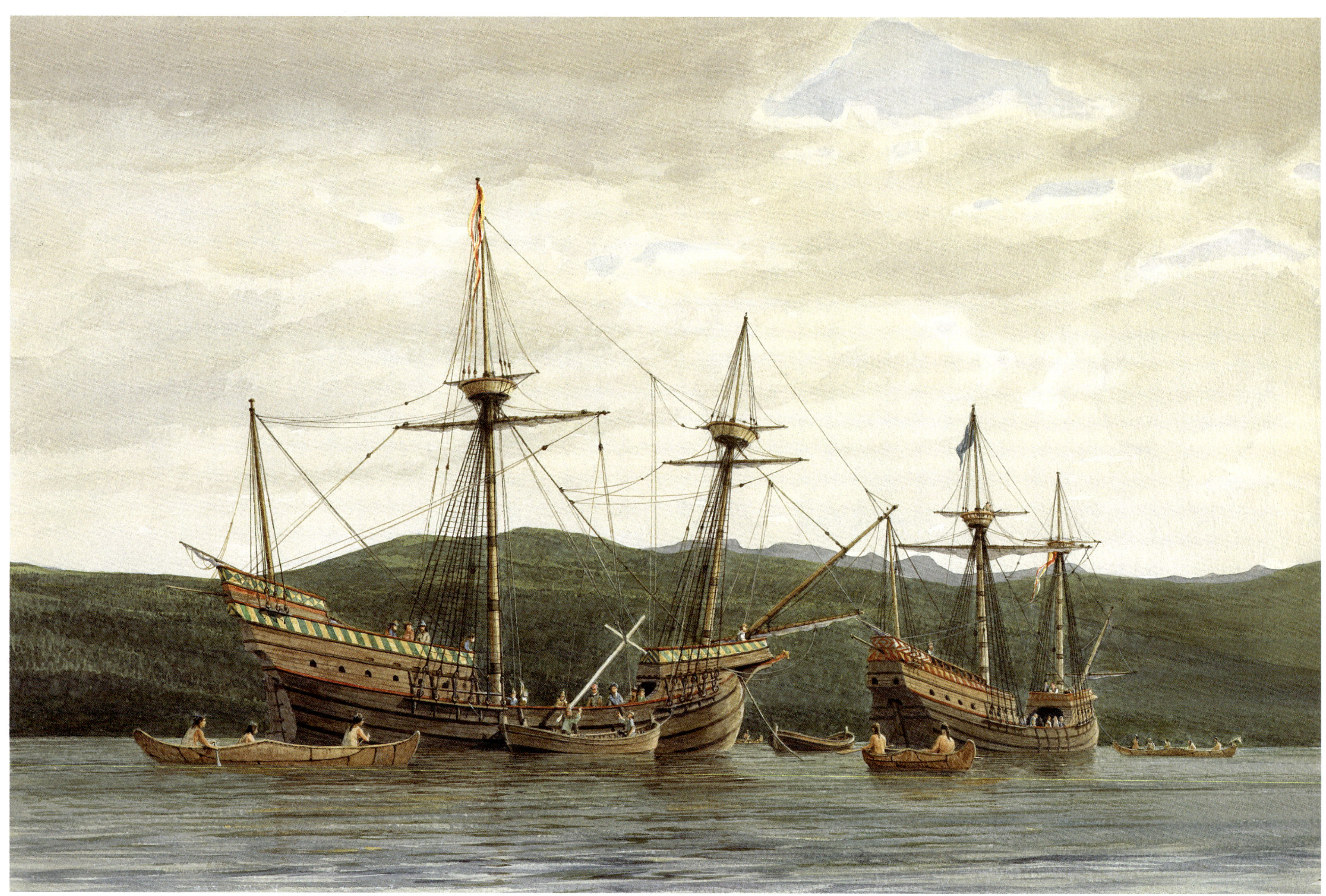

It was ten years before France mounted another serious attempt to find a western ocean passage to the Orient. Verrazzano had claimed that the land contained great riches, and that claim alone may have whetted French interest. In 1534 Jacques Cartier, a Breton mariner from St. Malo, was given a royal commission and two ships with instructions to find a northern passage to China. The two ships sailed from St. Malo on April 20. They must have been blessed with a fine easterly wind, for they made landfall at Cape Bonavista, Newfoundland, after only twenty days at sea. Cartier came on to the coast at 48°30′ north, almost the same latitude as St. Malo, suggesting he had followed that parallel all the way across.

After anchoring for ten days to avoid ice and to make repairs, Cartier and his men sailed around the top of Newfoundland, through the Strait of Belle Isle and down the west coast of the island. At midnight on June 25 they left the strait and sailed past Magdalen Island, and on June 30 made landfall on the north shore of Prince Edward Island. They rounded North Cape and followed the coast to the south before crossing the Northumberland Strait to present-day New Brunswick. This was new territory to Europeans, and as Cartier sailed into Miramichi Bay he believed he had found the strait leading to the Orient.

The two ships sailed north from Gaspé instead of west into the river and ended up on the south shore of Anticosti Island. There headwinds and strong currents discouraged further progress, and on August 2 they decided to return to France. Sailing back up the Strait of Belle Isle, they reached St. Malo on September 5.

The information gained on this voyage persuaded the king to commission a second one, and this time Cartier was provided with three ships: *La Grande Hermine*, *La Petite Hermine* and *L'Emerillon*. On May 19, 1535, Cartier sailed from St. Malo, and seven weeks later he and his men were back where they had left off the year before. On August 10, the feast day of St. Lawrence, they found a good anchorage on the north side of the river and named the place *La baye sainct laurens*. The name "St. Lawrence" would later be applied to the gulf, the river and a mountain range. "Canada" was also recorded for the first time, the name of the land as it was known to the Iroquois.

The three ships continued up the river to the native village of Stadacona, the site of present-day Quebec City. Cartier left the two largest ships and continued on to Hochelaga, a large fortified Iroquois village, now the site of Montreal. That was as close as he was ever to get to China. Returning to Stadacona, where a fort had been built in his absence, he prepared to stay the winter. There the men discovered the fierceness of winters and the devastating effects of scurvy. Only the natives' knowledge of the use of the bark of the arborvitae tree prevented disaster. As it was, when they sailed for home on May 6, *La Petite Hermine* was left behind because there were not enough men to handle two ships.

‹ **Cartier in Gaspé Bay, July 24, 1534**
(WC, 15″ × 22″)
In Baie des Chaleurs, Jacques Cartier's crew encountered friendly Mi'kmaq in canoes who were eager to trade. A little farther north, in Gaspé Bay, they met Chief Donnacona with two hundred of his Iroquois, down from his village of Stadacona on a fishing expedition. On the shore of this bay, and witnessed by the Iroquois, Cartier erected a large cross, taking possession of the country for the king of France. By this act—and over Donnacona's objections—France gained a foothold and claim to a significant piece of North America.

➤ ***Golden Hind*** **in Southern Ocean storm**
(wc, 15″ × 22″)
Whenever possible, Golden Hind *would have carried tiny scraps of sail to maintain steerage way and to keep off the coast, the rocky lee shores of Tierra del Fuego. Francis Drake's three ships were in some of the most dangerous waters on Earth, and the northwesterly storms drove them inexorably south and east, at one point as far as latitude 57° south. Drake was aware that he had been in open water well below the American continent. That lonely stretch of the Southern Ocean is now called Drake Passage.*

Cartier had not found a route to the Orient, but he had penetrated deep into the continent, added some significant new names to the maps and created an important French presence in North America. He had also captured the Iroquois chief, Donnacona, and brought him back to France. Donnacona, a curiosity and a celebrity, became adept at feeding the French court stories of riches and abundance in his "Kingdom of Saguenay," and he was instrumental in instigating a third voyage to America. However, a war with Spain delayed the launch of the next expedition, which didn't sail until 1541, and Donnacona died before he could be returned to his homeland.

The third voyage was also led by Cartier, but this time the objective was to found a colony in Donnacona's kingdom. A French nobleman, Jean-François de la Roque, Sieur de Roberval, was appointed overall commander and governor of the new lands. Roberval delayed his own departure for a full year. This time Cartier attempted to penetrate farther inland than he had before, but the Iroquois were uncooperative and the terrain too difficult. Near Stadacona Cartier built a stockaded settlement, but the Iroquois, realizing he meant to stay, became increasingly hostile. Cartier lost thirty-five men to their attacks over the winter. Discouraged and undermanned, in the spring of 1542 he sailed for home for the last time.

Roberval's attempt to colonize the New Land, when he did arrive on the continent, was even less successful than Cartier's, and after a terrible winter he too returned home, thus ending France's first attempt to establish a settlement in present-day Canada.

Francis Drake: Privateer to Circumnavigator

The sixteenth century had belonged to Spain. Its exploitation of the New World filled its homebound ships with silver and gold, and by the midpoint of the century Spain was a globe-girdling imperial power. But as the century ended, the nation was in decline. It was a turbulent time, and the continuing conflict between the Roman Catholic Church and rebellious Protestants in the Netherlands, Germany and England, as well as with the Turks, had drained Spain's treasury. In England, eighteen-year-old Henry VIII assumed the throne in 1509 and spent much of his reign vying for power with the Catholic Church.

His daughter Elizabeth, crowned queen in 1558, inherited her father's campaign against his continental enemies. This was the time of the English adventurers and buccaneers—Cabot, Frobisher, Drake and Hawkins—many of whom, after major ocean explorations on their own, later combined to help defeat the Spanish Armada. No longer threatened by Spain's attempt to invade and to reimpose Catholicism on the heretics, little Protestant England began to probe the seas for trade and treasure. This was the beginning of the rise of the British Empire.

In the 1570s England was officially neutral towards Spain, although for almost a decade English marauders

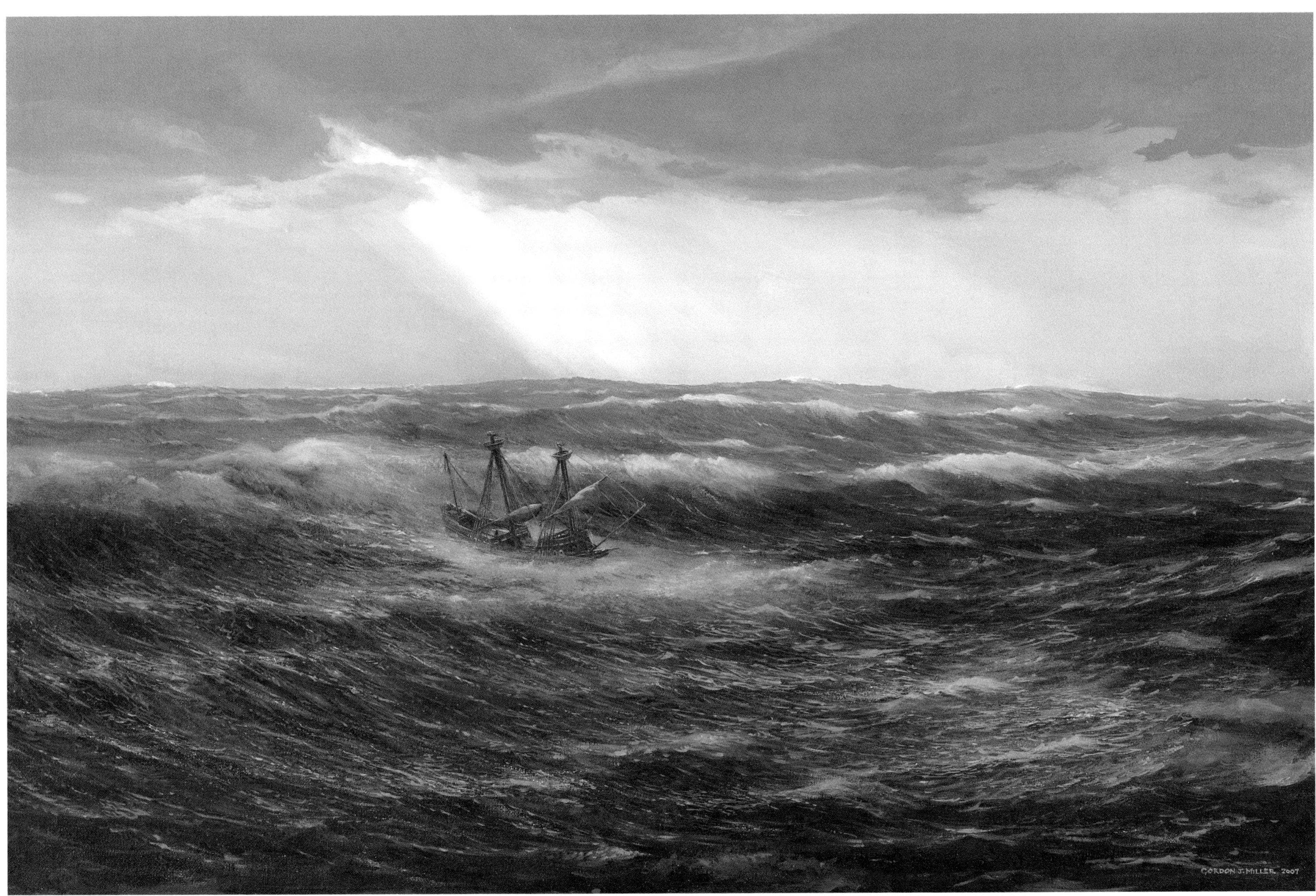
GORDON J. MILLER 2007

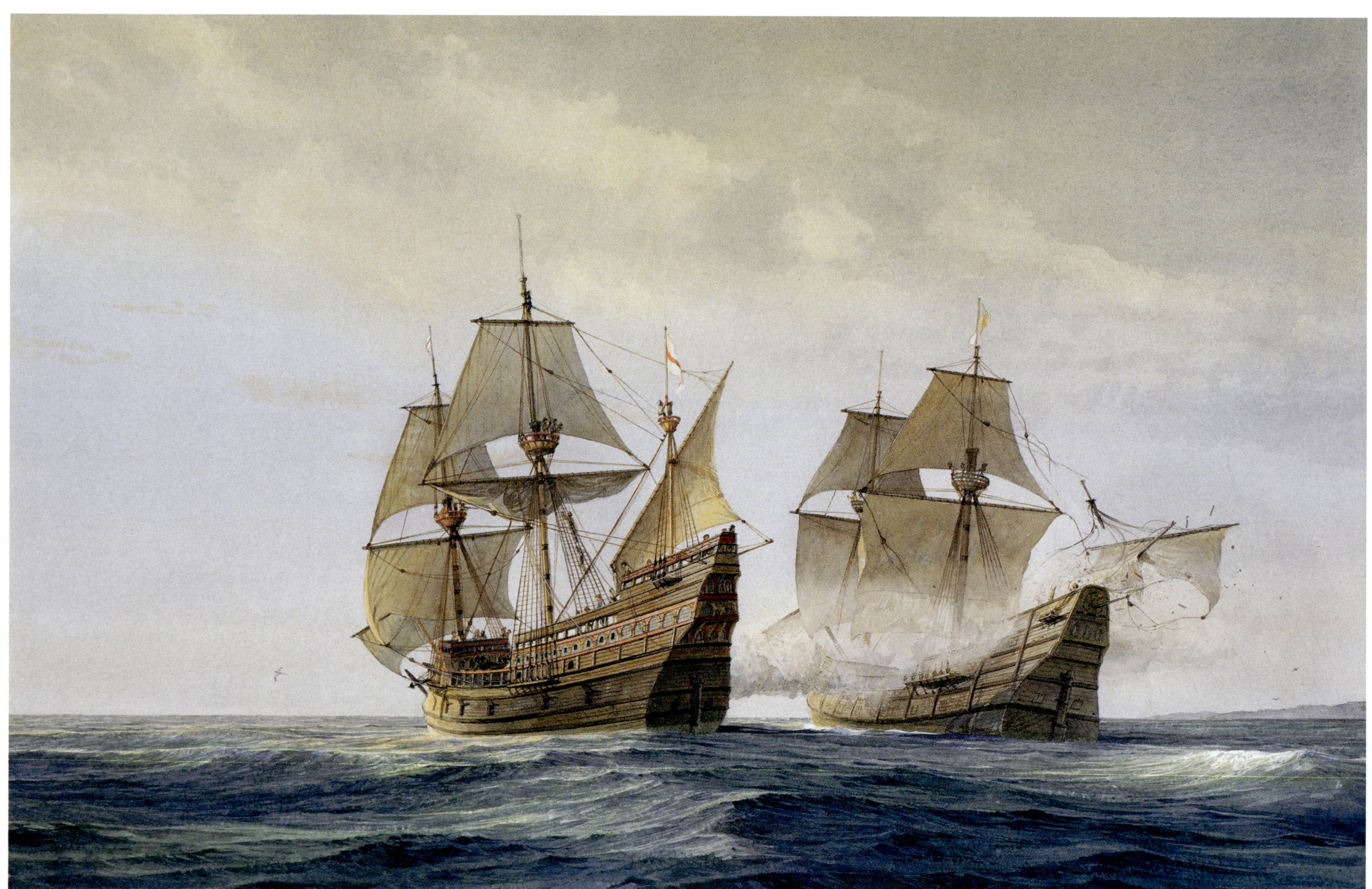

had been raiding Spanish ships and settlements in the New World, and Spain had been capturing and imprisoning English "pirates." The most successful of the Elizabethan captains was Francis Drake. In 1572–73 he had rampaged through the Caribbean, briefly capturing a Spanish port and waylaying bullion-loaded mule trains that were crossing the Isthmus of Panama. At one point Drake had hiked far enough west to see the Pacific Ocean, and he vowed one day to sail it in an English ship. He returned to England a hero and with a fortune in Spanish treasure.

Queen Elizabeth, while secretly praising Drake for his success, officially exiled him to Ireland to appease the incensed Spaniards. While in Ireland Drake nurtured an already well-established hatred of the Catholics and began to formulate a plan to challenge them in the Pacific. The scheme, which had been promoted for years by other advisers of Queen Elizabeth, was hugely ambitious: enter the Pacific via the Strait of Magellan, find and claim the unknown continent *Terra Australis,* sail north while plundering Spanish settlements on the west coast of the Americas, find the Northwest Passage and use it to return to England. Although Drake apparently agreed to this plan, his real ambition was likely to privateer freely among the unprepared Spaniards in the Pacific.

With Queen Elizabeth's unofficial blessing but with the intent of the voyage kept secret, Drake assembled a fleet of five ships. The flagship was the 120-ton *Pelican.* The others were *Elizabeth,* 80 tons; *Marigold,* 30 tons; *Swan,* 50 tons; and a pinnace, *Christopher,* 15 tons. They departed Plymouth on December 13, 1577, and after a difficult passage down the Atlantic reached Brazil on April 5, 1578. At Port San Julian, Drake put down a mutiny that had been brewing since the beginning of the voyage. Many of the gentlemen, some of whom had money invested in the enterprise, were unhappy with Drake's assumption of overall authority and were quietly fomenting dissension through the fleet. The chief instigator was Thomas Doughty, whose influence in the English court had helped Drake obtain backing for his venture. Doughty had joined Drake expecting to be his equal in command. In the ensuing showdown, Doughty was found guilty of intriguing to overthrow the venture and was executed. He was buried under the gibbets that were still standing at Bay San Julian, the ones that had been erected to hang the mutineers of Magellan's voyage fifty-eight years earlier.

The voyage continued on August 17 without *Christopher* and *Swan,* which had become unseaworthy. The remaining ships arrived off the entrance to the Strait of Magellan three days later, and there *Pelican* was renamed *Golden Hind* to honor Sir Christopher Hatton, Drake's patron, whose principal figure on his coat of arms was a golden deer, or hind. The ships passed through the strait in a remarkable sixteen days, compared with Magellan's thirty-eight, and entered the Pacific Ocean on September 6.

The next day they were struck by the first of a succession of fierce storms that raged constantly for almost

‹ **Capture of *Cacafuego*** (WC, 15″ × 22″)
The Spaniards employed a fleet of unarmed merchantmen to transport bullion and other treasure from Chile and Peru to the port of Panama. For more than thirty years they had sailed the coast unmolested, so they were taken completely by surprise when Francis Drake's Golden Hind *sailed into view in 1579. In El Callao, the port for Lima, Drake learned that the ship* Nuestra Señora de la Concepción, *affectionately known as* Cacafuego *("fireshitter"), had sailed thirteen days earlier with twenty-six tons of silver bars, thirteen chests of silver coins and eighty pounds of gold and jewels. The unsuspecting Spaniards allowed* Golden Hind *to sail alongside, and a broadside of chain shot took out her mizzen, ending any resistance before it could begin. Drake transferred* Cacafuego's *treasure to* Golden Hind *and allowed the Spaniards to go on their way.*

› **A fair and good bay** (Oil, 24″ × 36″)
Drakes Estero is a shallow estuary on the coast of Drakes Bay, California, protected by a shifting sandbar and with a navigable entrance channel when Golden Hind *visited in 1579. Francis Drake spent five weeks there in June and July, cleaning the bottom and repairing leaks to the ship. He was able to revictual the ship with the aid of the Coast Miwoks, the natives of the area. A peaceful people of hunters and gatherers, they were constantly around the encampment. Although neither side could understand the other, trust was established after elaborate gift exchanges, and friendly trade was conducted over the course of* Golden Hind*'s stay.*

two months. In this first encounter with the tempestuous Southern Ocean the three ships were separated. *Elizabeth* limped back to the strait and returned to England, but *Marigold* was never heard from again. Finally, on October 24, the winds eased and turned southerly, and *Golden Hind* found shelter behind Horn Island, where the crew rested for three days. When they sailed again they began a four-month reign of terror among the unprepared Spanish settlements. Fair winds and the Peru Current drove Drake easily northward, successfully capturing ships and ports and filling the hold of *Golden Hind* with treasure. Most of these settlements were small and barely protected. When everything of value was looted, Drake would sail away without harming the citizens but would leave the vessels in the harbor disabled and unable to pursue him or warn others to the north.

At the end of this foray, Drake was well north of Panama. From there he sailed far out to sea, possibly as far as 48° north, and regained the coast off Oregon, far beyond any Spanish settlements. He may have intended to sail home by the mythical Strait of Anian, but adverse winds, cold weather, a discontented crew and a foul and leaking *Golden Hind* forced him to turn south along the west coast, seeking a protected bay to repair the ship. He found a suitable cove, now known as Drakes Estero, on the California coast just north of San Francisco. There he stayed for thirty-six days, built a small fortification and careened *Golden Hind*. Before leaving he nailed a brass plate to a post engraved with the day and year of his arrival, and named the land Nova Albion because of its similarity to the cliffs facing the English Channel. This was the first act of possession by an Englishman on what would later become the United States.

With a sound and revictualed ship, Drake faced the problem of getting back to England. To the south lay the aroused and very angry Spaniards, whose settlements and ships he had plundered; to the north lay cold and uncertainty. The alternative was to cross the Pacific and Indian Oceans and sail north up the Atlantic. On July 23, 1579, Drake sailed, sighting no land until he reached Palau, five hundred miles east of the Philippines, sixty-eight days later. After loading six tons of cloves in the Moluccas, his luck ran out. Heavily laden, *Golden Hind* struck a reef off the island of Celebes on January 9, 1580. The crew jettisoned the least valuable cargo and guns and was able to get her off the reef undamaged. Their last port of call was Tjilatjap, on Java.

From there Drake embarked on what was the longest nonstop ocean passage to that time, crossing the Indian Ocean, rounding the Cape of Good Hope and not landing again until he reached Sierra Leone, West Africa, north of the Equator. *Golden Hind* arrived back in Plymouth on September 26, 1580. In her hold were twenty-six tons of silver coins and bars—Elizabethan England's greatest single acquisition of Spanish plunder. *Golden Hind*'s

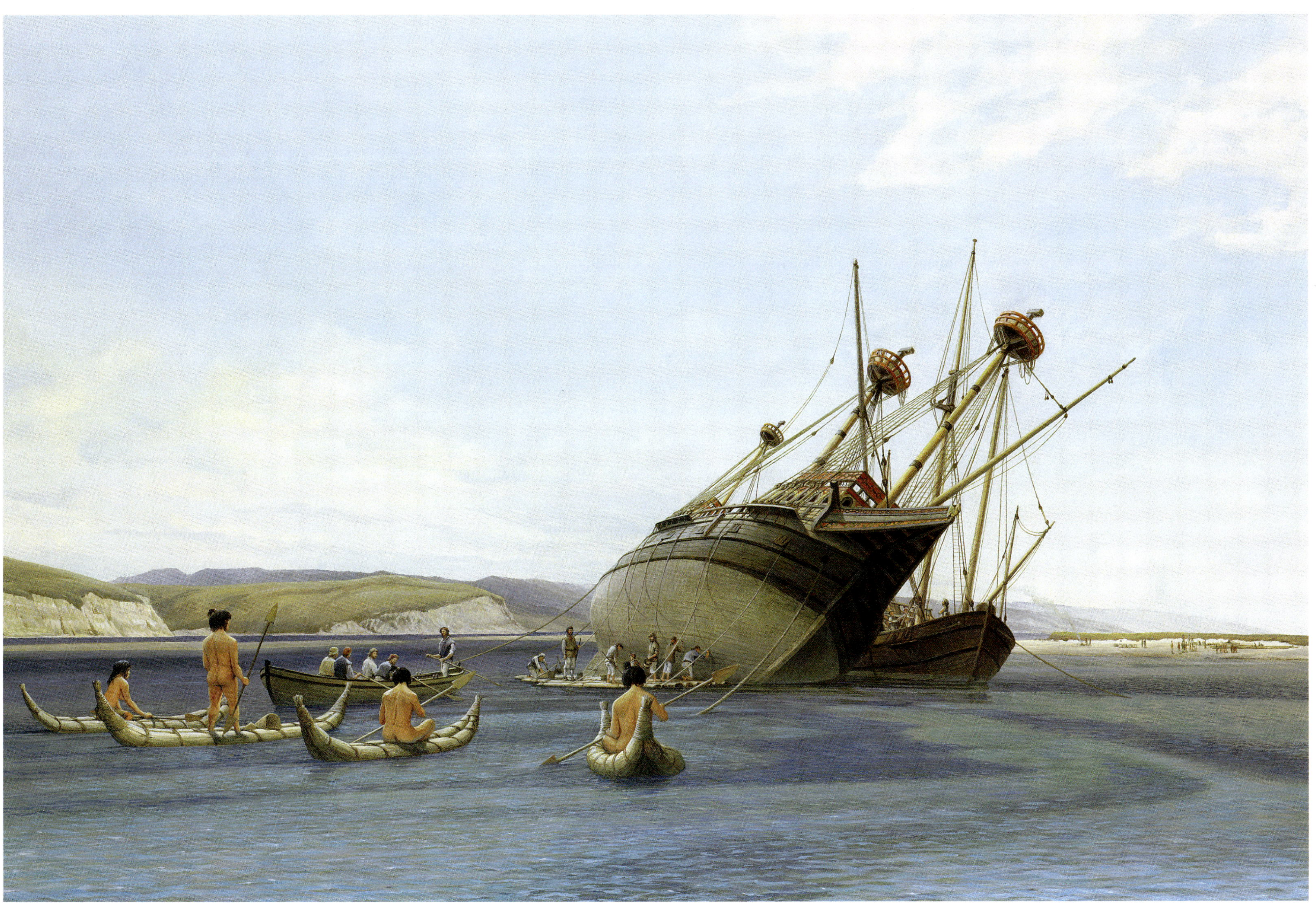

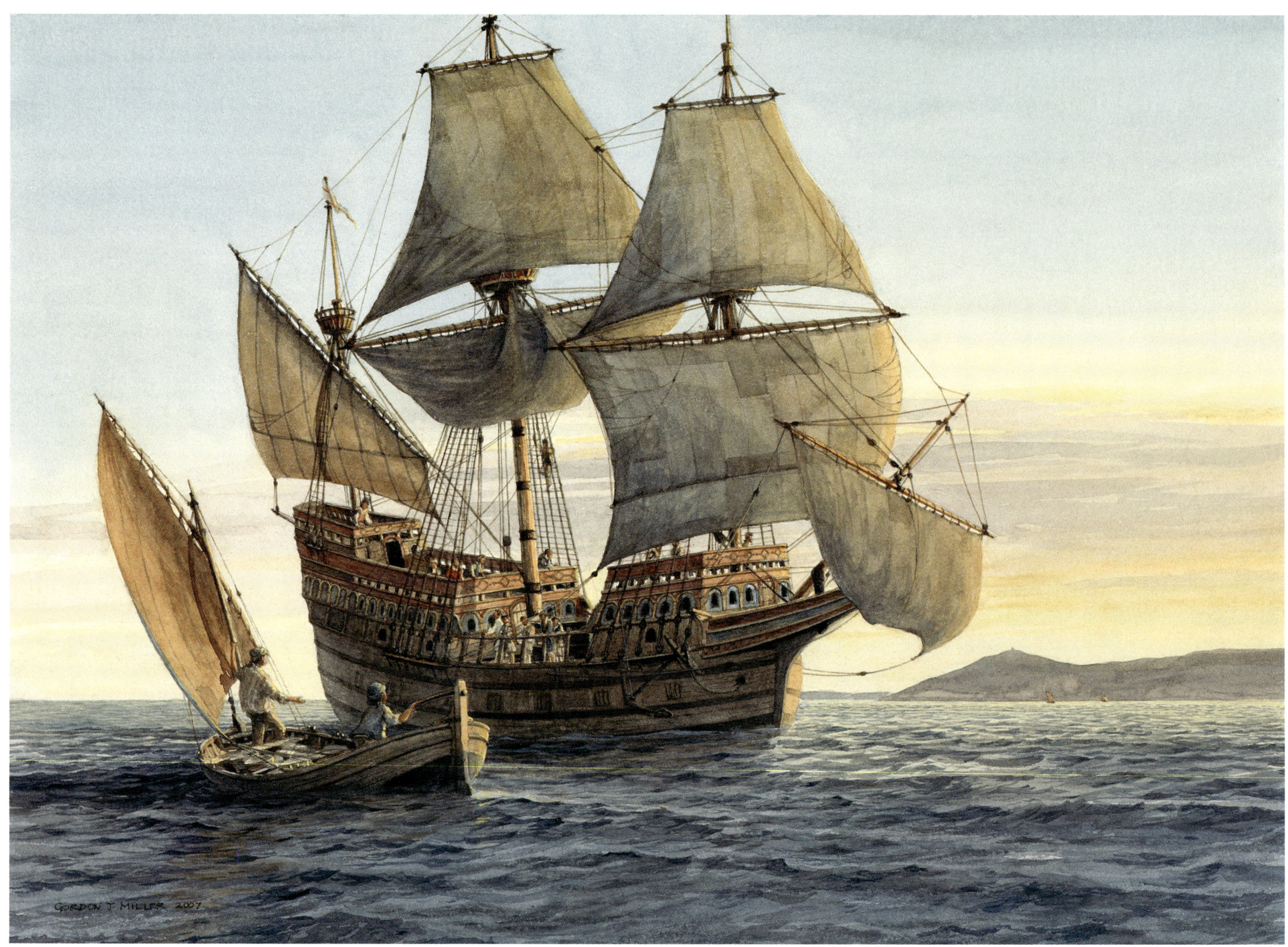
GORDON J. MILLER 2007

circumnavigation had taken almost three years, and, amazingly, more than half her crew survived.

What has not survived is any record of the captured treasure or any official accounts or charts of the voyage. The surviving journals differ in details, which has led to a great industry of speculation and myth-making about Drake's whereabouts in the North Pacific. Because there is more than one farthest-north latitude mentioned in the accounts, some believe that Drake reached the coast of Vancouver Island before turning south.

Martin Frobisher: The Quest for Arctic Gold

By the middle of the sixteenth century it was obvious to Europeans that the Americas were not part of Asia. The voyages of Verrazzano and Cartier had established that there was no ocean passage to the west between present-day Florida and Labrador. The only other route, through the Strait of Magellan, was controlled by Spain. Englishmen, with nowhere else to look, turned their efforts to the north. Foremost among these searchers was Martin Frobisher.

Frobisher was a tough Yorkshireman from a family of country gentry. Born in the late 1530s, before the age of fourteen he was sent to sea by an uncle with connections to trading enterprises to Africa, where he survived an attack of yellow fever he had picked up on Africa's west coast. Eleven years later, on another African venture, he was left as a hostage with the Portuguese and imprisoned for several months before being released. Sometime after that he became captain of a privateer and accepted commissions from anyone willing to engage his services. His seizure of a London merchant's cargo of wines landed him a short stretch in jail; his capture of a Spanish ship, when England was not yet officially at war with Spain, caused some embarrassment for Queen Elizabeth.

The existence of a Northwest Passage to Asia was being actively promoted in England, and Frobisher was anxious to lead an expedition to find it. He had gained an audience at court and the support of the Earl of Warwick. He was also supported by Michael Lok, a member of a substantial London mercantile family. Lok raised £875 from a group of private speculators and provided £739 of his own money. Frobisher, who had been dreaming of this opportunity for fifteen years, was given command.

Three very small vessels were purchased and prepared for the voyage. Their precise dimensions are unknown, but they were all much smaller than John Cabot's *Matthew*. Frobisher's *Gabriel* was thought to be about twenty-five tons, *Michael* about twenty tons, and an unnamed ten-ton pinnace was too large to be carried on deck. *Gabriel* carried an impressive list of books and navigational instruments: a cross-staff, a mariner's astrolabe, twenty compasses, eighteen half-hour glasses, an adjustable sundial, a *compassum meridianum* and a *holometrium geometricum*. A "carta of navigation . . . ruled playne" was provided to record the voyage, and the observations of

◂ **Does the Queen live?** (WC, 15″ × 22″) *On the evening of September 26, 1580,* Golden Hind *arrived off Rame Head, Plymouth Sound, 1,046 days after Francis Drake had sailed her from England. Drake became the second European to circumnavigate the globe. On entering the sound he hailed the first fishermen to ask, "Is the Queen still alive and well?" Drake was hailed a hero and knighted by Queen Elizabeth aboard the* Golden Hind.

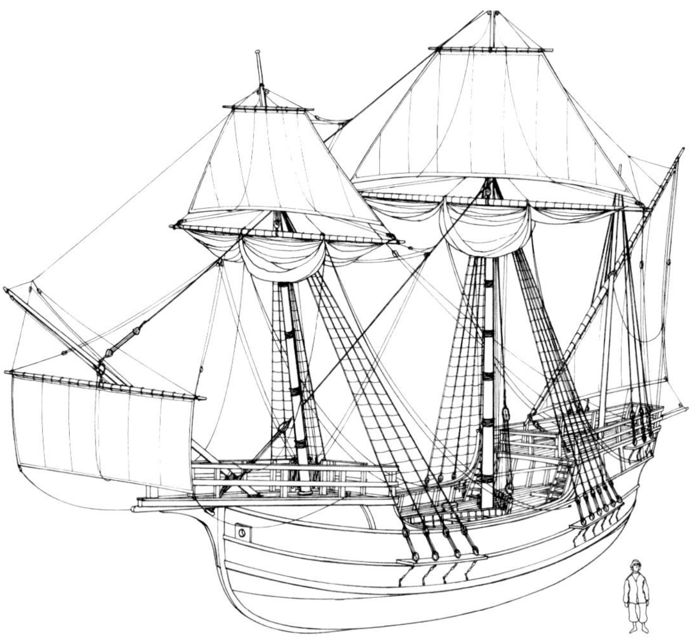

Martin Frobisher's *Gabriel*

› **Frobisher in *Gabriel*, Frobisher Bay, 1576** (WC, 15″ × 22″)
While anchored off a small island in Frobisher Bay, Martin Frobisher's men found ore they were sure was gold. They also encountered their first Inuit, with whom they traded for a few pleasant days. The pleasantness ended when the Inuit enticed ashore the ship's boat and five men, who were never seen again. The English retaliated by luring a man in a kayak alongside Gabriel *and then snatching him aboard, kayak and all. The Englishmen returned home with their captive, who soon died.*

compass variations and the lands encountered were kept on it by Frobisher. This map survived and is the only pre-seventeenth-century explorer's map known to exist.

In early June 1576 the three ships sailed from Ratcliff on the Thames. Passing Greenwich they fired a royal salute to the queen, who waved back graciously from her window in the palace. Foul winds delayed them at Harwich and Yarmouth, but they had a good run to the Shetland Islands before sailing into a severe eight-day gale that proved too much for the pinnace. She was lost with all four hands.

Gabriel and *Michael*'s intended course would have been as close to north as they could sail, to 60° north, on which latitude Frobisher believed the Northwest Passage to lie, then west. They had fair strong winds that carried them past the Faeroe Islands and Iceland and up to the southeast coast of Greenland, where landfall was made under a full moon on July 11. The coast was obstructed by pack ice, and the land was described as "rising like pinacles of steeples, and all covered with snowe." At this point, *Michael*'s master lost his courage and ran for home, reaching London on September 1. There he excused his behavior by saying that *Gabriel* had been "cast awaye" and that all was lost.

Frobisher carried on, nearly losing *Gabriel* in an extreme storm off Cape Farewell, the southernmost point of Greenland, only saving the ship from foundering by cutting away the mizzen mast. The storm blew her south, but after repairing the rig the crew again turned westward. On July 20 they sighted Resolution Island, at the southwestern cape of Baffin Island, which Frobisher named Queen Elizabeth's Forelande. Although the seas were ice choked, the explorers made their way for fifty leagues through the dead-end sound now known as Frobisher Bay, all the time convinced they were in the fabled passage. Ice finally ended their progress.

"Tyred and sik with laboure of their hard voyage" and with the loss of their only boat and a quarter of his crew—five of them lured ashore by Inuit—Frobisher abandoned the search for the fabled passage. On August 27, after spending a further forty-eight hours searching for the missing party and with a foot of snow on her deck, *Gabriel* sailed from the mouth of Frobisher Bay, arriving in London on October 9.

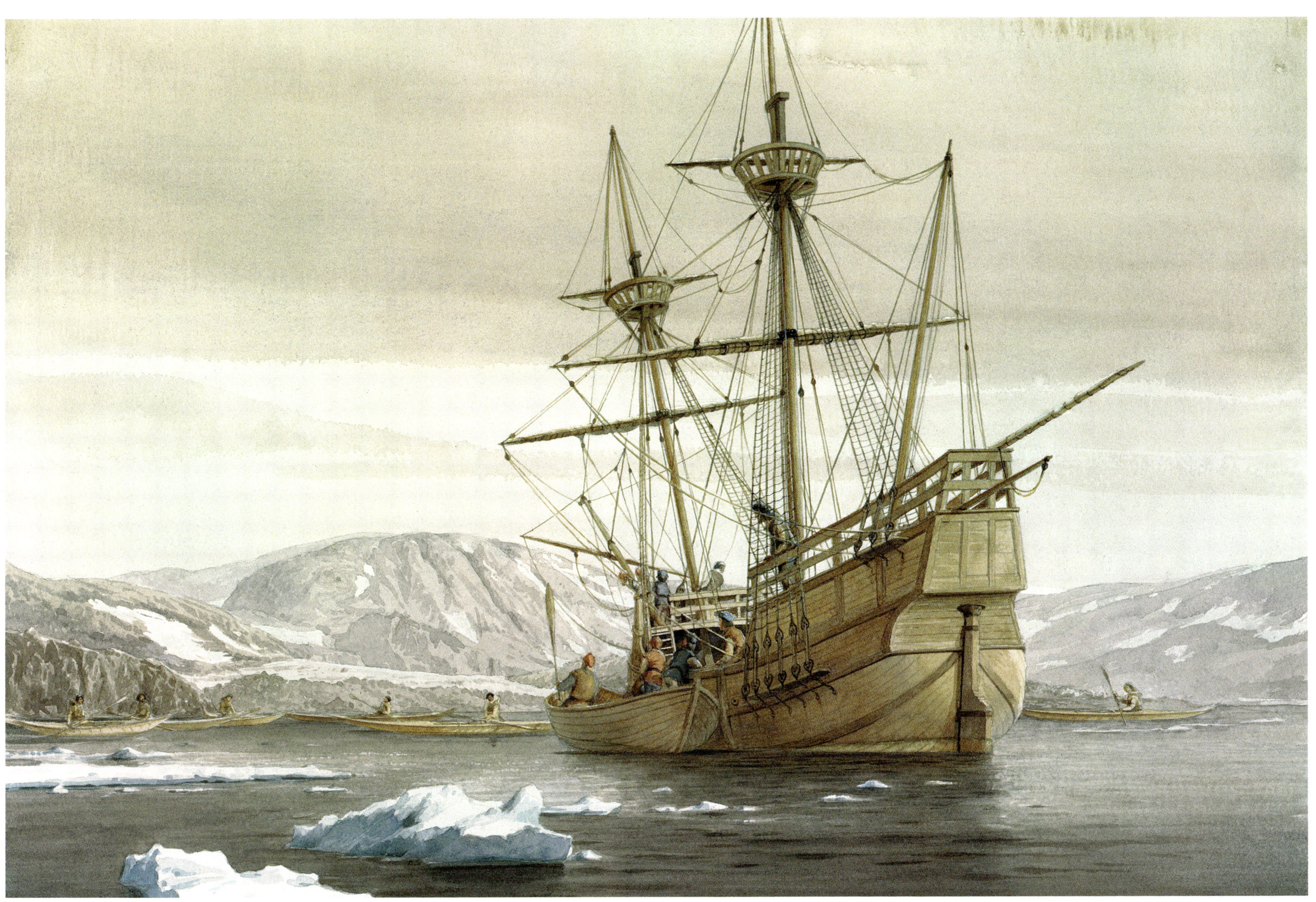

At some point the crew had been ashore long enough to collect souvenirs of the voyage, including a heavy black stone that altered the direction of the next two expeditions. The little lump of ore collected in Frobisher Bay became the subject of intense conjecture. Three English metallurgists declared that it was worthless, but Michael Lok found an Italian who proclaimed it rich in gold. Frobisher's certainty that he had found the route to the Orient was enough to secure funding for another voyage, and the excitement over gold made it a certainty. The original group of speculators was joined by others, and the Company of Cathay was incorporated with a charter from the Crown. A total of £4,275 was invested, including £1,000 from Queen Elizabeth, who also gave a royal ship, *Ayde,* as part of her contribution. Nine members of the Privy Council backed the venture. This time sailing to the Orient would be secondary; mining for gold was now Frobisher's main objective.

Three ships were prepared and provisioned with a complement of about 120 men: *Gabriel* and *Michael,* which were returning for a second time, and *Ayde.* Thirty of the men were miners and refiners, needed for working the mines. Also aboard was John White, an artist and member of the Painter-Stainers' Company of London. His were the first European pictures of Inuit and are a treasured record of the second voyage. White went on to be famous for making the first visual recordings of the first Virginia colony.

The three ships weighed at Blackwall on the Thames on May 25, 1577. After a slow and difficult passage across the Atlantic, and through dangerous ice near Halles Island, they finally found anchorage in Frobisher Bay on July 19. To celebrate their safe arrival and deliverance from disaster, Frobisher called a special service of thanksgiving, the first ever recorded in the Americas, preceding the more famous *Mayflower* event by forty-four years. For ten days the ships explored the area around the mouth of Frobisher Bay. On July 29 they anchored in what they named Countess of Warwick Sound, off Kodlunarn, the Inuit name for "white men's island." There, for the rest of their stay, the crew dug up two hundred tons of rock and stowed it in the three ships.

Frobisher's second summer in the Arctic was most noteworthy for his encounters with the Inuit. It appears he attempted to take hostages, as he had done a year earlier, to recover his lost men, grabbing two natives who immediately got away. Recovering their weapons, the two Inuit chased Frobisher back to the boat, wounding him in the buttock with an arrow. A soldier guarding the boat was unable to outrun one of his pursuers and was captured. Frobisher's men rallied, capturing one Inuit man who was taken aboard *Gabriel.*

On Halles Island, *Michael*'s Captain Yorke came upon Inuit tents and items of clothing from the five men left behind the year before. Hoping to establish friendly relations, he left some simple gifts and took nothing away, but to no avail. At a place they called Bloody Point his men were assaulted by natives with arrows and darts. The Englishmen responded with arquebuses, which so terrified the natives that they either fled to the hills or leaped into the sea. One Englishman was badly hurt, and several natives died. Two women were captured; one, very old, was released, but the other, a young mother with a baby, was taken aboard the ship.

By August 21 preparations were made to leave. The ships sailed for home the following day. The captured Inuit man, woman and child survived the crossing to England, but all three died soon after. The ore was offloaded, assayed at a profit of £5 per ton, and plans were immediately begun for another more ambitious voyage by the Company of Cathay. If there were any skeptics' concerns about the real value of the ore brought back, they were easily drowned out by enthusiasts. Queen Elizabeth was especially pleased. She had personally commended Frobisher on his return and contributed half the funds pledged for the third voyage. Fifteen vessels made up the 1578 fleet.

The ships assembled at Harwich on the southeast coast. They sailed on May 31, 1578, proceeded west down the English Channel and made their departure from Ireland's Cape Clear on June 6. A two-week passage brought them to Greenland, their "Weast Freeselande." Frobisher landed, assumed they were the first Christians to do so and named it "Weast Englande." Except for the ship *Salomon* striking a whale on June 30, the passage from there to Baffin Island was uneventful. The fleet sighted Resolution Island on July 2.

The summer of 1578 was especially cold. Frobisher's "Strait" was choked with ice, and the fleet was soon enclosed in the pack, where a southeasterly gale compacted the sea ice. This is an area of dangerous overfalls and strong tides, and the ships were in serious danger. *Dennis* "received such a blowe with a rocke of Ise, that she sunke downe therewith, in sighte of the whoale fleete." All her men were saved, but many of the much-needed winter supplies went down with her. *Judith* and *Michael* managed to find their way through into Frobisher Bay, but the ice prevented all but four of the remaining ships from gaining sea room, and they endured forty-eight hours of extreme danger and anxiety before a change of wind set them free. It wasn't until July 31 that most of the fleet finally sailed into Countess of Warwick Sound, where they found *Judith* and *Michael* already at anchor. Great volleys of ordnance were exchanged between the ships to proclaim their joy at being reunited.

By this time it was getting late in the season. Storms were frequent, the bay was never completely free of ice and several of the ships were damaged from constant contact with it. Half the timbers to build a winter house and much of the food had gone down with *Dennis*, so the plan to spend a winter was wisely abandoned. Mining began on Kodlunarn Island on August 1, and the fleet dispersed to look for other more likely sites. Of the 1,200 tons of rock

➤ **Bound for the Arctic: Frobisher's third expedition** (WC, 22″ × 30″)
Frobisher's third expedition to the Arctic in 1578 was a major enterprise, with the primary objective being the colonization and exploitation of Meta Incognita, *as Queen Elizabeth named it. The fleet of fifteen ships, the largest maritime expedition ever mounted to the Arctic, was expected to transport miners, carpenters, soldiers and seamen, plus one hundred colonists with a clergyman and a governor who were to remain behind at the mine site, as this was also intended to be a colonizing venture. They had no idea that while they were away the ore mined the previous year would be judged worthless.*

dug up that summer, only sixty-five came from Kodlunarn. It was all loaded on the thirteen remaining ships, Captain Tanfield on *Thomas of Ipswich* having deserted and fled for home.

The fleet sailed from the sound on August 31 and rendezvoused the next day at Beare Sound. While some of the men were ashore the ships were struck by a sudden storm—the worst encountered that season. A terrible night was spent hove to or trying to keep the ships off the rocks. Frobisher was ashore when the storm struck. In the chaos of trying to get back aboard the ships, a number of men, as well as nearly twenty boats and pinnaces, were lost. Frobisher was not able to join *Ayde* and had to sail home in *Gabriel*. *Emanuel* was given up for lost, having been caught on a lee shore, but she managed to find her way through the rocks and sail free. Although she successfully crossed the Atlantic, *Emanuel* was wrecked on the west coast of Ireland. The remaining ships experienced a boisterous Atlantic crossing and soon became separated. Because not all the men who had been caught ashore were able to regain their own ships, many of the smaller vessels were overcrowded and short of food, and almost forty men died on the passage home.

The fallout from this whole enterprise was disastrous for many of the investors. The 2,100 tons of rock were found to be worthless, and the costs of the expedition were unrecoverable. Futile attempts to smelt precious metal from the ore continued for five years; much of the rock can still be seen built into a wall at Dartford, England. In the end the Company of Cathay went bankrupt, and the treasurer, Michael Lok, was ruined. Frobisher did not escape unscathed; his reputation was attacked unmercifully by Lok, who held him responsible for all the losses, even though the blame most probably should have fallen on incompetent assayers and unconscionable promoters. Although Frobisher did receive a gold chain from Queen Elizabeth for his efforts, he too was essentially bankrupt.

His record is not unblemished, but Frobisher was a remarkable seaman and leader, and an honorable member of Elizabeth's little band of sea captains. The waterway on Baffin Island that he mistakenly thought was the fabled route to the Orient now carries the name Frobisher Bay.

The Dutch Rebels

Until 1581 the Netherlands was a province of Spain, the greatest colonial power at the time. Although the Dutch under Spain were energetic traders and competent seamen, they were content to trade no farther afield than Lisbon. The spices imported by Portugal were profitably distributed, in turn, in Dutch ships to the countries of northern Europe. In 1580, however, Philip of Spain seized the Portuguese crown and forbade the merchants of Lisbon to continue trading with the Protestant Netherlanders, hoping to cripple the economy of the seven

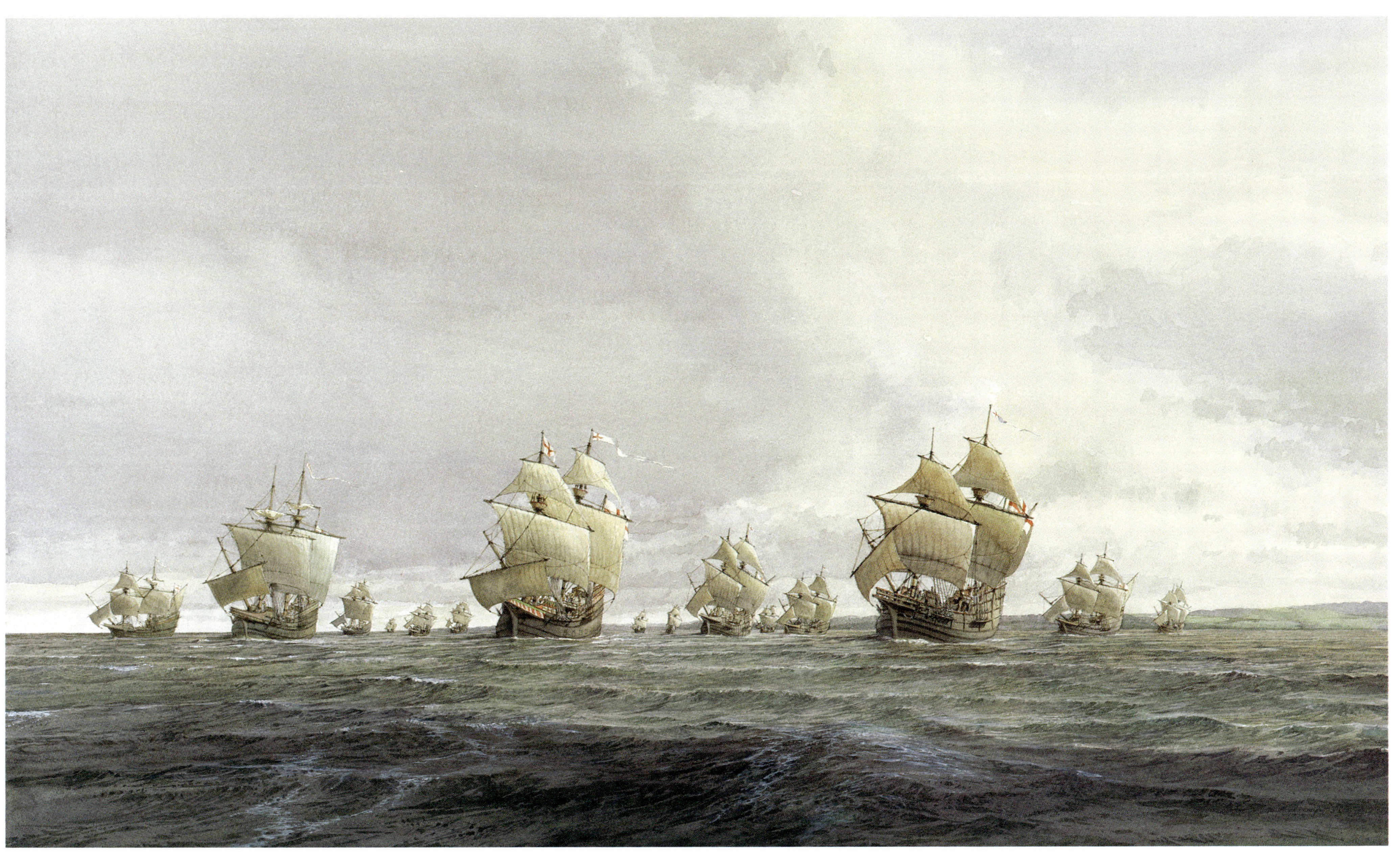

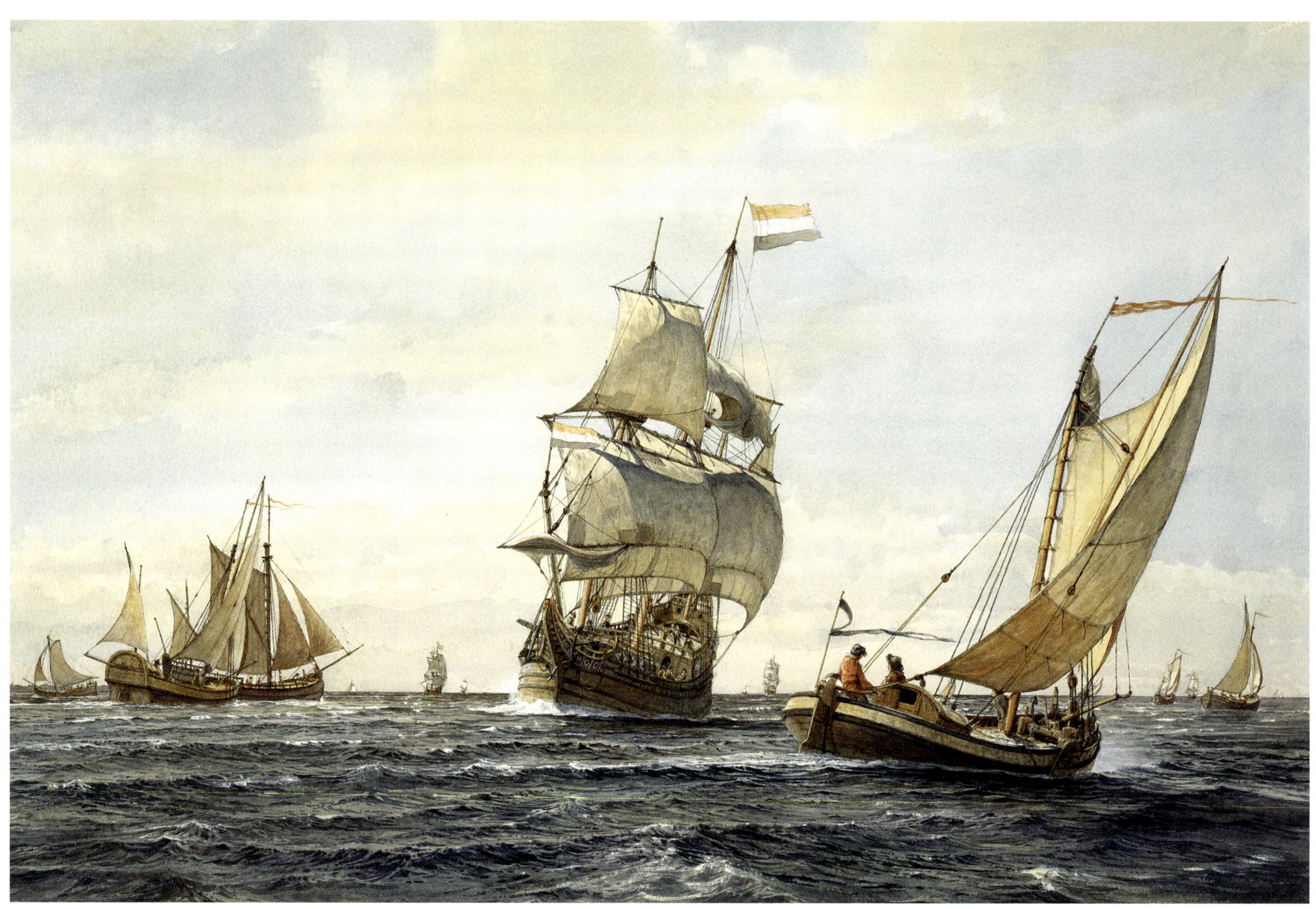

rebellious Dutch provinces. Instead the Dutch declared their independence and began challenging the Portuguese and Spanish monopoly of world trade. An English army helped sustain the Dutch revolt, and an English fleet defeated the Spanish Armada in 1588.

The Portuguese and Spanish enterprises were in decline when the period of Dutch expansionism began. The Dutch fleet was ten times the size of Portugal's and ready to challenge it for control of the spice trade. In 1595 four Dutch ships under the command of Cornelis de Houtman made it to the Spice Islands via the Cape of Good Hope and traded for a fortune in spices. The success of that voyage laid the foundation of the Dutch Empire. In 1598, buoyed by Houtman's success, Dutch merchants sent thirteen more ships around the cape, and two other expeditions tested the route through the Strait of Magellan. Of this latter group, the first fleet of five ships gave up after transiting the strait and returned home. The second fleet of four ships was commanded by Oliver van Noort on *Mauritius*. Only *Mauritius* completed the circumnavigation, but by then the Dutch had gained the confidence to take on their Catholic enemies in the far corners of the world.

The Dutch concentrated their offshore energies on trade and commerce, seeing no profit in colonization. They established private trading companies with full authority to conduct business, to establish and fortify trading posts and to wage war to protect those posts. The first of these businesses was the Dutch East India Company, founded in 1602, with the full approval of the States General to disrupt and destroy Portuguese or Spanish rivals on land or at sea. Because trade was the company's only motive, it wasted no time on converting natives, and as long as the local rulers cooperated the Dutch traders made no attempt to overthrow them. For this reason they were not seen as a threat, and the locals often enlisted them to help oust the Spaniards or Portuguese from their territories.

The Portuguese were the first to feel the effects of the company's ambition. Although they had been operating with little competition in the East Indies for a century, they were no match for the determined Dutch with their superior ships. The English proved to be more difficult and competed for a while, but they too eventually withdrew and left the spice trade to the Dutch. In 1619 Jan Pieterszoon Coen, governor of the company's operations in the East Indies, led a force against the town of Jacatra at the western end of Java, drove out the indigenous rulers and destroyed the city. Renamed Batavia, the city became the center of Dutch operations in the East Indies for the next three hundred years.

With all European competition eliminated, the Dutch set about defending their empire. Routes to the Indies were blocked at the Strait of Magellan and Cape of Good Hope, where a settlement was established at Cape Town to replenish their fleets. Profits soared with the Dutch East India Company's territories being brought under firm control, and as a result the company turned its attention

◂ ***Mauritius* off Rotterdam** (WC, 15″ × 22″)
In 1600 Mauritius *was one in a fleet of four ships under the command of Oliver van Noort that fought their way through the Strait of Magellan and tried to imitate Francis Drake's success in raiding Spanish settlements on the west coast of South America. This expedition found little to plunder and headed west across the Pacific. By this time only* Mauritius *and a smaller consort remained of the fleet, and the smaller ship was lost to Spanish galleons in the Philippines. Bloodied after the battle and with only a few men left,* Mauritius *crossed the Indian Ocean, rounded the Cape of Good Hope and arrived back in Amsterdam on August 26, 1601. Van Noort thus became the first Dutch navigator to circumnavigate the world and only the fourth of any nation to do so.*

➤ **The Roaring Forties: *Batavia* in the Southern Ocean, 1629** (WC, 22″ × 30″)
On the night of June 4, 1629, the Dutch ship Batavia *ran aground on the Houtman Abrolhos Islands off the coast of western Australia. The ship was a total loss, but most of her 332 passengers and crew were landed ashore safely. There,* Batavia's *captain, Jeronimus Cornelius, intoxicated with blood lust and with thirty-six men under his command, began the systematic killing of all who opposed him, including women and children.*

to the uncharted lands often reported by incoming ships. It dispatched a series of probes to determine the extent of the territories to the south and east of Java and into the western Pacific north and east of Japan.

One Dutch ship that gained some infamy during this time was *Batavia,* a heavily armed merchantman of approximately 1,300 tons displacement. She was built by the Dutch East India Company, and in 1629 she was making her maiden voyage from the Netherlands to Java. On board were 332 men, women and children—and the seeds of a mutiny. In command of the voyage was a senior merchant, Francesco Pelsaert. The ship's captain was Arien Jacobsz, who took offense at being given orders by a merchant. Also on board was Lady Lucretia van der Meylen, on her way to join her husband in Batavia, and her maid Zwaantie Hentrix. Added to this mix was Jeronimus Cornelius, third in command and the leader of the impending mutiny.

On the way to the Cape of Good Hope, Captain Jacobsz tried to seduce Lady Lucretia but was rebuffed. Lady Lucretia apparently turned to Pelsaert for comfort, and Jacobsz turned to Hentrix. At the cape, Jacobsz, Hentrix and Cornelius went on a wild drinking spree that ended in a fight. Jacobsz received a public dressing-down from his old enemy Pelsaert after a complaint was lodged. It was not difficult for Cornelius to enlist Jacobsz's support to take over the ship.

Before the mutiny could be launched, *Batavia* ran aground off the coast of western Australia. Most of the passengers and crew, and some food and water, were landed ashore safely. Pelsaert and Jacobsz took the two ship's boats and sailed to Batavia for help. The remaining survivors were in a dreadful situation, spread out among the small islands with almost no water.

Jeronimus Cornelius revealed his true character when he and the men under his command embarked on a spree of murder, rape and torture against the other survivors, killing over 120 in this reign of terror. At the same time, two dozen unarmed soldiers who were not involved in the mutiny had been left to die on the only island that contained any water. Led by Wiebbe Hayes and reinforced by escapees from the massacre, they successfully repulsed the ensuing attacks by the mutineers, until on September 17 they were relieved by Pelsaert, who had reached Batavia and returned on the rescue yacht *Sardam.*

A well-documented trial was held on the islands. The most senior of the mutineers, including Cornelius, were hanged after having one or both hands cut off. The lesser mutineers were simply hanged, and a few were taken to Batavia for further investigation. Two mutineers who pleaded for mercy were put ashore on the mainland and never heard from again. They were the first permanent European residents of Australia.

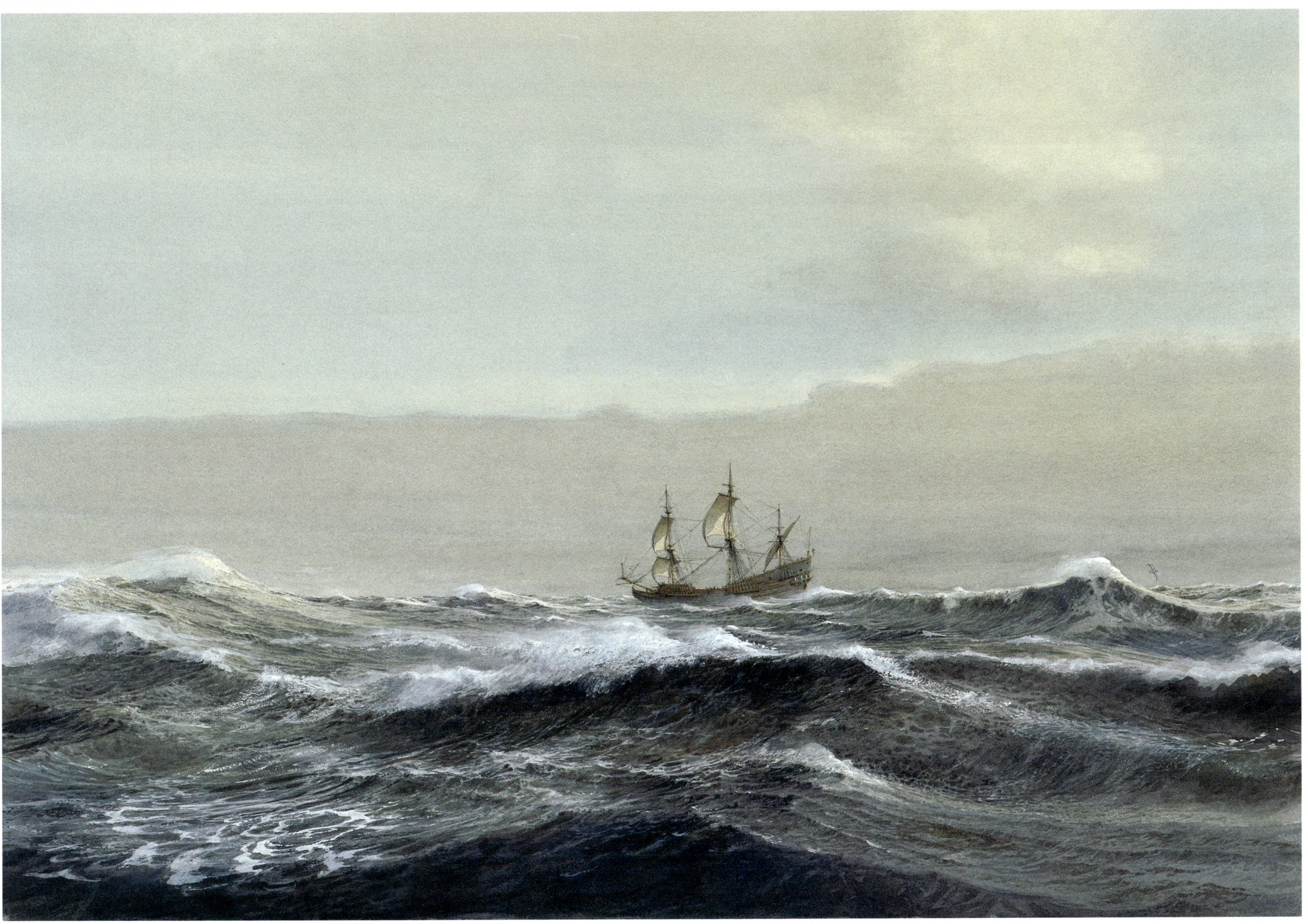

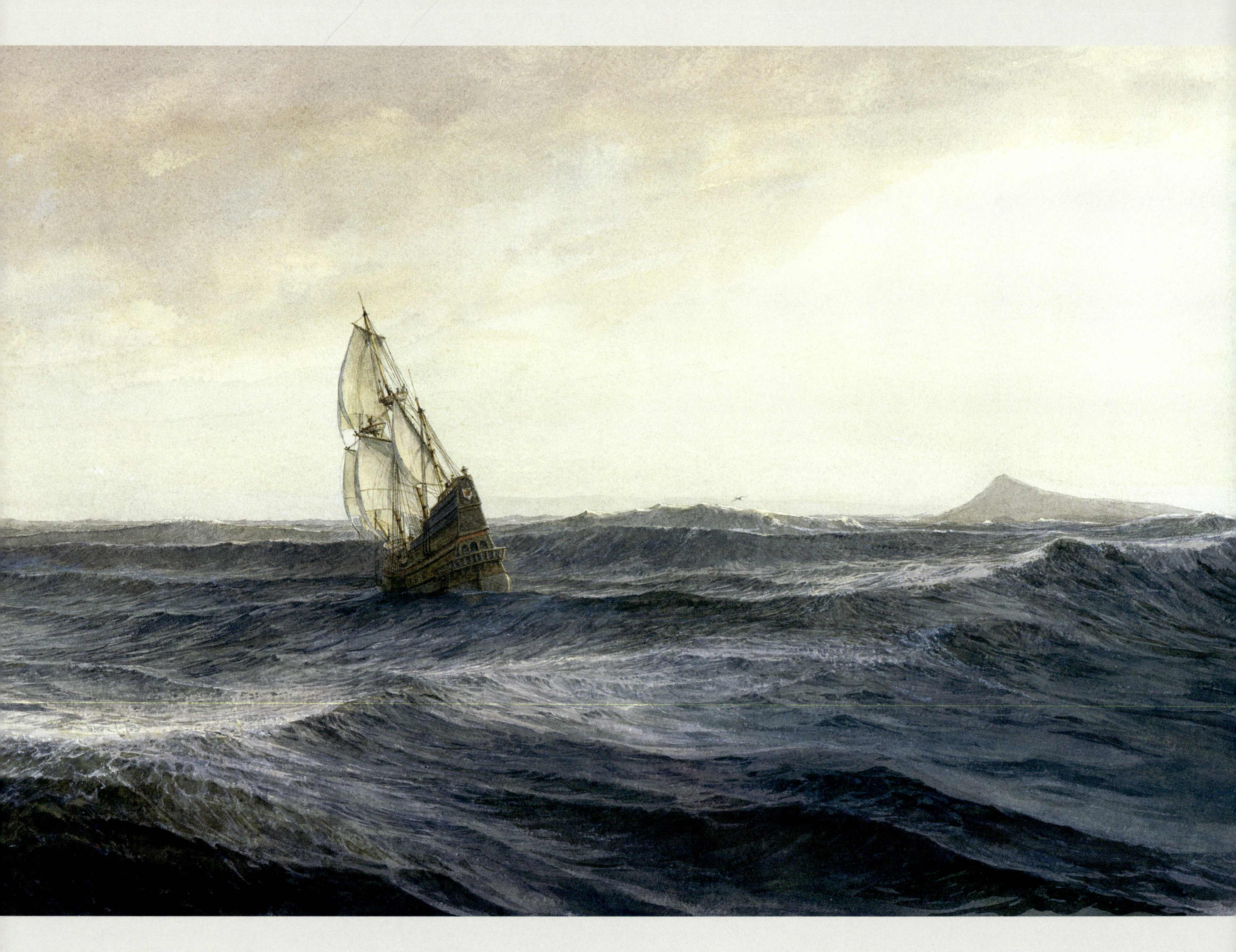

CONQUERING CAPE HORN

THE CONTINENT OF Antarctica is roughly the size of the United States and Mexico combined, but only 2 per cent of its rocky core rises above 1,500 feet. Weighing down and compressing this continent is a permanent mantle of solid ice up to ten thousand feet thick.

Over this cold mass the air is constantly chilled, and it pours down the edges of the continent, at times with incredible velocity, then mixes with warmer air and is moderated by the seas. The downdraft is bent into a clockwise direction by the earth's rotation and, with no land to interrupt it, blows almost constantly around the continent. This is a violent region of open water, where the frequency and duration of storms is not equaled anywhere else in the world. It circles the globe below the Pacific, Atlantic and Indian Oceans in a belt between latitude 40° and 60° south. This is the Southern Ocean, and its winds are compressed at only one place, the southern tip of South America. At its worst, there is no more fearful place for a ship to find herself. Sailors have a name for it: "Cape Stiff." This is Cape Horn.

In 1615 Isaac Le Maire, a disgruntled ex-officer of the Dutch East India Company, and Willem Schouten, an experienced navigator who had spent many years in the company's service, formed a competing company to trade in the Indo-West Pacific. On June 14, having fitted out two ships, *Eendracht* and *Hoorn,* they planned to circumvent the Dutch East India Company's prohibition on entering the Pacific through the Strait of Magellan by sailing south of the continent.

December found the two ships being careened on the coast of Patagonia, where *Hoorn* was lost to fire during graving. What could be salvaged was transferred to *Eendracht*, and she continued on alone. She passed the entrance to the Strait of Magellan and pressed on with no sign of another opening to the west. On her port side a new land began to appear, and with it the fear that she was sailing into a dead end on the coast of the undiscovered southern continent. Gradually the seas took on the blue of deep water and a heavy ocean swell could be felt running against the ship. *Eendracht* was feeling the first effects of the great ocean to the west, and on January 24, 1616, the strait later named Le Maire opened before them. On January 29 Cape Horn was observed for the first time. This uneventful passage was the first of what was to become the most traveled route into the Pacific Ocean until the opening of the Panama Canal 298 years later.

‹ ***Eendracht* off the Horn** (WC, 15″ × 22″)
At sunset on January 29, 1616, the land to Eendracht*'s starboard ended abruptly in a barren, rocky point. Only the vast Southern Ocean lay beyond. Accompanied by albatross and bucking the constant wind from the west, the little ship sailed past the point named Cape Horn and out into the Pacific.* Eendracht *had arrived in the strait at one of the rare moments of almost ideal conditions and had entered the Pacific without a hint of the dangerous waters she was in.*

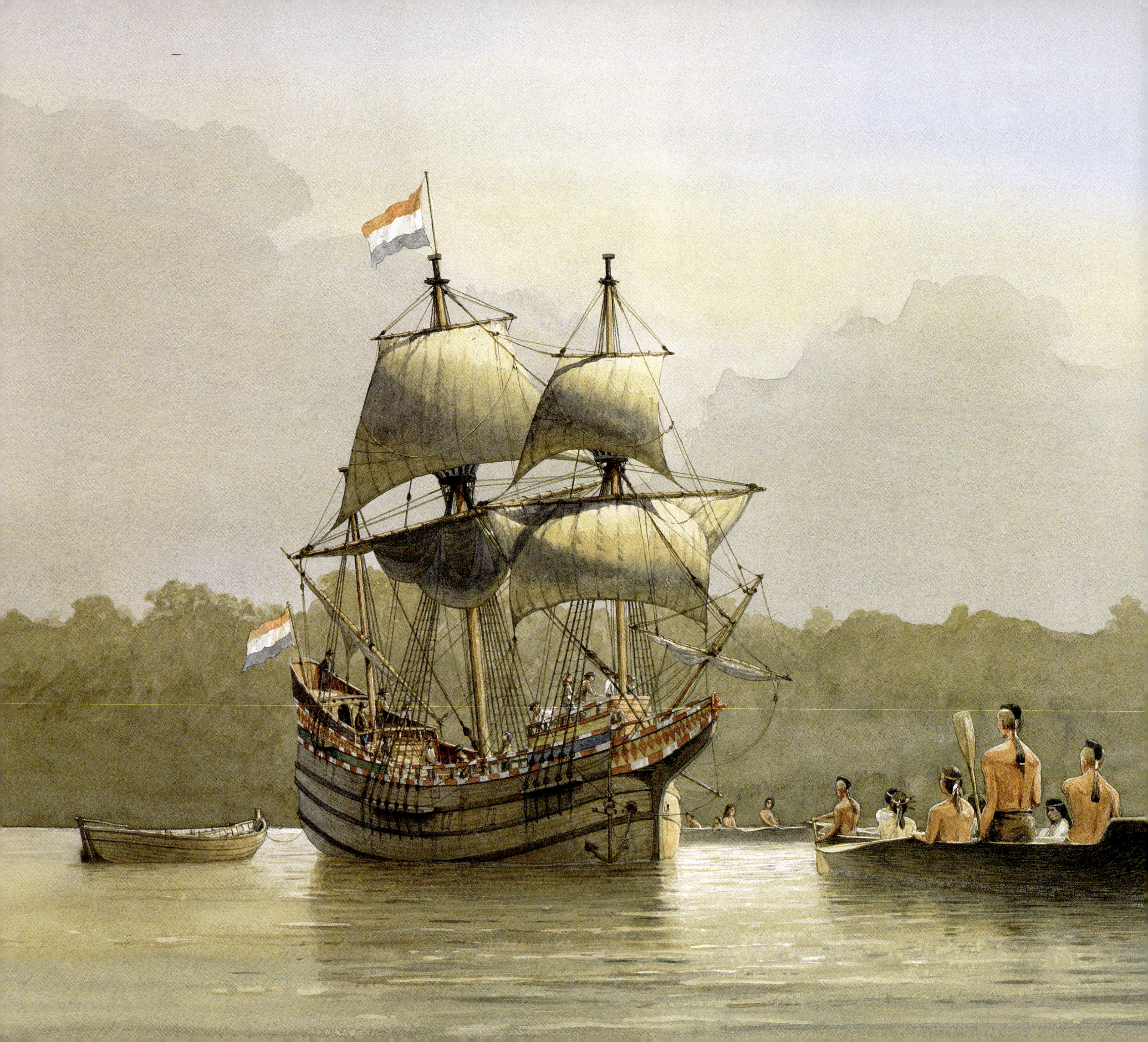

Half Moon in the Hudson River, 1609 (WC, 15″ × 22″)
In 1609 Henry Hudson's crew made contact with natives on several occasions on the coast and the river. Their relations were typical of the time; each group regarded the other with suspicion, and thievery was practiced on both sides. Some encounters were friendly; others ended in hostilities. In the peaceful encounters, the Europeans were introduced to green tobacco and corn and were supplied with berries and fish.

3

SETTLING THE NEW WORLD: THE NORTHERN VOYAGES

For most of the sixteenth century, Europeans focused their energies on searching for a northern route to Asia through the American continent. Ships visited the Atlantic seaboard in ever-increasing numbers through the 1500s, but the visits were seasonal, and except for a few ill-prepared attempts to overwinter the ships returned home every fall. As a result, at the beginning of the seventeenth century, the only permanent settlements in North America were Spanish.

Sailors arriving on the New World shores marveled at the abundance of fish, game and fine timber. After their initial disappointment at finding a land mass blocking their way to Asia, northern entrepreneurs began to contemplate the advantages of permanent settlements. England, France and the Netherlands began to stake out their own territories

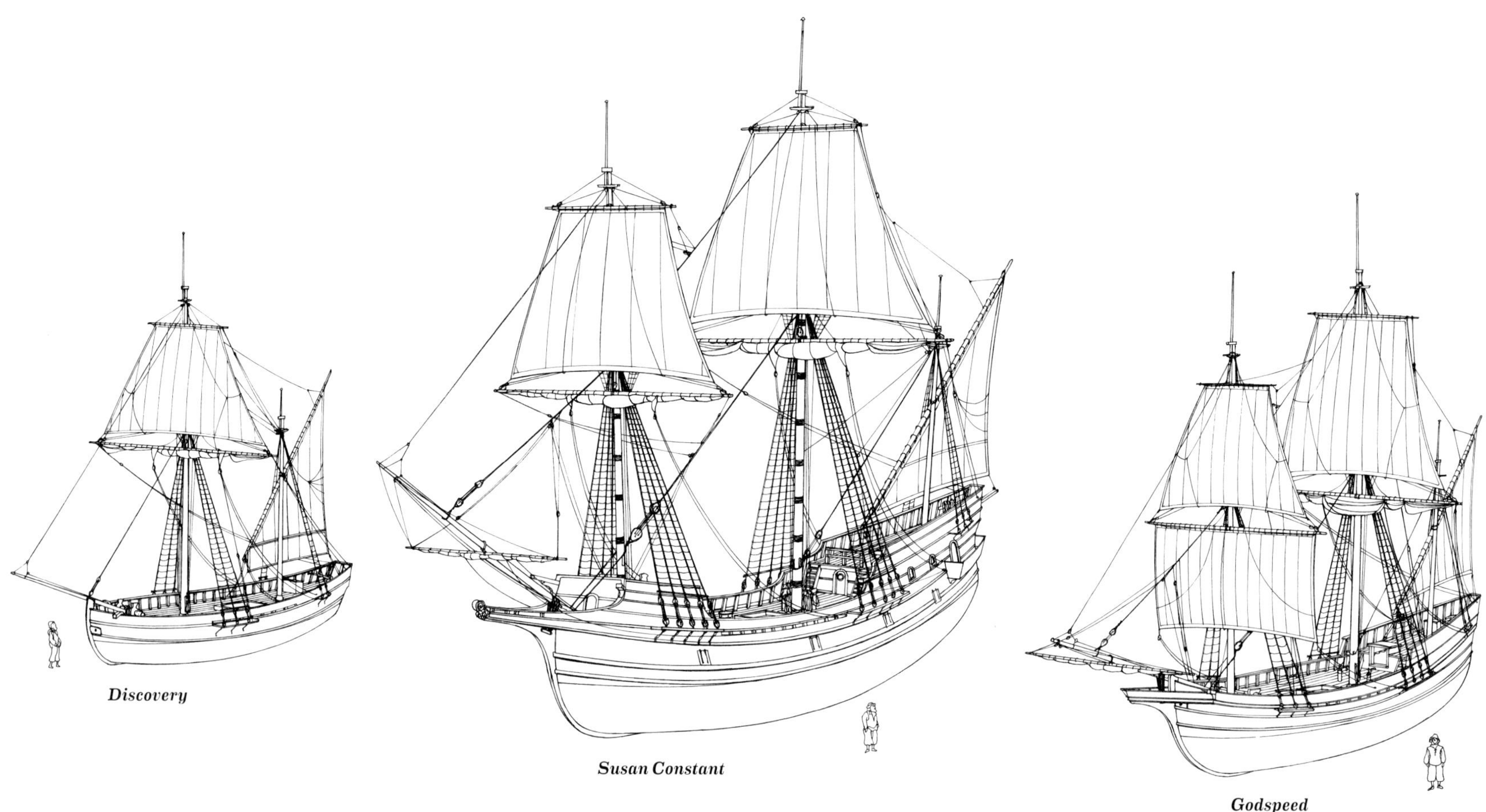

˄ *The three original ships of the Jamestown colony.*

north of the Spanish settlements. In 1541, after Jacques Cartier's explorations in the St. Lawrence, Sieur de Roberval, with several hundred colonists, had tried to establish a settlement in present-day Canada. He in fact dawdled until 1542 and returned to France in 1543, defeated by hostile Iroquois, scurvy and a harsh winter.

In 1584 Queen Elizabeth granted Sir Walter Raleigh, one of her favorite courtiers, a patent to colonize lands on the east coast of America, lands that he called Virginia. The leader of this enterprise, Sir Richard Grenville, in the summer of 1585 landed colonists, cattle, plants and supplies there and built a fort on Roanoke Island. This first small group of Englishmen nearly starved, and the next year all of them sailed back to England with Sir Francis Drake, who was on his way home from privateering in the West Indies. Later that year eighteen men arrived to

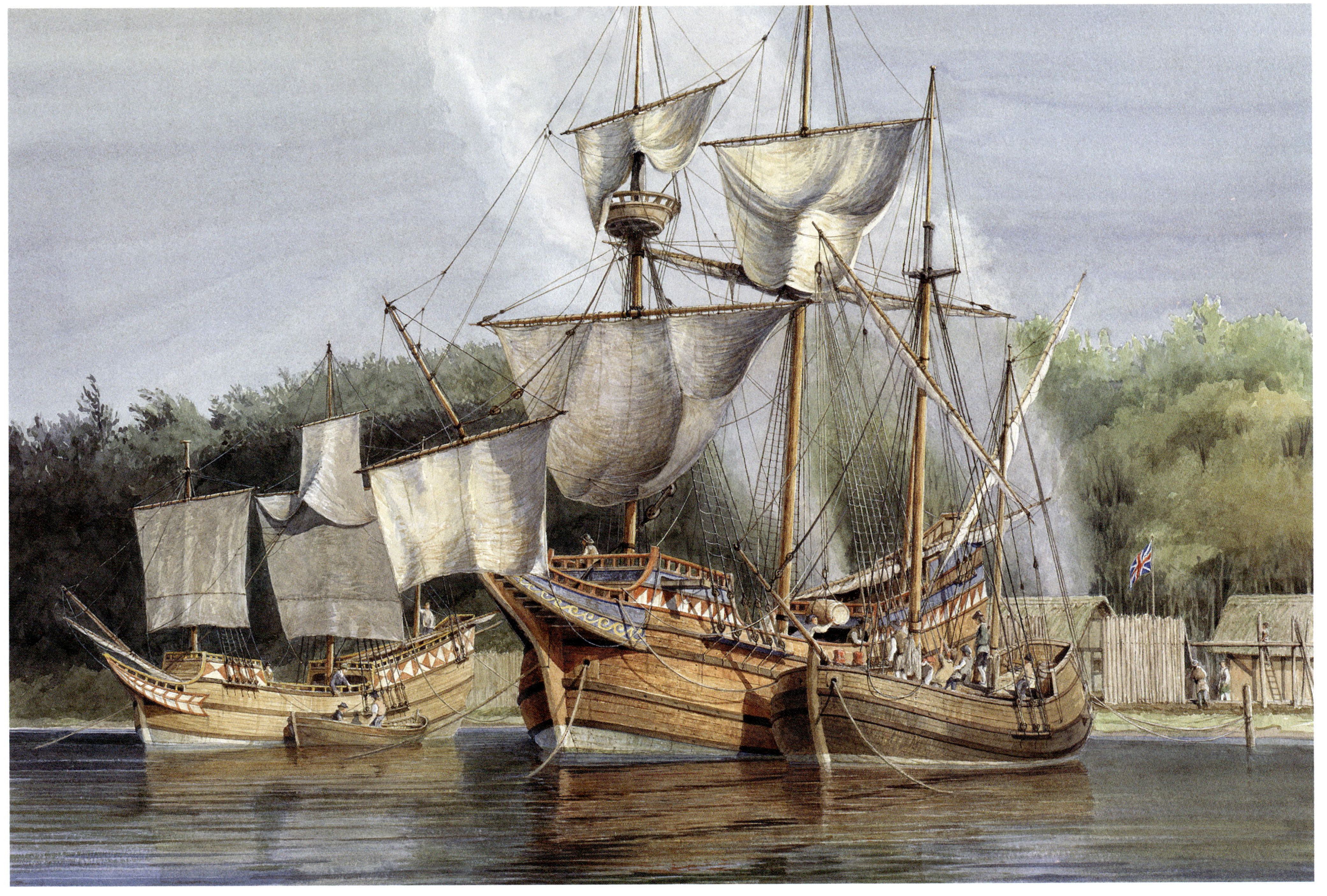

Jamestown (WC, 15″ × 22″)
The site selected for Jamestown was a swampy, mosquito-infested peninsula that was difficult to defend against the natives. It was chosen partly because the water was deep up to the shore, where the ships could be moored without building a wharf. In a land blessed with an abundance of food, by the end of the year half the settlers were dead from starvation, attacks by the local natives or disease. In 1608 reinforcements arrived; John Smith took command and immediately imposed discipline on the inefficiently run colony. Because he better understood the natives and was able to barter for food, the colony's fortunes improved. Smith returned to England in 1609; the winter after he left was called "the starving time," in which only sixty of the original 490 colonists survived. More settlers arrived in 1610, barely saving the colony from extinction; the cultivation of tobacco, begun in 1612, was their financial salvation.

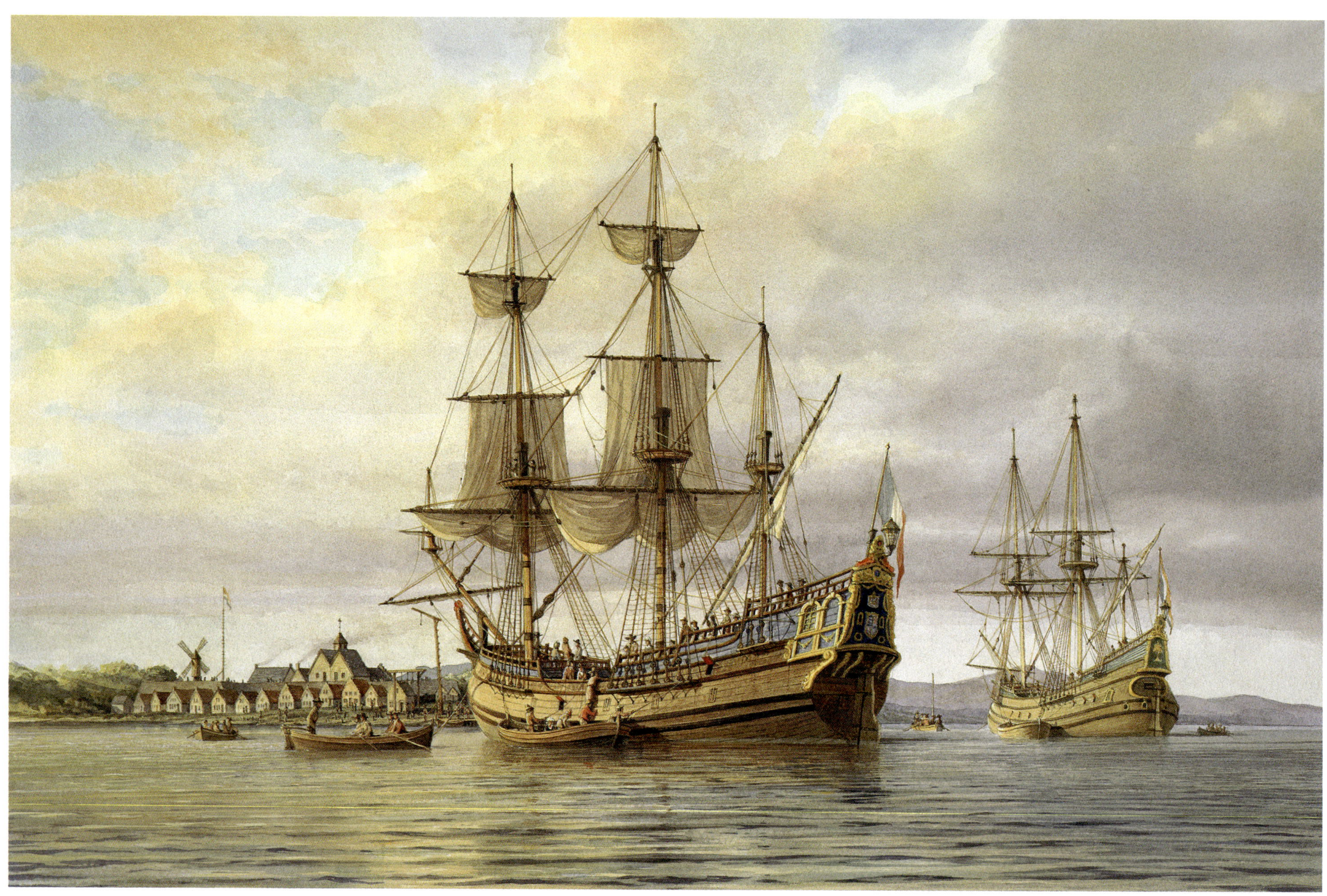

defend the fort, but in 1587, when more colonists arrived, these men had vanished. These latest colonists included women and children, and on August 18 Eleanor Dare gave birth to Virginia, the first English child born in the New World. The fleet that would have brought relief to this colony in 1588 was detained in England to help repel the Spanish Armada, and no aid was sent in 1589. When relief finally reached Virginia in 1590, no trace of the 1587 colonists could be found. Their fate remains a mystery.

The Promised Land: Europeans on the East Coast

A new series of voyages that began in 1602 were a prelude to the first permanent English settlements in the New World. Glowing reports of fertile lands, rivers teeming with fish and ships returning with cargoes of skins and sassafras stirred the interest of speculators back home. In 1606 they formed the Virginia Company, a joint-stock company, and on December 20 the ships *Susan Constant, Godspeed* and *Discovery* sailed for Chesapeake Bay. Almost five months later, 144 English colonists stepped ashore on the banks of the James River. Despite the colony's first years of near disaster, Jamestown survived to become the first successful English settlement in America, the site of the first capital of Virginia and, with its sale of land grants, the location for the beginnings of private enterprise in America.

To the north the French, interested in the profits of a fur trade, were also attempting to colonize the territories they had claimed. In 1605 they built a fort at Port Royal, on the Bay of Fundy shore of Nova Scotia, but it was occupied only until 1607. In 1608 Samuel de Champlain established a trading post at Quebec, the oldest site in Canada occupied by Europeans, but for decades it remained only an outpost of the fur trade.

While the English were settling in Virginia and the French were attempting to do the same in the north, the navigator Henry Hudson, sailing for an English organization known as the Muscovy Company, was attempting to find a northeast passage through the Arctic. Twice, in 1607 and 1608, the company backed him on voyages, but both attempts ended with his ships being stopped by ice. On the first attempt, in *Hopewell,* he was turned back at 80°23′ north. This was just 577 miles from the pole, as close as anyone would get for another 166 years. Hudson would have continued to sail west to find the Northwest Passage, but his crew had had enough of cold and ice, and they returned to England having made no significant discoveries. At this point the Muscovy Company lost confidence in Hudson as a commander.

The Dutch, keen trading rivals of the English, were also eager to find the northern passage to the Orient. On three occasions—in 1594, 1595 and 1596—they had sent

◂ ***St. Catrina* and *Pereboom*, New Amsterdam, 1654** (WC, 15″ × 22″)
The United Provinces of the Netherlands was remarkable for its spirit of religious and ethnic tolerance. These ideals extended to New Netherland, and anyone willing to work and observe the laws of the growing colony was welcome. In 1639 a Muslim owned a farm on Manhattan Island, and 1654 saw the arrival of the first Jews in New Amsterdam. Around August 22 the fluyt Pereboom (Peartree) *arrived from Amsterdam. Among her passengers were Jacob Barsimon, and probably Asser Levy and Solomon Pieterson. A couple of weeks later* St. Catrina *anchored off the beach; on board were twenty-three Jews, "big as well as little." They were ferried ashore to begin their life in the New World.*

› ***Kalmar Nyckel* off Fort Christina**
(WC, 15″ × 22″)
The voyage that established New Sweden began in late December 1637 in Kalmar Nyckel, *a pinnace built in 1625, one of several Dutch-built ships purchased by Sweden. She proved to be sturdy, swift and seaworthy, making four round-trip crossings to the colony—a record for the colonial era. In March 1638 Peter Minuit built Fort Christina on Minquas Kill and summoned the local natives to negotiate a treaty for their land by firing a cannon from* Kalmar Nyckel.

William Barents north of Novaya Zemlya into the western entrance of the Northeast Passage. All three voyages were stopped by ice, so in 1609 the Dutch East India Company hired Henry Hudson to search for the Northeast Passage and provided *Half Moon* for the voyage. On March 25 Hudson sailed from Amsterdam and headed north, but at the first sign of ice and bad weather, his men began to grumble and threatened to mutiny if they were forced to continue. To forestall any more trouble, Hudson sailed for the east coast of North America, where he had always believed the Strait of Anian would be found.

Half Moon touched at the east coast of Newfoundland, Cape Sable, Nova Scotia, Cape Cod, Delaware Bay and Chesapeake Bay, where she turned about to retrace her track. She was sailing a coast almost unvisited since Verrazzano had been there in 1524. On September 10 she anchored near Sandy Hook, and the next day entered the mouth of the river that now bears Hudson's name. Hudson was the third explorer (after Verrazzano and Estêvão Gomes) to visit the sound, but he claimed the area for the Dutch who employed him.

Half Moon's crew explored the river as far as present-day Albany before abandoning the notion that they had discovered a passage to the Orient. When Hudson left the New World, he returned to England instead of Holland. The British detained him and the English crew members but allowed the remaining Dutch crew to return *Half Moon* to Amsterdam.

Hudson's legacy was to leave his name on a major strait, bay and river, and to provide the Dutch with their claim to a foothold in the New World. In 1621 the Dutch West India Company was granted a charter to the land on the American coast from Chesapeake Bay to Newfoundland, between the territories claimed by France to the north and England to the south. It built forts and trading posts up and down the Hudson River, and the land was formally proclaimed New Netherland in 1623.

The company was interested in colonization only insofar as it supported trade, but to support the garrisons at the forts it encouraged farming settlements. In 1624 thirty families that had left the Netherlands to establish colonies in the Hudson River Valley settled around the fort being constructed at the southern end of Manhattan Island. The island was purchased from the natives for the price of sixty guilders, and the town that was to become New York City was incorporated in 1626 as New Amsterdam.

Peter Minuit was the very able governor of New Amsterdam, but in 1631 he had a falling out with the Dutch West India Company's directors and was discharged. Another dissatisfied company director enlisted Minuit in another commercial venture, this time on behalf

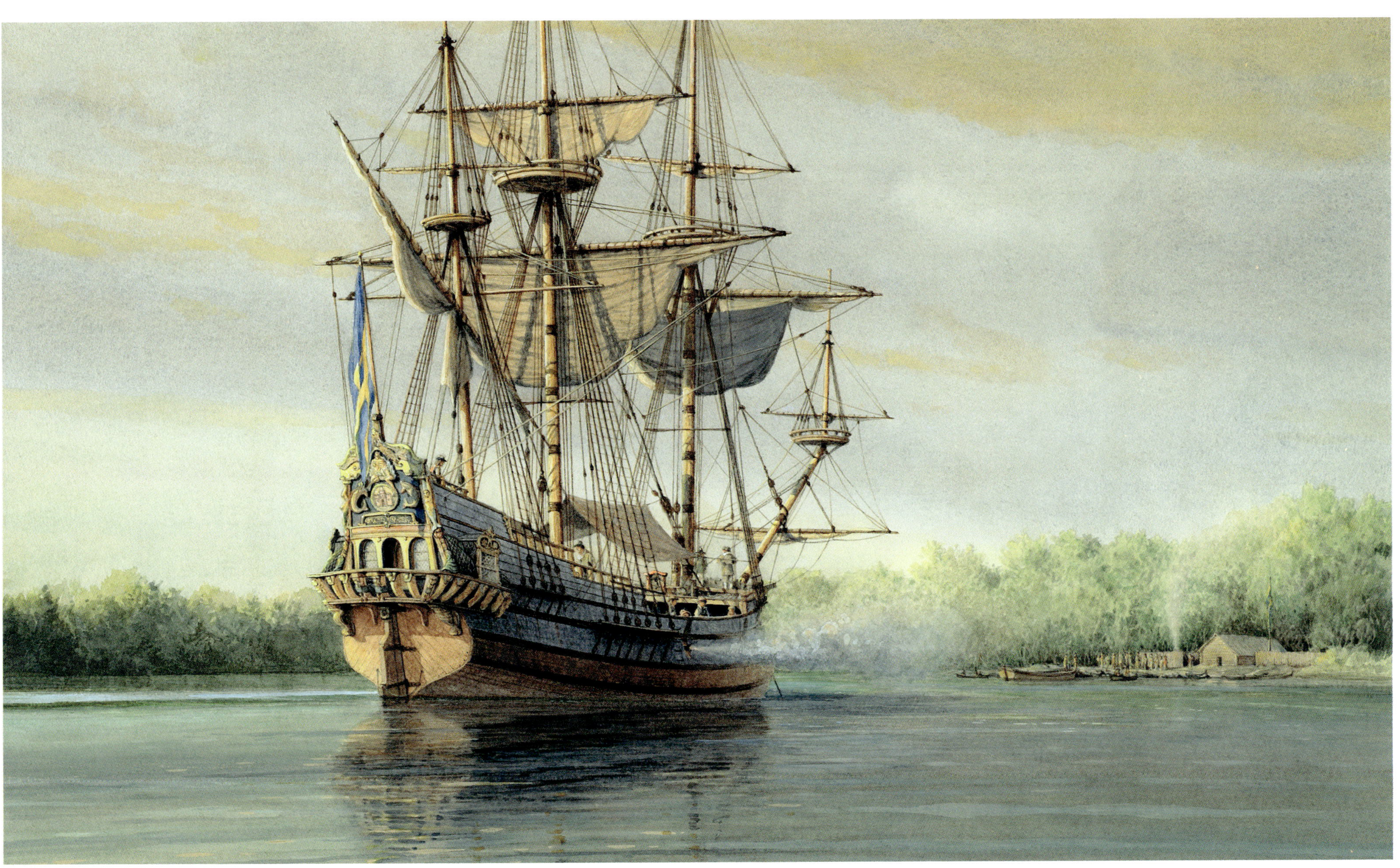

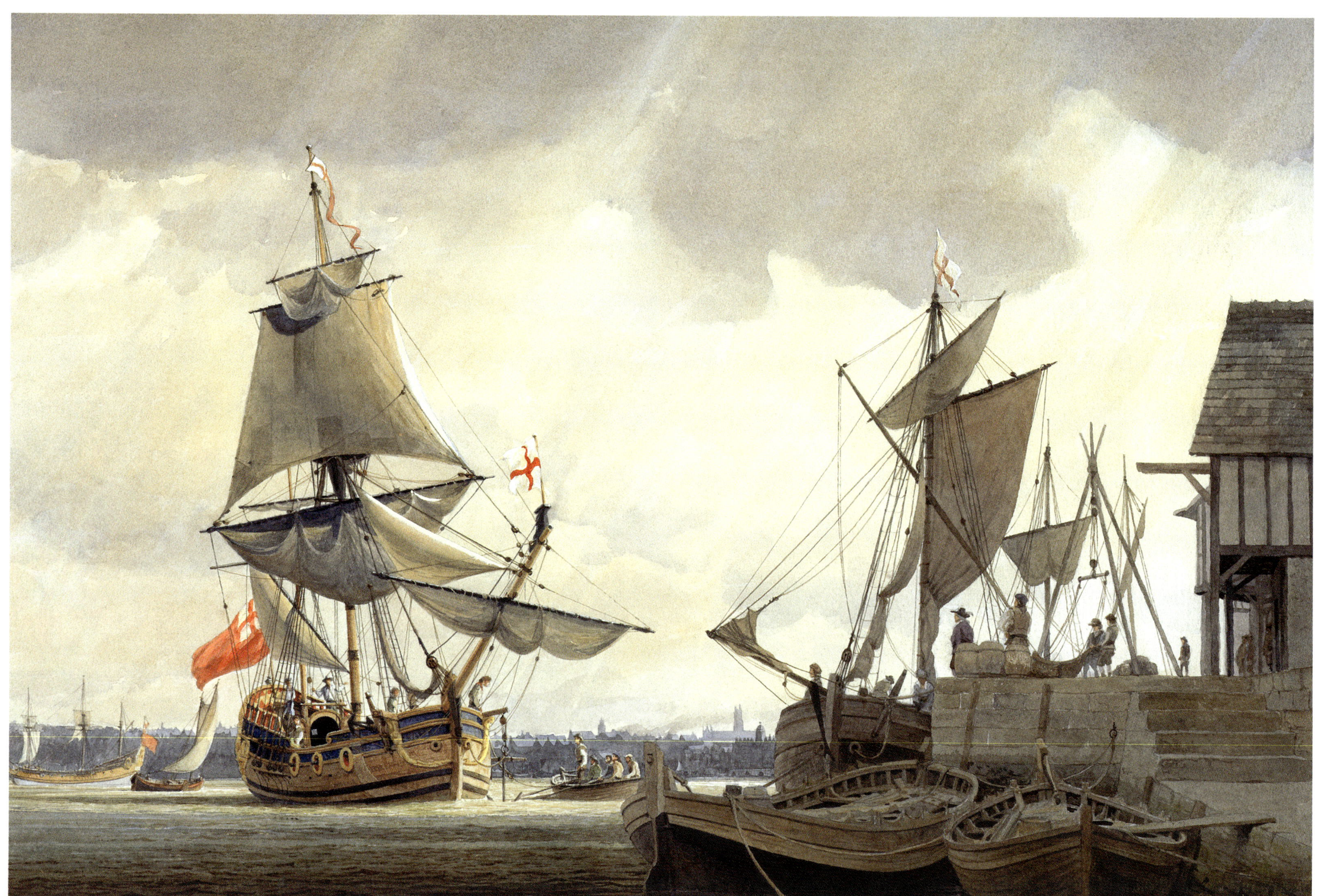

of the Swedish government. In 1637 Sweden joined England, France and Holland in gaining a foothold in America. On the Delaware River it planted a colony between the Dutch and the English colonies. At the site of present-day Wilmington, Delaware, Minuit negotiated a land purchase with the natives, built a small trading post, Fort Christina, and planted barley, wheat and corn. The tiny settlement, a colony known as New Sweden, survived until 1655, when it was seized by the Dutch, who in turn lost it to the British in 1664.

To the north, France's success in the fur trade caught the attention of the British. In 1665 two French fur traders, Pierre Esprit Radisson and Médard Chouart des Groseilliers, frustrated by French government trading restraints placed on them, were in London seeking backers for a proposed fur trading venture in Hudson Bay. Their tales of easy fortunes in furs persuaded a group of English investors to back a trial voyage and led to the chartering and sailing of two ships, *Eaglet* and *Nonsuch*, to Hudson Bay in 1668.

Eaglet turned back before completing the voyage, but *Nonsuch* successfully overwintered in James Bay, returning to London in 1669 laden with beaver furs that found a ready market. The sale did not return a profit, but this first voyage had shown the potential, and the king was approached for a charter to trade. On May 2, 1670, Charles II granted to the "Governor and Company of Adventurers of England Trading into Hudson's Bay," better known as the Hudson's Bay Company, a monopoly to trade in all the lands with rivers that drained into Hudson Bay. This area, known as Rupert's Land, comprised almost 40 per cent of all the land of modern Canada, and the Hudson's Bay Company was a major influence in the development of western Canada for the next two centuries. Today "The Bay" remains the oldest incorporated joint-stock merchandising company in the English-speaking world.

‹ ***Nonsuch* arriving in London, 1669**
(WC, 15″ × 22″)
On October 11, 1669, the London Gazette *reported from Deal on Dover Strait: "This last night came in here the* 'Nonsuch Ketch'…" Nonsuch*'s return from Hudson Bay heralded a new era in the fur trade. No original plans for* Nonsuch *exist. Built originally as a merchant trader, from 1654 to 1667 she had been an eight-gun ketch in the navy. Nothing is known of her career after her one voyage to Hudson Bay.*

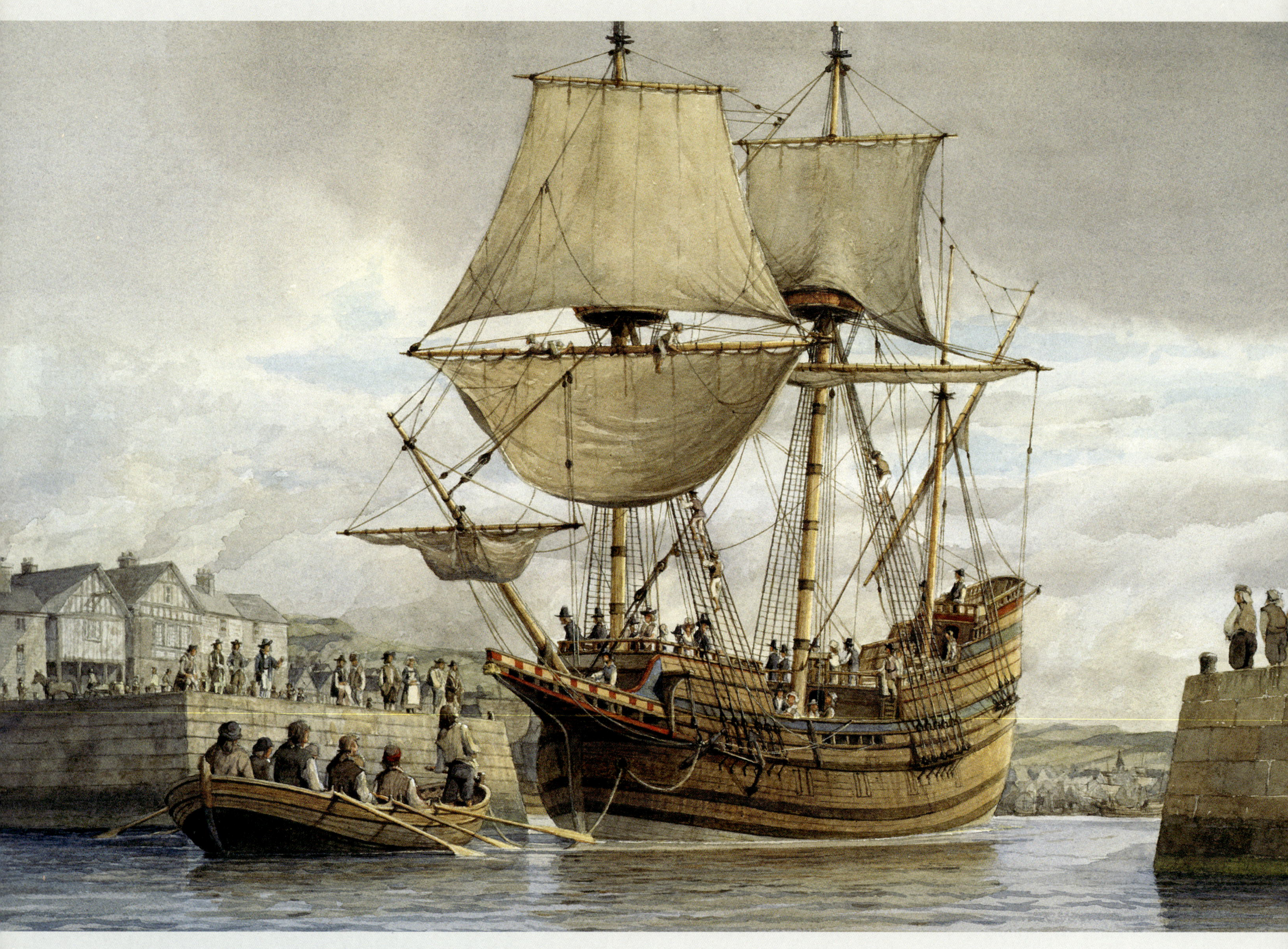

THE LITTLE SHIP *MAYFLOWER*

MAYFLOWER PLAYED A minor role in the grand theme of world exploration, and it is only because she carried a group of disenchanted Puritans from England to the New World that this ship is remembered at all. But she is a very good example of the ordinary trading vessels of the early seventeenth century, and a good deal is known about her.

Mayflower would have been a rather tubby merchant ship—high-pooped, deep-bellied, with a carrying capacity of 180 tons—and indistinguishable from the typical traders that sailed in and out of English ports. Before her famous voyage to America, she plied the waters around Spain, France, Ireland, Norway and the Baltic. Outbound from England to the continent, she would have carried cloth, furs, iron and pewter goods, and often would have returned fully laden with French wines, and occasionally with salt and vinegar.

The earliest record of *Mayflower* is of a 1609 voyage to Trondheim, Norway, although she is known to have been several years old at the time. She was hired to deliver hats, salt, wine, hemp and vinegar and to return with a cargo of lumber, tar and herring. During a severe storm in the North Sea, her cargo had to be jettisoned to save the ship. The loss resulted in a lawsuit, and the surviving court documents are the first authentic record of *Mayflower*'s existence.

The men and women who intended to settle the first Plymouth colony wished to practice a simpler and less ritualistic form of worship. Most were poorly educated farmers with little property or social standing. Too poor to finance the cost of emigration, they negotiated an agreement with investors in the London Virginia Company and agreed to establish a settlement at the mouth of the Hudson River, on land on which the Dutch also had designs.

Mayflower sailed for America on September 6, 1620. On November 9, after a stormy passage, her crew sighted Cape Cod, a landfall well north of the group's intended Hudson River destination. There *Mayflower* became entangled and was nearly lost in the shoals known as Tucker's Terror. Turning north she rounded the cape and came to anchor on November 11 in present-day Provincetown harbor.

The ship finally anchored in Plymouth Bay on December 16. The little band of Puritans and the ship's company endured a brutal winter, losing almost half their number to sickness and starvation. In April 1621 *Mayflower* sailed for England to resume her regular trading voyages in the wine trade.

◂ *Mayflower* leaving Plymouth, England (WC, 15″ × 22″)
The Puritans made two attempts to cross the North Atlantic. Both times they were forced to return to England to repair the leaking Speedwell, *a second vessel they had chartered to make the crossing.* Mayflower *finally sailed alone for America on September 6, 1620, late in the season to be making the crossing.*

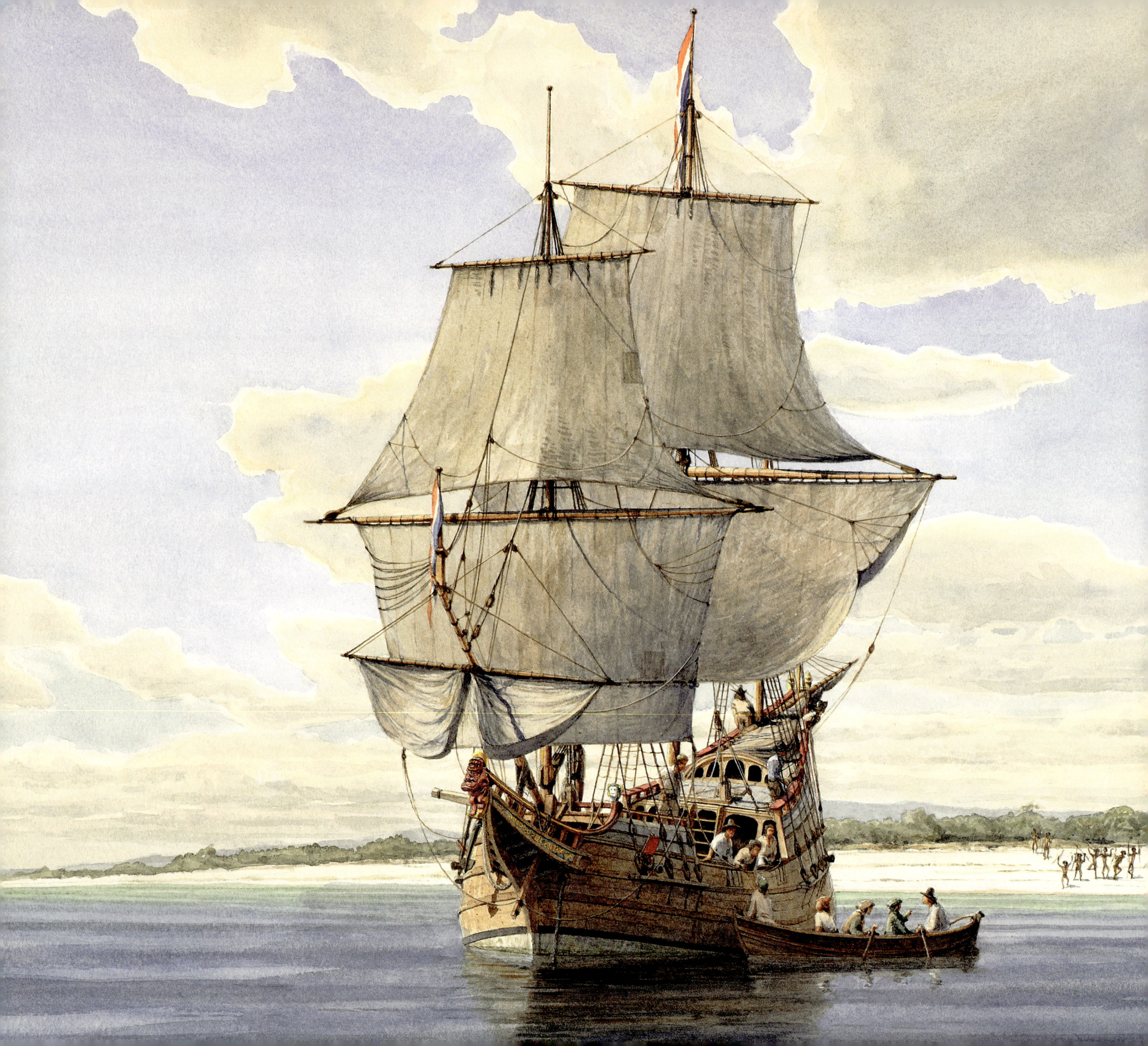

◂ ***Duyfken* at Cape Keerweer** (WC, 15″ × 22″)
In 1606 the Dutch East India Company's Duyfken *was dispatched from Bantam in the East Indies to search for gold and spices among unexplored islands to the southeast. Her course took her into Australia's Gulf of Carpentaria, where she made landfall on the west coast of the Cape York Peninsula at the Pennefather River. A boat was sent ashore for wood and water, and for the first time Europeans set foot on the continent of Australia.*

4

CHARTING THE GREAT SOUTHERN OCEAN

DOMINATING THE imaginations of geographers in the seventeenth and eighteenth centuries was the belief in the existence of *Terra Australis Incognita*, an immense southern continent that was supposed to cover almost all of the unexplored temperate zones of the southern Pacific Ocean.

In 1606 the Dutch East India Company ship *Duyfken* sailed south from the island of Banda into Australia's Gulf of Carpentaria. Her crew explored the Cape York Peninsula and made the first documented European landing on Australia. They surveyed southward as far as Cape Keerweer, where an encounter with aborigines, who were never friendly, may have convinced the Dutch to turn back. Dutch navigators continued to explore this unknown land, if only fitfully. Dirk Hartog, sailing north on Australia's

> **Abel Tasman in Southern Ocean ice**
(WC, 15″ × 22″)
In April 1642 Tasman's two ships, Heemskerck *and* Zeehaen, *called at Mauritius. They were repaired and then left for the high southern latitudes on October 8. Although it was springtime, the two ships struggled for months through icy seas, often surrounded by icebergs shrouded in fog, and the seamen were cold and exhausted. At about 49° south, Tasman relented and took the ships north to warmer climes, where at 44° south he ran east before the steady westerlies.*

west coast in 1616, found that on his starboard side land stretched north and south as far as he could see. Noting his position, he named it Eendrachtsland, after his ship. In 1619 Frederick de Houtman came upon the same coast far south of Hartog's landfall, which he charted while making his way towards Batavia.

Three years later, in 1622, the ship *Leeuwin* raised a cape even farther south than Houtman's discovery. The extent of this coast suggested that it was the western edge of a land of continental dimensions, which raised the age-old question of the existence of *Terra Australis*. Was this the long-sought southern continent? During the rest of the 1620s the Dutch made several voyages to the south and east of Java, along the south coast of New Guinea, into the Gulf of Carpentaria and to the area named Arnhem Land. For at least a decade these discoveries excited little interest in the practical Dutch. The natives were hostile, and the visible coast appeared to be barren and inhospitable.

The Search for *Terra Australis Incognita*

By the 1630s the little Dutch republic was entering its golden age. Its fleets were masters of the seas, and it had established commercial enterprises on every continent. In North America, it challenged Spain in the Caribbean and established New Amsterdam on Manhattan Island, and in South America it settled in western Guyana. It was also very active in the Dutch East Indies.

Anthony van Diemen, head of the Dutch East India Company, was fascinated by the *Terra Australis* mystery. Curious about the extent of the unexplored lands of New Holland, the vast blank area on the charts south of Java, van Diemen instructed Abel Janszoon Tasman to sail west to Mauritius, then south to 54° south and back east across the Pacific, where the continent was expected to be found. Tasman sailed on August 14, 1642, in two ships, *Heemskerck* and *Zeehaen*, calling first at Mauritius before sailing south. After a cold and difficult passage sailing eastward through the high southern latitudes, on November 24 his crew sighted high, wooded land. Tasman landed, performed an act of possession and named it Staat's Land (now known as Tasmania).

Continuing east, on December 13 Tasman's ships faced another high, forested coast rising ahead of them. This time it was capped by magnificent, snow-covered peaks. Tasman named this discovery Staten Land (now New Zealand), and followed it northward looking for signs of habitation. In early January 1643 his ships reached the northern end of the islands and struck off in a northeasterly direction, towards what he hoped were the Solomon Islands. Two weeks later they were among the Tonga Group, where water and victuals were readily procured. From there the ships made their way back to Batavia along the familiar north coast of New Guinea, discovering the Fiji Islands on the way.

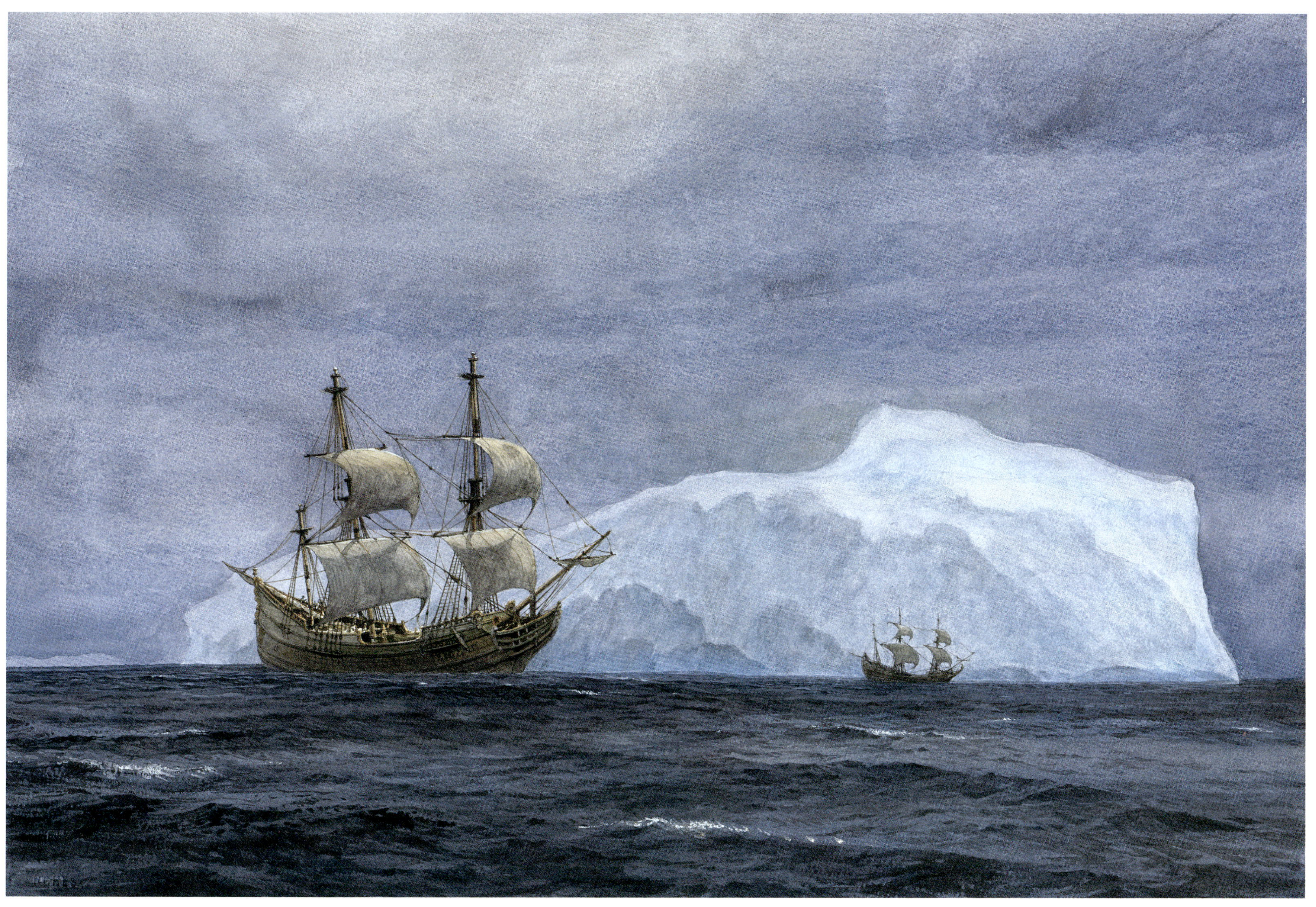

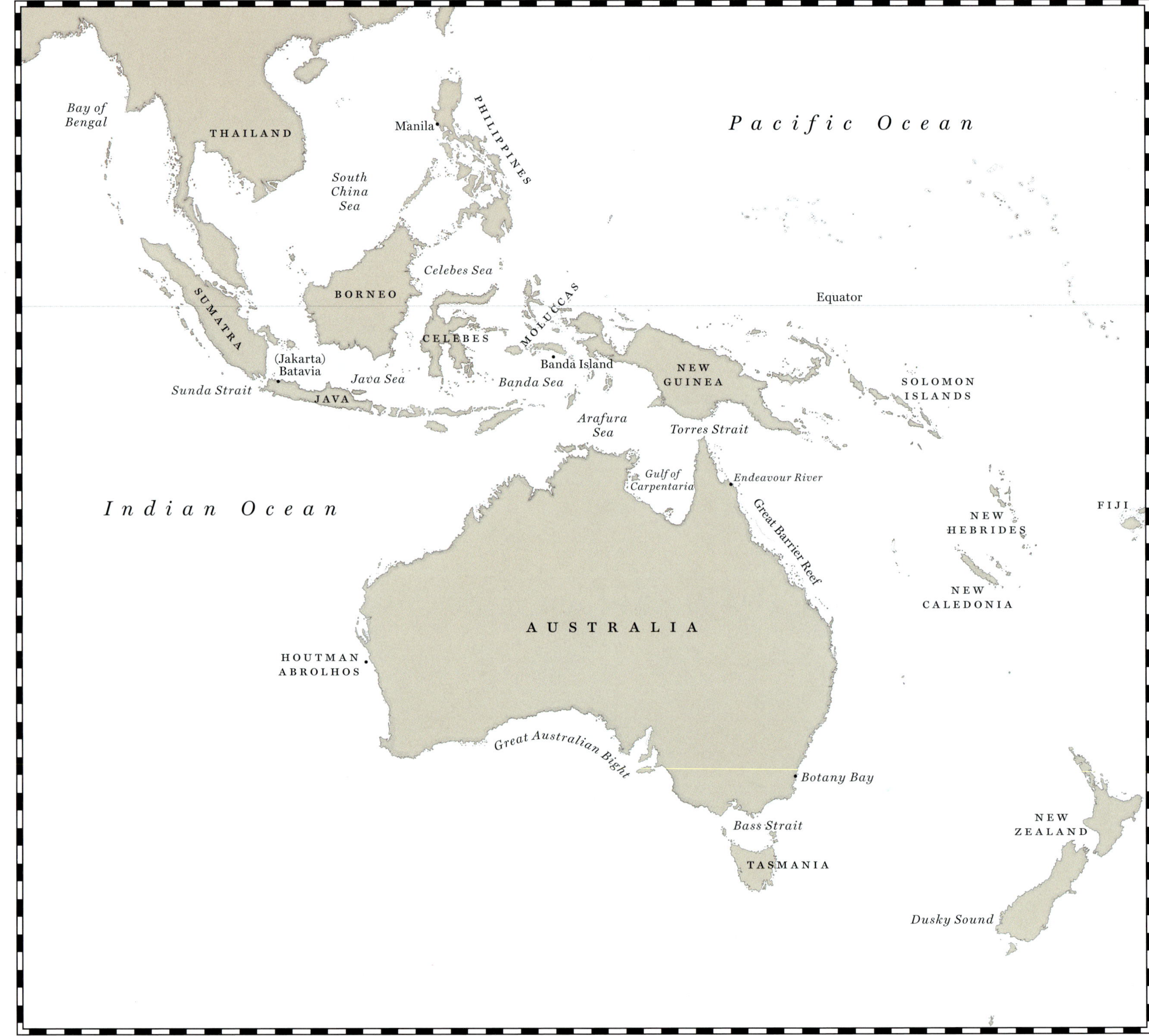

Bay of Bengal
THAILAND
Manila
PHILIPPINES
Pacific Ocean
South China Sea
Celebes Sea
SUMATRA
BORNEO
Equator
CELEBES
MOLUCCAS
(Jakarta) Batavia
Banda Island
NEW GUINEA
SOLOMON ISLANDS
Sunda Strait
Java Sea
Banda Sea
JAVA
Arafura Sea
Torres Strait
Gulf of Carpentaria
Endeavour River
Indian Ocean
Great Barrier Reef
NEW HEBRIDES
FIJI
NEW CALEDONIA
AUSTRALIA
HOUTMAN ABROLHOS
Great Australian Bight
Botany Bay
Bass Strait
NEW ZEALAND
TASMANIA
Dusky Sound

Tasman's discoveries met with little approval from the Dutch East India Company. Although he had added Tasmania, New Zealand and the Fiji Islands to the charts, he had failed to discover the southern continent, and in fact had completely circumnavigated Australia without laying eyes on it. The following year Tasman made another exploratory voyage along the south coast of New Guinea, south to the bottom of the Gulf of Carpentaria and back to Batavia by the north coast of New Holland. Again the official response to his discoveries was negative. The company could see little profit to be made in what appeared to be inhospitable territories populated by poor, naked and hostile natives.

It was almost eighty years before another Dutch administration showed any interest in the lands of the South Pacific. By that time, the Dutch East India Company's profits were in decline and Dutch sea power was being challenged by the English and French.

By 1763 England was no longer engaged in war with France, and once again its thoughts turned to the far Pacific. To answer the question of the whereabouts of the great southern continent as well as a northwest passage, in 1764 the Admiralty chose John Byron to mount an expedition. Byron's secret orders called for him to survey the Falkland Islands, sail to Sir Francis Drake's New Albion, find a northwest passage and return through it to England. If the passage wasn't discovered, Byron was to return via the Cape of Good Hope, all the while searching for the mythical southern continent. In the end, commanding the thirty-two-gun frigate *Dolphin*, Byron ignored all his orders and, preferring to cruise in more agreeable climates, crossed the Pacific too far north to make any significant discoveries. He returned to England in 1766, having circumnavigated the world.

Undeterred by Byron's lack of success, England again readied the newly returned *Dolphin* for sea. This time she was put in command of another dependable if undistinguished captain, Samuel Wallis. *Dolphin*, freshly coppered, was provisioned for a long voyage and ordered into the Pacific to search the high southern latitudes for the mythical continent. She was to be accompanied by *Swallow*, under the command of Philip Carteret, a young lieutenant who had previous Pacific Ocean experience. Also along was a store ship, which was only intended to travel to the Falklands before returning to England. *Swallow* was so unseaworthy that she was not expected to survive beyond the Falkland Islands and was to be abandoned there.

The three ships sailed from Portsmouth on August 22, 1766. They made a slow passage down the Atlantic, much delayed by *Swallow* and the store ship, and arrived in the Falklands after the replacement ship had already come and gone. When the replacement ship failed to materialize, Wallis reluctantly sent the store ship home and decided to continue with *Swallow* as consort. They made sail for the Strait of Magellan, where they battled

◂ *Spanish, Dutch and British discoveries and settlements in Australia, New Zealand and the East Indies.*

➤ ***Dolphin* in Matavai Bay, Tahiti, June 18, 1767** (WC, 15″ × 22″)
In 1767, during her search for Terra Australis, *the British ship* Dolphin *discovered Tahiti and dropped her hook in Matavai Bay. Captain Samuel Wallis landed, planted a flag and named the island King George the Third Island. There were some hostilities at the beginning of the visit—the islanders were prone to stealing, and watering parties were stoned—but when the power of the ship's guns was demonstrated, peaceful relations were established and no lives were lost.*

a nightmare of headwinds for four months. Finally, on April 11, 1767, *Dolphin* cleared the strait only to sail immediately into dense fog, with *Swallow* a dozen miles behind. To avoid the dangers of the lee shore at the entrance to the strait, Wallis headed off into the Pacific, leaving the hapless *Swallow* behind to fend for herself.

Carteret, his ship damaged by battling four months of storms in the strait, now embarked on one of the most harrowing and incredible feats of seamanship in British naval history. He nursed *Swallow* north, looking for safe refuge to make repairs. Finding that the Spanish had occupied the Juan Fernandez Islands off the coast of Chile, he was forced to pass them by. This led to his discovery of Pitcairn Island, later of *Bounty* fame, but *Swallow* could not land on the steep, cliffy shore. *Swallow* sailed on, leaking and trailing weed, her men discouraged and weakened by scurvy.

Finally, on August 12, 1767, four months after separating from *Dolphin* and six thousand miles into the Pacific, Carteret sighted the island of Santa Cruz in Melanesia. Although the natives were hostile, *Swallow* was desperate for water and a boat was sent ashore. In the ensuing skirmish the sailing master, three of his men and a number of islanders were killed.

Carteret was again forced to sail without obtaining needed supplies. A few days later, in the Solomon Islands, *Swallow* captured a canoe filled with coconuts. On August 26 she sailed into St. George Bay, the strait between New Britain and New Ireland. In a cove the crew was finally able to make temporary repairs to the ship and partially replenish her stores. On this passage across the Pacific they had been 137 days at sea and farther south in that part of the Pacific than any ship before, but they had sighted no great continent.

Carteret's trials were far from over. His crew was exhausted and sick, *Swallow*'s gear was rotten and the nearest shipyard where Carteret could hope to make proper repairs was still over a thousand miles away in the Dutch East Indies. He was among hostile and dangerous natives, and the monsoon season was preventing his making headway. Not until December 17 was he able to bring *Swallow* to anchor at Macassar, on the Dutch island of Celebes. After their sixteen months at sea, only twenty-five men, including officers, were healthy enough to work the ship. The Dutch at first refused to help them, but after begging for assistance they were allowed to move to the nearby port of Bonthain. Over the next five months the crew began to recover and some minor repairs were made to the ship. If she were ever to reach home, however, *Swallow* would require a complete overhaul, which could only be accomplished at a fully equipped shipyard.

In May 1768 *Swallow*—wormy, rotten and her bottom covered with weed—limped into the Dutch port of Batavia. The Dutch reluctantly helped repair the hull and rig and

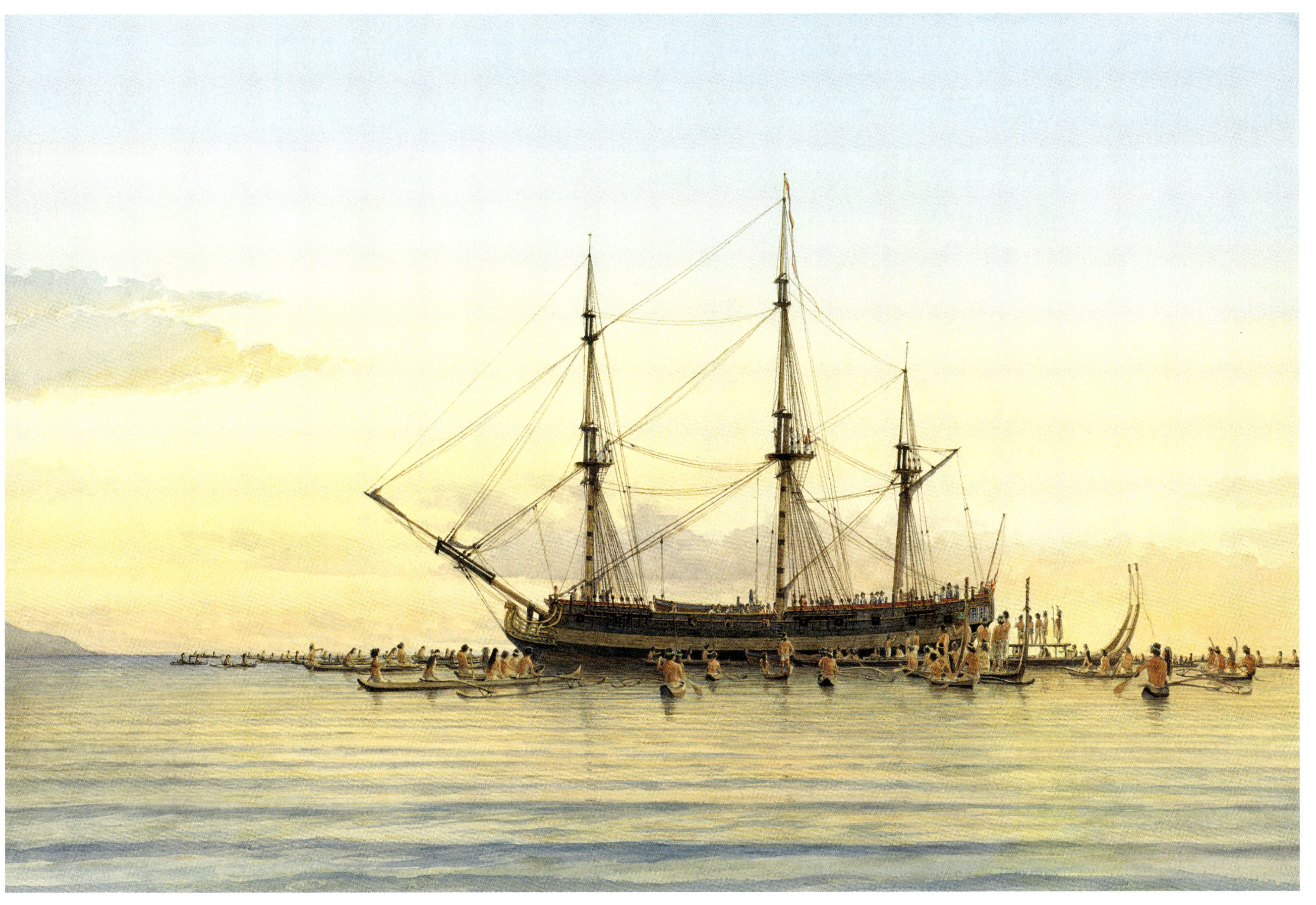

enlisted stranded British sailors to replace the men who had died on her voyage. Batavia was a notoriously disease-ridden port, and after four months, before repairs were complete, Carteret decided that life at sea on an unseaworthy ship was safer than staying in this port. In September he raised anchor and headed for home. For another six months they nursed the sad and sinking ship along, pumping almost constantly. Seven more men died. Finally, in March 1769, thirty-one months since she had sailed as consort to *Dolphin*, *Swallow* anchored in the Thames—to find that *Dolphin* had been home for almost a year. It was entirely due to the heroics of *Swallow*'s crew and Carteret's determination and talent that she made it home at all.

Dolphin's voyage had not been hindered by disease, but it had been just as eventful. After having abandoned *Swallow* to her fate, Captain Wallis was many miles north of where the Admiralty wanted him to be. It was believed that the undiscovered continent for which he had been sent to search lay at about latitude 40° south—it *had* to exist, in order to keep a balanced global equilibrium, a "conformity of hemispheres," as the Scottish geographer Alexander Dalrymple expressed it. Wallis had orders to sail west near that latitude until he found land, claim possession of it for England and then sail immediately for home. But 40° south was the middle of the belt of strong westerly winds that circled the earth in the southern hemisphere, which would have stopped *Dolphin* in her tracks. In order to gain any distance to the west, Wallis shaped a course to the northwest. After sailing for two months through empty seas, *Dolphin* sailed into the southern chain of the Tuamotu archipelago. At sunset on June 18, 1767, again in empty seas, her lookouts sighted high land on the horizon.

They sailed on through the night, and in the morning found themselves surrounded by canoes filled with hundreds of handsome, friendly and curious islanders. They had stumbled upon one of the loveliest islands on Earth, Tahiti, the largest of the group later named the Society Islands. The climate was delightful and the native people attractive and peaceful. For several weeks the ship lay at anchor, constantly surrounded by canoes, and her decks crowded with outgoing Tahitians. The availability of the women became legendary; they would trade sexual favors for a nail, and *Dolphin* consequently was in danger of being destroyed by sailors anxious to gain female attentions. In order to protect the ship, Wallis was forced to restrict shore leave to watering and wooding parties. He eventually sailed on July 27, 1767, arriving back in England on May 20, 1768.

Tahiti was the most significant discovery of Wallis's long voyage. The island paradise became the destination of almost every voyage to the Pacific over the next century.

Meanwhile, France was also entertaining ideas of overseas expansion. After its defeat in the late war and looking for ways to reestablish its fortunes and empire, France believed that the discovery and possession of the phantom southern continent would be the instrument of its renewal. Foremost in advancing the proposal was Louis-Antoine de Bougainville, a remarkable mathematician, author, soldier, sailor, statesman and member of the Royal Society in London. Recently returned to France from his position as aide-de-camp to General Louis-Joseph de Montcalm at the battle for Quebec, Bougainville persuaded the government to establish a colony in the Falkland Islands—which he then proceeded to do at his own expense, believing the islands would be a key base for supplying expeditions to the South Seas. During this adventure in 1765 he was surprised to discover Byron's ships in the Strait of Magellan, where both parties were watering.

On these voyages Bougainville may have sharpened his skills as a navigator and whetted his appetite for exploration, for the next year he sailed in command of the French expedition to search for *Terra Australis* on the twenty-six-gun frigate *Boudeuse*, accompanied by the store ship *Étoile*. On board were an astronomer, Pierre Antoine Vernon; a botanist, Philibert de Commerson; and Commerson's mistress and valet, Jeanne Baré, the last disguised as a boy and who thus became, if accidentally, the first recorded woman to complete a circumnavigation of the world.

Bougainville's mandate was to cruise the South Pacific and chart and claim for France any new discoveries. This was to be the first real scientific voyage of discovery, and the naturalists on board were well equipped with scientific instruments and books. Bougainville's two ships sailed from Nantes on November 16, 1766, three months after Wallis and Carteret had sailed from England, and from the start they were dogged by bad luck. Storm damage and accidents delayed them in the Atlantic and on the west coast of South America. They were eight months behind the two English ships when they encountered frustrating gales and cold in the Strait of Magellan, where they began to see debris left behind by *Swallow* and *Dolphin*. They also found other disturbing evidence that the English were ahead of them: dead campfires, and names and the date "1767" carved on a tree. It took the French fifty-two days to beat through the strait before finally emerging in the Pacific on January 26, 1768.

Bougainville took his ships north and west, roughly following in *Dolphin*'s wake, and had no more luck than Wallis in making significant discoveries. Late in March the French found themselves among the Tuamotus, which Bougainville named the Dangerous Archipelago, claiming them for France. On April 6 they anchored on Tahiti's east coast, in Hitiaa Lagoon, a roadstead so poor that they were forced to cut short their stay after only nine days. While there they enjoyed the same hospitality the

➤ ***Swallow* and *Boudeuse*—Atlantic encounter, February 25, 1769**
(WC, 15″ × 22″)
On February 25, 1769, the French ship Boudeuse *caught up with the British ship* Swallow *a few days north of Ascension Island, in the South Atlantic.* Swallow *was a pitiful sight, wallowing along, trailing long tendrils of weed, barely making headway in the Atlantic seas.* Boudeuse's *captain, Louis-Antoine de Bougainville, sent a boat with offers of assistance, but the suspicious British captain, Philip Carteret, refused them. Bougainville sailed on, not revealing that he had crossed the Pacific in* Swallow's *wake.*

Tahitians had accorded the English and made the same assessment of the beauty of the land and its people, giving rise to the myth of the "noble savage." Unaware that Wallis had already claimed Tahiti for England, Bougainville named it New Cythera and claimed it for France.

Bad weather dogged the passage of *Boudeuse* and *Étoile* to the west, past Samoa and through the New Hebrides. The ships sailed uncharted territory through the Coral Sea and would have been first to sight the east coast of Australia if they had not turned north just short of the Great Barrier Reef. But Bougainville was experiencing the common affliction of explorers of the day: disintegrating ships, hunger and rapidly sickening men. He was forced to make for Batavia, sailing north over the top of New Guinea, reaching the port on September 28, 1768.

At Batavia Bougainville nursed his ailing men back to health and replenished the ships' stores, but the dysentery endemic in the port forced him to leave before *Étoile* had finished repairs. The ships were reunited at Mauritius in November, and on December 12 they sailed for home. On January 9, 1769, *Boudeuse* reached the Cape of Good Hope, where Bougainville learned he was only three days behind the hapless *Swallow*. They had seen many signs of Wallis and Carteret's expedition along the way, but their presence had been confirmed at Batavia. Carteret had left only twelve days before *Boudeuse* arrived. A brief stop at Ascension Island confirmed that *Swallow* was still ahead, and on February 25 Bougainville caught up to her.

On March 16 Bougainville arrived at St. Malo to huge acclaim as the first Frenchman to circumnavigate the globe. He had not, however, found *Terra Australis Incognita*, and he had added little to the knowledge of the Pacific. Bougainville never sailed there again.

The Voyages of James Cook

While Bougainville, Wallace and Carteret were still at sea in the 1760s, the British government was planning yet another expedition to the Pacific, this time under command of James Cook. With the possible exception of Horatio Nelson, Cook remains the most famous and revered of all of Britain's captains. Without ever commanding a fighting ship, he brought great prestige to England. He was the consummate seaman, navigator, cartographer and observer. In one decade, between 1768 and 1779, he made three great scientific voyages to the Pacific Ocean that defined its vastness, fixed clearly the outline of its coasts and almost completely discounted the possibilities of lost continents and mythical straits. He defined for the first time the coasts of New Zealand, eastern Australia and the Hawaiian Islands; the west coast North America from California to the Bering Sea; and many undiscovered islands in the South Pacific. He was expert at accurately determining longitude, eliminated the problem of scurvy from his ships and was devoted to protecting the health and conditions of his crew. In fact, men who sailed with Cook were more likely to survive than if they stayed ashore.

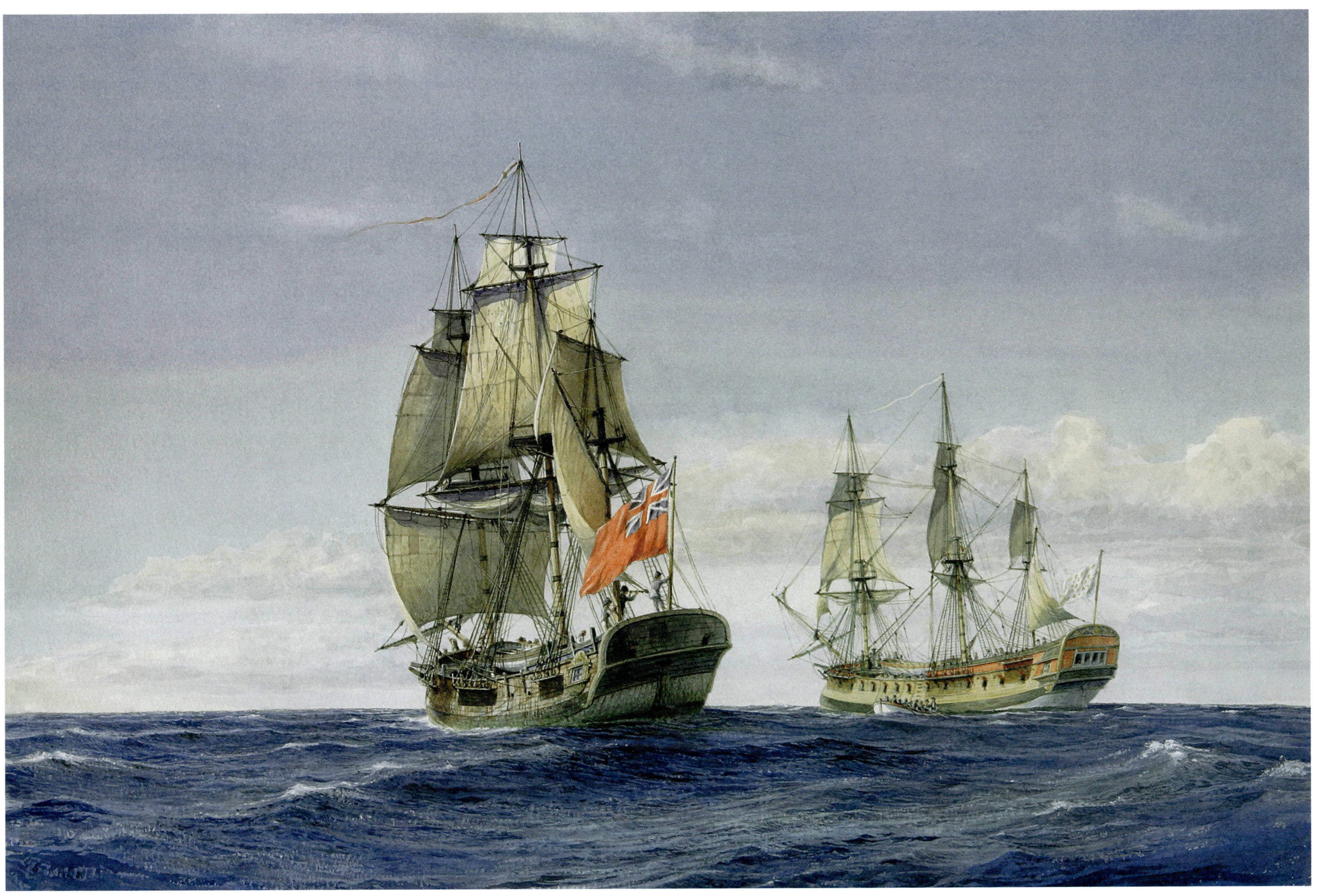

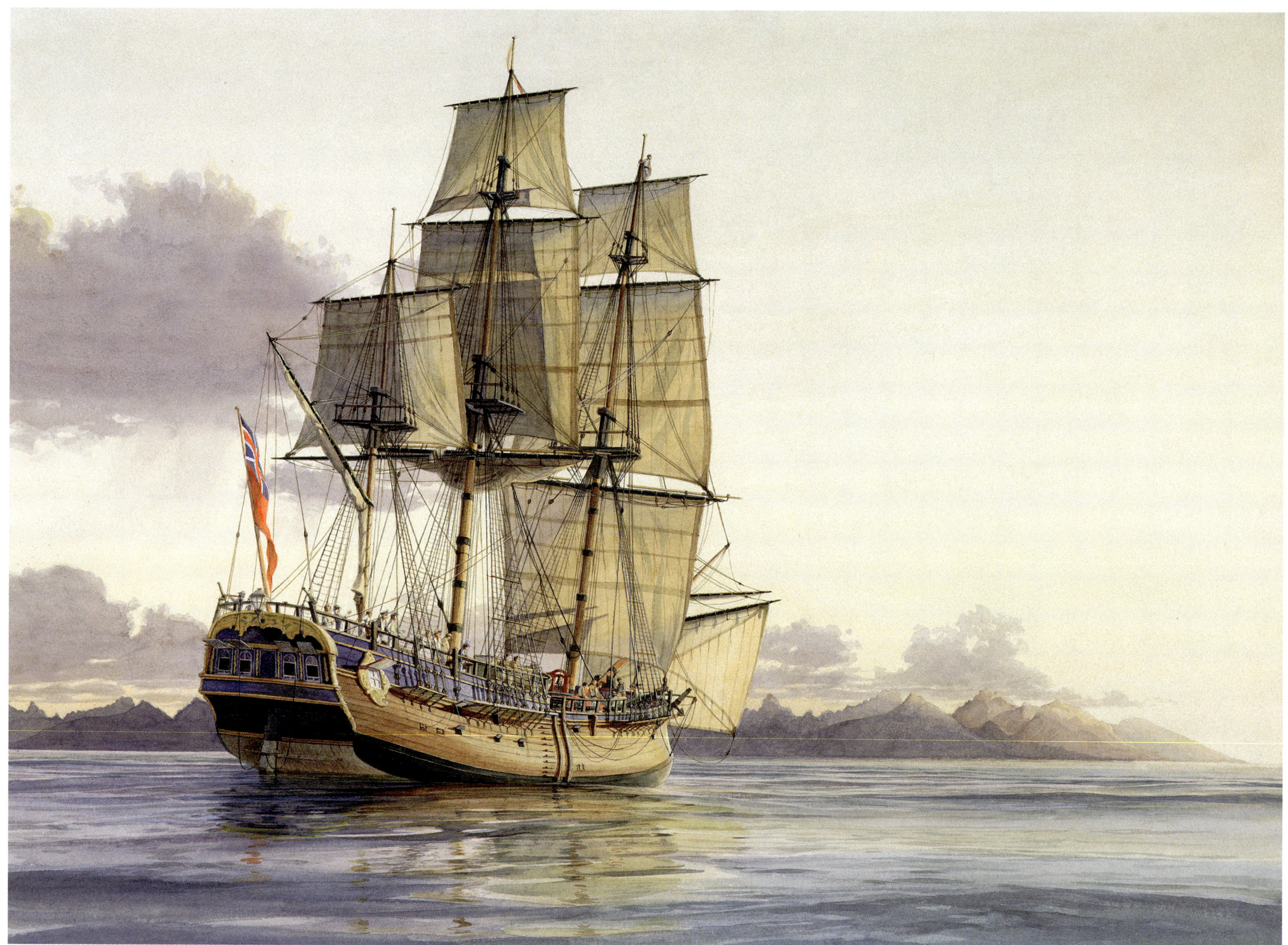

The ostensible purpose of Cook's first voyage was to observe the transit of Venus from Tahiti, but secretly he was also expected to search for the legendary southern continent at 40° south. On board his ship, *Endeavour,* for the duration was Joseph Banks, a young and wealthy natural scientist and member of the Royal Society, accompanied by his personal servants, plus an astronomer, two botanists and two artists. *Endeavour* sailed from Plymouth in August 1768, easily cleared Cape Horn in late January 1769 and on the morning of April 11 had the high peaks of Tahiti in sight. The trade winds were gentle, and it wasn't until the morning of April 13 that the anchor splashed into the clear water of Matavai Bay. The crew and scientists enjoyed the pleasures of paradise for ninety-one days, obviously not anxious to depart.

Cook sailed from Tahiti on July 13, taking his ship westward through the Society Islands before beginning the long, tough slog south into the high latitudes. The weather became increasingly cold and squally as *Endeavour* pounded through the strong westerlies known as the Roaring Forties. On September 1, at latitude 40°22′ south and with no sign of land where Dalrymple's "necessary continent" was supposed to be, Cook turned back to a warmer and gentler latitude to relieve the ship and rest the crew. Then he headed west in search of Tasman's discoveries. On October 6, 1769, land was sighted ahead; *Endeavour* had come upon New Zealand at the latitude of Poverty Bay, approximately the midpoint of the north island. The native Maori, who considered all strangers to be enemies, were not friendly, which is what Tasman had discovered 126 years earlier. Despite the chilly reception and the often adverse weather, Cook spent over six months on an exhaustive charting of the challenging New Zealand coast.

Cook had now fulfilled his orders and was free to go home. He chose the westward route, partly to avoid the Horn in midwinter, and hoping to discover the eastern coast of New Holland and a westward passage above it. Sailing across the Tasman Sea, *Endeavour* raised the southeastern tip of Australia. Cook bore away to the north and began a running survey of the two thousand miles of coast. *Endeavour* anchored in the first convenient opening, which Cook named Botany Bay, on April 28, 1770. The naturalists had a field day collecting new and exotic specimens, another act of possession was performed, and *Endeavour*'s water was replenished. Cook kept close to the coast on the passage north, noting but not entering possible anchorages.

The weather was mostly benign, but Cook was sailing into a trap that almost ended the voyage. Along the coast of Queensland stretches the Great Barrier Reef, a hundred miles wide and twelve hundred miles long, the gap of safe water gradually closing towards the northern end. Into this dangerous coral labyrinth Cook was carefully feeling

‹ ***Endeavour* approaching Tahiti, April 12, 1769** (WC, 22″ × 30″)
James Cook's ship Endeavour *was a Whitby collier purchased by the Admiralty and outfitted for an extended scientific voyage.* Endeavour's *approach to Tahiti was slow, as the trade winds were gentle.*

his way. On a clear June night, under a radiant moon in perfect night-sailing conditions, *Endeavour* struck fast on a coral head. Everything heavy and expendable was jettisoned, and after twenty-three anxious hours she floated off on the next night's high tide. Several agonizing days of constant pumping were spent searching for a suitable bay to careen her.

On June 16 *Endeavour* was grounded safely in a river mouth; there the crew made repairs, replaced what stores they could, surveyed the reefs for a way out and waited for a fair tide and breeze that would free them from the river. On August 4 they sailed. For the next sixteen days they were never free of the dangerous coral, but at noon on August 21, with the boats sounding ahead, they cleared the last dangerous shoals, with the northernmost point of Australia bearing a little south of west. Cook had found Endeavour Strait, and though his worst problems were at last behind him, home was still half a world away.

On October 10 Cook reached Batavia, where three months were spent in a thorough refit of *Endeavour*. The diseases of the port struck hard; seven men died of fever, forty were very ill and most of the rest were sickly. Cook sailed as soon as he could, but men continued to die all the way into the North Atlantic. Finally, on July 13, 1771, *Endeavour* anchored in the Downs.

Joseph Banks took all the credit for the success of the voyage, was written about extensively in the press and was presented to the king. The arrival of "*Endeavour*, Captain Cook, from the East Indies," was all the recognition Cook was given. The Admiralty was more impressed, however, and Lieutenant Cook, promoted to commander, was eventually presented to the king. Dalrymple savaged Cook for not being more diligent in looking for his continent, and demanded another voyage. The Admiralty, aware of several more French expeditions already looking for undiscovered lands, quickly approved a second voyage and ordered Cook to sea again. Two new Whitby merchantmen were purchased and converted: the 462-ton *Resolution* and the 336-ton *Adventure*. This time the ships were given suitable decoration, more in keeping with a king's ship, and a figurehead and quarter galleries were added to *Resolution*.

Joseph Banks expected to be given command of this second voyage, but neither the Admiralty nor Cook would accede to his demands for a larger ship more suited to his exalted station, and Banks stayed home in a huff. This second voyage was to be a circumnavigation in the high southern latitudes, as close to the South Pole as possible, explicitly to look for the large continent still believed to be there. An artist, a naturalist and his son and two astronomers were accommodated, and for the first time each ship had two chronometers for keeping time. Also on board was fourteen-year-old midshipman George Vancouver, who would go on to make his own reputation.

Resolution and *Adventure* sailed from Plymouth on July 13, 1772, and were anchored in Table Bay at the Cape of Good Hope on October 30. From the cape the ships began their search to the south into unknown waters. They soon were well into the ice, ceaselessly bearing away from growlers and bergs and often in fog, snow, sleet and intense cold in the area later called the Shrieking Fifties. On January 4, 1773, they crossed the Antarctic Circle, the first ships ever to do so. At 66°36½´ south, pack ice ended any attempt to continue, stopping them only seventy-five miles from the continent of Antarctica.

On February 8, in thick fog, the two ships lost sight of each other. Cook continued alone on *Resolution,* east and as far south as he dared, mostly in gales, always cold, but discovering no land. On March 17, after more than three months in the most dangerous seas in the world, he at last turned north. High seas and heavy westerly gales prevented a course for Tasmania, and the first landfall was the southern end of New Zealand. *Resolution* spent six weeks anchored in idyllic Dusky Sound, she and her crew recovering from the Antarctic ordeal. In mid-May Cook found *Adventure* in Queen Charlotte Sound, at anchor and rigged down, with her captain, Tobias Furneaux, expecting to spend "a few Months in Ease & Quietness." Cook had other ideas; it took a month to put *Adventure* back together and for her sickly crew to recover.

The next part of the voyage was a swing through the Pacific east of New Zealand at about 45° south, still in a search of the continent, then north to Tahiti for a rest. No continent was found, and in mid-August Tahiti was in sight. The crews rested in Matavai Bay until *Adventure*'s scurvy patients recovered. The Tahitians, still masters of thievery, wept when the ships left, but generously gave what fresh supplies they could. It was already September, and the ships were bound for New Zealand and another summer in the Antarctic.

Resolution anchored in Ship Cove, Queen Charlotte Sound, but there was no sign of *Adventure.* The ships had been separated in a violent storm within sight of the islands, and weeks later, when *Adventure* limped into the bay, Cook had already left. Furneaux returned to England through the Pacific by a southern route—adding to the charts more empty ocean where no land was found—called at the Cape of Good Hope and was home a full year before Cook. Cook again headed down below the Antarctic Circle, back in the ice and freezing gales, searching for Dalrymple's continent. The weather was relatively pleasant on the last days of January 1774, with good visibility. On January 30, at longitude 106°10´ west, latitude 71°10´ south, they came to the edge of a field of ice, unbroken as far as they could see. It was as far south as they were ever to get, and much farther than anyone had ever been before. George Vancouver always claimed that on that

› **Watering party in the southern ice, 1773**
(WC, 15″ × 22″)
In January 1773 James Cook's ships Resolution *and* Endeavour *came within seventy-five miles of Antarctica. Cook discovered that sea ice was fresh, and when the seas were calm his ships filled their casks from the unlimited supply of fresh water.*

momentous occasion he had made his way to the end of the bowsprit, and thus could claim to have been closer to the South Pole than any other man.

Cook could now claim that his ship had gone as far south as was possible, and turned north to make a great counterclockwise sweep through the eastern Pacific before sailing for home. *Resolution* touched at Easter Island, rediscovered the Marquesas Islands, stopped at Tahiti and the Friendly Islands, discovered New Caledonia and Norfolk Island, and in New Zealand was made ready for the run to Cape Horn and Cape of Good Hope. Cook kept the ship well to the south, where he added South Georgia and the South Sandwich Islands to his discoveries. Almost three and a half years after she left, *Resolution* anchored at the Cape of Good Hope, and after a five-week refit she sailed for home. On July 30, 1775, Cook dropped anchor at Plymouth, after a voyage of three years and eighteen days.

This time on his return, Cook was rewarded with the fame he deserved. He was elected a Fellow of the Royal Society, awarded the society's Copley Gold Medal, promoted to post captain and given a captain's berth at Greenwich Hospital, where he could have retired comfortably for the rest of his life. Instead, he volunteered for a third voyage to the Pacific. This one would traverse the North Pacific into the high Arctic, completing his exploration of the last of the major unexplored oceans.

Cook had more or less dispelled all hopes that *Terra Australis* existed, but there was still one idea that refused to die: the Northwest Passage. Many attempts to locate it from the east had failed, but no one had looked seriously on the west coast of America. The Admiralty was committed to another voyage of exploration, *Resolution* was already being readied for sea and another Whitby ship, purchased and renamed *Discovery*, was being converted. Cook's obligations ashore allowed him no time to oversee *Resolution*'s refit, and the naval dockyards were under pressure to supply vessels for the American war now in progress. As a result, *Resolution* didn't get the attention she required. The poor material and shoddy work done on her plagued Cook from the start.

Resolution sailed on July 12, 1776, nine months behind schedule. No scientists were shipped, but on board was the Polynesian Omai, who had been brought to England by Furneaux and was going home. John Webber was the artist, and the sailing master was William Bligh, later to be captain of the *Bounty*. Cook's first lieutenant was John Gore, James King his second. Commanding *Discovery* was Charles Clerke. George Vancouver was making his second voyage, as a midshipman in *Discovery*.

In Cape Town, *Resolution* was completely recaulked and waited for *Discovery* to catch up, and by November 30 the ships were ready. They sailed east in the wild winds between latitude 45° and 50° south on the way to

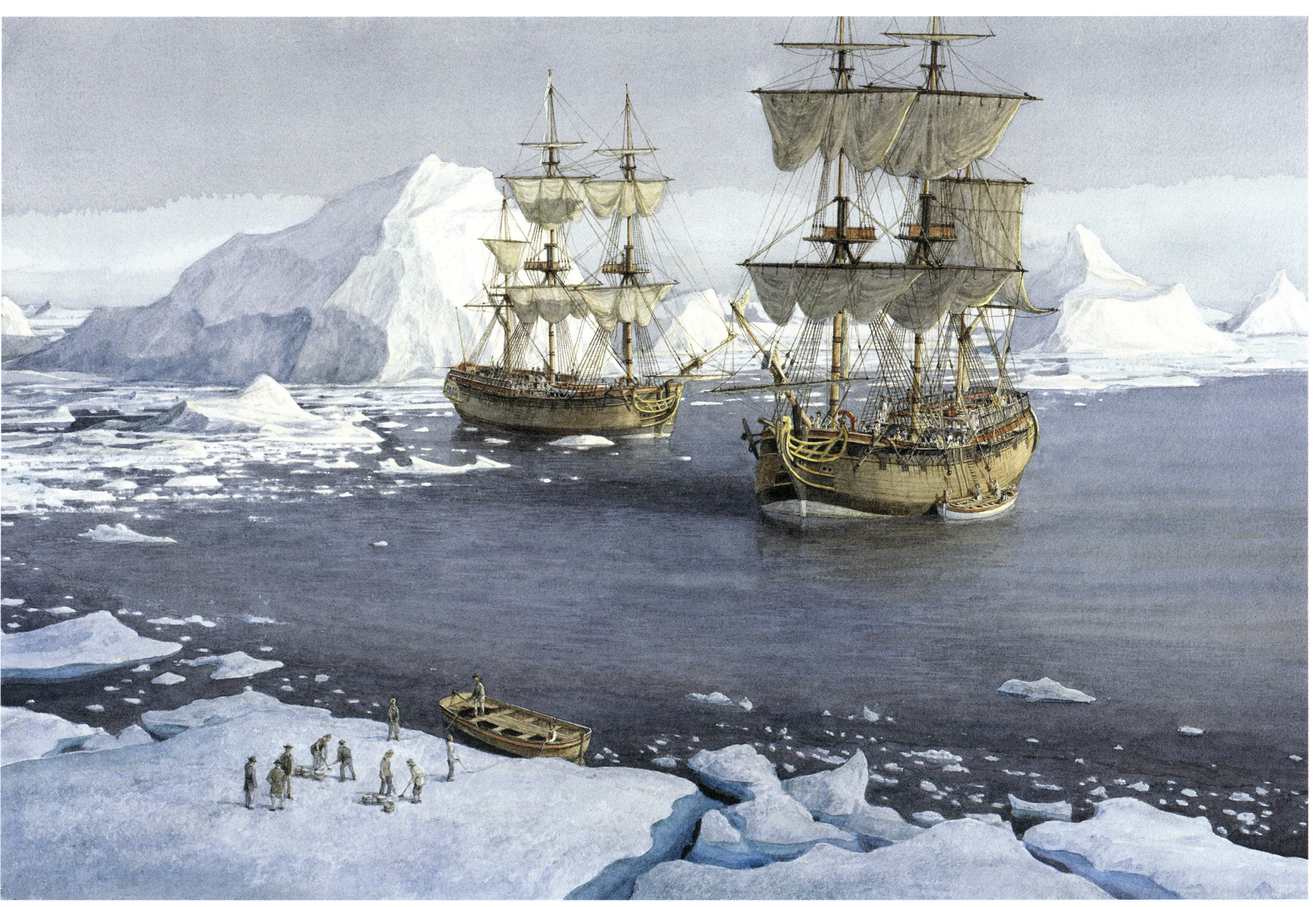

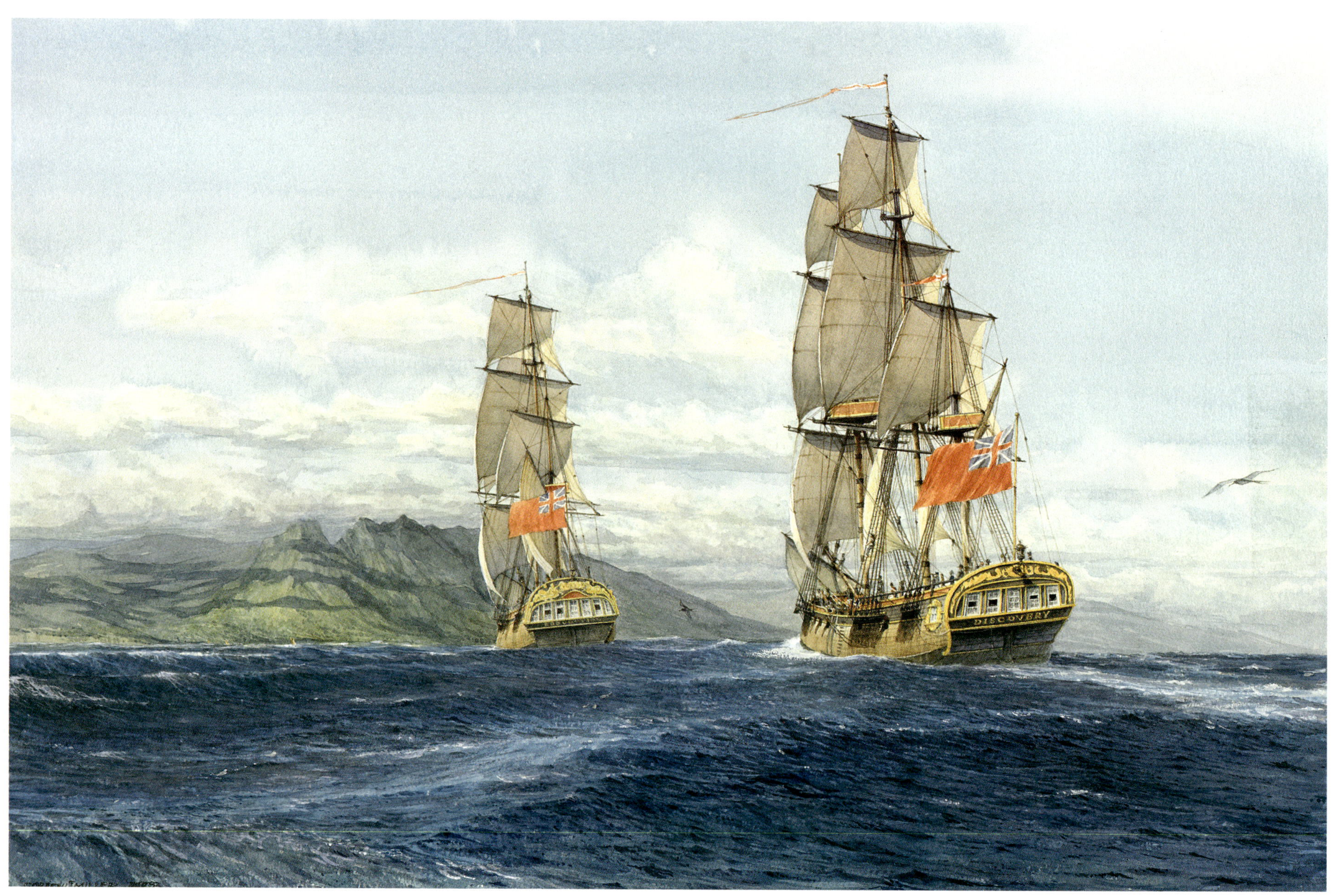

Tasmania and New Zealand. In these stormy seas, *Resolution*'s mizzen topmast came down, and in a later gale the fore topmast went, taking the main topgallant mast with it. This was another sign of the poor work done back in England that was to trouble Cook for the duration. They stopped briefly in Adventure Bay, Tasmania, to cut new spars and replenish wood and water. On February 12, 1777, the ships anchored in Ship Cove, Queen Charlotte Sound. There they lingered only eleven days.

By this point Cook was aware that he was too late to reach the American coast by June and would have to wait another whole season. With time in hand, he took a north-easterly course from New Zealand—past a new discovery, the Cook Islands—and arrived at Nomuka in the Tonga Group, where two and a half months were spent exploring and documenting island life. Early in the voyage Cook had experienced severe stomach pain, possibly from an ulcer, and some uncharacteristic behavior in these islands suggested he was still suffering. He dealt more harshly with the thievery by the Tongans than was his norm, flogging, humiliating and holding chiefs for ransom. Although his actions did not seem to affect the generally friendly relations, they were noted as unusual by his crew.

In July the ships left for Tahiti, an uphill sail against light trade winds. It took four weeks and resulted in one new discovery, Tubuai. After a short stop at Vaitepiha to put ashore three cows for a bull left by a Spanish ship in 1774, they anchored in Matavai Bay in August 1777. There they were at last relieved of the remaining livestock that had been fouling the decks all the way from Cape Town: a bull, a horse, a mare, a sheep, a turkey cock and hen, a gander and geese, ducks and a pair of breeding peacocks, the last a gift from Lord Bessborough. The time at Tahiti was spent mending sails, repairing water casks and fixing *Discovery*'s main mast, which had been damaged in a squall. The ships were well stocked by the generous Tahitians and were ready for sea on September 29, when a fair breeze took them out of the bay.

They made a brief and regrettable visit to the beautiful island of Moorea. There some natives took a liking to the ship's goats that were taken ashore to graze, and Cook retaliated by destroying several canoes and houses. The goats and friendly relations returned, but Cook's reputation for fairness was compromised. His last stop was at Raiatea, where the attractions of the native women proved too great for his crew, and desertions from the ships delayed him for a month. The ships finally sailed in December and set off into the vast ocean to the north.

After they crossed the equator, on January 18, 1778, a large island rose in the northeast. Cook had encountered the Hawaiian Islands, his last major discovery in the Pacific Ocean. He was received with typical Polynesian hospitality, and although pilfering was common, fair trading relationships were soon established. His first

‹ **Cook's discovery of Hawaii** (WC, 15″ × 22″) *On January 18, 1778, James Cook sighted the big island of Hawaii. As the day wore on, more islands began to appear. A course was laid for the islands to the north, and on the afternoon of the next day the ships were close to the east coast of Kauai. Canoes soon surrounded the ships, and to Cook's surprise he found the natives were Polynesian.*

› ***Resolution* and *Discovery* approaching Nootka Sound** (WC, 22″ × 30″)
On the morning of March 29, 1778, Resolution *and* Discovery *were looking for a secure anchorage to make repairs and obtain wood and water. James Cook made for an indentation that promised shelter, with just enough of a breeze to make the anchorage under sail. Before the sun set, the ships were greeted with traditional songs and the ceremonial scattering of eagle down by Nuu-chah-nulth canoes from the village of Yuquot. Cook had found Nootka Sound, where Juan Pérez had stopped four years earlier.*

anchorage was off Waimea, but a change of wind put them on a lee shore, and they got off with difficulty. They experienced the same conditions off Niihau, where they tried to land for water. On February 2 they gave up and made sail for America. Cook had no doubt that Hawaii was a significant discovery, and left with the hope of returning to make a thorough survey.

The ships first sailed north looking for the westerlies and then east to the California coast. At daybreak on March 7 the continent was visible about thirty miles ahead. As Cook approached it he encountered a long stretch of foul weather (he named the point Cape Foulweather), and working north he saw little of the coast. His chart has many blanks where his ships were forced out to sea or encountered fog. He did not see the entrance to Juan de Fuca Strait, though he knew he was in the vicinity.

The dishonest workmanship to *Resolution* in the naval dockyard at Deptford plagued Cook for the whole of the final voyage; she had begun to leak through her seams with the first blow she met. Finding reasonably secure anchorage in Nootka Sound, Cook set about making much-needed repairs. By April 26 the ships were ready to sail and were towed out of the cove by the boats, back into squalls and rain. This storm lasted almost five days, by which time they had been blown north of the Queen Charlotte and Prince of Wales Islands. When they sighted land again it was May 1 and they were at 55°20′ north. From there, in more favorable weather, Cook searched for any opening that might be the Northwest Passage. The first possibility surveyed was Prince William Sound.

Farther to the west Cook came to an even larger and more promising opening, but surveys suggested it was only a river estuary. George Vancouver later surveyed it to the end and named it Cook Inlet. Cook all this time was looking for an opening to the Arctic Ocean, a way to 65° north, and was trying to rationalize what he was seeing using two confusing Russian charts he had been provided with. Continually hampered by fog and gales, he spent the month of June inching along the grim coasts of Kodiak Island and the Alaska Peninsula. Off the Shumagin Islands the ship was surprised by a native in a canoe who handed them a note, presumably in Russian, and paddled off. Cook had no one on board who could translate it.

They missed the first pass into the Bering Sea and narrowly avoided disaster in the pass they eventually navigated. Cook's track shows a slow and torturous course to the middle of the Bering Sea, where they raised St. Matthew Island. They came onto the mainland again in the first week of August and anchored below Cape Prince of Wales, the westernmost point of America. When the winds permitted, Cook followed the American shore to the northeast. At noon on August 17, a telltale brightness in the northern sky announced the presence of ice ahead.

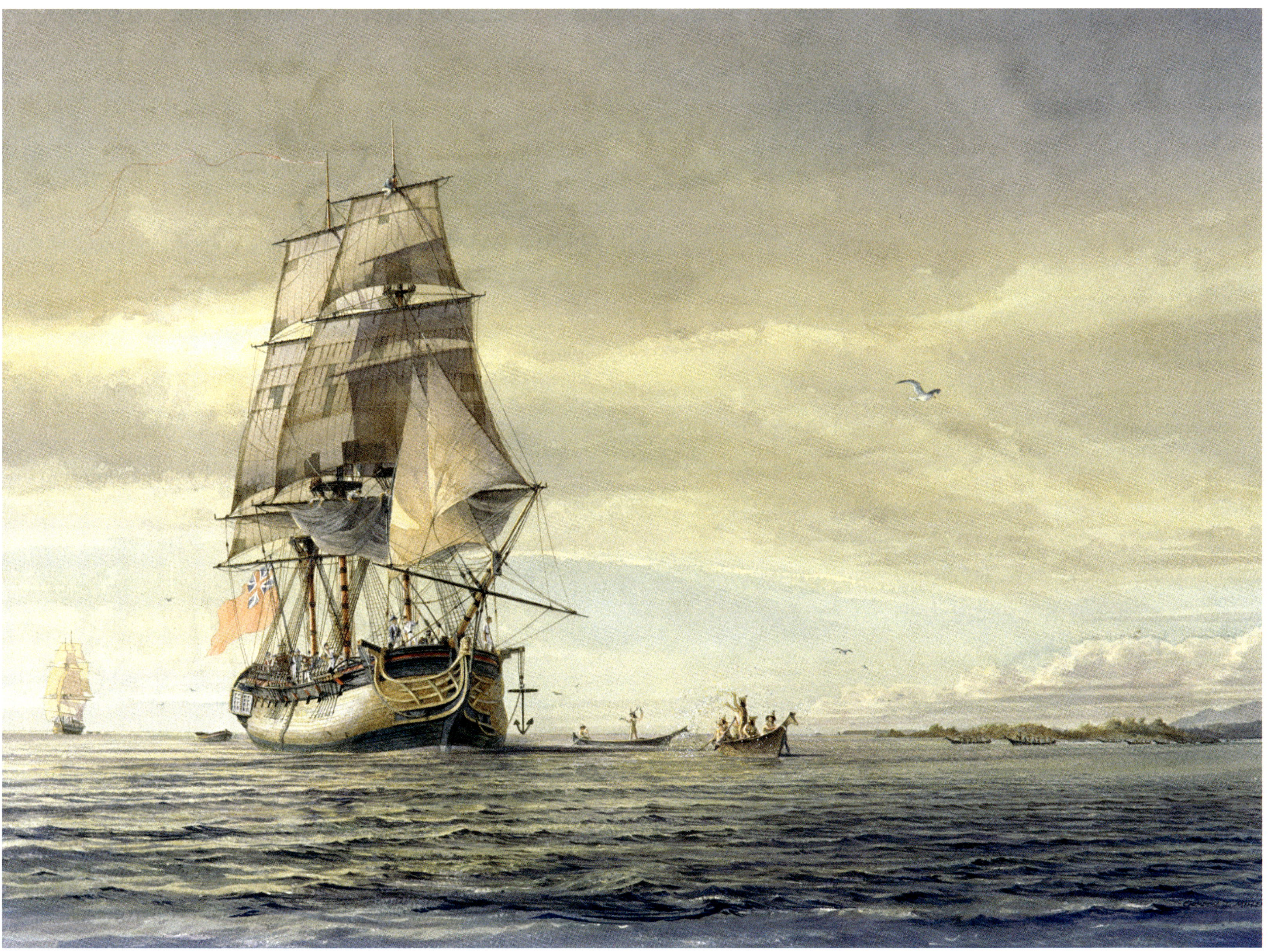

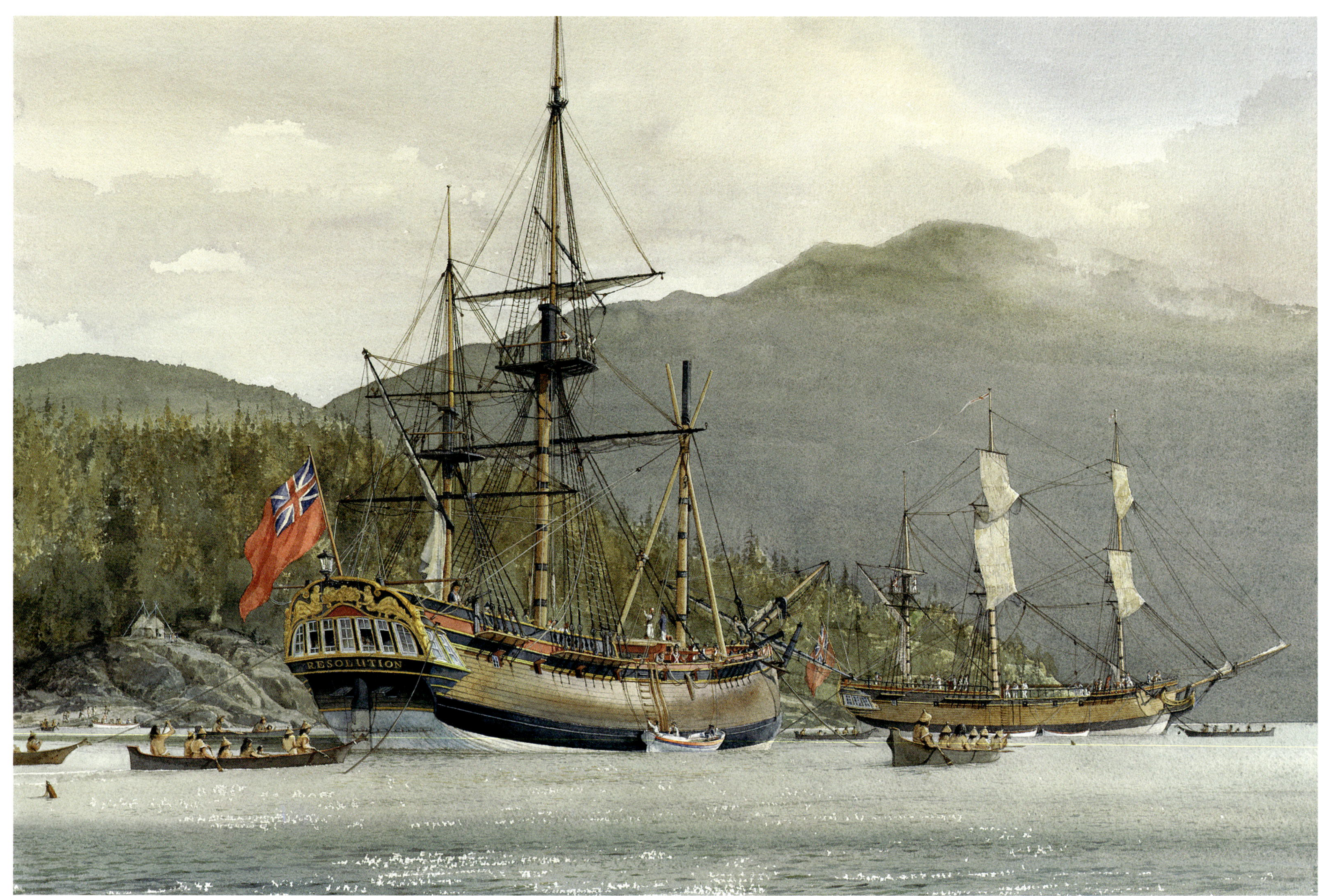
RESOLUTION

Next day they were stopped by an immense field at 70°44′ north, the farthest north they were ever to reach. Off Icy Cape both ships were almost trapped in the drift on a lee shore, but were saved by a providential change of wind.

With the summer coming to an end, Cook turned the ships south. He charted the Chukchi Peninsula where it was visible, fixed accurately East Cape and picked up the west side of Bering's St. Lawrence Island before returning to the American shore. He was then ready to leave the Arctic; it had been five months of cold, miserable weather with few days of sun, and the Sandwich Islands were beckoning. He stopped again for three weeks at the Russian-Aleut community on Unalaska Island for wood, water and seam caulking, and exchanged charts with the Russian factor. He also left charts and an account of the voyage to be delivered to St. Petersburg and eventually to London.

The long sail south began at the end of October. The ships rig and sails were wearing out, and four days of one of the worst storms of the voyage added to their stress. They sailed on, repairing what they could, the days gradually warming, and on November 25 they were four degrees east of the Hawaiian Islands. At sunrise the next morning, Haleakala volcano on Maui was showing above the clouds to the west. Cook needed a well-protected anchorage in the lee of the islands to carry out repairs. For eight weeks he was forced to tack offshore at night, back to the coast at dawn to trade, gradually working around the south and west of the big island. Not until January 17, 1779, in Kealakekua Bay, were they finally able to anchor.

The ships were at once surrounded by a huge flotilla of canoes, filled with thousands of rejoicing Hawaiians. Their reception was extraordinary, and for the next two weeks Cook was celebrated like a god. The ships were gifted with more fresh produce than they could stow, so much that the local communities were in danger of being impoverished. Thievery from the ship was rampant and serious but repairs were begun, and early in February they were again ready for sea. On February 4, escorted by a fleet of canoes, they sailed out of the bay. Although Cook had been treated like royalty, the people were relieved to see him leave.

After two days of light and variable winds they sailed into increasingly violent squalls, and on the morning of February 8 *Resolution*'s foremast was found to be badly sprung. It was not damage that could be repaired at sea, and reluctantly Cook returned to Kealakekua Bay. The ships were anchored and work began immediately on getting the mast ashore. This time there were noticeably fewer natives in attendance, and these became increasingly belligerent and bold. The insolence came to a head with the theft of *Discovery*'s cutter. For Cook, this was the last straw. Uncharacteristically, he armed himself and, with Lieutenant Philips, led nine armed marines ashore to take Chief Kalei'opu'u hostage to the ship. They were

◂ **Resolution Cove** (WC, 22″ × 30″)
In April 1778 Resolution *and* Discovery *were anchored in Ship Cove (later named Resolution Cove) on Bligh Island, on the west coast of Vancouver Island. Most of the month was spent replacing* Resolution's *masts and all of the rigging on the main. A tent was set up ashore for astronomical observation, and the sound was charted from the ship's boats. The Nuu-chah-nulth were around them every day, and James Cook made a visit to Chief Maquinna's village in Friendly Cove. Sea otter furs obtained from the natives here were later traded in Canton for huge profits, and the news, when it reached Europe, set off a fur trade rush to the Northwest Coast in the 1780s.*

met on the beach by a large hostile crowd, which followed Cook into the village.

The old chief willingly accompanied them back to the waiting boat, but the Hawaiians were becoming alarmingly bold and agitated. Weapons appeared, and one of the mob threatened Cook with a dagger. Cook fired one barrel of small shot from his musket that did no damage, but at the shot the crowd erupted. Daggers, spears and stones were met with a volley from the marines. The enraged Hawaiians overwhelmed the men, leaving four dead on the beach. Cook's final shot killed a man, and as he turned towards the beach he was clubbed from behind. A stab from a dagger felled him, and in the ensuing tumult he was hacked to death.

A shocked and saddened Charles Clerke assumed command of the expedition and moved onto *Resolution*. He wisely decided against retaliation, and after a few days tensions began to ease. The Hawaiians, even after Cook's death, held the captain in high regard and treated his body in the manner reserved for their highest priests. It was burned, and the head and large bones were treated as relics. On February 20 a procession of natives led by a chief came down to the beach waving flags, beating drums and bearing gifts of hogs, fruit and roots.

A bundle covered with a cloak of black and white feathers was presented to Clerke. The bundle held the remains of Cook: scalp, long bones, thighs, legs, arms, hands and skull. The priest returned with Cook's jawbone, feet and shoes and the battered barrels of his musket. The remains were put in a coffin, and late on February 21, with all the ceremony of a naval burial, it was slipped into the bay.

Work resumed on the two ships, and when it was finished Clerke took them back to the Arctic to complete exploring what Cook had left unfinished. They reached Kamchatka late in April and were in the icy waters of Bering Strait six weeks later. On August 22, heading for home, Clerke died and command of *Resolution* was passed to Lieutenant Gore, while King took over *Discovery*. Their long passage home was by way of China, the East Indies and the Cape of Good Hope. The voyage of almost three and a quarter years ended on October 4, 1780, when the two ships anchored in the Thames.

The reputation of James Cook has not diminished over the years. The Yorkshire farmhand's son who had risen to become a famous seaman and the recipient of a gold medal from the Royal Society revealed more of the undiscovered world in his three famous voyages than anyone before or since.

Defining Australia: Matthew Flinders

Captain James Cook, the consummate seaman and explorer, passed his skills on to many officers who sailed with him. Two of these men became exceptional commanders in their own right: George Vancouver and William Bligh, of *Bounty* fame. William Bligh, in turn, inspired Mathew Flinders, who sailed with Bligh on his second voyage to Tahiti. Bligh introduced Flinders to the art of marine surveying, an interest that would become the focus of his career. These three exceptional seamen set the standards of navigation and hydrography for their time and gave detail to much of the uncharted Pacific. It was Flinders's accurate survey from 1801–03 that finally defined the shape of the great continent of Australia.

Matthew Flinders was born on March 16, 1774, at Donington, Lincolnshire. It is believed that his determination to go to sea, against his family's wishes, came after reading Daniel Defoe's novel *Robinson Crusoe* at age fifteen. That year he signed onto the navy aboard HMS *Scipio* as a lieutenant's servant. Eight months later he was promoted to midshipman on HMS *Providence* under Captain Bligh. Flinders's voyage on *Providence* took him to Tahiti by way of the Cape of Good Hope, and back to Jamaica through Torres Straits and the Indian Ocean. On his return he was taken as the captain's personal aide onto *Bellerophon*, part of the fleet that had defeated the French in the naval conflict known as the Glorious First of June.

By 1795 Flinders had become a competent navigator and signed as master's mate on HMS *Reliance*, the ship taking the second governor of Australia out to Port Jackson. On board *Reliance* was George Bass, a surgeon and naturalist with a keen interest in exploration. He and Flinders formed a close friendship. Together, in very small boats, they began making surveys of the coast around Port Jackson. Over the next six years the pair began bestowing names to discoveries in the new land, including Bass Strait, a discovery that confirmed Van Diemen's Land was an island.

In 1797 Flinders passed examinations for lieutenant. He returned to England in 1800, fired with the ambition to accurately chart the coasts of Australia, the last major part of the world to be explored. He solicited the assistance of Joseph Banks (now Sir Joseph, his having been knighted in 1781), who was able to persuade the Admiralty to mount the expedition, partly because of their fears that the French might beat them to it. In fact, in October 1801 France dispatched Capitain Nicolas Baudin on *Géographe* and *Naturaliste* on just such an expedition. This French voyage produced exceptional botanical studies, and its narrative and charts of Australia were published three years before Flinders's.

The British expedition was to be a scientific voyage in the manner and style of Cook's, and Banks was given virtually a free hand to equip and man it. Flinders was promoted to the rank of commander, and a naturalist, his assistant, two artists, a mineralogist and an astronomer were appointed. A noteworthy member of the crew and a cousin of Flinders was midshipman John Franklin, later to become an admiral and governor of Tasmania and who died in 1847 searching for the Northwest Passage.

A north-country collier—*Fram*, first renamed *Xenophon* by the navy and finally named *Investigator*—was chosen for Flinders's voyage. Although well equipped, she

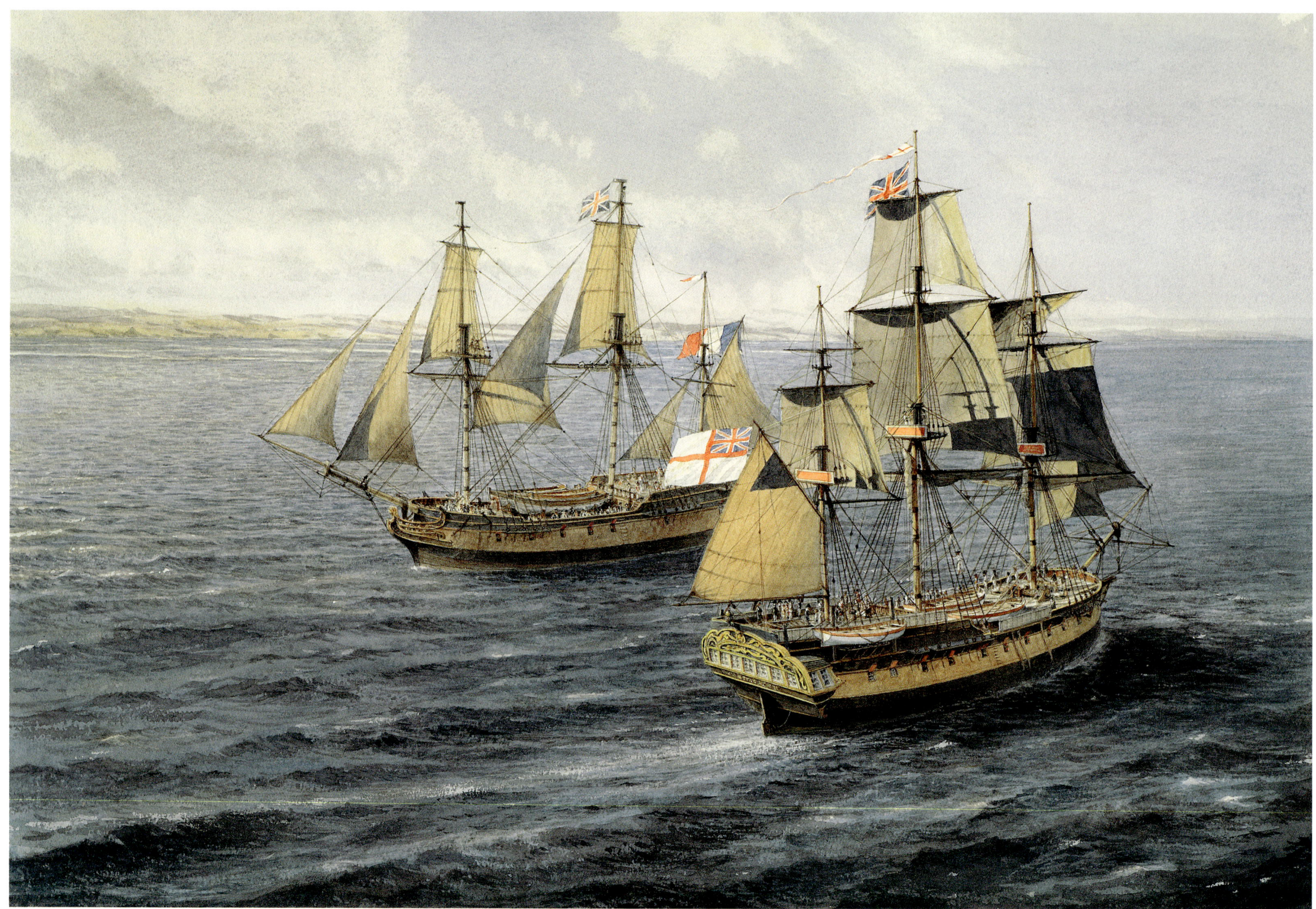

leaked badly. Nevertheless *Investigator* sailed for Australia in July 1801, and after stops at Madeira and Cape Town, Flinders began his survey around the Great Australian Bight, arriving back at Port Jackson on May 9, 1802.

Investigator required extensive refitting for the second phase of the voyage, which was to accurately chart Australia's east coast and a route through the Great Barrier Reef and Torres Strait, the Gulf of Carpentaria and the north and west coasts of the continent. She sailed in July, late in the year for the approaching monsoon season. As a result the surveys of the east coast and Torres Strait were somewhat rushed. A worse problem for Flinders was the condition of *Investigator*. In a sheltered bay in the Gulf of Carpentaria he ordered a survey of the ship and found her to be so rotten that she would not have survived a strong gale. Nevertheless Flinders completed a careful survey of the coasts of the Gulf of Carpentaria and Arnhem Land.

Seven months into the voyage Flinders's health was deteriorating and his crew was showing signs of scurvy. Sickness, the dangerous condition of *Investigator* and the approaching monsoons forced Flinders to abandon the survey in Arnhem Bay. He sailed in March 1803 for Timor, hoping for fresh provisions and a vessel to replace *Investigator*, but he found mainly dysentery instead. Flinders returned to Port Jackson via the west coast, becoming the first to circumnavigate Australia. He arrived in June with barely enough healthy men to man the ship.

Investigator was condemned, and Flinders and what remained of his crew sailed for England on HMS *Porpoise*. They left in company with two other ships, *Bridgewater* and *Cato*. About seven hundred miles north of Port Jackson, *Porpoise* and *Cato* were lost on a reef, but *Bridgewater* sailed on, knowingly leaving the crews of the other two ships to their fate. Flinders salvaged what he could of his records, rigged the cutter and, with the carpenter, *Cato*'s second mate and eight men, set out for Port Jackson, arriving after a month. A rescue fleet reached the wreck survivors six weeks later. *Cumberland* was provided to take Flinders directly to England, but at only twenty-nine tons she had to make frequent ports to reprovision. One of the stops was at Mauritius, where the French, again at war with England, held Flinders captive for six and a half years.

Matthew Flinders had married Ann Chappelle in 1801, just weeks before he sailed in *Investigator*. When they were reunited in 1810, they had been separated for nine and a half years. Flinders had only four more years to live. He spent them preparing his charts and his book for publication. He died in 1814, on the day the first copies of his journal came off the press.

◂ **Flinders and Baudin in the Great Australian Bight** (WC, 15″ × 22″)
From Cape Leeuwin, Matthew Flinders began his survey of the Australian coast by sailing eastward around the Great Australian Bight. On April 8, 1803, at Encounter Bay, he met Nicolas Baudin's Géographe, *part of a French expedition surveying the coast from east to west. The two ships spent a courteous but strained two days in company, exchanging information and then departing to continue their separate surveys.*

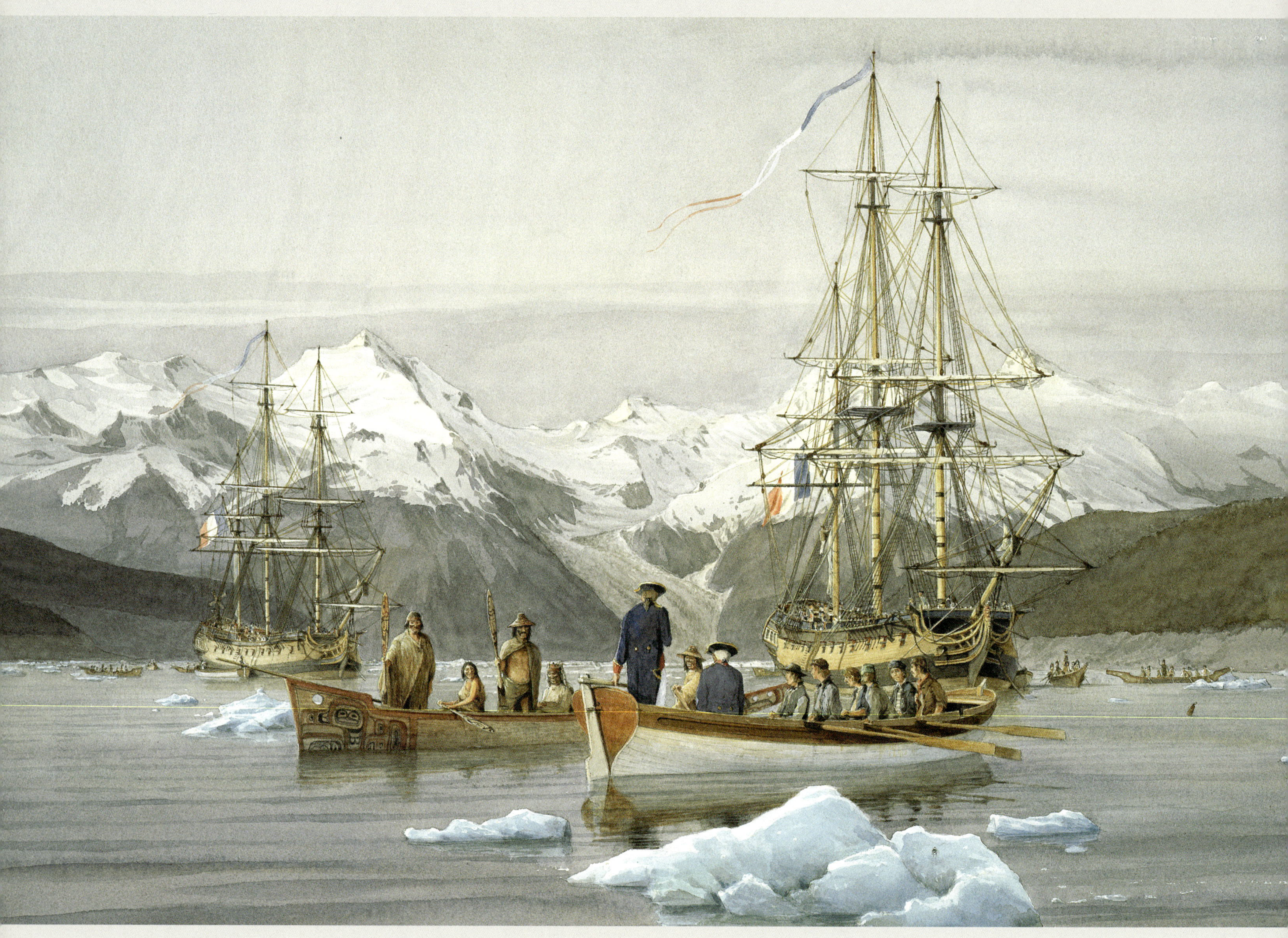

FRANCE EXPLORES THE PACIFIC

THE FRENCH WERE anxious to capture some of the prestige James Cook had gained from his three voyages. They selected Jean-François de Galaup, compte de La Pérouse, to command a round-the-world scientific voyage that would determine the true positions of the Aleutian and Kuril Islands and areas of the northwest coast of America not surveyed by Cook. La Pérouse was provided with two frigates, *Boussole* and *Astrolabe,* and recruited eleven scientists and artists for what was intended to be a significant scientific voyage.

The two ships sailed from Brest in August 1785, made an easy passage around the Horn, called at Easter Island and Hawaii and, on June 23, 1786, sighted the snowcapped coastal mountains of southeastern Alaska in the vicinity of Mount Saint Elias. For the next week they followed the coast southeastward, trying to match what they were seeing with their copy of Cook's chart. On July 2 they were off the very narrow entrance to a large inlet, which La Pérouse entered with trepidation the next day.

The expedition stayed in the inlet for several weeks, made extensive notes, traded with the natives, surveyed the bay and made a wonderful chart and sketches. On July 30 it sailed south for Monterey, making a running survey of the coast on the way. It left Monterey on September 23 for Macao, which it reached early on January 3, 1787. On the western side of the Pacific, the ships carried out extensive surveys from Manila to Kamchatka before making a wide sweep south to Botany Bay, Australia.

In Kamchatka and Botany Bay, La Pérouse sent back to France all the notes, charts and drawings made on the expedition. If he had not done so the voyage's entire achievement would have been lost, for when the two ships sailed from Australia they were never heard from again. (In the 1960s the remains of both ships were found on a reef in the Solomon Islands; they were probably the victims of a Pacific cyclone.)

The achievements of La Pérouse's ill-fated expedition were considerable: precise and beautiful charts and drawings, and extensive observations of native customs and appearance.

La Pérouse in Lituya Bay, 1786 (WC, 15″ × 22″)
On July 2, 1786, La Pérouse's two frigates Boussole *and* Astrolabe *entered a large inlet in southeastern Alaska. The inlet, which La Pérouse called Port des Français, is today known as Lituya Bay. It is a deep, majestic T-shaped fjord with a very narrow and dangerous outlet. Five glaciers hang on the steep sides of the mountains. Ice dislodged by frequent earthquakes creates massive waves, which have kept the lowest two hundred feet of the shores denuded of all vegetation, and the constricted entrance creates dangerous tidal overfalls that may only be attempted near slack water. On this voyage, a boat and a surveying party of twenty-one sailors were lost in the narrows while sounding the entrance.*

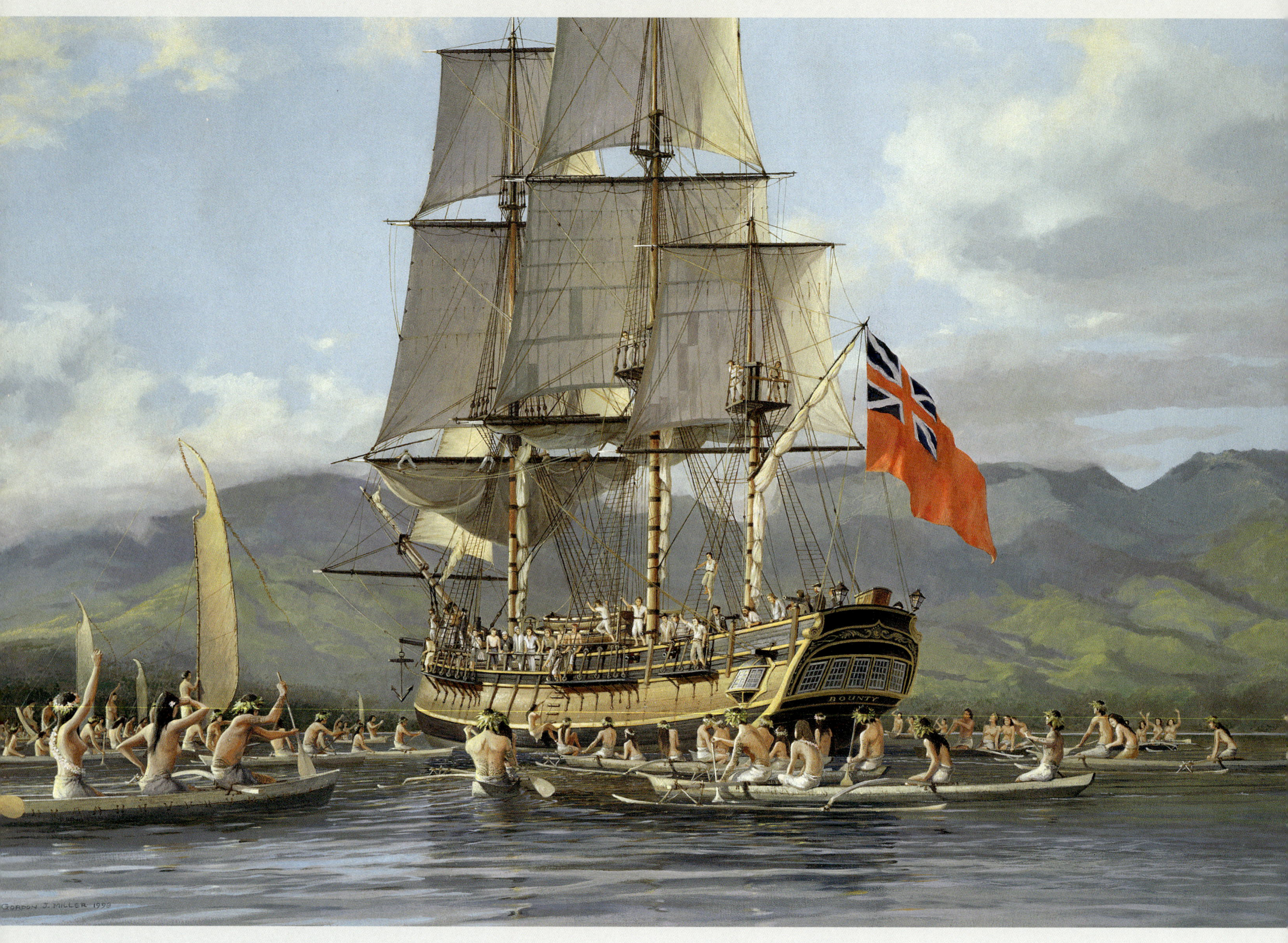
BOUNTY
GORDON J. MILLER 1998

HMS *BOUNTY*: FROM BREADFRUIT TO MUTINY

WHILE IN TAHITI Captain James Cook had noticed that the breadfruit tree was an easily grown source of nutritious food. In 1787 a group called the West India Planters and Merchants persuaded the British Admiralty to undertake a voyage to transplant breadfruit seedlings from Tahiti to their plantations in the West Indies. The Admiralty purchased the ship *Bethia* and had her fitted out at Deptford, where she was renamed *Bounty.* Lieutenant William Bligh was named to command her.

Bligh was an exceptional and experienced seaman, surveyor, draftsman and navigator. His talent had been recognized by Captain Cook, who had taken Bligh on as sailing master of *Resolution* on Cook's third voyage. As a result there are several geographical features named after Bligh, including the largest island in Nootka Sound. Unfortunately, Bligh seems to have had some deficiencies of character that contributed to the later mutiny of his crew.

On December 23, 1787, *Bounty* sailed from Spithead, England, bound for Tahiti via the Horn. How soon the seeds of mutiny were sown has never been satisfactorily answered, but things did not go well right from the start. *Bounty* left too late in the year to be off the Horn at the most desirable season, and severe storms southwest of the Canary Islands further delayed her. Bligh's harsh character was revealed when he handed out very severe punishments for some minor and questionable misdemeanors.

Off Cape Horn, *Bounty* encountered a continuous succession of westerly storms. Bligh's stubbornness kept her battering against cold and heavy seas for over a month. The conditions aboard were appalling: the already inadequate food was cold and putrid; the crew's fingers froze, their bedding and clothes never dried and the constant working of the ship in both daylight and darkness was exhausting. When Bligh finally relented and ran for the Cape of Good Hope, the crew had endured thirty-two days of icy winds, snow squalls and mountainous seas. Bligh put in to False Bay at the cape, where for a month *Bounty* was refitted and provisioned, leaving again on June 28, 1788.

On October 26 *Bounty* arrived at Tahiti, where she was warmly received by the uninhibited Polynesians. When it came time to set sail from Matavai Bay six months later, not many of the crew were happy to leave. Mutinous feelings surfaced among some of the men, and on the morning of April 28, 1789, under the leadership of Fletcher Christian, *Bounty* was seized. Captain Bligh and eighteen of his crew were set adrift in *Bounty*'s launch.

Bligh successfully navigated the twenty-three-foot boat through 3,618 miles of hostile waters to Timor—one of the greatest small-boat voyages in history. Fletcher Christian and the mutineers returned to Tahiti, where they recruited a few of the Polynesians and made for the uninhabited Pitcairn Island. There they burned *Bounty* and lived out the rest of their days.

‹ ***Bounty* in Matavai Bay** (Oil, 24″ × 36″)
William Bligh's ship Bounty *arrived at Tahiti on October 26, 1788, where she received a typical warm and joyful greeting from the uninhibited Polynesians. She anchored for almost six months in Matavai Bay, where the crew's harsh memories of the voyage out may have been forgotten.*

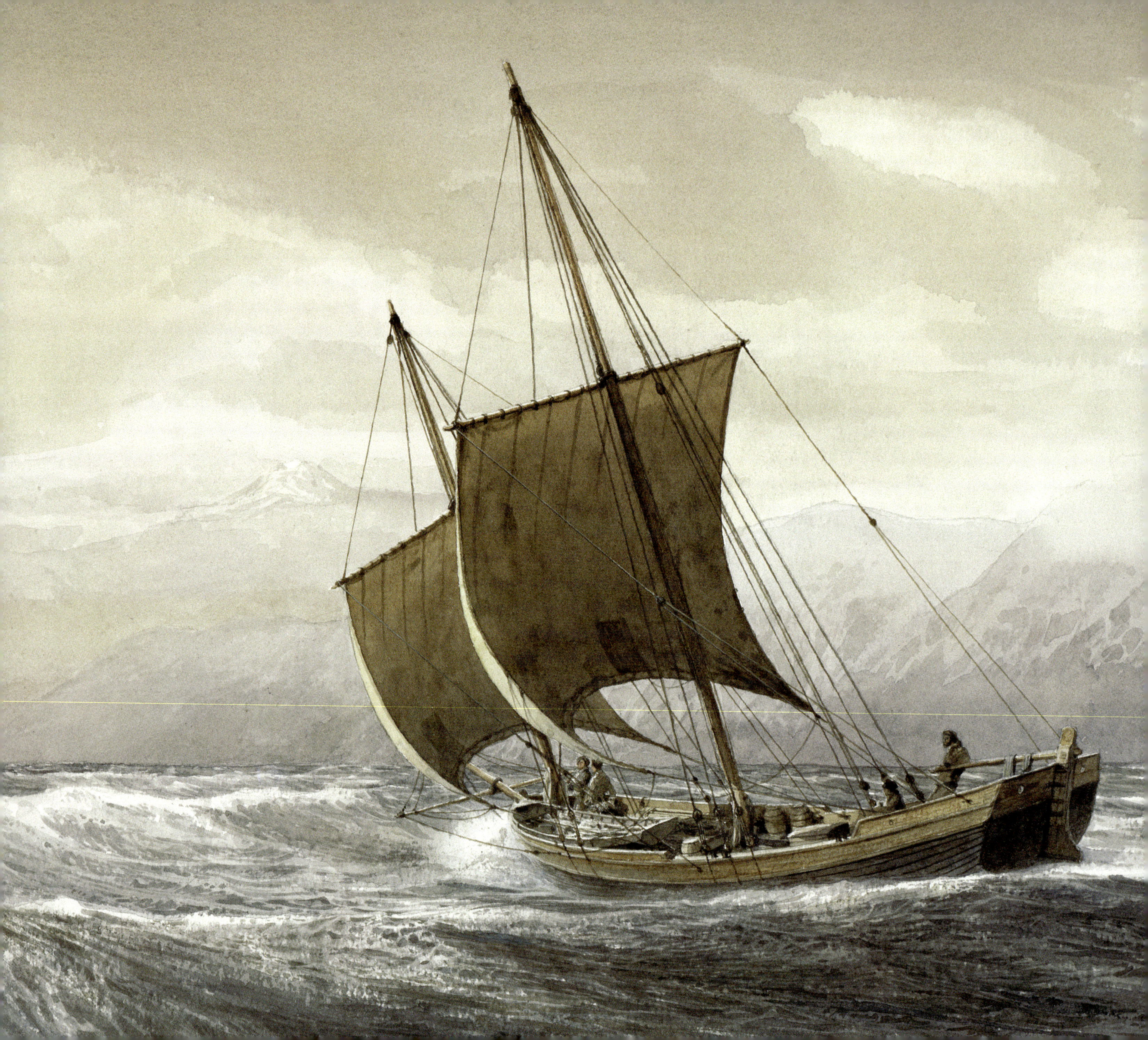

◂ **Pomor *kotch* off the Chukchi Peninsula, 1647**
(WC, 15″ × 22″)
Russia finally entered the Bering Sea in 1647, when an expedition led by Semeon Dezhnev and organized by Fedor Popov and Aleksei Usov set out to reach the mouth of the Anadyr River by sailing around the Chukchi Peninsula. This voyage was repeated annually for another twenty years, and gradually knowledge of a great land to the east, across the sea, entered local folklore. It prompted the first official Russian government interest in exploring what is now Alaska.

5

EXPLORING THE NORTH PACIFIC OCEAN

By the mid-eighteenth century the voyages of Vitus Bering, and of the many fur-hunting Russian *promyshlenniki* who followed him, were occurring on America's northwest coast—a coast that Spain had thought of as its own. Spain's dominant position in the Americas was also being challenged by Britain, but its ability to withstand these challenges was seriously impaired by the absence of a North Pacific fleet. Still, Spain clung stubbornly to its claims over all the northern coasts—even though it had never ventured beyond San Diego and had not even been that far north since Juan Rodríguez Cabrillo had anchored off Ballast Point in 1542.

The countries of Europe kept envoys in foreign courts in times of peace, as well as spies in times of war, so it was inevitable that news of Russia's incursions into the North

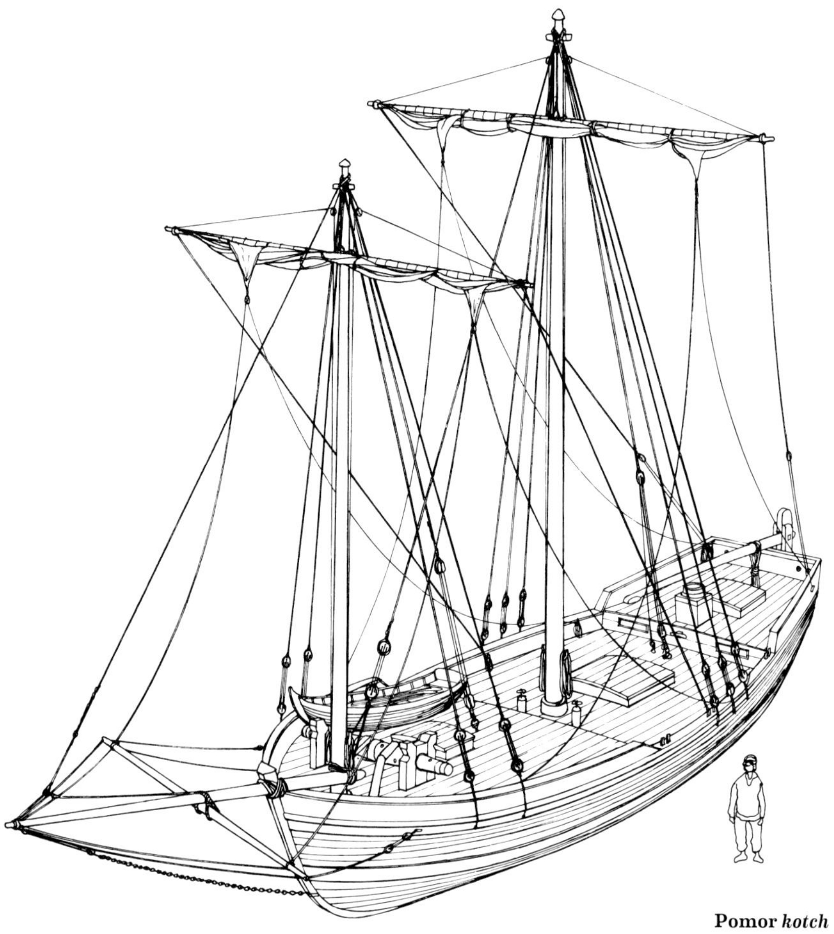

Pomor *kotch*

Pacific Ocean would get back to the court of Spain. Not until it learned that the Russians were building permanent trading posts in Alaska and were threatening to expand southward, perhaps as far south as Alta California, did Spain show much interest in these cold waters. But it was competing with a nation that had a long history of sailing in northern waters.

To Russian America: The Northeast Passage

The region known as Pomorie—the land around the White and Barents Seas—was first settled by Russians about the same time the Norse voyagers were establishing bases in Iceland and Greenland. The Pomors, who were trappers and fishermen, developed boats specifically for sailing in ice-infested waters. These small, flat-bottomed boats were built for inshore and river use, but soon the Pomors designed larger, round-bilged hulls for longer voyages, and over time Pomorie became the center of Russian shipbuilding.

The Barents Sea was often ice-free in summer, and by the thirteenth century the Pomors were voyaging to Novaya Zemlya for walrus and to Spitsbergen for cod, halibut, walrus and whales. The vessel they used was the *kotch,* a small two- or three-masted boat, usually with a single square sail on each mast. The *kotch* was developed from the more ancient *lod'ia,* a single-masted, clinker-built vessel of Scandinavian origin. Gradually, in the search for sea mammals, the Pomors extended their passages to the east, and by the fifteenth century they were beginning to imagine a sea route to China across the top of the continent. While the British and Dutch were vainly trying to breach the ice barrier above the Norwegian Sea, the Russians were yearly extending their way towards the Pacific.

When Peter the Great became czar in 1696, Russia was a huge and insular country whose cultural and political power was centered in Moscow. Although it claimed all of northern Asia from the Baltic Sea to the Pacific Ocean, it had no real knowledge of its eastern territories. Those lands had been gradually occupied by eastward-moving *promyshlenniki* who were interested only in furs, not in maps or exploration. Peter was resolved to rectify this ignorance and particularly to determine whether Asia and North America were connected.

One of the most arduous and amazing feats of exploration ever undertaken was a scientific expedition begun in 1725 under the command of Vitus Bering, a Danish captain in the Russian navy. Before Bering could even begin the voyage, he had to organize and transport everything needed to build and provision the ships across Siberia, from Saint Petersburg to the Kamchatka Peninsula, a distance of over four thousand miles. This was a trackless region of endless steppes, rugged mountains, swamps, muskeg and unbridged rivers, fly-infested in summer and bitterly cold in winter. The expedition took three and a half years just to transport the men and supplies to the east coast of Kamchatka.

The ship they built there was *St. Gabriel.* She sailed on July 14, 1728, and went north until the Siberian shore turned westward. On August 16, just above the Arctic Circle, Bering gave the order to turn back. He had found no connection between Asia and North America and had sailed through the strait that bears his name. The expedition that had taken three and a half years to execute was over after only fifty-one days at sea. Bering reversed the whole journey back to St. Petersburg, where he made his report to the Russian Academy of Sciences, which apparently was not impressed with his efforts.

In 1730 Bering proposed a second and more ambitious expedition to explore the northwest coast of America. After many years of preparation and a repetition of the horrendous journey to the east, in June 1740 he launched two new and larger ships, *St. Peter* and *St. Paul,* at Okhotsk. They were sailed around to the harbor of Petropavlovsk on the west coast of Kamchatka, where they were iced in for the winter. From there, in the spring of 1741, the two ships set sail, *St. Peter* under command of Vitus Bering and *St. Paul* under Alexei Chirikov. They followed a course to the southeast in a futile search for land that didn't exist, adding many miles to their voyage to the American coast. On June 20 they were separated in a storm, and the two ships did not see each other again.

Chirikov sighted land first, on July 15 making landfall on the most westerly point of Baker Island, off the west coast of Prince of Wales Island, now named Cape Chirikov. He sent both his boats in search of an anchorage, but they

› ***St. Paul* off Baker Island, July 1741**
(wc, 15″ × 22″)
Alexei Chirikov was probably the first European to encounter natives on the northwest coast of America. On July 15, 1741, he sent one of St. Paul's *boats ashore at Baker Island to search for a safe anchorage, but it failed to return. Five days later he sent a second boat to search for the first, and it too did not come back. Some time later* St. Paul *was approached by two canoes, likely manned by Tlingit, but they could not be coaxed alongside the ship.*

failed to return. With no boats to go ashore for wood and water, Chirikov reluctantly turned back for Kamchatka. He roughly followed the chain of the Aleutian Islands and sighted land on several occasions, but was still unable to go ashore. With many of her crew ill from scurvy and water running low, *St. Paul* limped into Petropavlovsk on October 12, 1741.

Meanwhile, Bering sailed cautiously eastward in *St. Peter*. His crew was also already short of water and concerned about running out. Finally, after twenty-eight days at sea, they sighted the American continent. On July 17 the ever-present fog lifted, and the St. Elias mountain range was revealed stretched across the eastern horizon. The jubilation of the men was not shared by Bering. He was ill and aware of the shortness of supplies, the lateness of the season and their distance from home.

They had arrived off Kayak Island, and the next day a watering party was sent ashore. In the party was Georg Steller, a naturalist who had for months waited impatiently for this opportunity to gather specimens. He had endured all of the hardships of getting to the coast and the privations on board the ship, but his total time ashore was to be a mere ten hours. Bering, not interested in local natives and wildlife, was anxious to be away. After watering, *St. Peter* sailed, against the objections of the bitterly disappointed Steller. Relations between the commander and the scientist, not good at the best of times, became dangerously strained. *St. Peter* then sailed to the northwest along the Aleutian chain. The water collected later in the Shumagin Islands was unfit to drink, and the delay while collecting it caused the ship to lose a rare favorable wind.

The weather, which had not been good, began to worsen. By mid-August more of the men were becoming ill, and Bering was too sick to stand. On August 30 the first death occurred. For the next two and a half months, with dispirited and indecisive leadership, the crew battled constant cold and adverse westerly gales, and more men began to die. By November almost no one was well enough to work the ship, and on November 6 *St. Peter* finally drove ashore on a small island that now carries Bering's name. He died there on December 8. *St. Peter* was a total loss, but the men who survived the winter built a boat from her remains and sailed it to Petropavlovsk the following spring.

Following this ill-fated expedition, Russia lost interest in its far eastern territories. The *promyshlenniki* of Siberia, however, were soon voyaging to the islands off Kamchatka in search of sea otter pelts. By 1745 they were building posts on the American coast as far south as the Russian River in California and maintaining a year-round presence in Alaskan waters, the first permanent European settlement on America's west coast north of Mexico. In 1778 James Cook sent his last dispatch to the Admiralty from Dutch Harbor, Alaska, and exchanged charts with the Russian factor there.

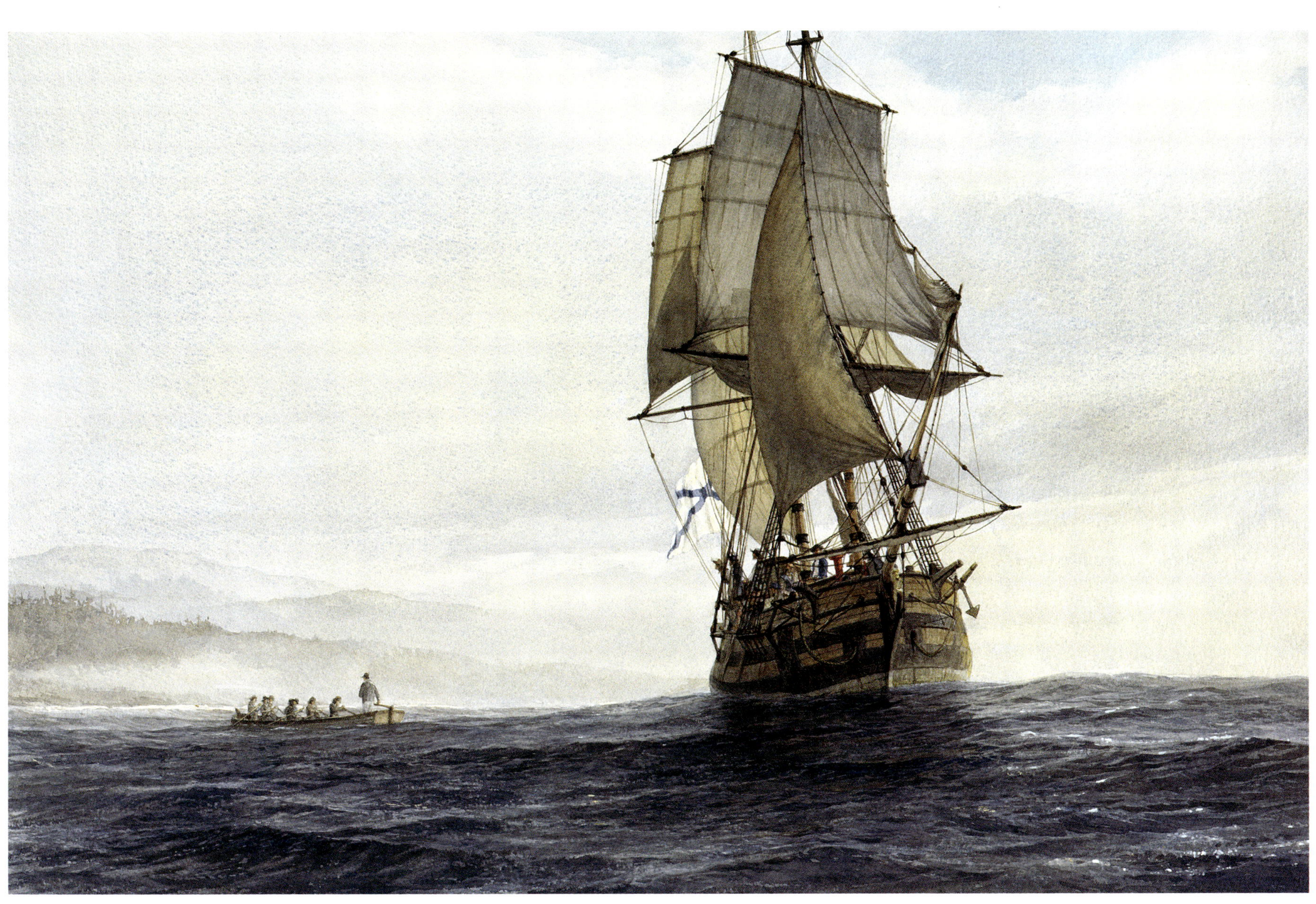

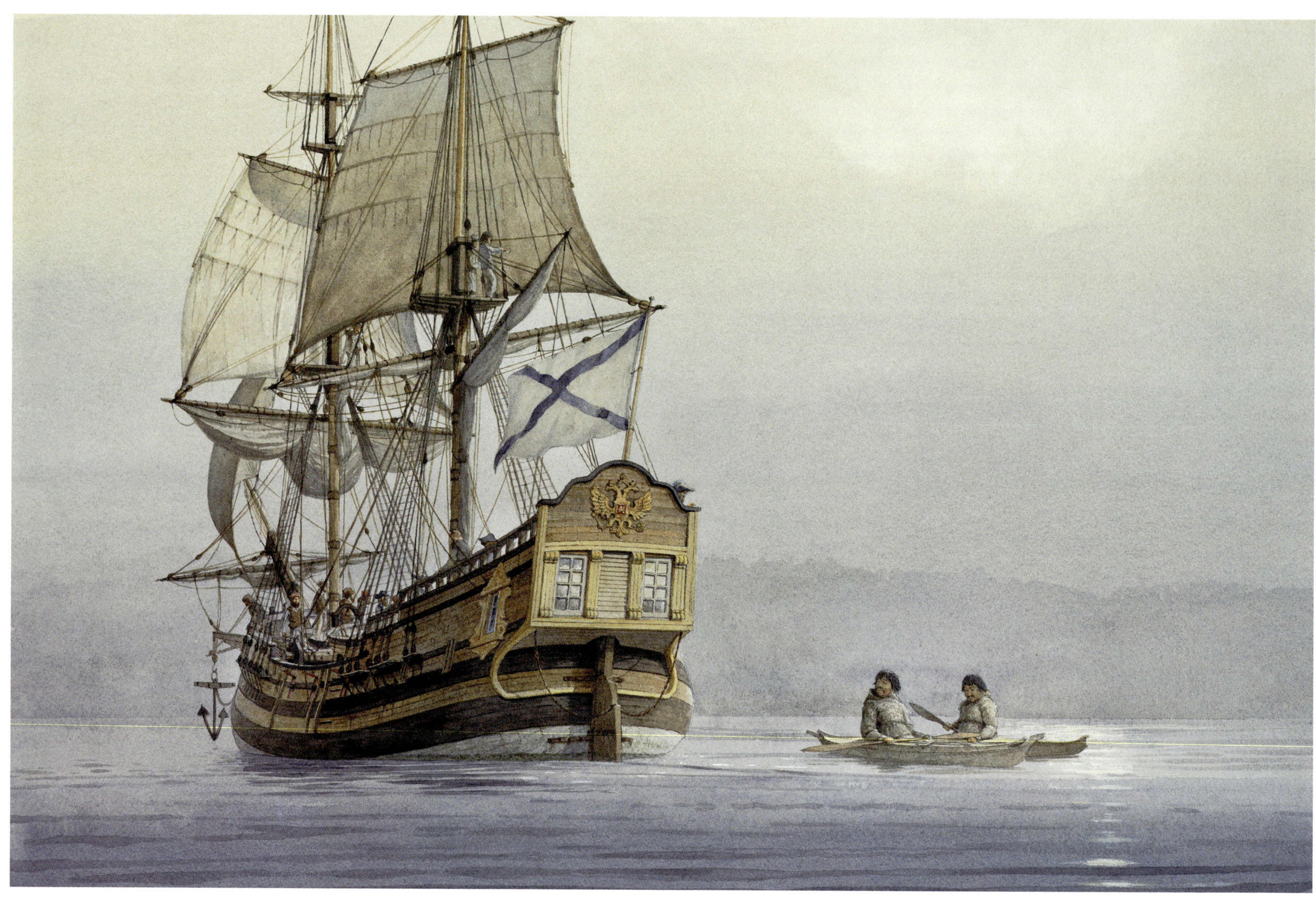

Spain's Northern Voyages

Spurred into action by Russia's eastward expansion across the Pacific, Spain began searching for a suitable port on the west coast of New Spain. It wanted a port closer to its northern aspirations from which its missions in Alta California could be supplied, and in 1767 San Blas was chosen as the base for its expansion. San Blas was located in a swampy, mosquito-infested estuary just north of present-day Puerto Vallarta, on one of the tributaries of the Rio Santiago. The river channel shifted frequently and silted up, the banks were covered with mangrove jungle and the steamy lowlands were almost uninhabitable, but the site had the advantage of a readily available supply of shipbuilding timber. For the first year the inhabitants endured storms, flooding and disease, finally fleeing to a higher inland village. In 1768 they tried again, formally announcing the establishment of the Naval Department of San Blas. For thirty years the shipyard built, repaired and supplied the ships that explored the northwestern coast of America for Spain.

Antonio Maria de Bucareli, the viceroy of New Spain, was responsible for the three major expeditions to the northwest coast of America that sailed from San Blas. In 1774, alarmed at the news of Russian activities in Alaska, Bucareli ordered the first northern expedition. Juan Pérez was given command of *Santiago* and ordered to sail to 60° north, determine the extent of the Russian incursions and take possession of any new discoveries for Spain not already occupied. To accomplish this he was instructed to return as close to the coast as was safe, taking note of all possible sites suitable for settlement. Pérez was expected to give presents to any natives he encountered, to take nothing from them by force and to inquire into their numbers, customs, government and religion.

Santiago, alias *Nueva Galicia,* was launched late in 1773, the first and largest frigate built at San Blas. Well stocked for an extended voyage, she sailed on the high tide of January 25, 1774, lingered twenty-five days at San Diego, arrived at Monterey on May 8 and sailed from there on June 11. She kept well out to sea, with favorable winds but with cold, rain and fog that caused much distress and sickness among the crew, who were not used to the northern latitudes. On July 15 Pérez altered course towards the coast, and three days later sighted land at 53°43′ north. This was the west coast of Graham Island, the largest of the Queen Charlotte Islands. The next afternoon, the ship was approached by three canoes. The natives were Haida, likely from the villages of either Dadens or Kiusta in Parry Passage, the area that fifteen years later became one of the principal destinations for ships in the fur trade.

Pérez remained off Langara Island for four days, frustrated by the lack of wind and adverse currents from making an anchorage or proceeding farther north. During this period canoes often came alongside, sometimes as many

‹ ***St. Peter* off Bird Island, 1741**
(wc, 15″ × 22″)
Off Bird Island in the Aleutian chain in 1741, Vitus Bering's St. Peter *was visited by two Inuit in kayaks. This was the first recorded meeting between Europeans and this native group on the northwest coast of North America.*

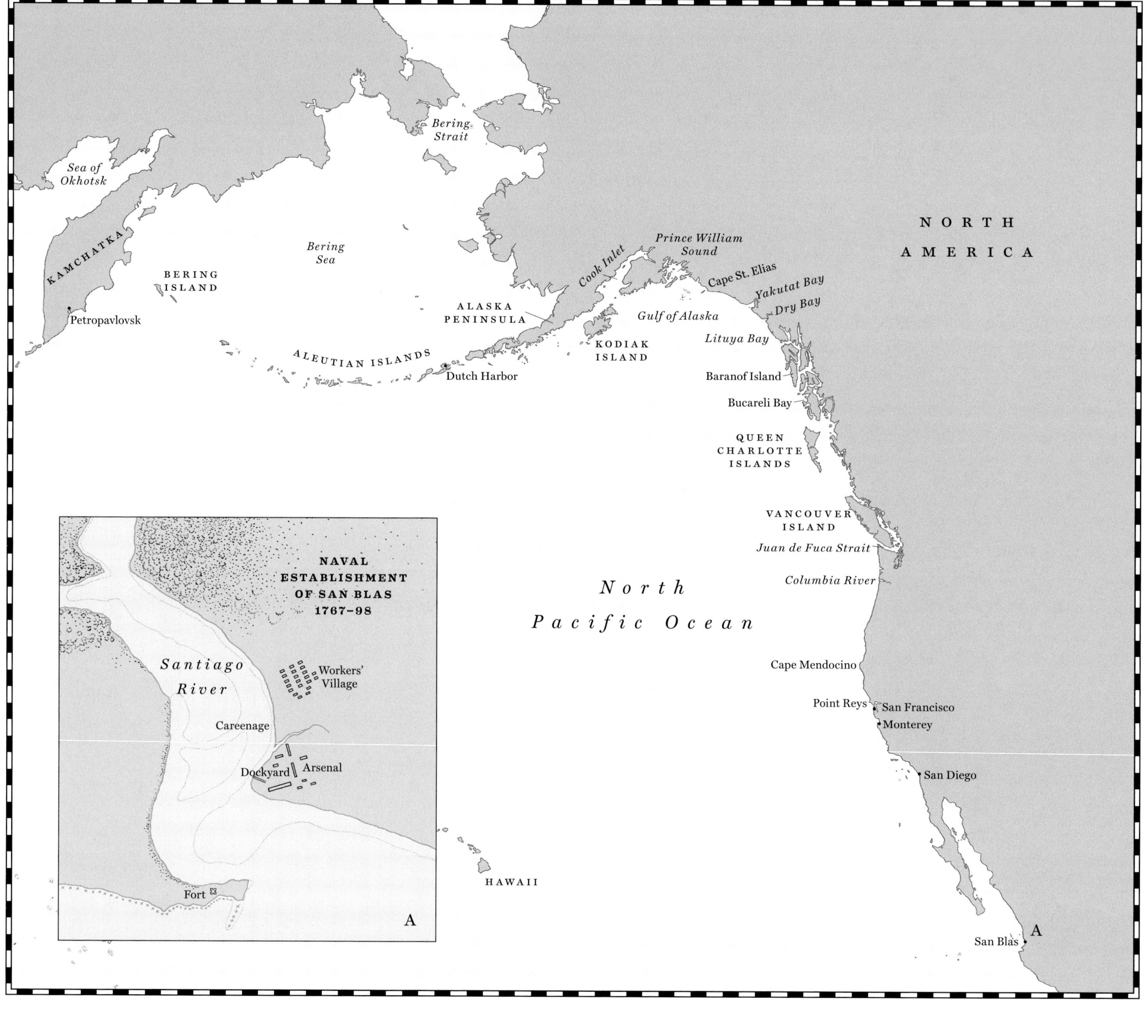

Bering Strait
Sea of Okhotsk
KAMCHATKA
BERING ISLAND
Petropavlovsk
Bering Sea
ALASKA PENINSULA
ALEUTIAN ISLANDS
Dutch Harbor
Cook Inlet
Prince William Sound
Cape St. Elias
Yakutat Bay
Dry Bay
Gulf of Alaska
KODIAK ISLAND
Lituya Bay
Baranof Island
Bucareli Bay
QUEEN CHARLOTTE ISLANDS
VANCOUVER ISLAND
Juan de Fuca Strait
Columbia River
NORTH AMERICA
North Pacific Ocean
Cape Mendocino
Point Reys
San Francisco
Monterey
San Diego
HAWAII
San Blas
A
NAVAL ESTABLISHMENT OF SAN BLAS 1767–98
Santiago River
Workers' Village
Careenage
Dockyard
Arsenal
Fort
A

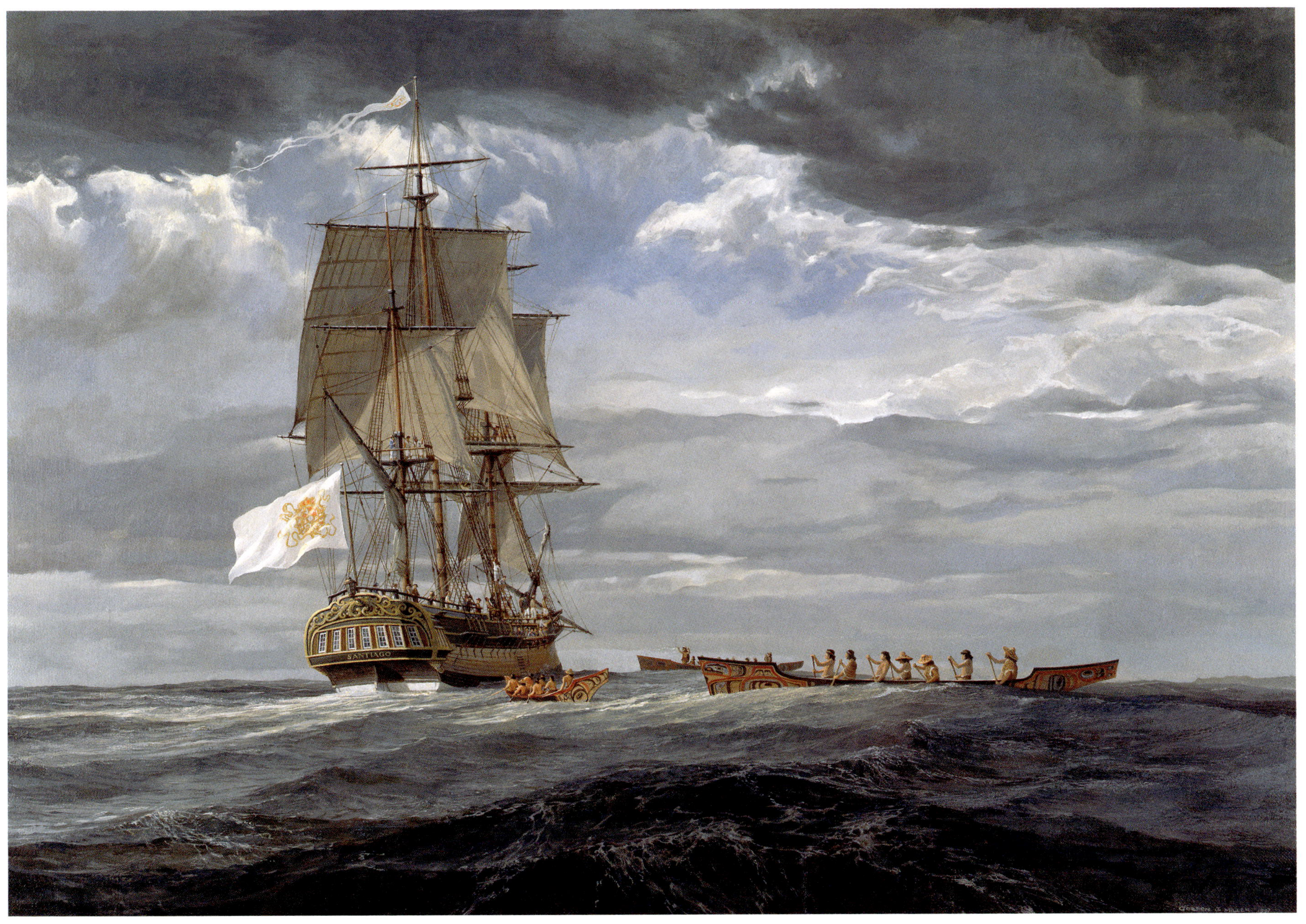

‹ *Spanish and Russian establishments on the northwest coast of North America in the 18th century. Inset: The Spanish naval establishment at San Blas.*

^ ***Santiago* off Langara Island, 1774**
(Oil, 24″ × 36″)
On July 19, 1774, in the late afternoon, Juan Pérez's ship Santiago *was approached by three canoes. Here, several miles southwest of Langara Island, occurred the first recorded contact between Europeans and Haida. The Haida sang, danced and paddled in time with the rhythm of drums and rattles, and sprinkled down and feathers in a sign of friendship. The largest of the canoes, at forty-four feet, was almost half the length of* Santiago*. After a half hour of trade, in which some furs were exchanged for European knives, old clothes and trinkets, the three canoes departed.*

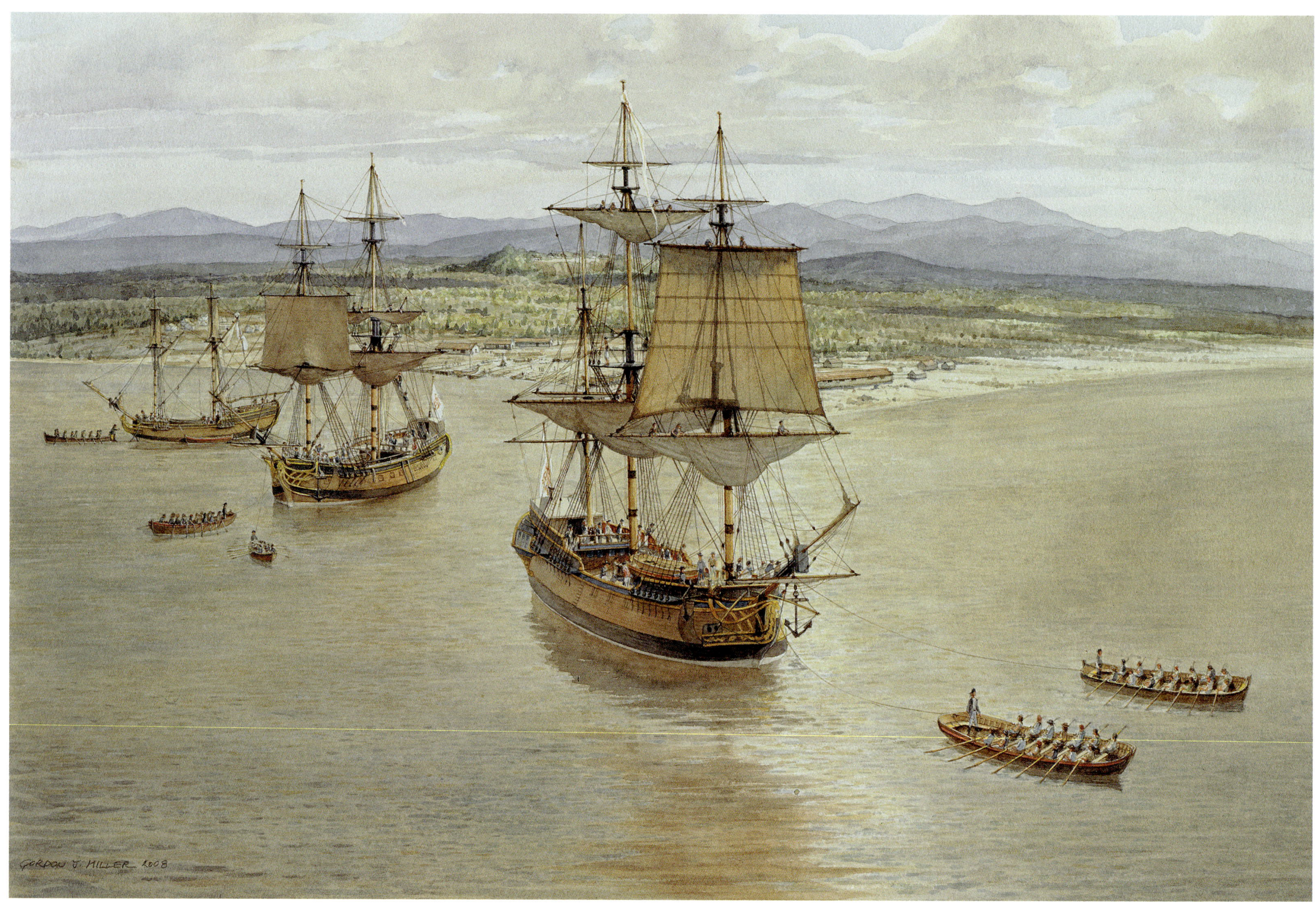
GORDON J. MILLER 2008

as twenty at a time. Trade was friendly, and each side was equally intrigued with the other. The journals kept by the two friars on board contain the earliest descriptions of the Haida's appearance and customs.

Pérez turned back at latitude 54°40′ north, not the 60° north he had been instructed to reach. On August 7 he anchored overnight near the entrance of Nootka Sound, in Nuu-chah-nulth territory, and again engaged in trade. (Silver spoons pilfered by the natives then were seen by James Cook when he entered the sound four years later and recognized as likely being from the Pérez expedition.) Pérez arrived back at Monterey on August 28, his instructions largely unfulfilled. Fearing hostilities with the natives he never went ashore anywhere, and he performed no acts of possession for Spain.

Unimpressed with Pérez's efforts, Bucareli ordered another expedition in 1775. *Santiago* was to sail again, under command of Bruno de Hezeta, and the small schooner *Sonora II*, under Lieutenants Ayala and Bodega y Quadra, with Francisco Mourelle as pilot, was to be her consort. Together with the packetboat *San Carlos*, the two ships left San Blas on March 19. Sailing in contrary winds and currents, they made very slow progress north. Their first landing was three months later at Trinidad Bay, California, where they stayed ten days, traded with the Yurok, charted the harbor and performed an act of possession. The cross they raised was still visible when George Vancouver visited the bay seventeen years later.

The next land they sighted was what is now the coast of Washington state just south of the Quinault River. A boat with seven men went ashore from *Sonora II*, but all of them were killed by a large group of natives. Nevertheless, a cross was erected there and another act of possession was performed before *Sonora II* sailed.

Leaving the coast, the two ships were often separated by heavy seas, and scurvy began to decimate *Santiago*'s crew. Hezeta, never very resolute, decided not to continue and, somewhere near Juan de Fuca Strait, turned *Santiago* south. *Sonora II* was expected to follow, but Bodega y Quadra and Mourelle slipped away and took the tiny schooner on an epic voyage north. On August 15 landfall was made at about 57° north, and on the northern end of Kruzof Island they took possession. (This was the northernmost point ever claimed by Spain.) Although scurvy was beginning to take its toll and the season was late, they still were able to examine much of the coast. On the way south they discovered and named Bucareli Bay, again performing possession ceremonies. When *Sonora II* limped into Monterey on October 7, many of her crew had died and the survivors were so weak they had to be carried ashore.

The positive result of this voyage was a chart of most of the coast from Monterey to Alaska; as well, *Santiago*, on her return, had found and made a simple chart of the entrance to the Columbia River. Nevertheless Britain did not acknowledge Spain's claim to the Northwest Coast, including Nootka. It cited Cook's actual four-week stay in

◂ ***San Carlos*, *Sonora II* and *Santiago* leaving San Blas** (WC, 15″ × 22″)
From San Blas, on the Pacific coast of New Spain, were launched the expeditions that established the settlements of San Diego, Monterey, San Francisco and Nootka, and where many of the vessels were built that carried them out. On March 19, 1775, the ships San Carlos, Sonora II *and* Santiago *sailed together on the ebb.* San Carlos *discovered the entry to San Francisco Bay, the little* Sonora II *sailed all the way to latitude 57° north and* Santiago *turned back at about 50° north, although she did chart the mouth of the Columbia River on her return to San Blas.*

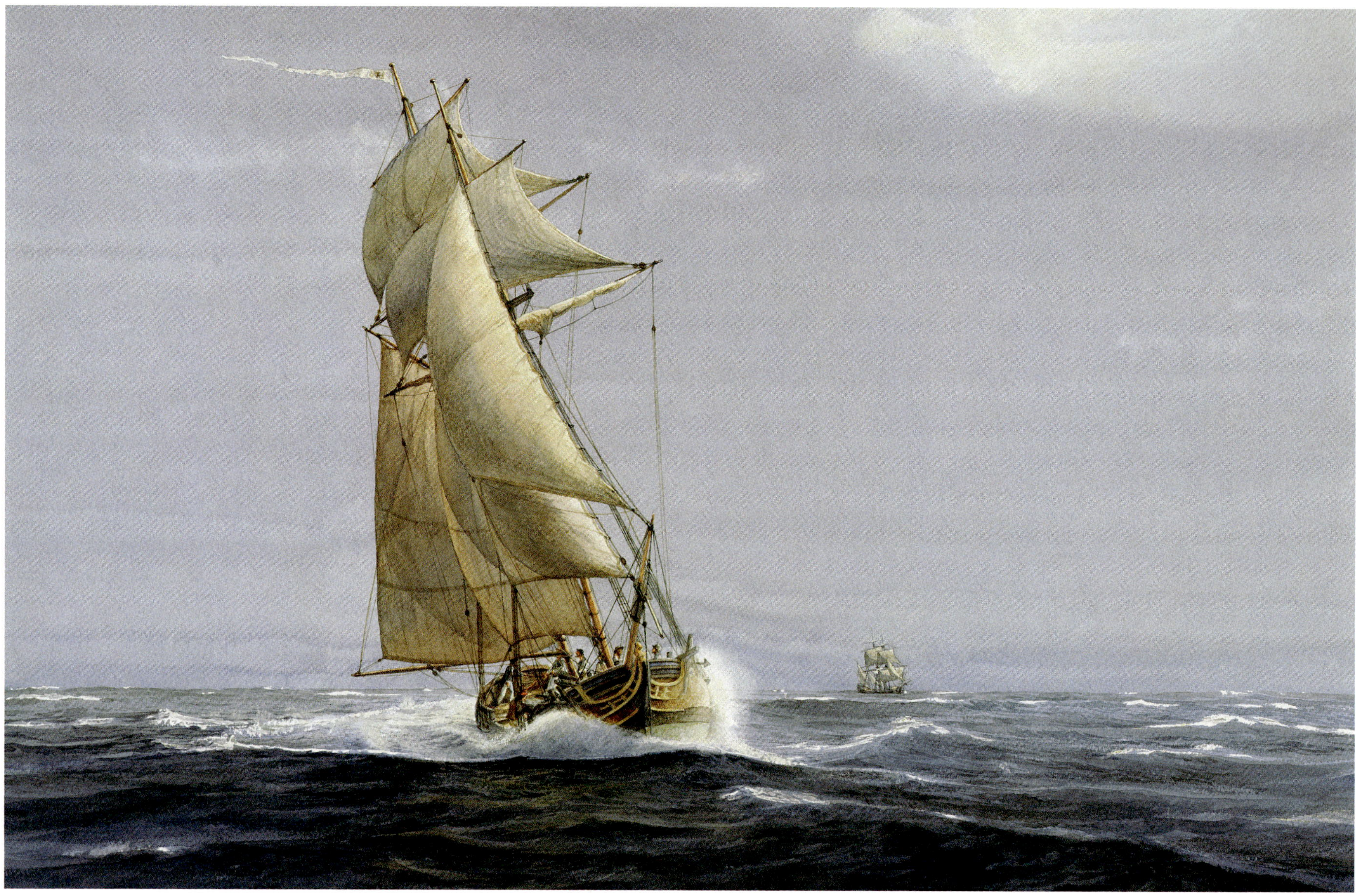

▲ ***Sonora* II** (WC, 15″ × 22″)
A small schooner, Sonora II, *was* Santiago's *consort on the 1775 voyage. Of the fourteen men in her crew, only four had been to sea; the others were Mexican ranch hands.* Sonora *was such a poor sailer that nothing could make her exceed three knots, and she had to be towed by* Santiago *for the first seventy-eight days. On the California coast she was given topmasts and sails, after which she was credited with the ability to carry full sail in a gale that caused the frigate to shorten sail.*

➤ ***Santiago* on the Columbia River bar, August 17, 1775** (WC, 15″ × 22″)
Sailing south past Cape Disappointment, Bruno de Hezeta realized Santiago *was in the mouth of a significant river. Her crew was weak from scurvy, and the dangerous conditions on the river's bar discouraged a detailed exploration, but a simple plan was drawn, the first chart of the mouth of the Columbia River.*

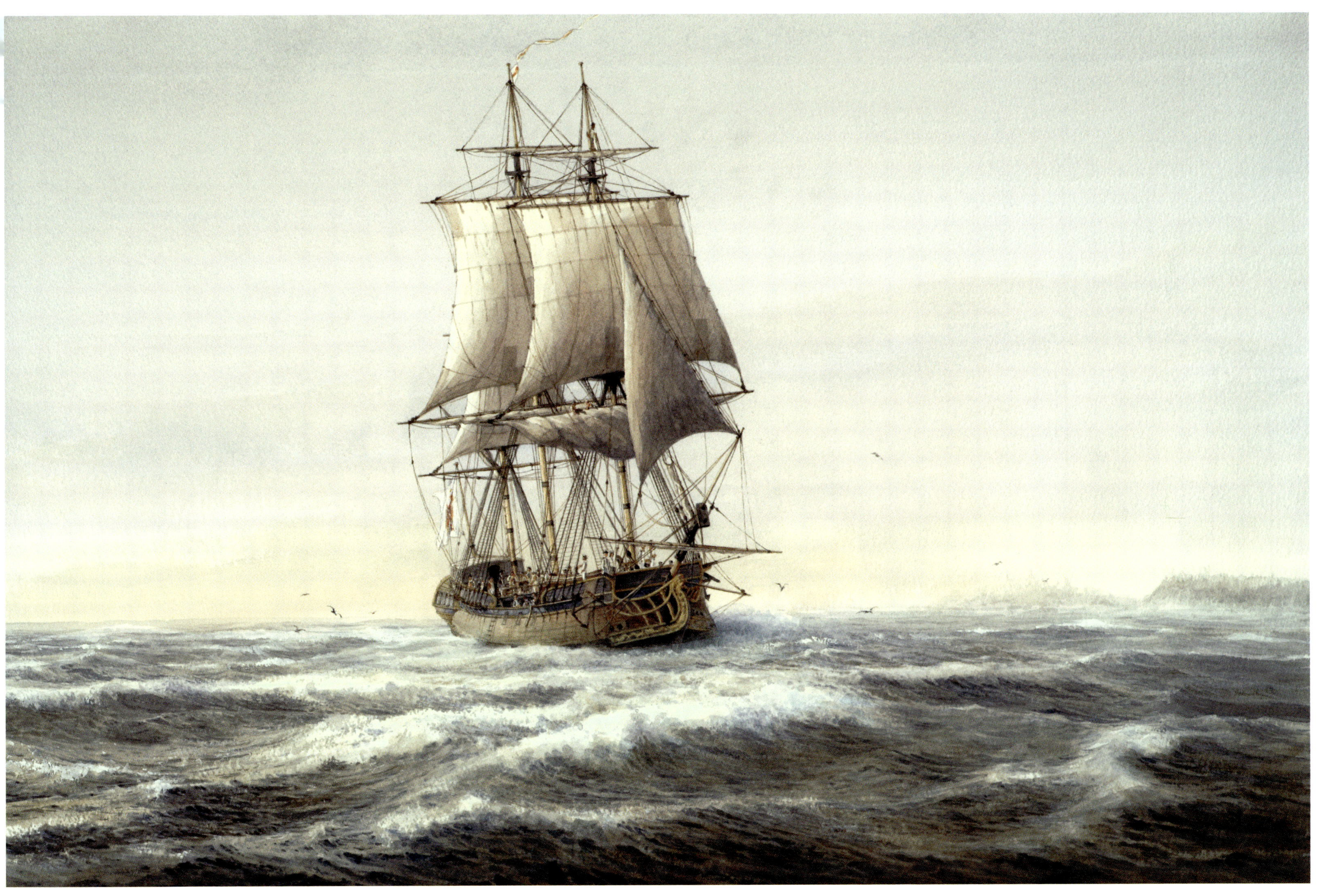

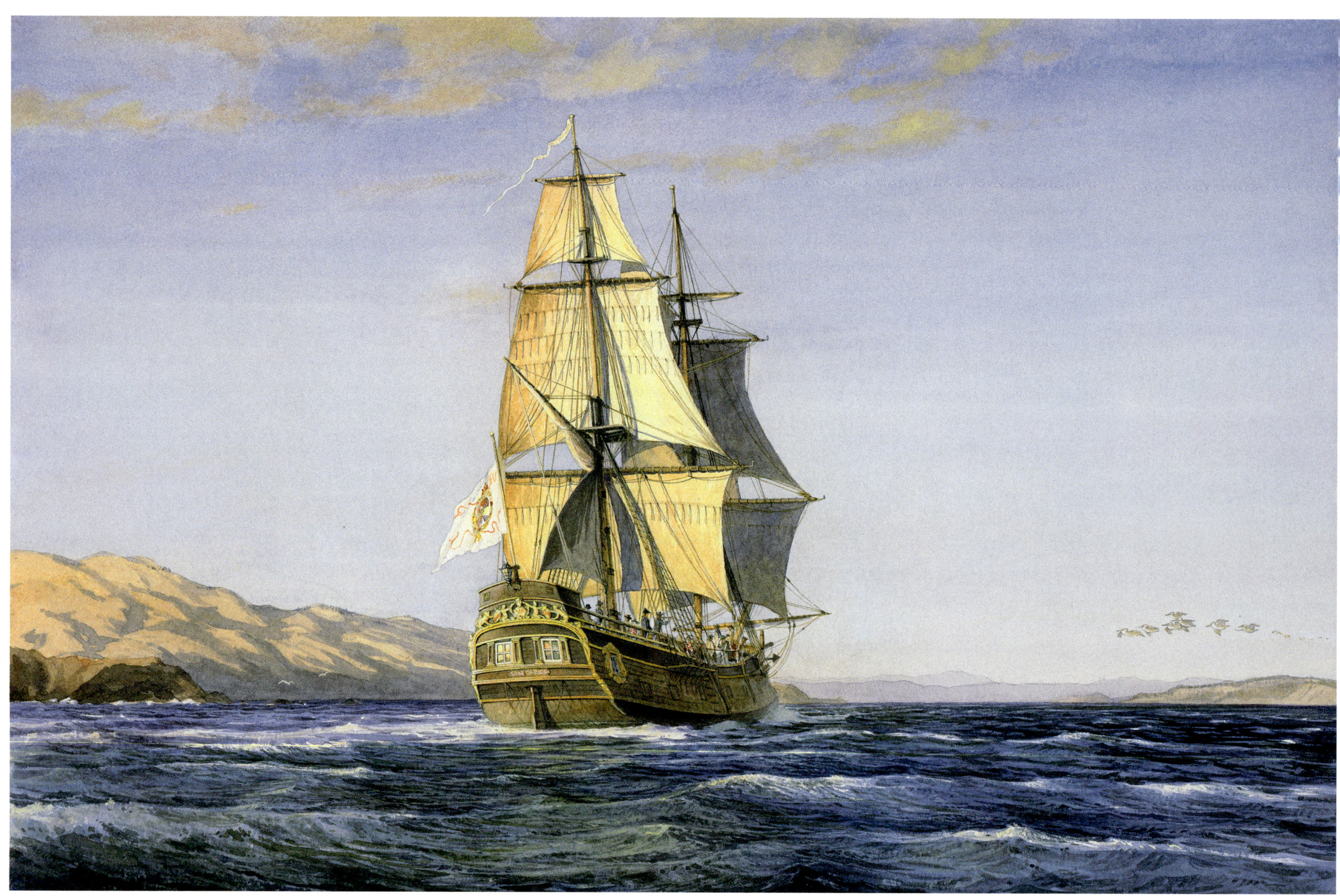

‹ ***San Carlos* approaching the Golden Gate**
(WC, 15″ × 22″)
On the evening of August 5, 1775, the Spanish packetboat San Carlos *became the first European vessel to enter San Francisco Bay. A half hour before sunset* San Carlos *was about two miles south of Bonita Point, with a good southwest breeze and fair tide, and the entrance to the bay in sight. The launch was sent ahead to sound the narrows, but when she disappeared behind Point San Jose the decision was made to continue anyway.*

˅ ***San Carlos* in the Golden Gate**
(WC, 15″ × 22″)
As darkness fell on August 5, 1775, the tide turned against San Carlos. *With a moon rising ahead in a clear sky, she passed through the narrows, holding close to the north shore until the wind died and the tide began to take her backwards. She dropped anchor and lay the rest of the night to the west of Presidio Shoal.*

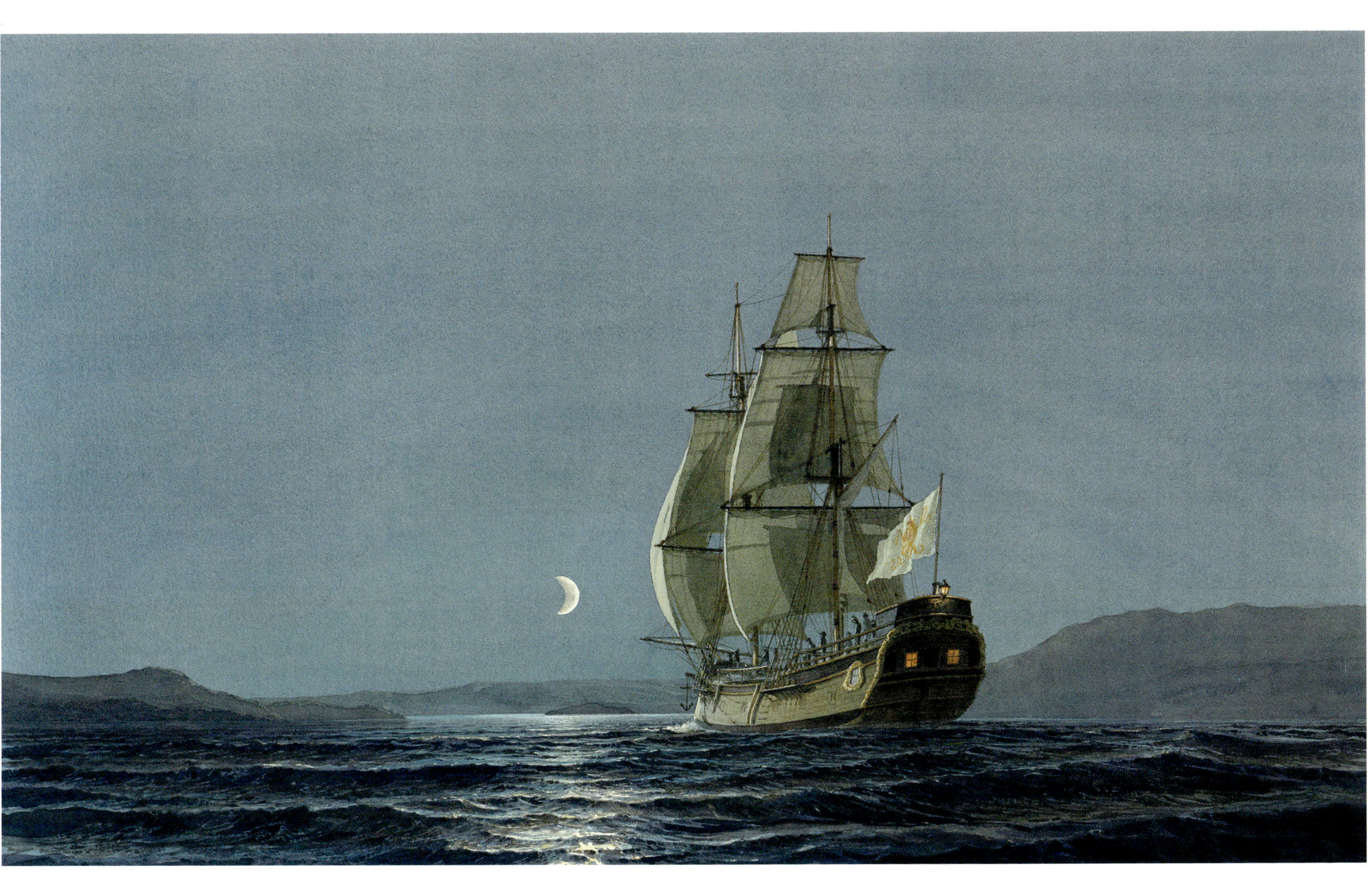

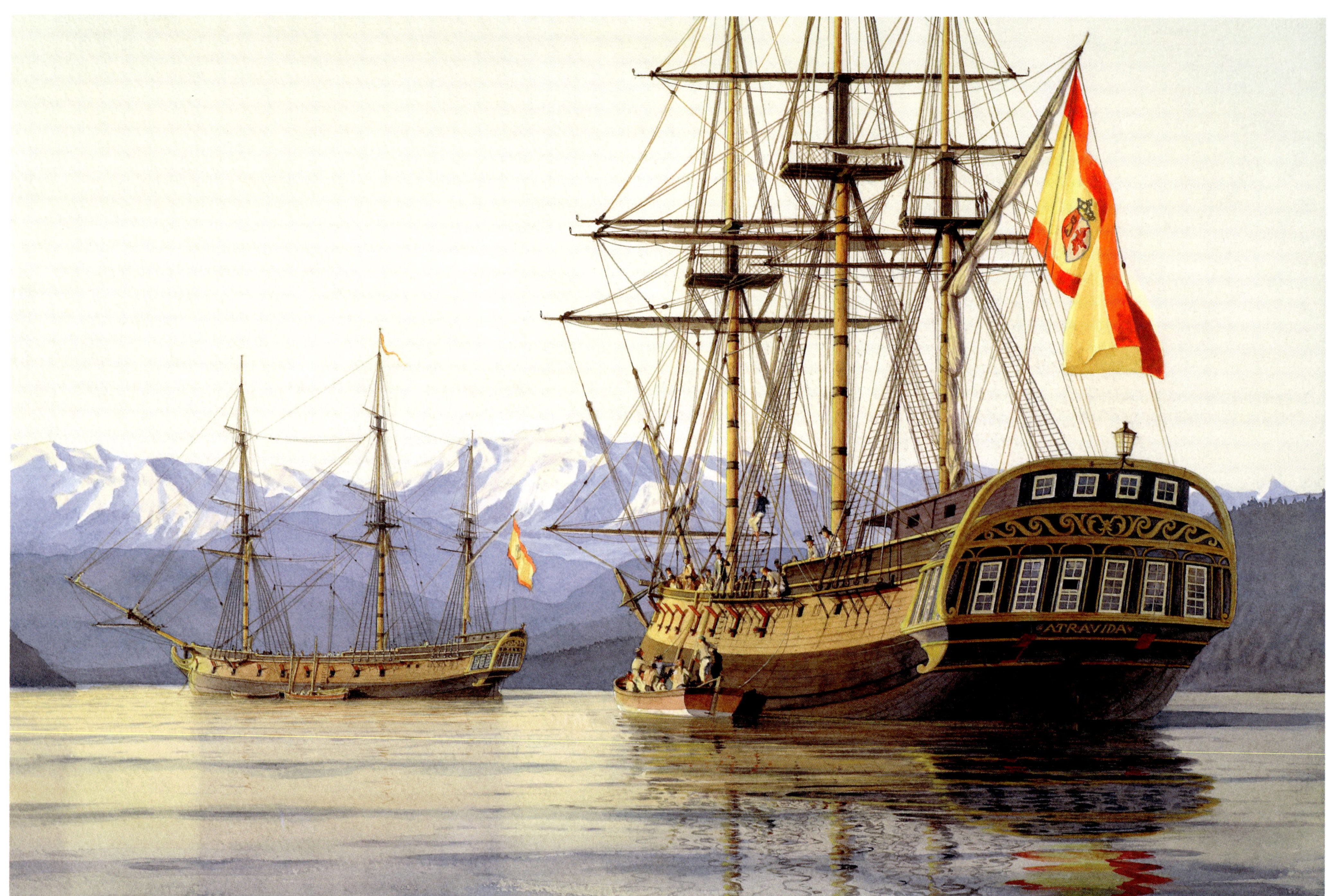
ATRAVIDA

1778, whereas Pérez had only anchored overnight outside the sound. In any case, neither nation had taken formal possession of the area.

Many years later, in an effort to strengthen her claim to the Northwest Coast, Spain decided to establish a permanent military base at Friendly Cove in Nootka Sound. In 1789 two ships, *Princesa* and *San Carlos*, were dispatched from San Blas. In command of *Princesa* and all of the Spanish forces was naval Lieutenant Esteban José Martínez, an irascible man of not very good judgment. He was expected to build a garrison on shore beside the native village, erect a small battery at the entrance to the cove and expel any traders not licensed by Spain. As an ardent promoter of Spain's interests in the Northwest Coast, his actions at Friendly Cove precipitated the Nootka Crisis.

When *Princesa* arrived on May 5 there were already two ships in the sound: the American ship *Columbia* and the British snow *Iphigenia*. Martínez examined and questioned their papers but did not act until May 14, when he arrested Captain William Douglas and seized the *Iphigenia*. He later allowed Douglas to leave on condition he quit the coast. Douglas sailed June 1 and, ignoring the Spanish orders, continued to look for trade to the north. He eventually anchored at Macao, where he reported the Spanish actions to John Meares.

On July 3 an event occurred that would have a profound effect on the history of Canada and nearly brought England and Spain to war. Martínez arrested James Colnett, captain of the British ship *Argonaut*, and seized his ship, which was licensed by the East India and South Sea Companies. More important, John Meares had a major interest in her. When Meares learned of this outrage from Captain Douglas on his arrival in Macao, he sailed for England on the first available East Indiaman, where he stirred up public opinion and the House of Commons. The news added fuel to the already smoldering British grievances against Spain.

At the same time, in France, Parisians were storming the Bastille, precipitating the French Revolution and effectively removing Spain's only ally. Britain seized the opportunity and the excuse, and forced Spain to sign the Nootka Sound Convention on the threat of war, forcing it to return all of the seized British properties with restitution. The treaty effectively ended Spain's territorial claims to northwestern America and led eventually to the British occupation of western Canada.

The final and most comprehensive of Spain's voyages took place between 1789 and 1794 under the command of Alejandro Malaspina. The Malaspina expedition was meant to emulate the great scientific voyages of Cook and La Pérouse and was meticulously planned and provided for. Two new ships, *Descubierta* and *Atravida*, were staffed with excellent officers, cartographers, artists and scientists. They left Cadiz in 1789, and before arriving

‹ **Malaspina expedition in Yakutat Bay, 1791** (WC, 15″ × 22″) *On June 27, 1791,* Descubierta *and* Atravida *anchored in Yakutat Bay. Alejandro Malaspina surveyed the entire bay, including the head, which ends at the Hubbard Glacier. In the ten days spent there, the crew made extensive contact with the local Tlingit, mostly in peaceful trade, although not all contact was friendly, and one Spanish survey party was forced to fire on a Tlingit attack.*

➤ *The major centers of trade and surveying on the northwest coast of North America in the 18th century. Inset: The Spanish naval establishment at Friendly Cove.*

off Mount Edgecumbe, Alaska, in 1791, had surveyed extensively the coasts and settlements of South America. The expedition visited Yakutat and Nootka Sound, where it made many fine drawings and charts, collected numerous artifacts and took extensive notes of native life and culture.

Sailing from Nootka, Malaspina visited Monterey, Acapulco, Guam, Manila, New Zealand, Australia and the Friendly Islands before returning to Spain. There, political distractions resulted in his arrest and imprisonment. As a result, the great scientific and cultural achievement of this voyage went unrecognized and unpublished for one hundred years.

Not all expeditions were as large or well prepared as Malaspina's, and some long and difficult voyages were made in the North Pacific in very small and poorly manned ships. Three small Spanish vessels built at San Blas also made significant voyages to the Northwest Coast. *Sonora II,* under forty-three feet on deck, sailed from San Blas to almost latitude 60° north on the Alaska coast, the farthest north reached by any Spanish vessel. *Sutil* and *Mexicana* were two small schooners identical except in rig, and were slightly over forty-six feet on deck. When George Vancouver encountered them in the Strait of Georgia, he commented that they were "the most ill calculated and unfit vessels that could possibly be imagined for such an expedition."

In the days of exploration and colonization, it was often the practice for ships making long voyages to carry prefabricated vessels, "in frame," in their holds. These vessels, often referred to as shallops, were single-decked, usually schooner-rigged and often under forty feet long on deck. The very first ship launched on the Northwest Coast, John Meares's *North West America,* was brought in frame and launched from the beach at Friendly Cove in 1788.

North West America was approximately forty tons, with a length on deck about forty-two feet and a beam of about fifteen feet. In spite of her small size, after a short trading excursion on the coast she sailed to Hawaii, where she spent the winter. She was back on the coast the following year, where she was captured by the Spanish lieutenant Esteban José Martínez at Friendly Cove. Beached, repaired and renamed *Santa Gertrudis la Magna,* she was sent to survey Nootka Sound and the entrance to Juan de Fuca Strait. She ended her days as a mission supply vessel in San Blas, New Spain.

Princess Royal was a fifty-ton sloop from London, between fifty and fifty-five feet on deck, and might have set topsails and topgallants above the gaff mainsail. The little sloop was seized by Martínez at Nootka, renamed *Princesa Real,* and sent to San Blas with the *Argonaut.* In 1790 she was part of the Eliza expedition returning to reoccupy Friendly Cove. She was required to be returned to James Colnett, but in 1791 she was first sent to probe

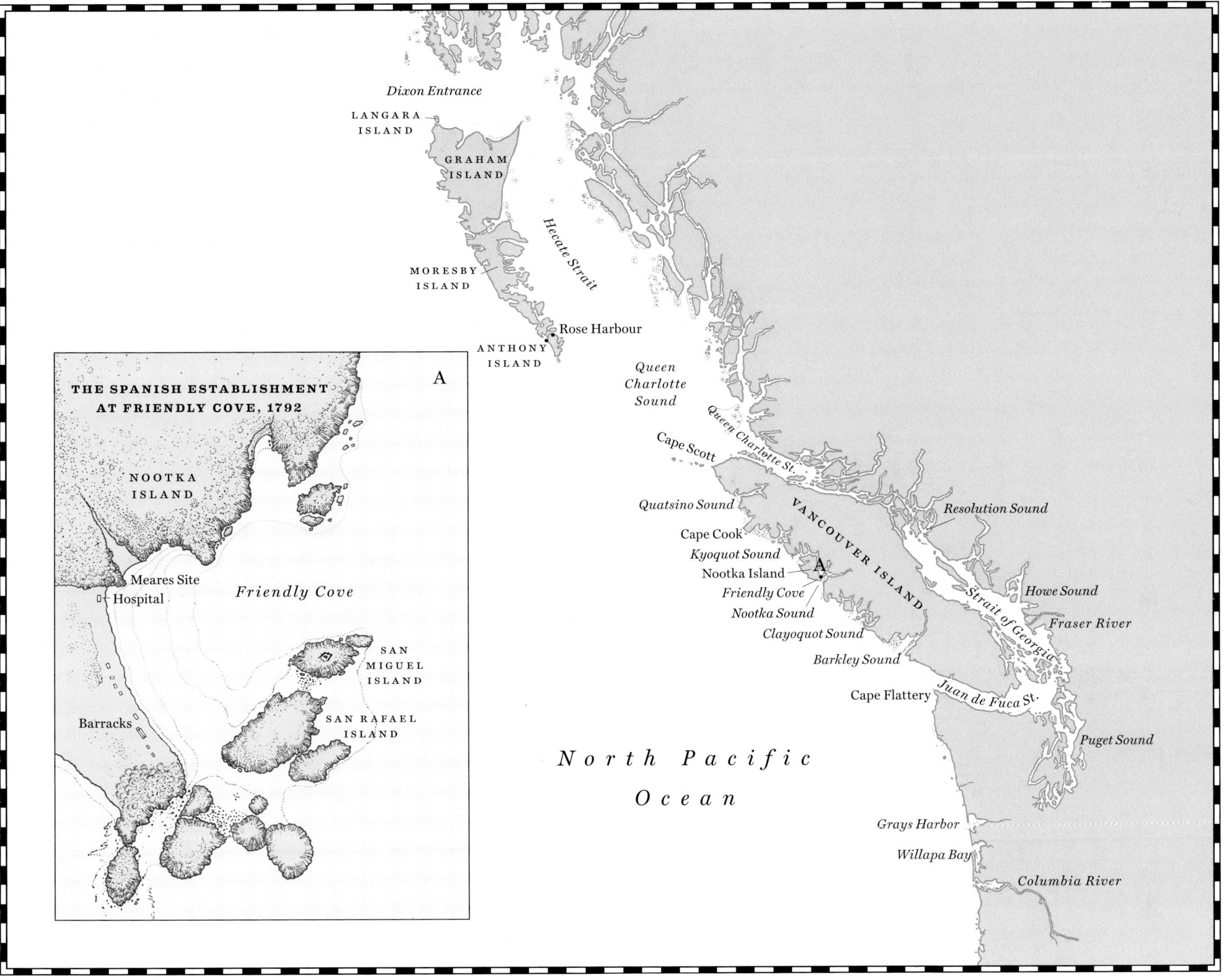
Dixon Entrance
LANGARA ISLAND
GRAHAM ISLAND
Hecate Strait
MORESBY ISLAND
Rose Harbour
ANTHONY ISLAND
Queen Charlotte Sound
Queen Charlotte St.
Cape Scott
Quatsino Sound
VANCOUVER ISLAND
Resolution Sound
Cape Cook
Kyoquot Sound
A
Nootka Island
Friendly Cove
Nootka Sound
Clayoquot Sound
Barkley Sound
Strait of Georgia
Howe Sound
Fraser River
Cape Flattery
Juan de Fuca St.
Puget Sound
North Pacific Ocean
Grays Harbor
Willapa Bay
Columbia River
A
THE SPANISH ESTABLISHMENT AT FRIENDLY COVE, 1792
NOOTKA ISLAND
Meares Site
Hospital
Friendly Cove
SAN MIGUEL ISLAND
SAN RAFAEL ISLAND
Barracks

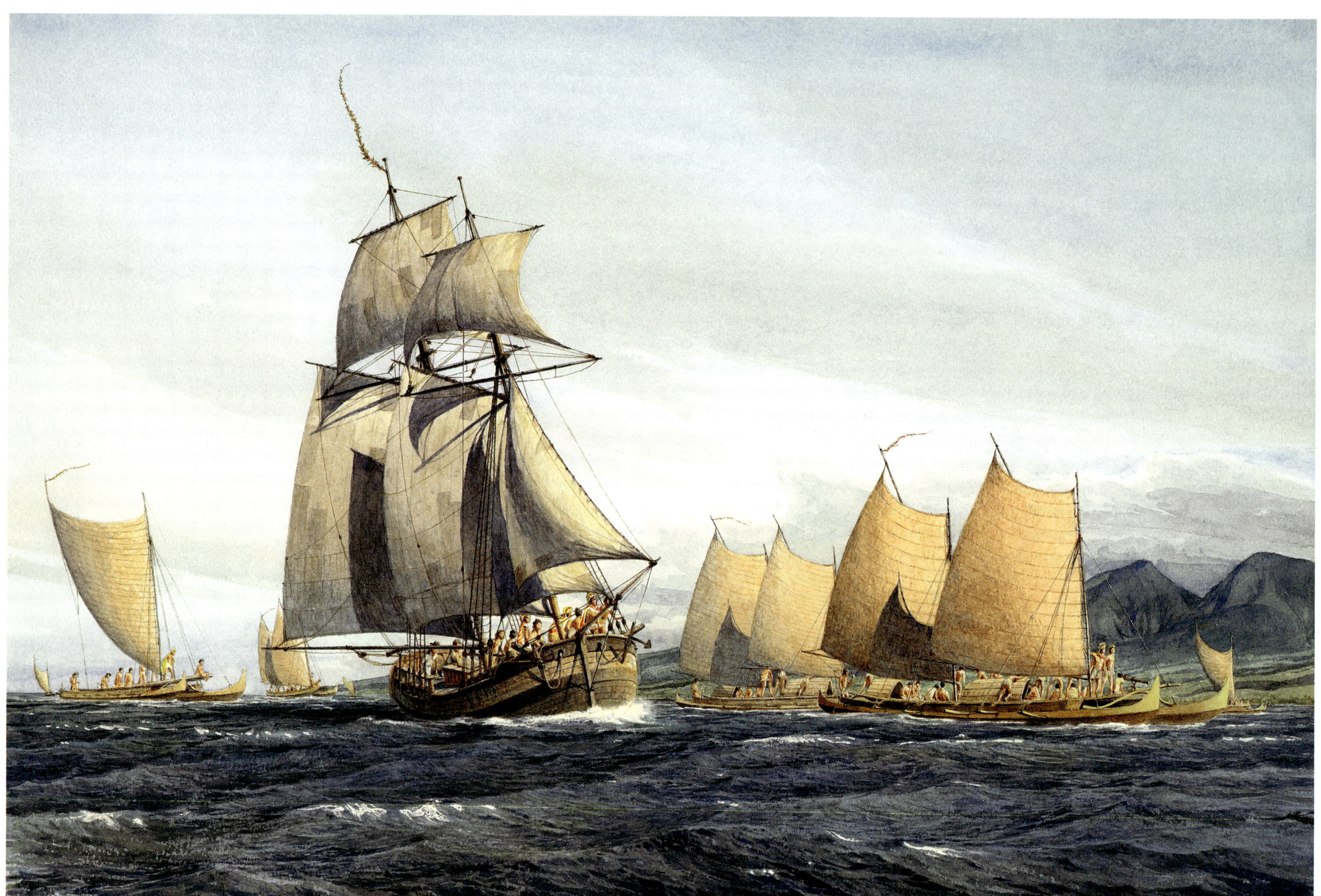

Juan de Fuca Strait. Colnett finally caught up to his ship in Hawaii, but by then she was in such poor shape that he refused to accept her.

Among the items on board *Argonaut* when she was seized in 1789 were frames for a small schooner, to be named *Jason*. *Argonaut* was sent to San Blas, the frames still in her hold. While Colnett was negotiating for his release and reparations, he sold the material for his schooner to the Spaniards. They were sent back in *Conception* to Nootka, where the schooner was built and, on September 26, 1790, launched and named *Santa Saturnina*. She was the second ship built on the Northwest Coast and was destined to make history as the first to sail in the Gulf of Georgia and see the future site of the city of Vancouver. At the end of the 1791 Eliza survey she sailed for San Blas, where she ended her days as a supply vessel. This little schooner was only thirty-six-and-a-half feet on deck, with a twelve-foot, four-inch beam, but on the survey voyages she carried twenty-two men, plus all their supplies, for three weeks.

The third ship launched on the coast was a small sloop of about fifty tons, built by the American fur trader Robert Gray. In the fall of 1791, he had *Columbia* rigged down for the winter in a cove in Clayoquot Sound. In her hold was the material for a small sloop assembled in Boston. On the beach Gray constructed Fort Defiance, built the sloop and launched her as *Adventure* in February 1791. She would have been about fifty feet on deck, with a seventeen-foot beam. *Adventure* made two coastal trading voyages before being sold to Bodega y Quadra for seventy-five prime sea otter and sea lion skins.

Another small schooner was on the coast in 1789: *Fair American*, about fifty-four feet long and twenty-six tons burthen. She was apparently purchased in Macao by the American Simon Metcalfe, owner of the brig *Eleanora*. The schooner was commanded by his son Thomas. *Fair American* arrived in Friendly Cove via Alaska, where she was seized by Martínez.

Eleanora arrived off Nootka Sound just in time for Metcalfe to see his *Fair American* under Spanish colors leaving for California. Metcalfe made directly for Hawaii, where his trading methods led to disastrous relations with the Hawaiians, eventually ending in his killing many natives and disgracing two high chiefs, who vowed to capture the next foreign ship to appear. The next vessel to arrive was *Fair American*. She was easily captured, and Thomas Metcalfe and three of the four crew were killed. After her capture, *Fair American* was employed by King Kamehameha in his campaign to unify the islands under his command.

Eleanora eventually left the islands, and Simon Metcalfe was later killed by natives on the Northwest Coast. He never knew that it was his own behavior in Hawaii that had led to the death of his son.

‹ ***Fair American* off Maui** (WC, 15″ × 22″)
The American schooner Fair American*, on arriving in Friendly Cove in 1789, was seized by the Spanish. They sailed her to California and then released her to Thomas Metcalfe, who sailed for Hawaii. She was captured there by Hawaiians, and the two crewmen who were spared helped King Kamehameha sail her in his campaign to unify the Hawaiian Islands.*

› ***Sea Otter* approaching Nootka Sound**
(WC, 15″ × 22″)
Sea Otter, *a sixty-ton brig under the command of James Hanna, approached the west coast of Vancouver Island on August 8, 1785: "land was seen, remarkably high," and the next day the brig was off Nootka Sound. "At nine o'clock in the evening three canoes approached," Hanna's journal recounts; "as the night was dark, the arms were got up. And they hallowed at a distance* 'Maakook'—*this was asking to trade. We soon got them alongside."*

China and the North Pacific Fur Trade

When Captain James Cook visited the Northwest Coast in 1768, the crews of his ships traded some relatively worthless trinkets for sea otter pelts. They were astonished at the price willingly paid for the pelts when *Resolution* arrived in China. After the publication of Cook's journals in 1784 news of the lucrative trade spread quickly, and within two years the first vessel to take advantage of this new commercial opportunity had reached the coast of Vancouver Island. She was a small British brig appropriately named *Sea Otter.*

The North Pacific fur trade had three major components. First was the outbound voyage to the Northwest Coast to trade for furs, principally sea otter, which were most prized by the Chinese. Second was the passage to China, often with a break in Hawaii for rest and to obtain fresh provisions. Third was China itself, where the furs were exchanged for high-value goods such as porcelain, silk and tea, which were brought home for the domestic market.

A complicated and oppressive system of inspections, customs and fees was in place in China. All transactions had to be made through an organization known as the "Hong," or "Cohong," and the exorbitant fees ensured that a merchant's representative, or "fixer," was more than adequately compensated. This system could keep ships bottled up in the anchorage for months, but such was the value of the trade that the captains suffered the inevitable indignities and obstructions and prayed for eventual release.

For the first few years the trade was almost all British, but after 1789 the Americans, principally from New England, took over. For the forty years the trade continued it was almost entirely a monopoly of vessels from Boston, so much so that the natives distinguished the traders as either "King George Men" or "Boston Men." Most of these trading ventures originated in England or on the American east coast and continued longer than any other deep-water commercial ventures of the period. Since the ships spent at least one season on the northwest coast of America and then crossed the Pacific to China, it was not unusual for them to be away from home for three years. It was the practice of the ships to leave in time to round Cape Horn in southern summer, be on the Northwest Coast for at least one summer season and return home via Canton, often stopping over in the Hawaiian Islands to rest and reprovision.

The trade with the natives took place mainly on the outer coast between the Columbia River and the Bering Sea. From Juan de Fuca Strait northward the coast is a labyrinth of rocky islands, hidden reefs, deep inlets and treacherous currents. In the north the tides can range up to twenty feet, and where they are restricted they can run at a terrifying fifteen knots. To further complicate the dangers, summer on the outer coast is the season of fog. In

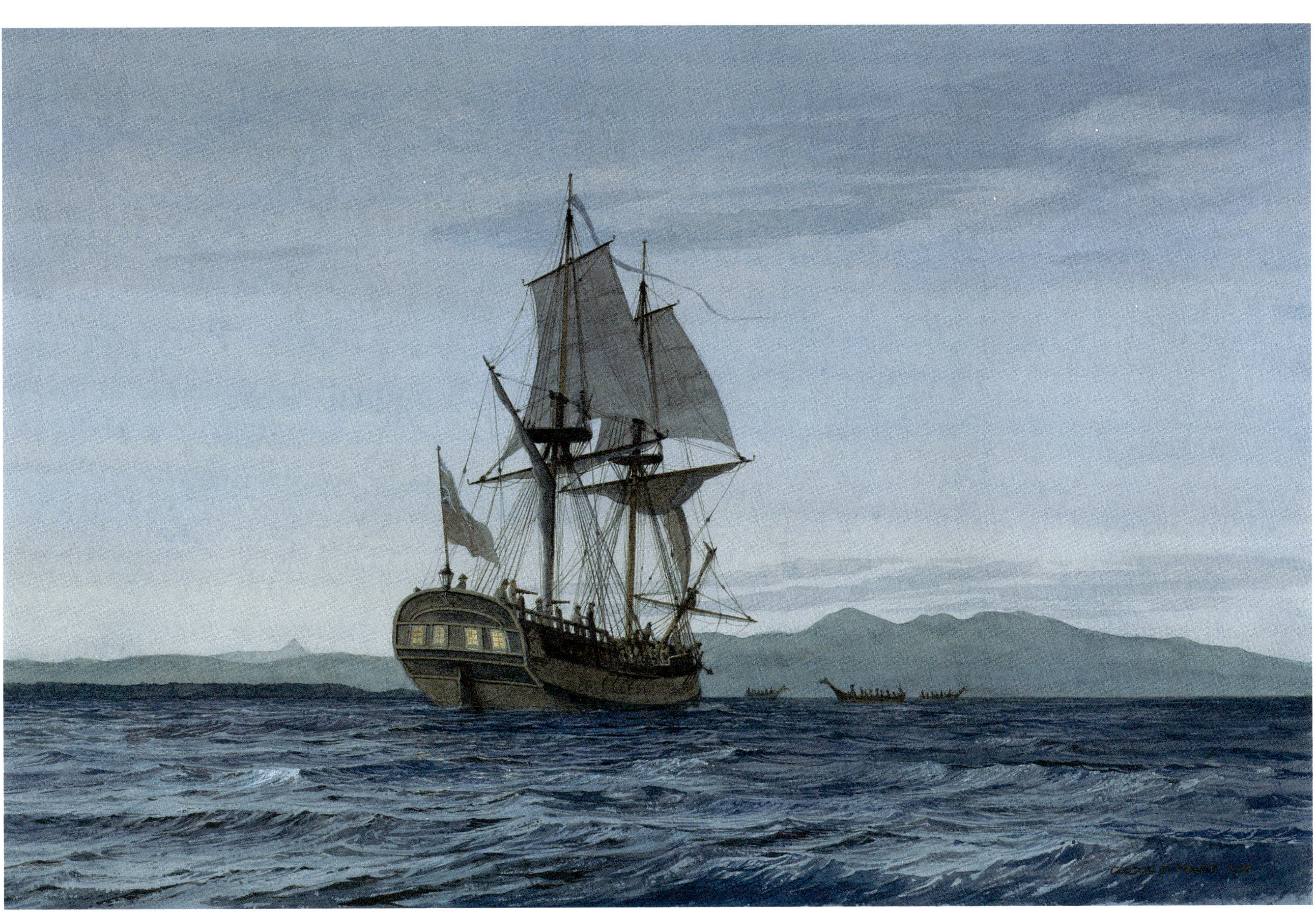

Whampoa Roads, Pearl River (WC, 15″ × 22″)
Canton, China, played a crucial role in the Northwest Coast fur trade. Outside of Macao it was the only Chinese port where foreigners were permitted to land their cargos, and the anchorage in the Pearl River was a hub of activity. Ships could proceed no further than Whampoa Roads, about twelve miles below Canton. Beyond that point, only ships' boats carrying captains or ships' agents were allowed to conduct the intricate business of trading furs.

Nuu-chah-nulth canoes, Vancouver Island's west coast (WC, 15″ × 22″)
The Nuu-chah-nulth were truly people of the sea. The rugged, rocky shores and nearly impenetrable forests of Vancouver Island's west coast forced them to take to the water, and they developed an elegant dugout canoe, carved from a single cedar log, of superb design and craftsmanship. Their traditional territory was the narrow coastal strip from Cape Flattery on Washington's Olympic Peninsula in the south to the island's Brooks Peninsula in the north. They were the people who paddled out to meet Juan Pérez in 1774 and who welcomed James Cook to Nootka Sound in 1778. Of all the coastal peoples, only the Nuu-chah-nulth were whalers, often spending days at sea in wait for the migrating gray whales.

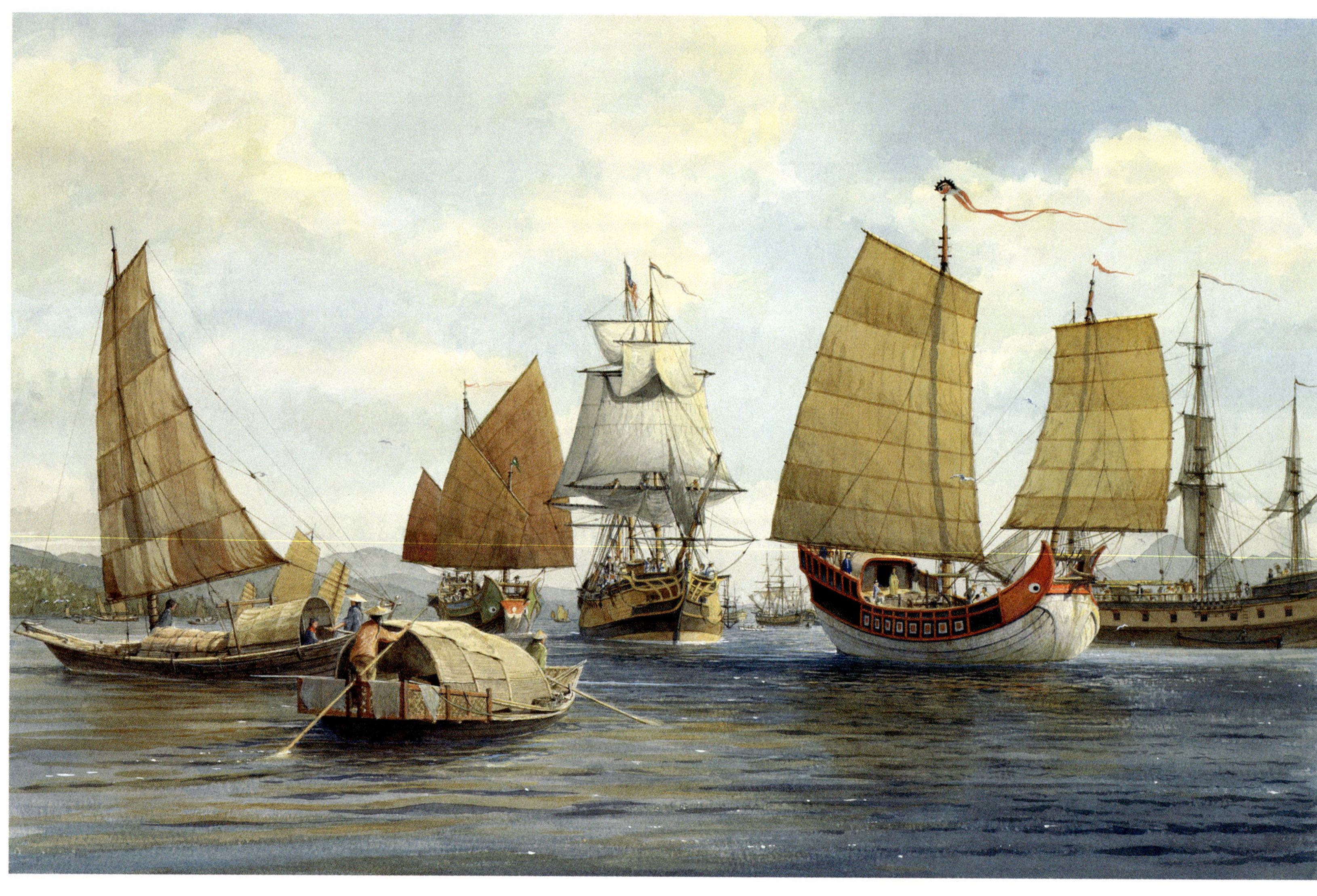

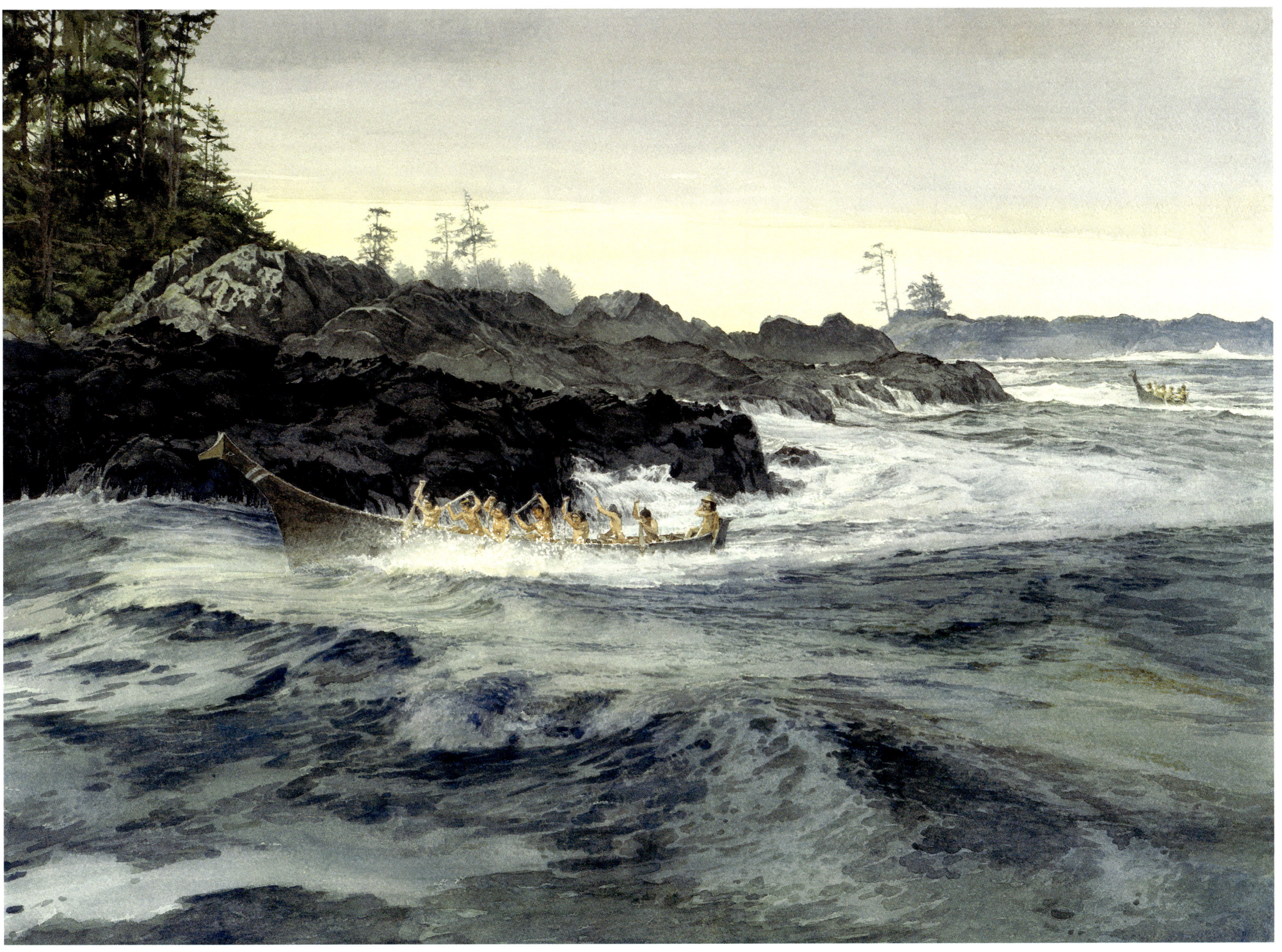

➤ ***Queen Charlotte* in Cloak Bay**
(WC, 15″ × 22″)
In 1787 Queen Charlotte, *commanded by George Dixon, was the first ship to anchor in Cloak Bay, at the north end of the Queen Charlotte Islands. The nearby waters around Langara Island were rich in sea otters, and the anchorages in Parry Passage became an important destination for traders.*

spite of these obstacles, and with no reliable charts of the coast, very few vessels came to grief.

Spread out along this coast, the various native peoples greeted the traders with curiosity, apprehension and, sometimes, open hostility. Although they were generally at war with each other, they were not usually aggressive towards newcomers unless provoked. When they were, revenge was the accepted response—and not necessarily against the original transgressor. The natives quickly became skilled barterers and soon learned the value of their furs and the desirability of the iron, copper and firearms that could be had for them. Some local chiefs became very wealthy and powerful as a result of the convenient location of their villages and the abundance of furs.

The native peoples in closest contact with the traders were the Tlingit on the Alaskan coast, the Haida in southeast Alaska and the Queen Charlotte Islands, the Kwagiuth and Tsimshian around Queen Charlotte Sound and the Nuu-chah-nulth on Vancouver Island's west coast. It was Cook who gave the Nuu-chah-nulth and the region the name "Nootka," in the mistaken belief that it was the name they applied to themselves. (In fact, the Mowachaht of Friendly Cove were attempting to explain their location to an uncomprehending Cook.)

On board *Resolution* in 1778 when Cook visited the Northwest Coast were several men who later played important roles in exploring and opening up the coast to Europeans. As well as George Vancouver, there was master's mate Nathaniel Portlock and armorer's mate George Dixon. When in 1785 a group of London merchants formed the King George's Sound Company, they obtained a five-year license to trade from the South Sea Company, acquired two ships and hired Portlock and Dixon to sail them on a trading venture to the Northwest Coast. Portlock was given overall command of the voyage and of the 320-ton *King George,* and George Dixon was given the 200-ton snow *Queen Charlotte.*

The two ships sailed from England in August 1785 and were in the Hawaiian Islands in May and June of the next year, acquiring fresh provisions. They first sighted the North American shore in mid-July 1786, near the approaches to Cook Inlet. The ships spent the summer of 1786 on the north coast and arrived back in Hawaii in November to winter in the islands. Back in Alaska the following April, they anchored off Montague Island in the entrance to Prince William Sound. After being beached for repairs, they left to pursue separate trading opportunities.

Portlock concentrated on the Alaskan coast, trading leisurely with good results, and Dixon took *Queen Charlotte* south, visiting and naming Port Mulgrave (Yakutat Bay), Norfolk Sound (Sitka Sound), Port Banks and Forrester Island. At the end of June Dixon found a large opening he named Dixon Straits, now Dixon Entrance,

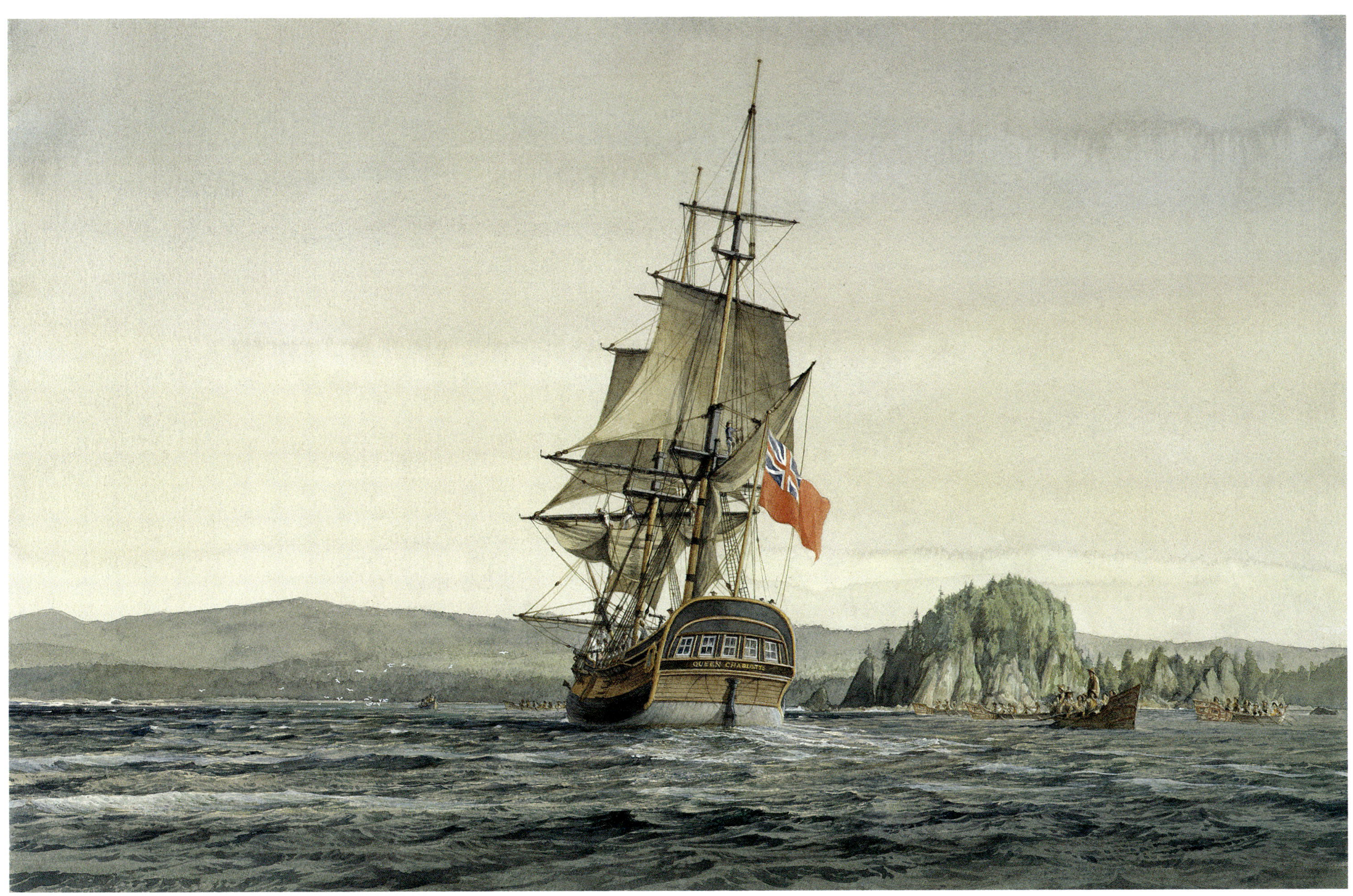
QUEEN CHARLOTTE

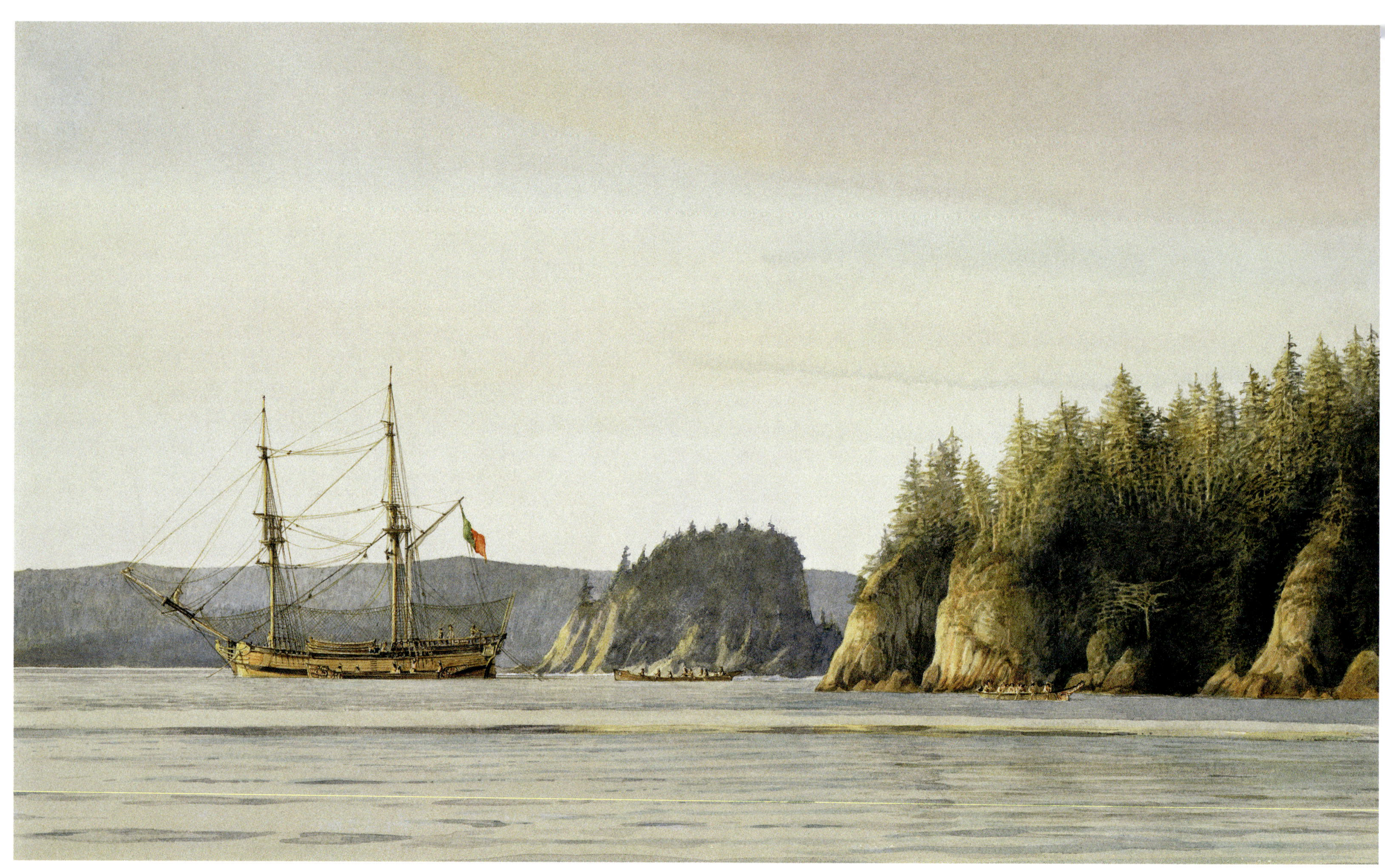

‹ ***Iphigenia* at Cloak Bay, Langara Island, June 1789** (WC, 15″ × 22″)
In June 1789 William Douglas's ship Iphigenia *dropped anchor "two miles from a small barren, rocky island which happened to be the residence of a chief, named Blakaw Coneehaw (Gunia), whom Douglas had seen on the coast in his last voyage. He came immediately on board and welcomed the arrival of the ship with a song, to which two hundred of his people formed a chorus of the most pleasing melody. When the voices ceased, he paid Douglas the compliment of exchanging names with him."*

⌄ **Kiusta, 1799** (WC, 11″ × 15″)
The journal of the ship Eliza *contains the first known drawing of a Haida village, Kiusta. It shows eight houses, two mortuary posts and one frontal pole. Ten years earlier, William Douglas had helped the Haida erect a pole in this village.*

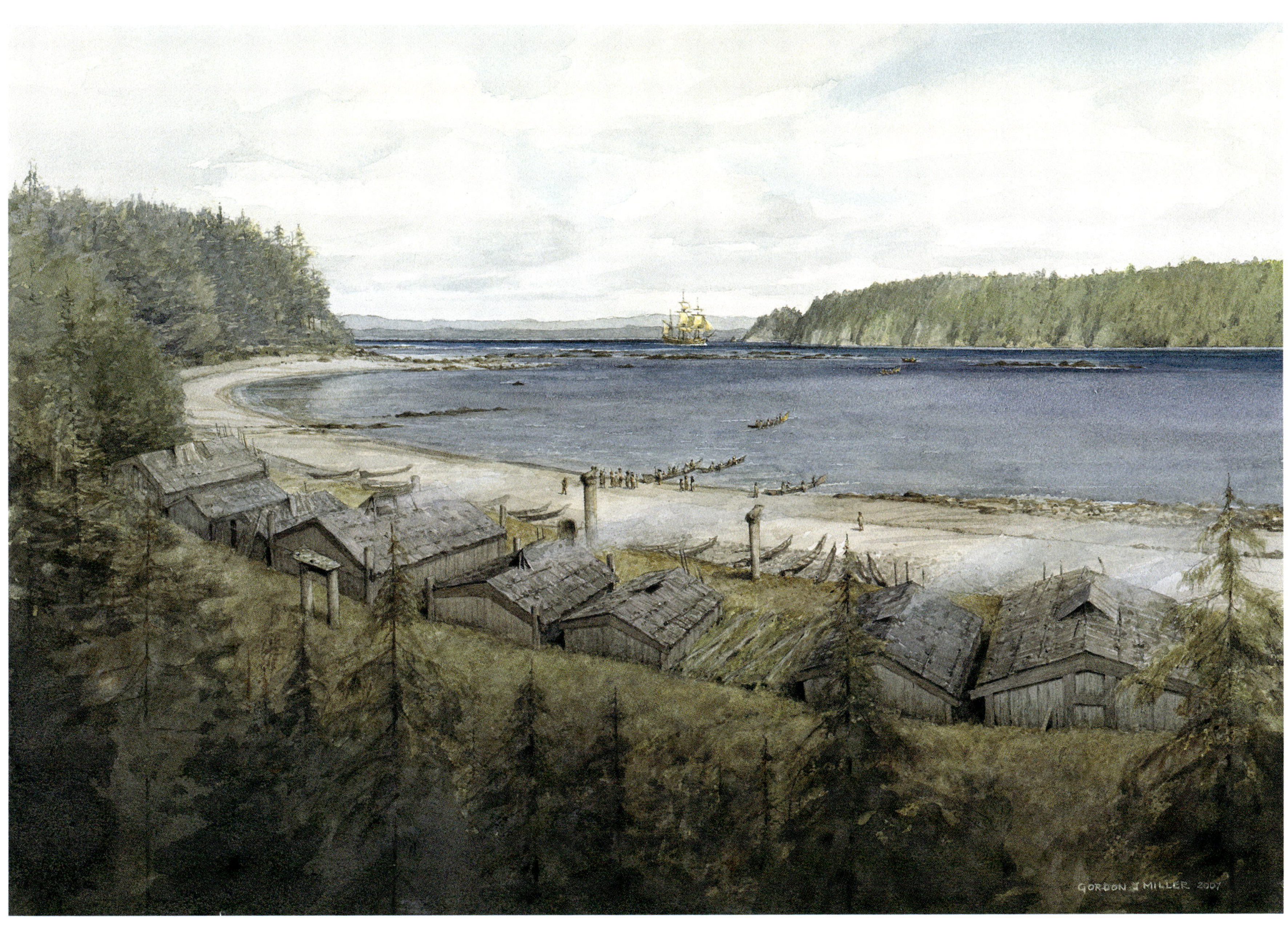

➤ ***Nootka* overwintering in Alaska, 1786–87**
(WC, 15″ × 22″)
John Meares had Nootka *rigged down and made secure for the winter of 1786–87. For a while the natives stayed around the ship, and the crew prepared her for cold weather. As the temperatures dropped, the men began to fall ill from the cold, scurvy and suffocating smoke created by the fires below deck. The cold and snow continued right through April, by which time twenty-three men had died. Another crew member died later.*

where the Alaska–British Columbia border now runs. *Queen Charlotte* was then off Langara Island, which had been named by Pérez in 1774. Dixon spent several profitable days anchored in Cloak Bay, between Graham Island and Langara Island. Named for the large number of prime pelts Dixon acquired there, Cloak Bay became one of the prime destinations for traders heading for the coast.

Dixon continued south from Cloak Bay, keeping close to shore and trading with the Haida who came to the ship in their canoes. On July 25, 1787, he came to the end of the land, Cape St. James, and heading north up the east coast surmised correctly that he had been sailing around an island archipelago. He named the archipelago the Queen Charlotte Islands, after his ship.

One of the more interesting and nefarious characters to engage in the fur trade was John Meares, an ex-Royal Navy lieutenant. Meares was in Calcutta when he heard of the fortunes being made on the Northwest Coast and immediately arranged financing for a venture of his own. With a group of merchants he formed the Bengal Fur Company, and to avoid the taxes and licensing requirements of the East India and South Sea Companies, his ships sailed under Portuguese colors. The company outfitted two ships, the 200-ton snow *Nootka*, with Meares in command, and *Sea Otter*, under the command of William Tipping.

In the summer of 1786 *Sea Otter* was seen with a good cargo of furs in Prince William Sound, but when she sailed from there she was never seen again, and her fate is unknown. That summer Meares had sailed *Nootka* north to the Aleutian Islands, then eastward along the archipelago. The weather was poor, and the Russians had already obtained most of the furs. Late in September Meares reached Prince William Sound with little to show for his time on the coast. There he made the near-fatal decision to overwinter in Alaska rather than sail for the warmer comfort of Hawaii. The local natives guided *Nootka* to a safe anchorage farther up the sound, where Meares had her rigged down and made secure. Salmon were plentiful in the streams and ducks and geese provided fresh meat, but the anchorage Meares had chosen was a poor one. Because it was off a freshwater creek, by November the bay was iced over, the salmon and the natives had left and the wildfowl had long since flown south.

Warmer weather brought relief to *Nootka* in May 1787, but by then twenty-three men, including the surgeon, had died of scurvy. The ship was barely seaworthy and the remaining crew were too ill to work her. A total disaster was averted with the arrival on May 7 of Nathaniel Portlock in *King George*, who had returned with George Dixon in *Queen Charlotte* for a second season on the coast. Portlock provided Meares with two healthy men, medical assistance and fresh provisions on Meares's promise to leave the coast and engage in no further trade.

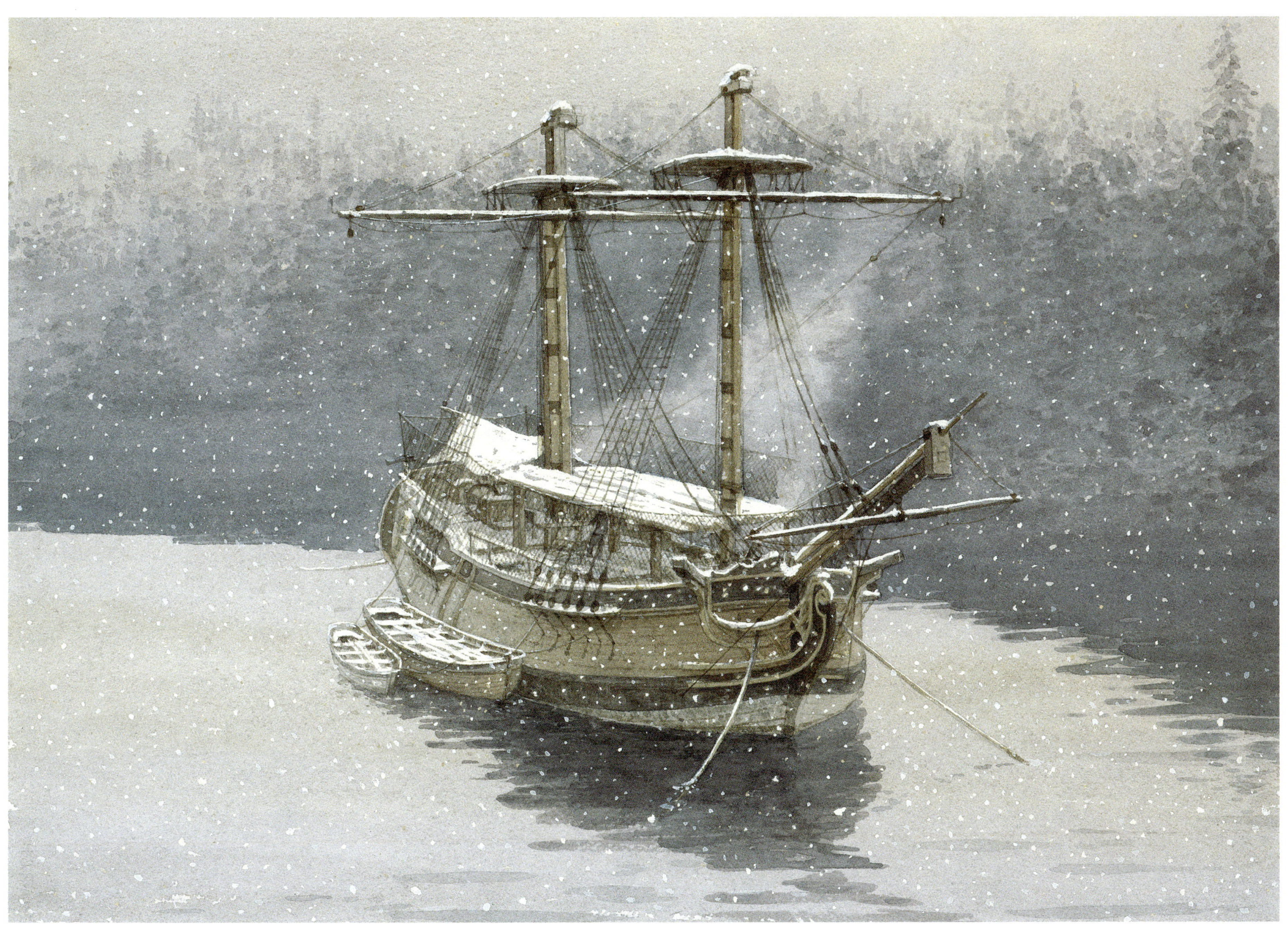

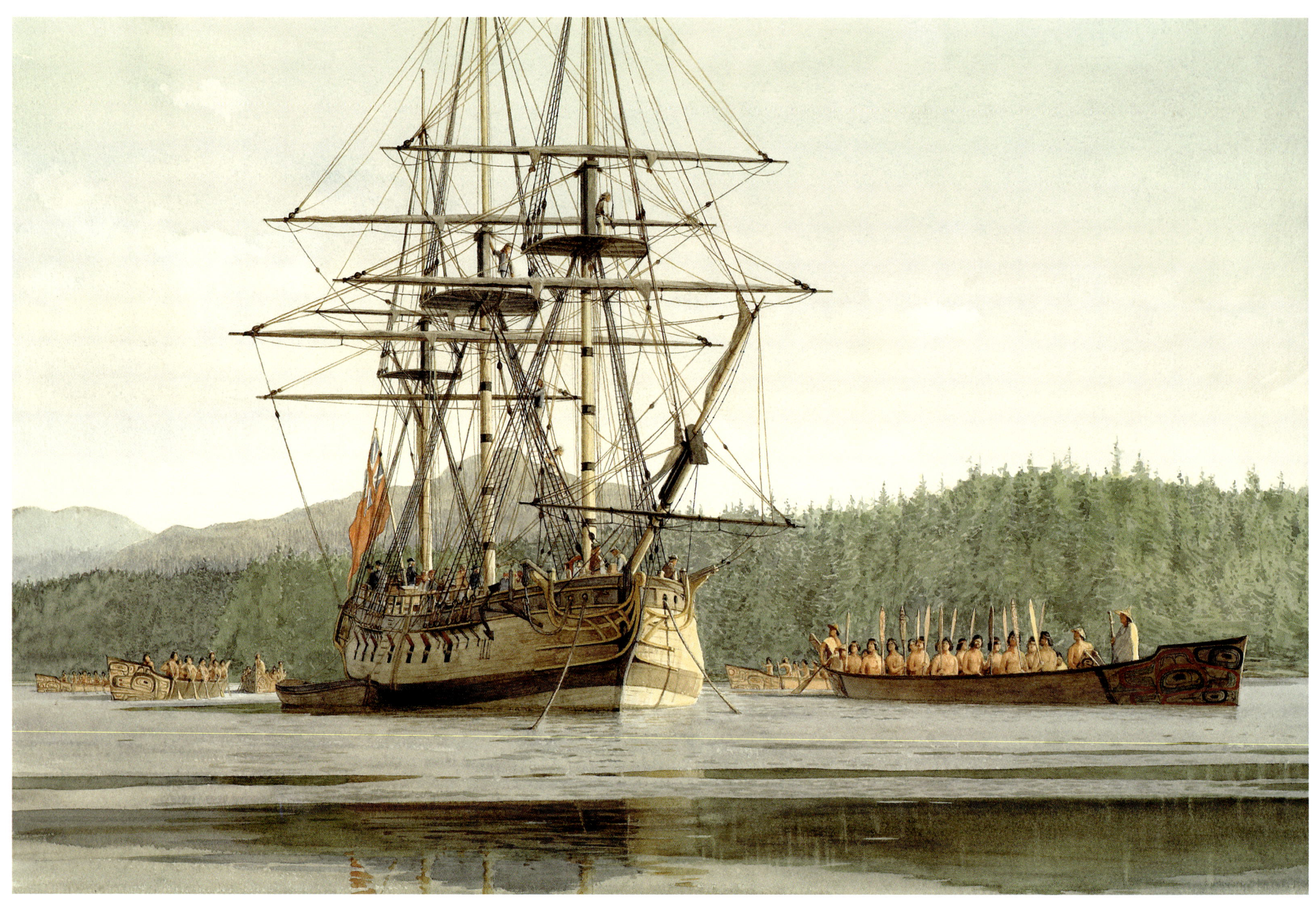

Nootka left Prince William Sound on June 21, but Meares, instead of honoring his promise, gathered more pelts before sailing for Hawaii and China. The Hawaiians treated *Nootka*'s crew with their typical hospitality, and although it had been nine years since James Cook had called at the islands, Europeans were still a source of intense curiosity. Many Hawaiians would have liked to join the ship on the voyage to "Britannee." That privilege was granted to Kaiana, a six-foot-five-inch chief of Kauai, who endeared himself to the crew and was an instant celebrity when they arrived in Macao.

Although the first venture of the Bengal Fur Company had turned out to be a disaster—*Sea Otter* and her cargo had disappeared with all hands, and *Nootka*, the first ship to winter over in Alaska, had lost twenty-four of her crew and collected few furs for her troubles—Meares was able to raise the funds for yet another trading venture in 1788. He had high ambitions, including control of the fur trade between the Northwest Coast and Canton. With Richard Etches, a leading shipowner, and Captain James Colnett, another ex–British naval officer, he formed a partnership called "The Associated Merchants Trading to the Northwest Coast of America."

Colnett had spent the summer of 1787 on the coast in the *Prince of Wales*, owned by Richard Etches and associates, with the little sloop *Princess Royal* as her tender. For the 1788 season Meares purchased two snows in China: *Felice Adventurer* and *Iphigenia Nubiana*. James Colnett was given *Argonaut*, a snow built in Calcutta, and overall command of the next expedition. Part of their plan was to establish permanent factories on land acquired from the natives, where furs could be collected year round. To this end, the *Argonaut* embarked with twenty-nine Chinese men to construct and man the posts, as well as material for a house and the frames for a small schooner.

In 1788 Meares's ships were again flying Portuguese colors to avoid high customs duties at Macao and to deceive the British and Spanish authorities. Meares arrived at Nootka Sound on May 13 in *Felice Adventurer*. The Nuu-chah-nulth chief, Maquinna, arrived three days later with much ceremony and exchanges of gifts. Meares had already staked out an area of beach and had set up tents for his men, who erected a small house inside a breastwork on which they mounted a small cannon. He later claimed this "spot of ground" had been purchased legally—that Maquinna had willingly given him the rights to the plot in exchange for a pair of pistols that had caught his eye—and it became central to Meares's claim of English sovereignty over Nootka Sound. Years later, however, in his dealings with the Spanish, Maquinna denied making this contract with Meares.

After finishing the house ashore, Meares began the work of framing the new schooner from material brought over aboard *Iphigenia Nubiana*. The schooner *North West*

‹ ***Prince of Wales* in Rose Harbour, 1787**
(WC, 15″ × 22″)
In 1787 James Colnett, commanding Prince of Wales, *was looking for trade at the south end of the Queen Charlotte Islands. On August 20 the ship was towed into Houston Stewart Channel and anchored in Rose Harbour, where she was soon visited by Haida canoes. Colnett noted, "At the coming of each Canoe, they carry a carved figure, on a staff in the Bow as an emblem of Peace, and paddle two or three times round the Ship, singing ere they come along side."*

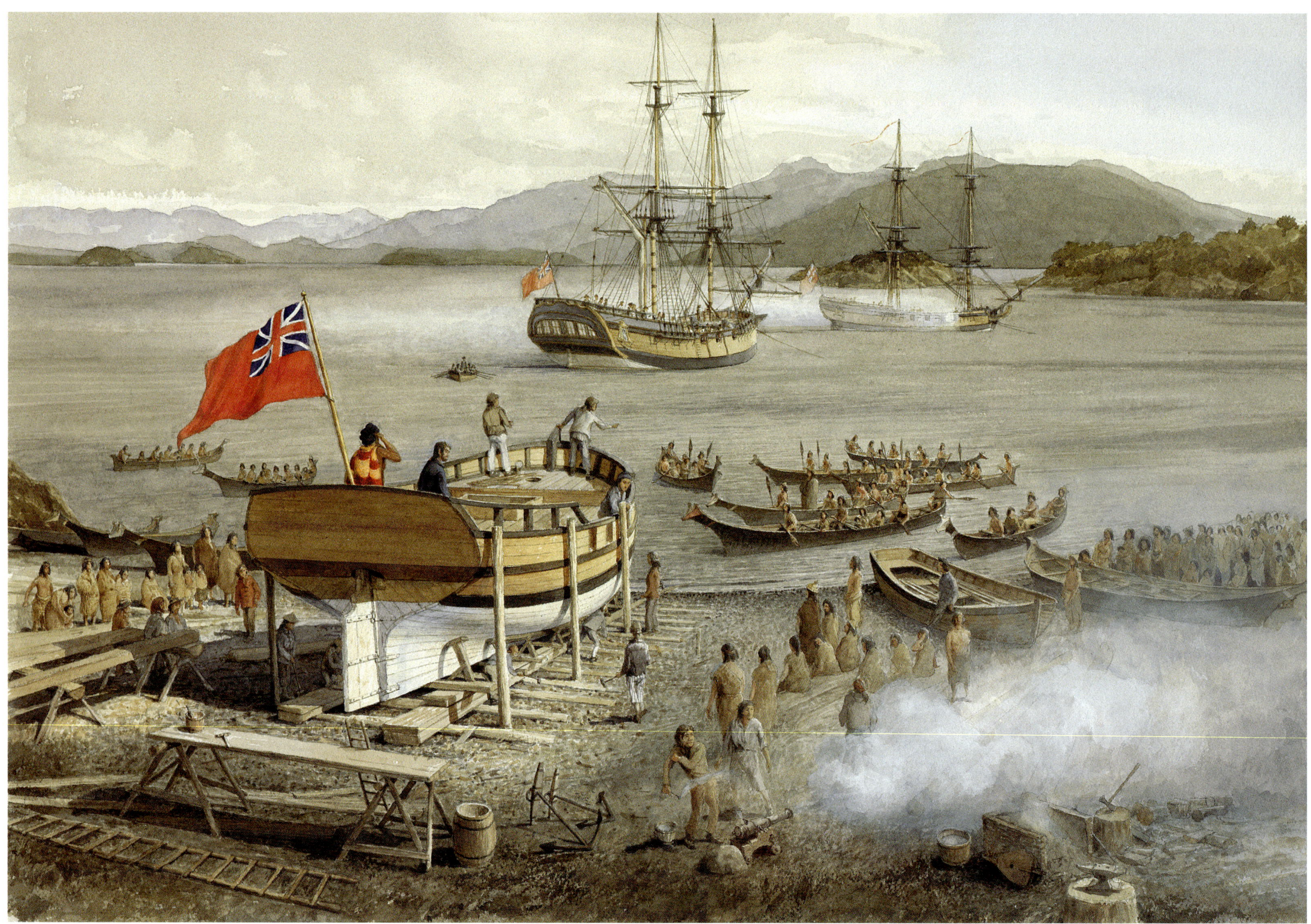

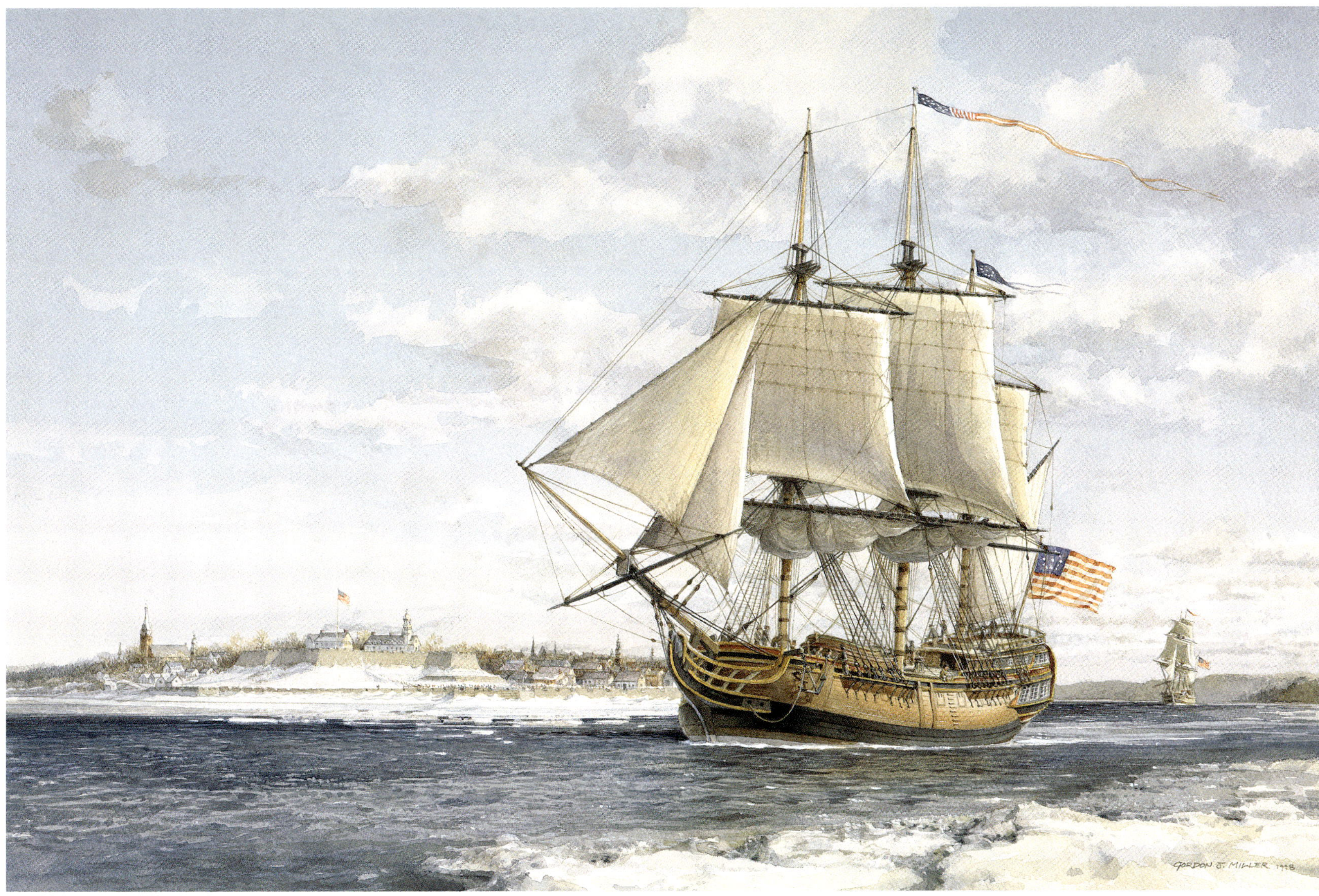

Launch of *North West America*
(WC, 15″ × 22″)
The first ship built on the Northwest Coast was launched at Friendly Cove, Vancouver Island, on September 19, 1788. The resident natives and the crews of the anchored British and American ships had gathered to witness the spectacle. At noon, on the firing of a gun, John Meares noted that "the vessel started from the ways like a shot—Indeed she went off with so much velocity, that she nearly made her way out of the harbour; for the fact was, that not being very accustomed to this business, we had forgotten to place an anchor and cable on board to bring her up." On board as she slid into the water was the Hawaiian Kaiana, dressed in a brilliant feathered cloak, who expressed his excitement by exclaiming "Mighty! Mighty!"

***Empress of China* sailing from New York**
(WC, 15″ × 22″)
Before the American Revolution, all American trade with the Orient was controlled by the British East India Company and was heavily taxed. It was these taxes, in part, that precipitated the famous Boston Tea Party. After winning their independence from Britain, the Americans were eager to test international trade, and a Philadelphia syndicate was the first to give it a try. They purchased the newly launched privateer Angelic, *moved her down to New York in the fall of 1783 and renamed her* Empress of China. *There she loaded a cargo that consisted mainly of ginseng. She arrived at Macao on August 23, 1784—the first ship to visit China under American colors—and arrived back in New York on May 11, 1785, with 200 tons of tea, plus chinaware, silks and spices. A 30 per cent profit on the voyage was encouragement enough, and the China trade was launched.*

➤ ***Columbia Rediviva* and *Lady Washington* leaving Boston** (WC, 22″ × 30″)
Columbia Rediviva *and* Lady Washington *sailed together on the morning tide, October 1, 1787. The two ships proceeded around Cape Horn and into the Pacific.* Lady Washington *anchored in Friendly Cove on September 17, 1788, becoming the first American ship to reach the Northwest Coast.* Columbia *arrived five days later; on her return voyage she became the first American ship to circumnavigate the globe when she arrived in Boston on August 10, 1790.*

America, the first ship built on the Northwest Coast, was launched at Friendly Cove in September. Robert Funter was given command, and he traded briefly on the coast before sailing for Hawaii on October 27. The ship was later captured by the Spanish and renamed *Santa Gertrudis la Magna.*

The first Americans to test the possibilities of the maritime fur trade were merchants from Boston, Salem and New York. Together they financed two vessels for a voyage to the Northwest Coast: *Columbia Rediviva,* under the overall command of Captain John Kendrick, and *Lady Washington,* under Captain Robert Gray. They sailed together from Boston on October 1, 1787, and entered the Pacific around Cape Horn. *Lady Washington* anchored in Friendly Cove on September 17, 1788, five days ahead of *Columbia.* They wintered in Nootka, the first ships ever to do so, where the contrasting character of the two captains emerged. In the spring, while Gray was trading for furs along the coast, for ten months Kendrick had *Columbia* rigged down and swinging idly at anchor.

Lady Washington returned to Nootka in July 1789, after trading for furs all season. The two ships sailed for Clayoquot Sound, where the captains exchanged commands; Captain Gray then sailed *Columbia* to Canton via Hawaii. Kendrick kept *Lady Washington* on the coast to finish the season, then joined *Columbia* in China in January 1790. After trading their furs, *Columbia* sailed for Boston, arriving on August 10, to "salvos of artillery and cheers." She was the first American ship to circumnavigate the globe. Although the first voyage was only moderately profitable, *Columbia* was immediately readied for sea and sailed again on September 28. In the meantime John Kendrick had spent the winter in China converting *Lady Washington* to a brigantine.

Kendrick appears to have had little respect for the natives. In one notorious incident in 1789, while *Lady Washington* was anchored off the village of Ninstints, he almost lost his ship to the villagers, who were intent on capturing her. It has been suggested that Kendrick was under the influence of alcohol, for he allowed more natives aboard than was prudent. Those on board engaged in some minor pilfering, and hostilities erupted when Kendrick discovered that among the items missing was some of his own laundry. The two chiefs, Koyah and Skulkinanse, were seized and held hostage until Kendrick's clothes and the other goods were returned. Kendrick, still unsatisfied, was determined to teach the natives a lesson. Captain Gray, who visited the village at a later date, was given the following account by the natives: Kendrick "took Coyah, tied a rope around his neck, whipped him, painted his face, cut off his hair, took away from him a great many skins, and then turned him ashore. Coyah was now no longer a chief, but an 'Ahliko,' or one of the lower class. They now have no head chief, but many inferior chiefs."

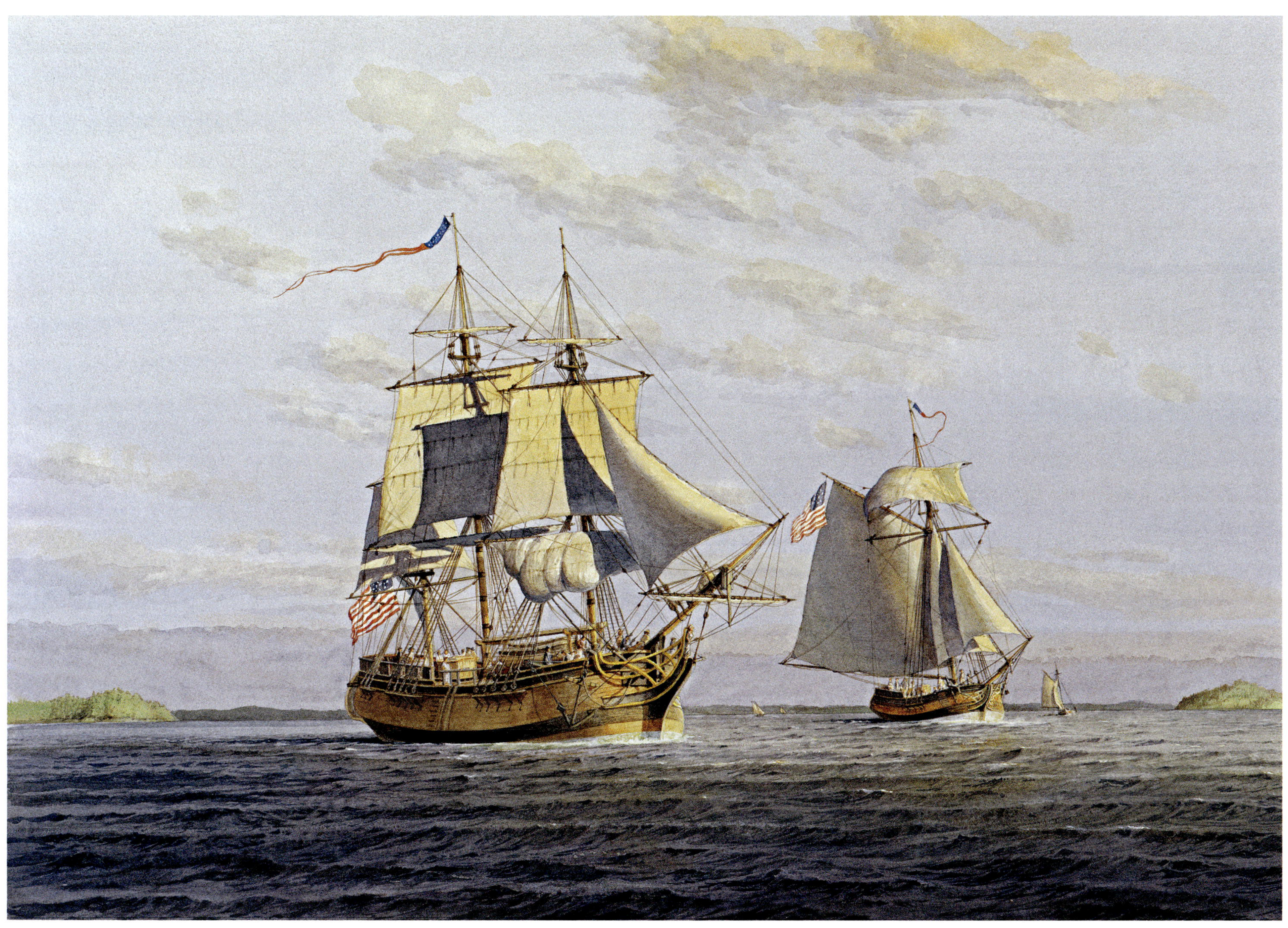

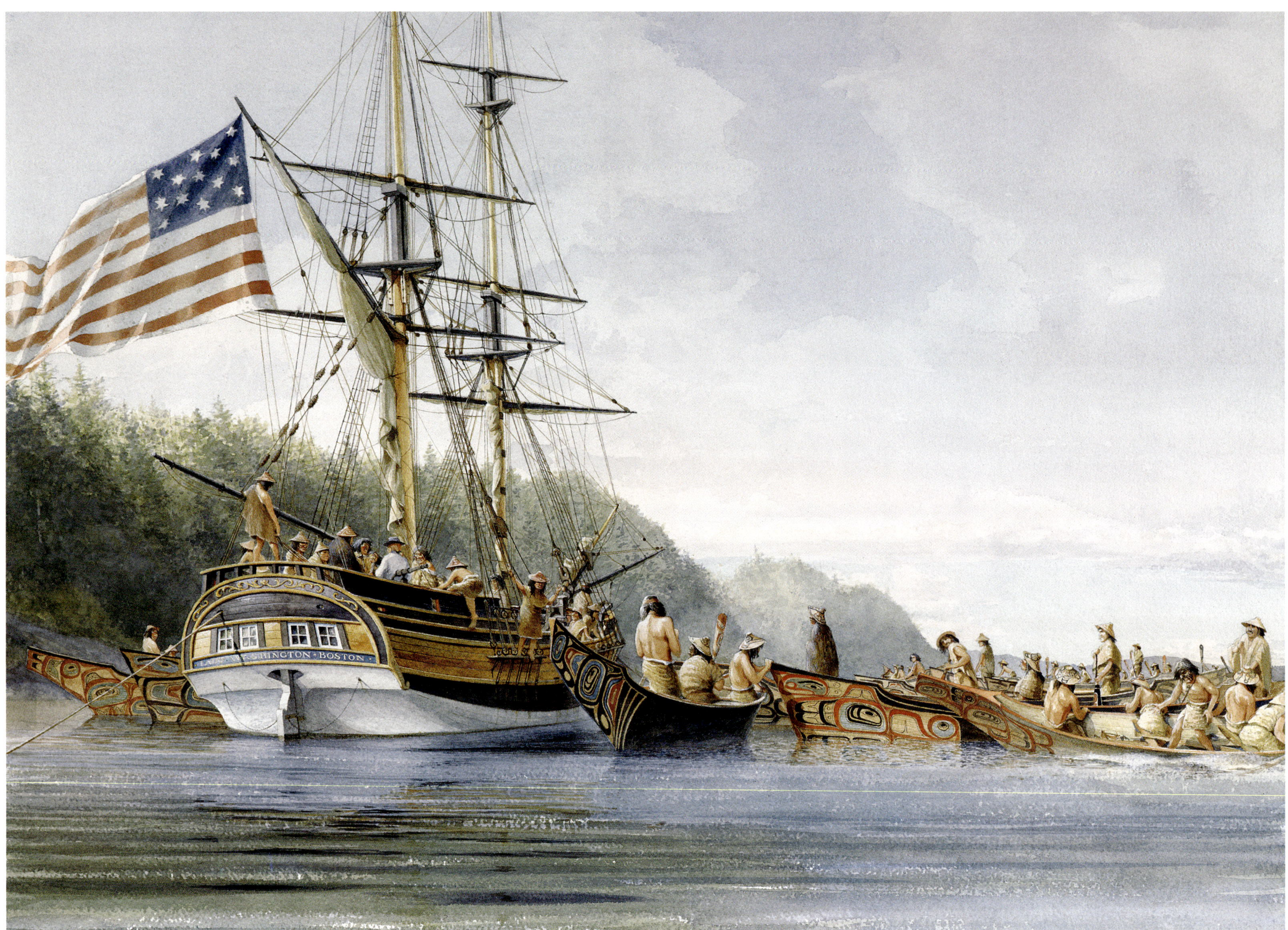
HINGTON · BOSTON

In June 1791 *Lady Washington* returned to Ninstints. Although re-rigged as a brigantine, she was recognized by Koyah, who was still smoldering from his earlier humiliation. Kendrick, who had likely been drinking but was certainly careless, again allowed far too many natives on board. Koyah seized the keys to the arms chest on deck and forced the outnumbered crew below. For a short time Kendrick was alone on deck, and he escaped only by dropping down a hatch and re-emerging with his armed officers and crew. The resulting incident was immortalized in the first sea chantey composed on the Northwest Coast, "The Bold Northwestman."

It is possible that Kendrick's relations with the Chinese were no better than with the natives, as he attempted to circumvent their trading customs and regulations. He seems to have used *Lady Washington* for his own private ventures, for he never returned any of the profits to the owners in Boston or made any attempt to return there. His life ended dramatically in Hawaii when a cannonball, fired from a loaded signal gun that was not supposed to be shotted, passed through his cabin and killed him.

In the spring of 1792 *Columbia Rediviva* was looking for furs off the Oregon and Washington coasts, where she met up with the two ships of George Vancouver's, HMS *Chatham* and HMS *Discovery*, surveying slowly northward along the coast. Captain Gray accompanied them as far as the entrance to Juan de Fuca Strait before returning to the south. On May 7 he discovered and entered Grays Harbor. There *Columbia* spent a night, sinking with cannon shot one of several canoes bent on capturing the ship.

On May 11 *Columbia* was off the river that was to bear her name. The river's presence had been suspected previously by signs of freshwater runoff and debris, but fog or breakers over the bar had denied access. This time conditions favored *Columbia*, and with the longboat sounding ahead she passed safely over the bar. Captain Gray remained in the river until May 20, exploring as far as thirty miles upriver from the mouth. The chart he drew he later gave to Bodega y Quadra at Nootka, and a copy was given to Captain Vancouver, who later that year sent *Chatham* over the bar to conduct a British survey of the river.

Exploring the Salish Sea

In 1592 Apostolos Valerianos, a Greek pilot in the service of Spain searching for the Strait of Anian, claimed to have sailed into a wide strait between latitude 47° and 48° north. The journals of the voyage were never found, and the claims were so improbable that they were not given much credence. But there is in fact a wide strait at that latitude, and when Captain Charles W. Barkley entered it in 1787 he named it Juan de Fuca, the name by which Valerianos was known by his Spanish employers.

Barkley was a twenty-seven-year-old captain who had been persuaded to resign his position with the British East

‹ **"Bold Northwestman": *Lady Washington* off Ninstints, 1791** (WC, 22″ × 30″)
"The vessel was immediately thronged with natives, a woman standing in the main chains urging them on. The officers and people all retired below, having no arms save the officers' private ones . . . Though the natives had taken the keys of the arm chests yet they did not happen to be lockt. They were therefore immediately opened and a constant fire was kept up as long as they could reach the natives with the cannon or small arms, after which they chased them in their armed boats, making the most dreadfull havock by killing all they came across": F.W. Howay, "The Ballad of the Bold Northwestman: An Incident in the Life of Captain John Kendrick" (1928).

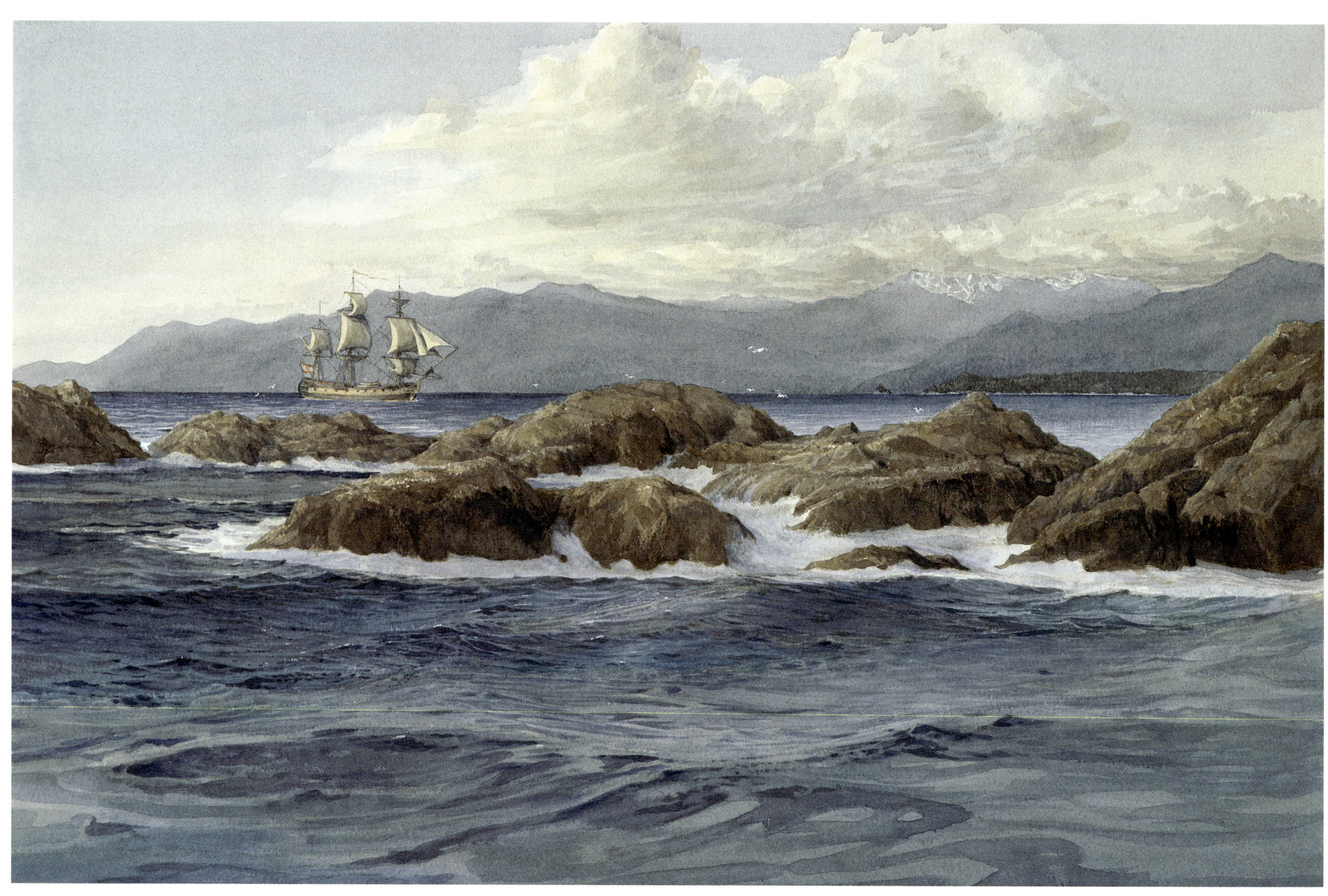

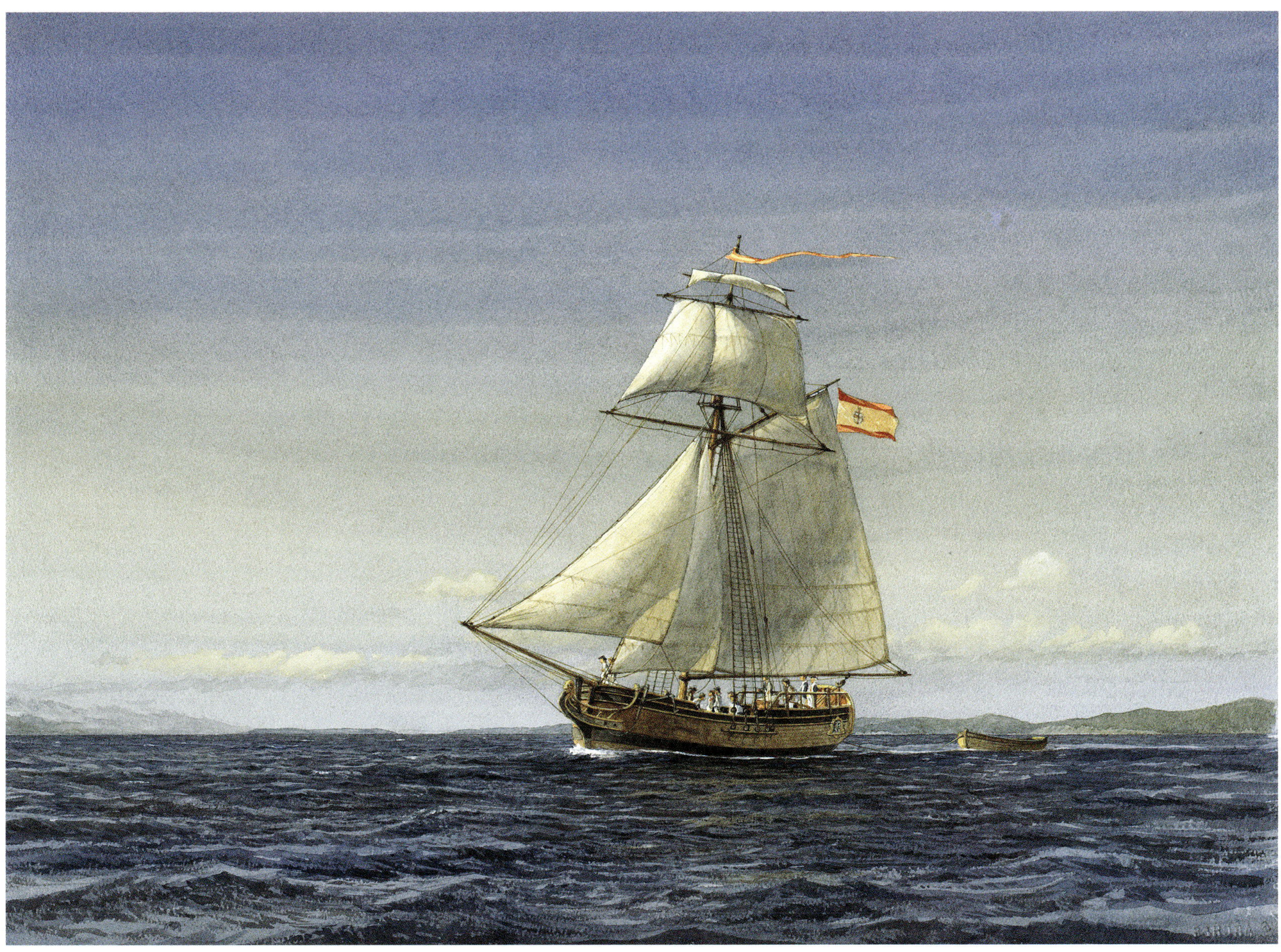

‹ ***Imperial Eagle* in Barkley Sound, 1787**
(WC, 15″ × 22″)
Imperial Eagle *was the first ship to arrive at Nootka in 1787, and the trade for furs went well. She traded in Clayoquot Sound before entering a large sound that her captain, Charles W. Barkley, named after himself, as well as naming a channel after the ship. Frances, Barkley's wife, was honored by having Hornby Peak, Trevor Channel and Frances Island named after her.*

^ ***Princesa Real* in Juan de Fuca Strait**
(WC, 15″ × 22″)
The full length of Juan de Fuca Strait was explored in 1790 by Manuel Quimper in Princesa Real. *She left Nootka Sound on May 31, called at Clayoquot Sound and then sailed into the strait, keeping to the northern shore. Quimper explored and named Puerto de San Juan (San Juan Bay), Puerto de Revillagigedo (Sooke Inlet) and Rada de Valdes y Bazan (Royal Roads). Princesa Real was required to be handed back to her British owners at Nootka, but fog prevented her from entering the sound and she sailed instead for Monterey. When she finally reached Macao, she was in such bad shape her British owners refused to accept her.*

› ***San Carlos*** **and** ***Santa Saturnina*** **off Royal Roads** (WC, 15″ × 22″)
Off Puerto de Cordova (Esquimalt Harbour), near the eastern end of Juan de Fuca Strait, Santa Saturnina *and the longboat were provisioned for three weeks. At dawn on June 14, 1791, the two little vessels cast off from* San Carlos *and made their way into Haro Strait. That day they made their way far enough to see up Trincomali Channel, where they anchored somewhere for the night.*

India Company to command a private trading venture to the northwest coast of North America. He acquired *Imperial Eagle,* a decommissioned East India Company ship with twenty guns, and at four hundred tons was very large for her intended use. Barkley purchased her in London, but in order to circumvent the trade restrictions and stiff license fees imposed on private English trading companies he sailed her to Ostend, Belgium, where she was registered under Austrian colors.

On November 24, 1786, *Imperial Eagle* sailed from Ostend and headed south into the Atlantic. Sailing with Captain Barkley was his wife of only four weeks, Frances Hornby Trevor. The daughter of a Protestant chaplain, Frances was only sixteen when she met and married Charles. She made two voyages with her husband over a period of eight years, and in the process established many historical "firsts." She was the first European woman to set foot on the Hawaiian Islands. There she employed Winee, a young Hawaiian girl, to sail as her maid. Winee and Frances thus became the first non-native women to visit the Northwest Coast when they arrived at Nootka in June 1787, and Winee also became the first Hawaiian woman to reach America.

A few days after the Barkleys left Nootka, sailing south in clear weather, they opened up the entrance to a wide strait at latitude 48° north. Barkley correctly assumed it was the long-lost Juan de Fuca Strait. Although he didn't explore it, Barkley gave the strait the name it is known by today.

The first European to enter the strait discovered by Captain Barkley was the Spaniard José María Narváez, in 1789, on *Santa Gertrudis*—the renamed *North West America,* which had been seized the previous year at Nootka. The full length of Juan de Fuca Strait was explored the next year by the Spaniard Manuel Quimper. In the captured *Princess Royal,* renamed *Princesa Real* by the Spanish, Quimper sailed the length of the strait, noting but not investigating any of the channels at the eastern end.

The stage was set for the final entry into the Strait of Georgia the following summer. Francisco de Eliza, who had been given command of the Spanish forces at Nootka, had instructions to explore the waters at the eastern end of the strait that Quimper had seen the year before. Deciding to undertake the survey himself, he took command of *San Carlos,* accompanied by a small schooner, *Santa Saturnina,* under José Maria Narváez. It was agreed the two ships would rendezvous at Puerto de Cordova (Esquimalt Harbour) near the eastern end of the strait. Eliza arrived first, and while waiting for the *Santa Saturnina* he sent a longboat on a short survey up Haro Strait.

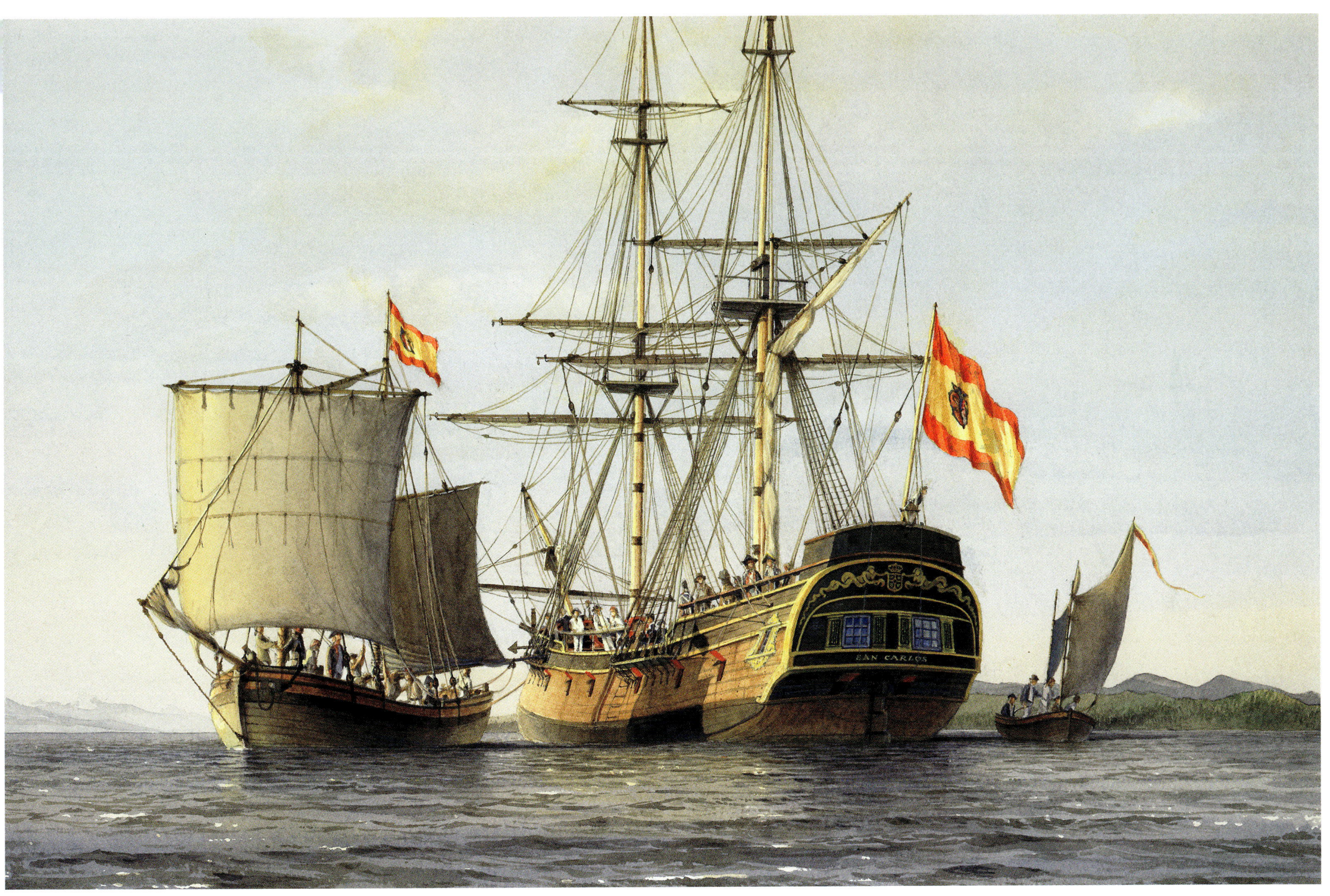
SAN CARLOS

➤ *The Salish Sea: Juan de Fuca Strait, Puget Sound and the Strait of Georgia. Area of Spanish and British exploration, 1790–92.*

➤ ***Santa Saturnina*** **and longboat off Saturna Island** (WC, 15″ × 22″)
In the evening of June 15, 1791, Europeans first saw what locals now refer to as "The Gulf," a grand expanse of open water, in contrast to the tortuous and restricted passages of the islands. The evening was clear, and across the eastern horizon stretched the snowcapped Coast Range, centered by the volcanic peak of Mount Baker. Beyond the lee of Saturna Island the two boats found a fresh northwest wind that took them across to Patos Island, where they anchored for the night.

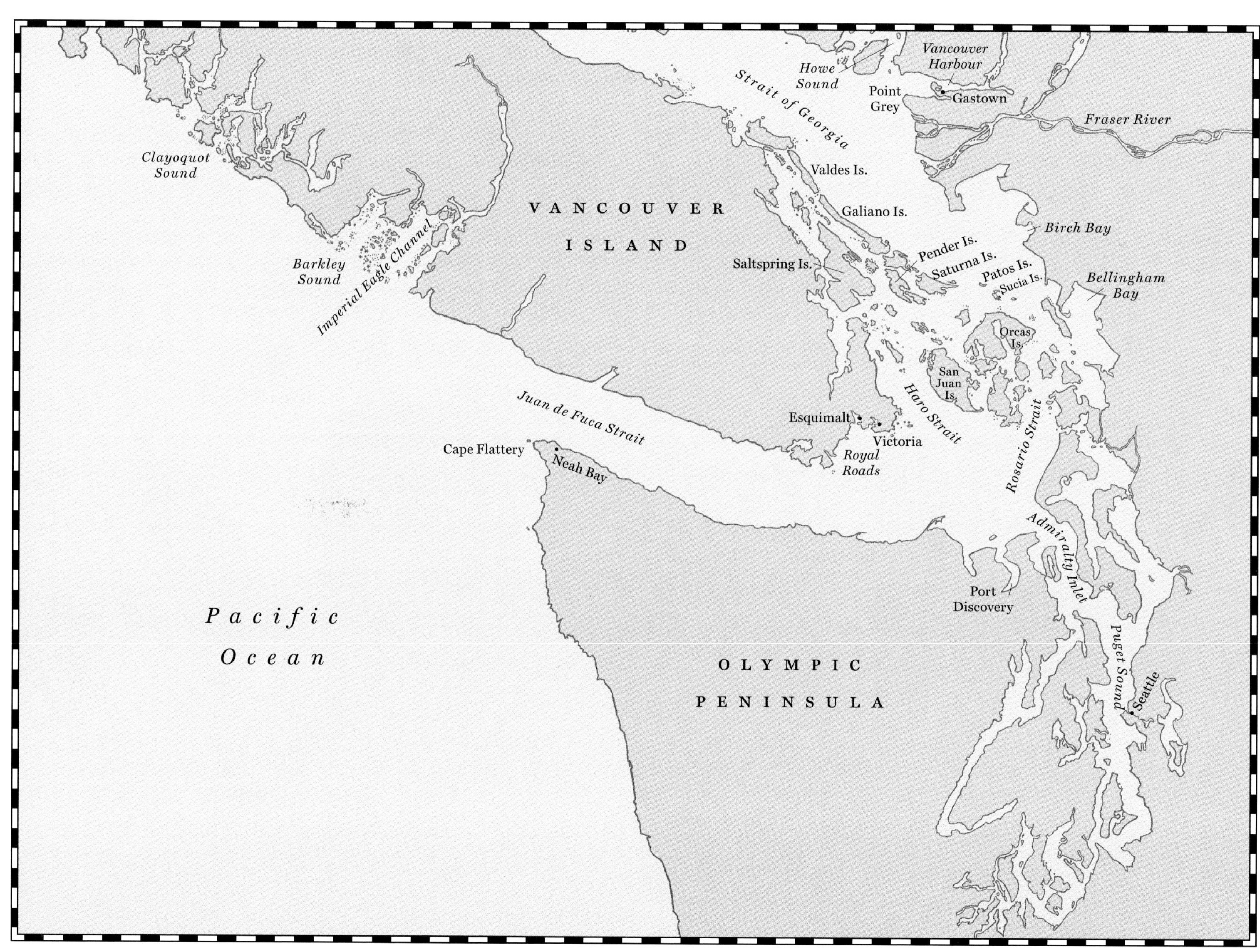

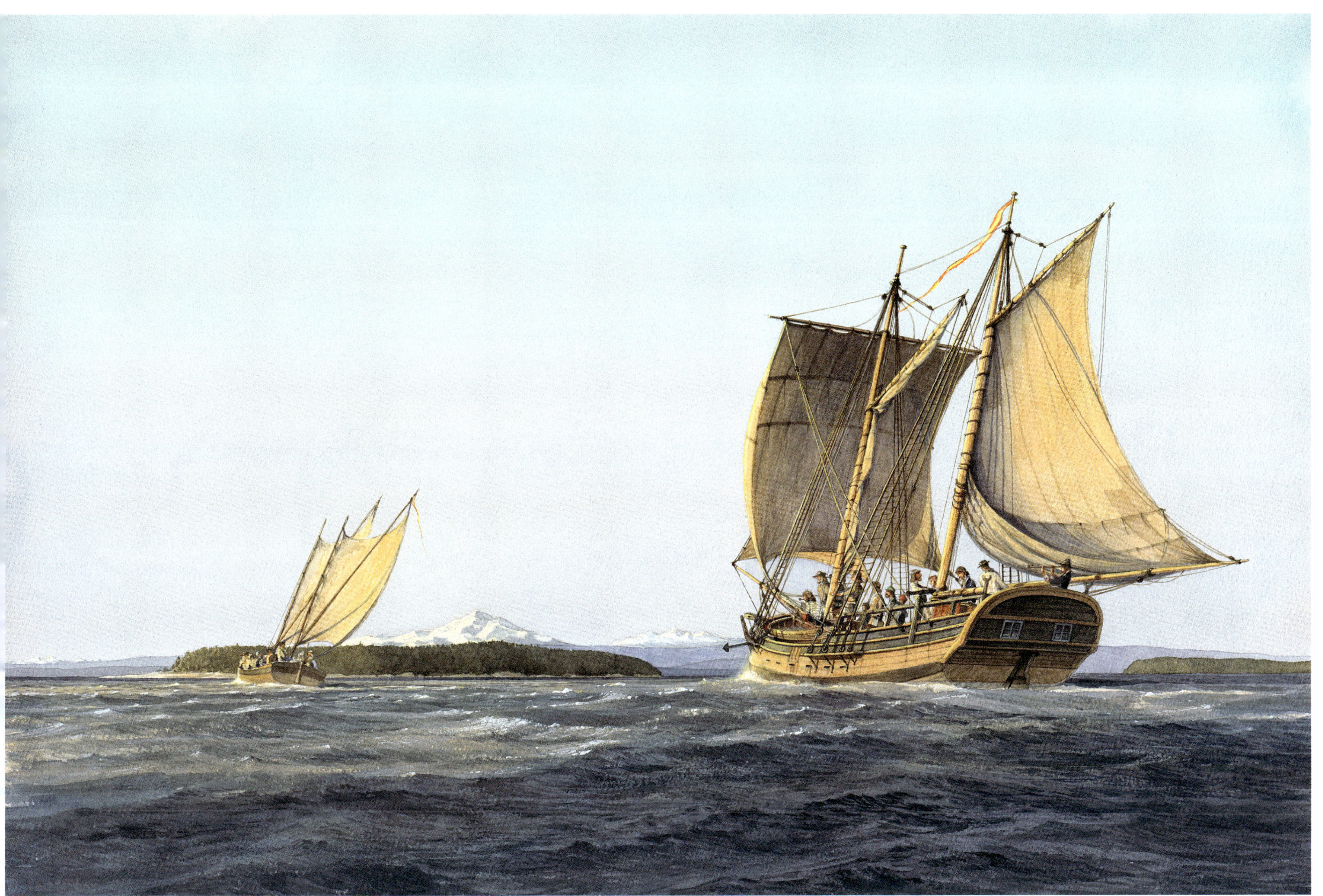

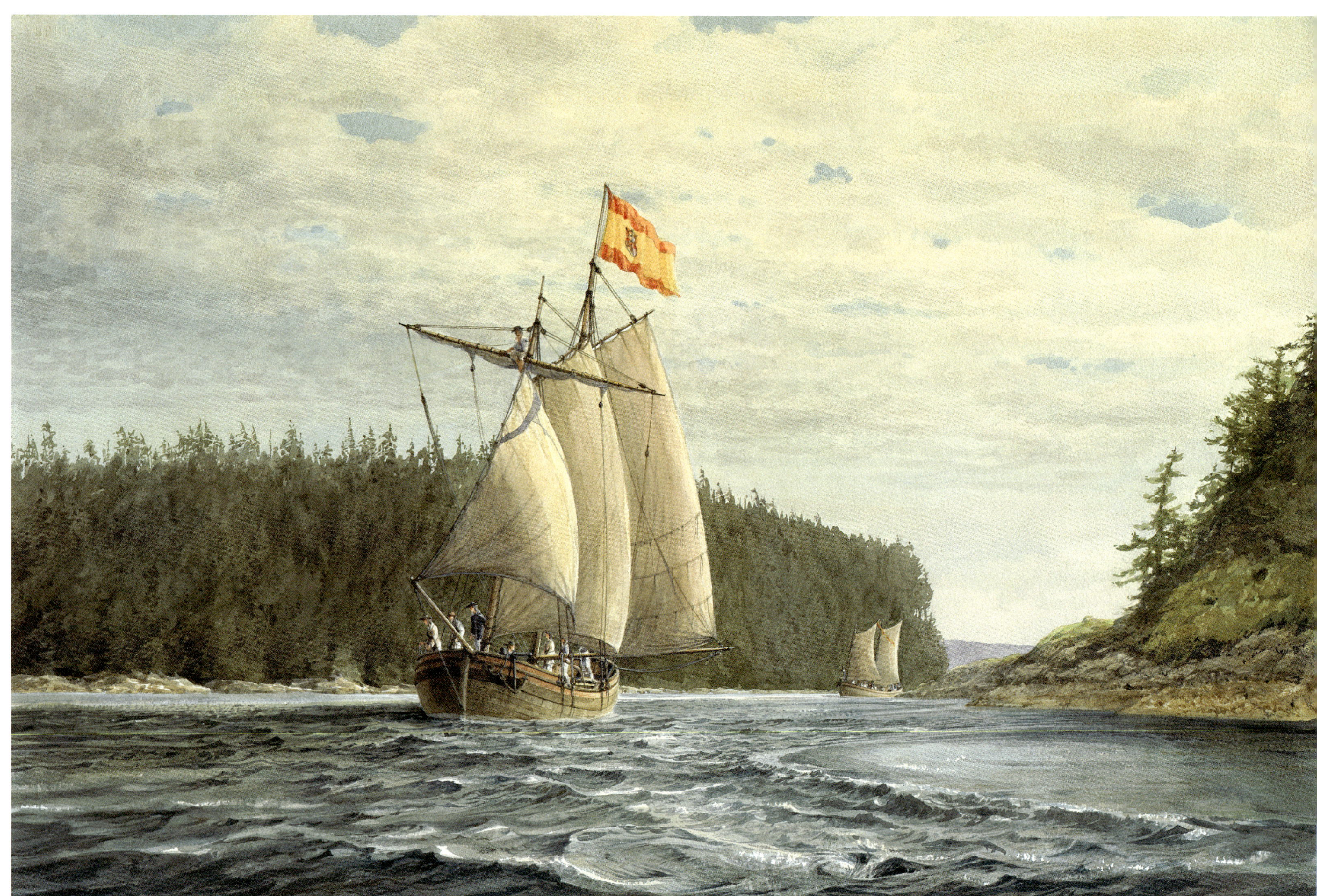

The first venture into what was later named the Strait of Georgia began on June 14, 1791, in *San Carlos*'s longboat and *Santa Saturnina*. Their chart shows that they sailed to the top of the Pender Islands, where they anchored for the night. The next day they sailed into Bedwell Bay and to the top of Plumper Sound, and in the evening they passed south of Saturna Island and into the Strait of Georgia. After anchoring overnight behind Patos Island, they sailed east towards the mainland, naming Sucia and Matia Islands. Anchors on their chart indicate that they examined the west side of Lummi Island and Bellingham Bay. They exited through the southern Gulf Islands and rejoined *San Carlos* at Port Discovery on June 24.

On July 1 a second excursion was begun by the two small boats. They sailed far enough in the strait, which they named Nuestra Señora del Rosario, to know that it was closed at the top, although they surmised correctly, because of the tidal actions, that there was another opening to the Pacific. Landmarks on both sides of the strait are easily identifiable on their chart, although they thought Point Roberts and Point Grey were islands. The achievements of all these surveys were compiled in one important chart, the *Carta que comprehende*. The following year, this chart was used aboard *Sutil* and *Mexicana* on their final and comprehensive survey of the waters east of Vancouver Island—Spain's last exploring expedition on the British Columbia coast.

George Vancouver's Voyages: Charting the Northwest Coast

The signing of the first Nootka Convention in 1790 averted war between England and Spain and allowed Britain to turn its attention to the Northwest Coast of America, where it was challenging Spain's claims of sovereignty. This event also set the stage for one of the most remarkable and underappreciated voyages of the eighteenth century.

In 1791 the British Admiralty launched a new expedition to the northeast Pacific to determine once and for all the existence of a northwest passage and to examine thoroughly the waters of the coast where Britain had a growing interest in the fur trade. Command of the new expedition and of the newly commissioned HMS *Discovery* was given to George Vancouver. He was ordered to

Santa Saturnina

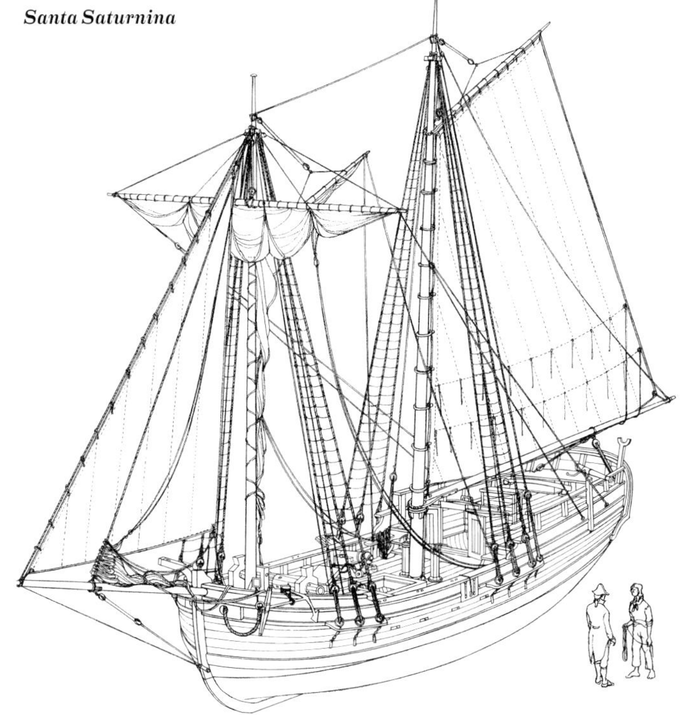

‹ ***Santa Saturnina* and longboat in Guemes Channel** (WC, 15″ × 22″) *The chart produced by* Santa Saturnina*'s commander, José María Narváez, in 1791 shows that these vessels likely sailed into Bellingham Bay through Rosario Strait, to the east of the San Juan Islands, then north into the Strait of Georgia past Lummi, Sucia and Patos Islands.*

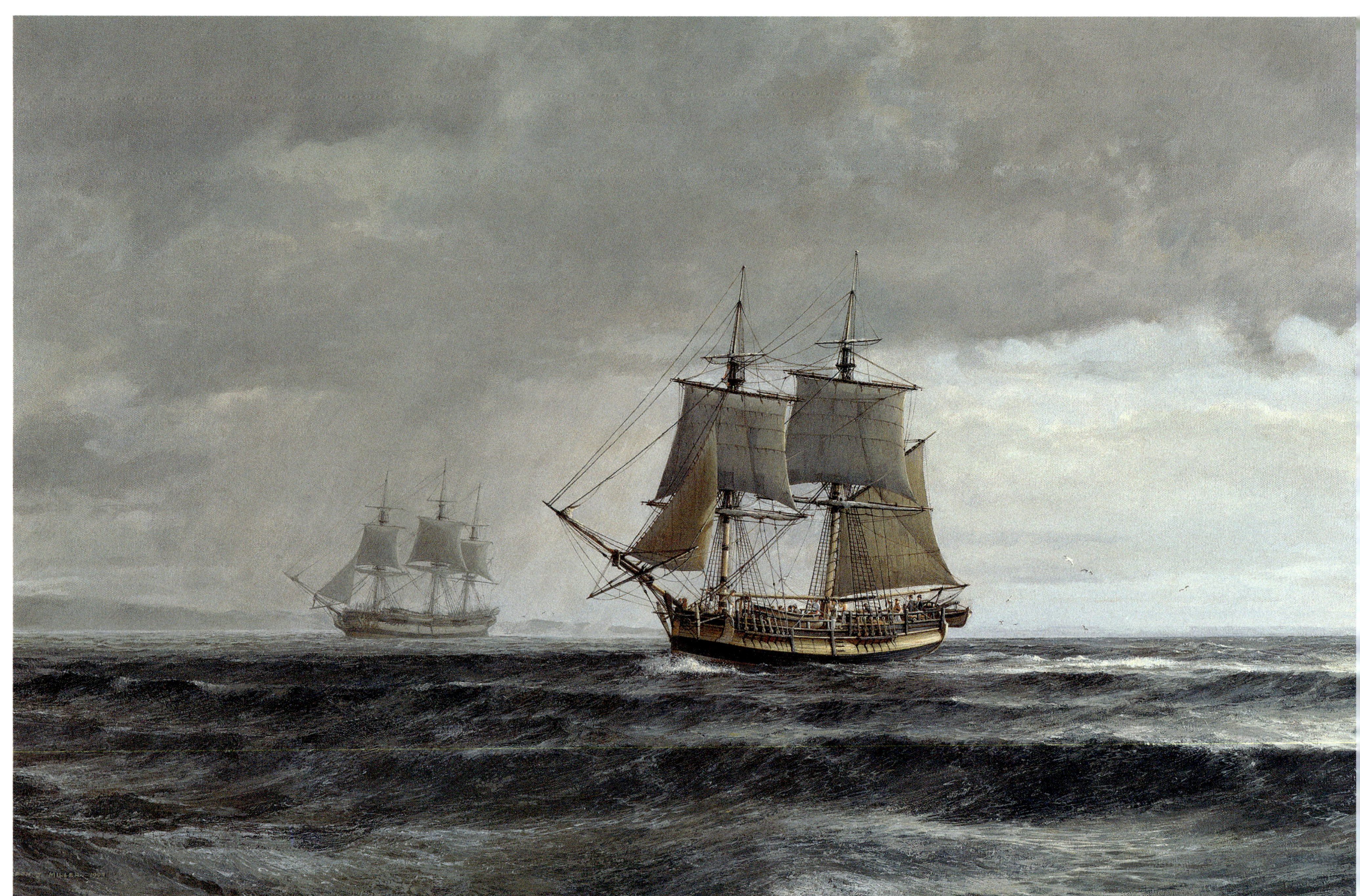

Landfall: *Discovery* and *Chatham* off California (Oil, 24″ × 36″)
The days before sighting land had been squally, with poor visibility. Unsure of their exact position, Discovery *and* Chatham *had been proceeding with caution. On April 16, 1792, Vancouver wrote, "The nearest shore was about two miles distant. The rain and fog with which the atmosphere was now loaded, precluded our seeing much of this part of the coast of New Albion. The shore appeared straight and unbroken, of a moderate height, with mountainous land behind."*

***Columbia*, *Discovery* and *Chatham* off the Olympic Peninsula** (WC, 15″ × 22″)
On April 28, 1792, off the Washington coast, about ten miles below Juan de Fuca Strait, Vancouver spoke with Captain Gray on the American ship Columbia. *Their three vessels sailed a short distance together to Cape Flattery, where Captain Gray turned back south.* Discovery *and* Chatham *headed east into Juan de Fuca Strait.*

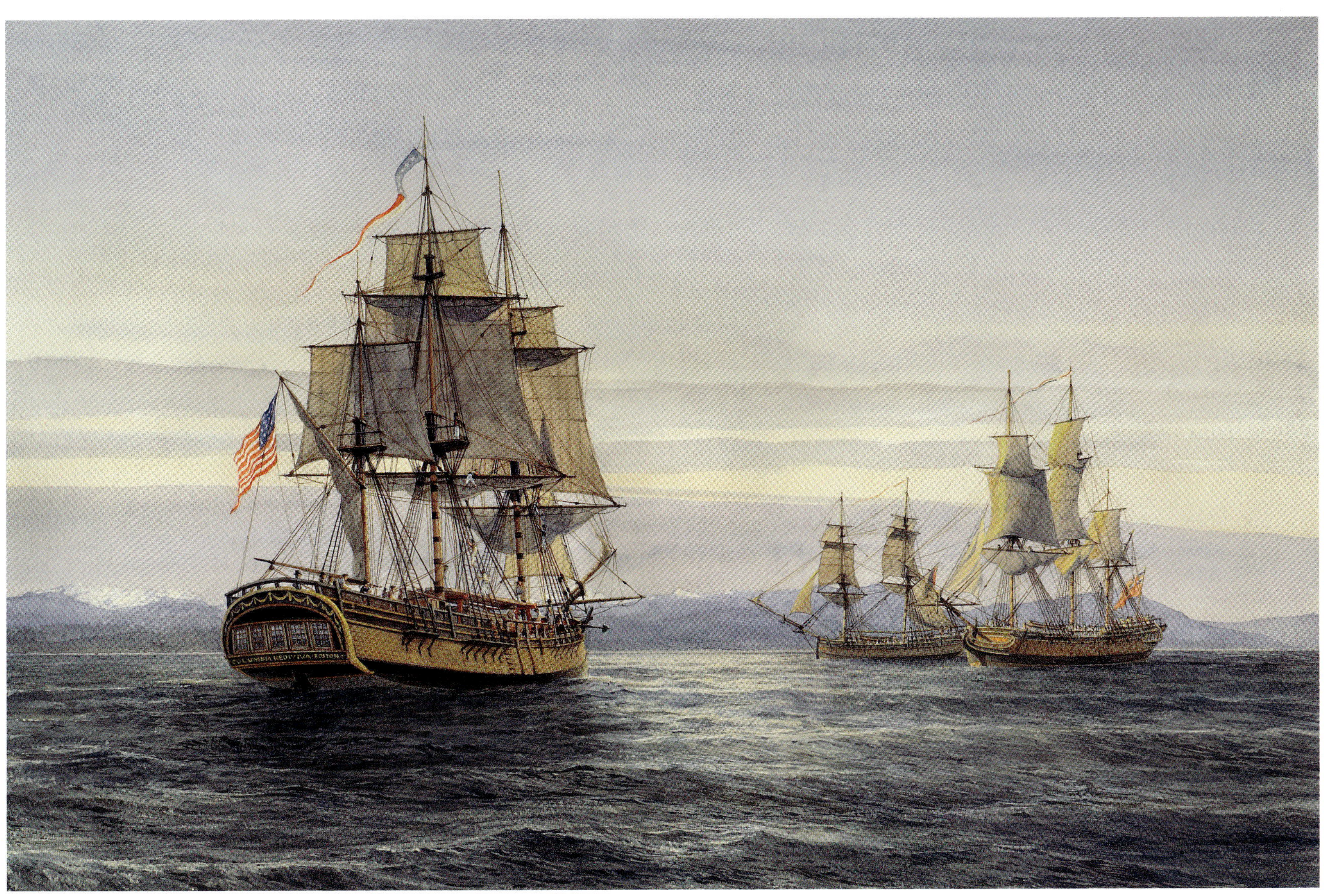

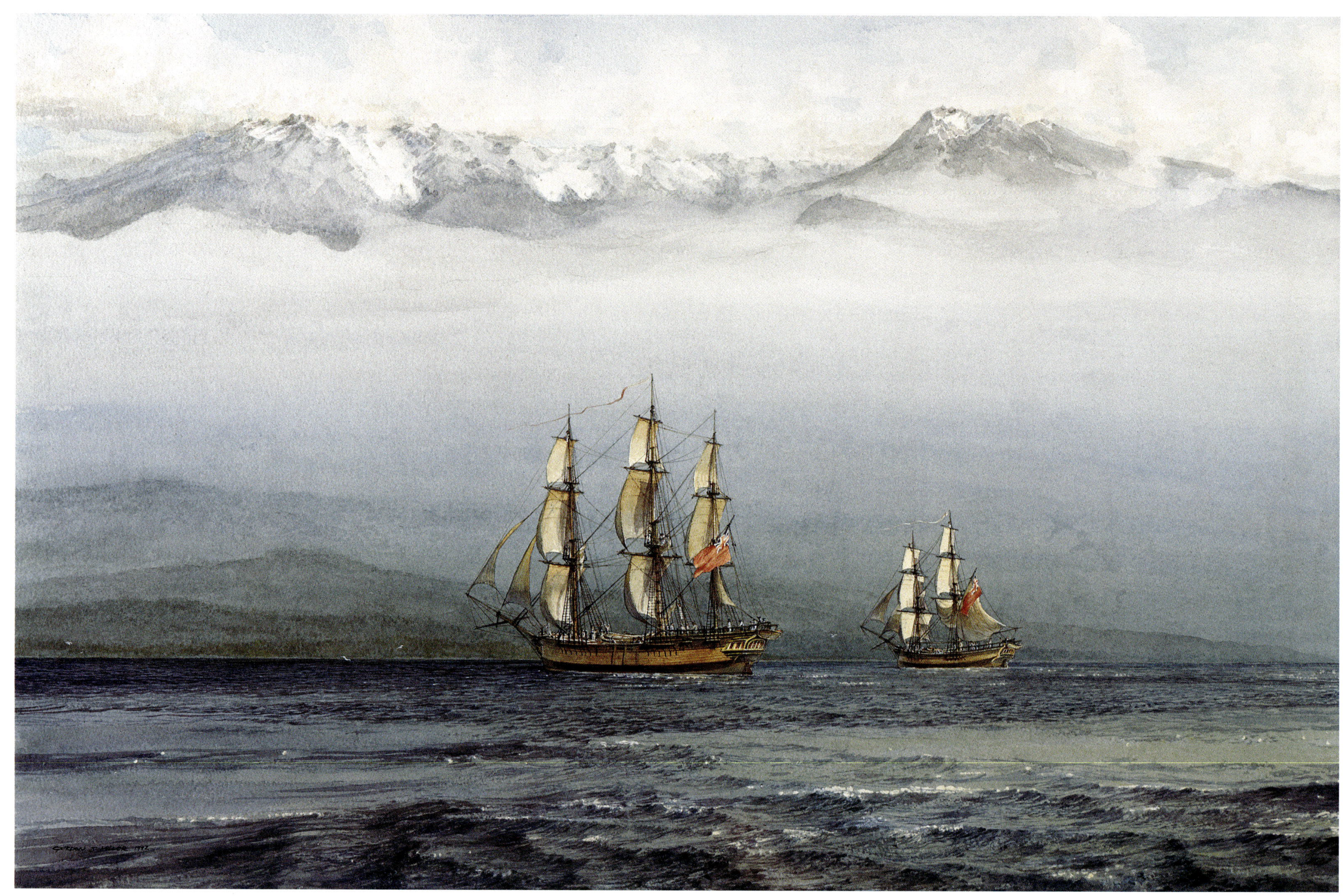

‹ ***Chatham* and *Discovery* in Juan de Fuca Strait, April 30, 1792** (WC, 22″ × 30″) *On April 30, 1792, Vancouver wrote in his journal, published after his death as* A Voyage of Discovery to the North Pacific and Round the World, *"As the day advanced, the wind, which as well as the weather was delightfully pleasant, accelerated our progress along the shore."*

˅ **Encounter off Spanish Banks: Vancouver meets Galiano and Valdés** (WC, 15″ × 22″) *"As we were rowing for Point Grey, purposing there to land and breakfast, we discovered two vessels at anchor under the land . . . on a nearer approach, it was discovered that they were a brig and a schooner, wearing the colours of Spanish vessels of war." Vancouver was welcomed aboard* Sutil *and* Mexicana *by the Spanish commanders, who gladly exchanged the results of their survey and informed him of the latest developments at Nootka, where the Spanish commander Juan Francisco de la Bodega y Quadra was awaiting him.*

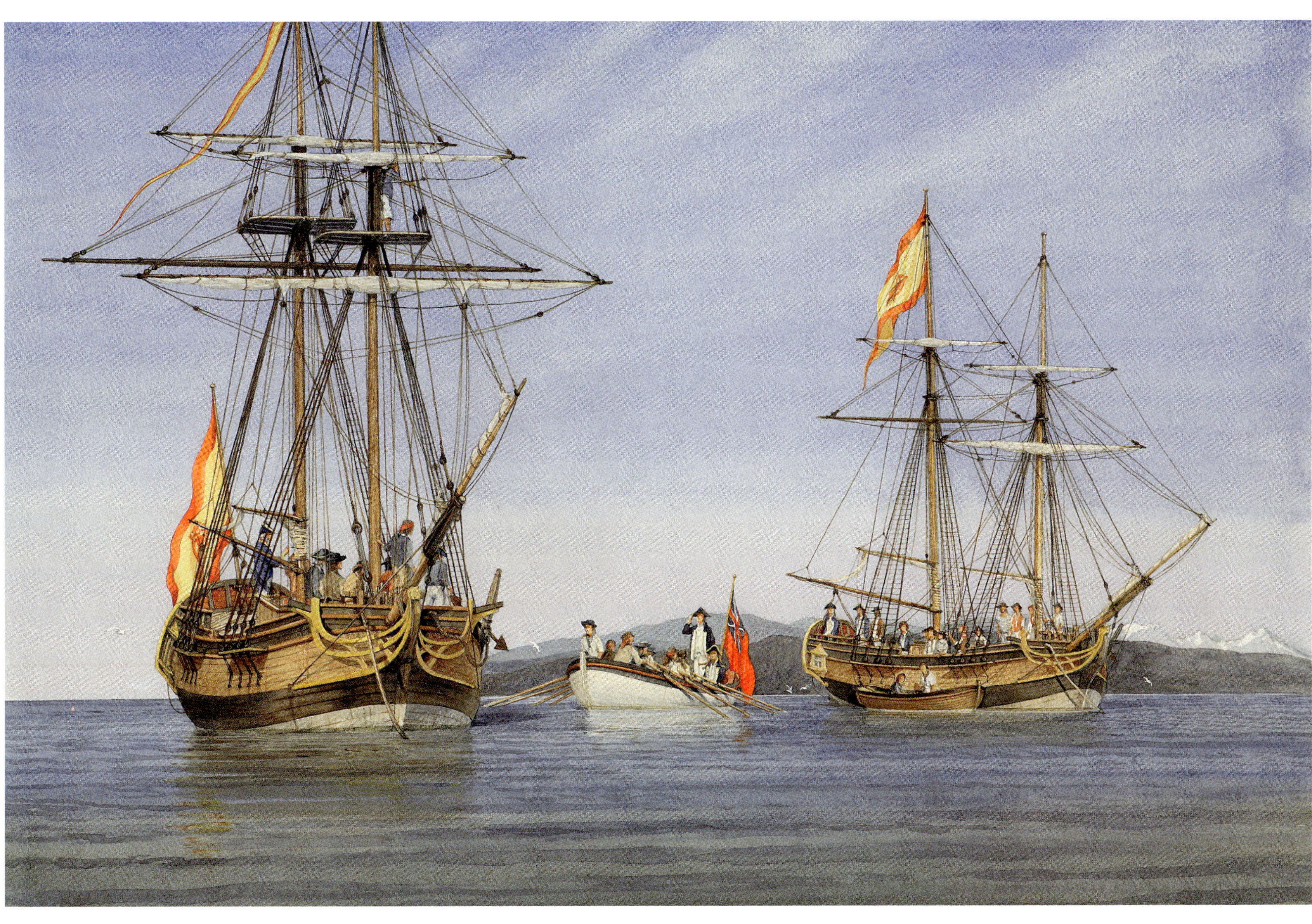

➤ **Friendly encounter off Point Grey, June 24, 1792** (WC, 30″ × 40″)
Vancouver remembered the encounter fondly: "With a fine breeze, and very pleasant weather, we sailed out of Birch Bay, on Midsummer morning: and with the wind from eastward, we directed our course up the gulf to the north-westward. About two in the afternoon of Sunday [June] 24th, [1792] we were joined by the Spanish vessels, who saluted by cheering. This was returned; after which their respective commanders favoured me with their company on board Discovery; *and we pursued our way up the gulf together."*

make a detailed survey of the west coast of America from California to the Aleutians and to meet the Spanish commissioner at Nootka to finalize the return of lands taken from English traders in 1789.

Vancouver had joined the navy at age fourteen, sailing first as a midshipman in *Resolution* on James Cook's second voyage to the Pacific and then as a midshipman in Clerke's *Discovery* on Cook's final voyage. Two weeks after his return from this latter voyage, Vancouver passed his exams for lieutenant. For the next ten years he served aboard a variety ships, ending his tour as first lieutenant on *Europa*. His lengthy experience in seamanship, navigation and surveying with Cook—the greatest seaman of his age—uniquely qualified him to lead the planned expedition to the Northwest Coast.

Discovery was accompanied by the brig *Chatham*, under command of Lieutenant William Broughton. The two ships sailed from Falmouth on April 1, 1791, and reached Hawaii via the Cape of Good Hope, the southwest coast of Australia, New Zealand and Tahiti. Vancouver made his landfall on the California coast on April 16, 1792, off Cape Mendocino, about 115 miles north of San Francisco Bay.

From there began a running survey to the north. On April 26 Vancouver noted the discharge from the Columbia River but chose to ignore its significance. Two days later he spoke with Captain Robert Gray on *Columbia;* their three vessels sailed together to Cape Flattery, where Gray turned back to the south to enter and name the Columbia River while *Discovery* and *Chatham* hauled to the east and entered Juan de Fuca Strait. The two ships charted their way along the south shore of the strait to Port Discovery, where they anchored on May 1.

In Port Discovery the real work began. While *Discovery* and *Chatham* were anchored, an observatory was erected ashore, and boats were provisioned and sent into Puget Sound to begin the survey. This became the routine that would be followed for the next three summers. The intricate nature of the coast meant the surveys had to be done from the ships' boats, which were dispatched from anchorages along the coast, often up to three weeks at a time. Twenty-hour days of rowing, in every kind of weather, were not uncommon. The men slept where and when they could, often in the boats. In this way, Vancouver charted accurately ten thousand miles of rugged, intricate coastline between Puget Sound and Cook Inlet.

It took five days to chart just Admiralty Inlet and Hood Canal. When the boats returned, *Discovery* sailed down close to the present site of Seattle, while *Chatham* examined the San Juan Islands before joining her. The rest of May and until June 4 was needed for the boats to complete the survey of Puget Sound.

They were then about to enter the waters explored the year before by José María Narváez and Juan Pantoja y Arriaga in *Santa Saturnina*. On June 10 they anchored in Birch Bay. That night their lights were seen by

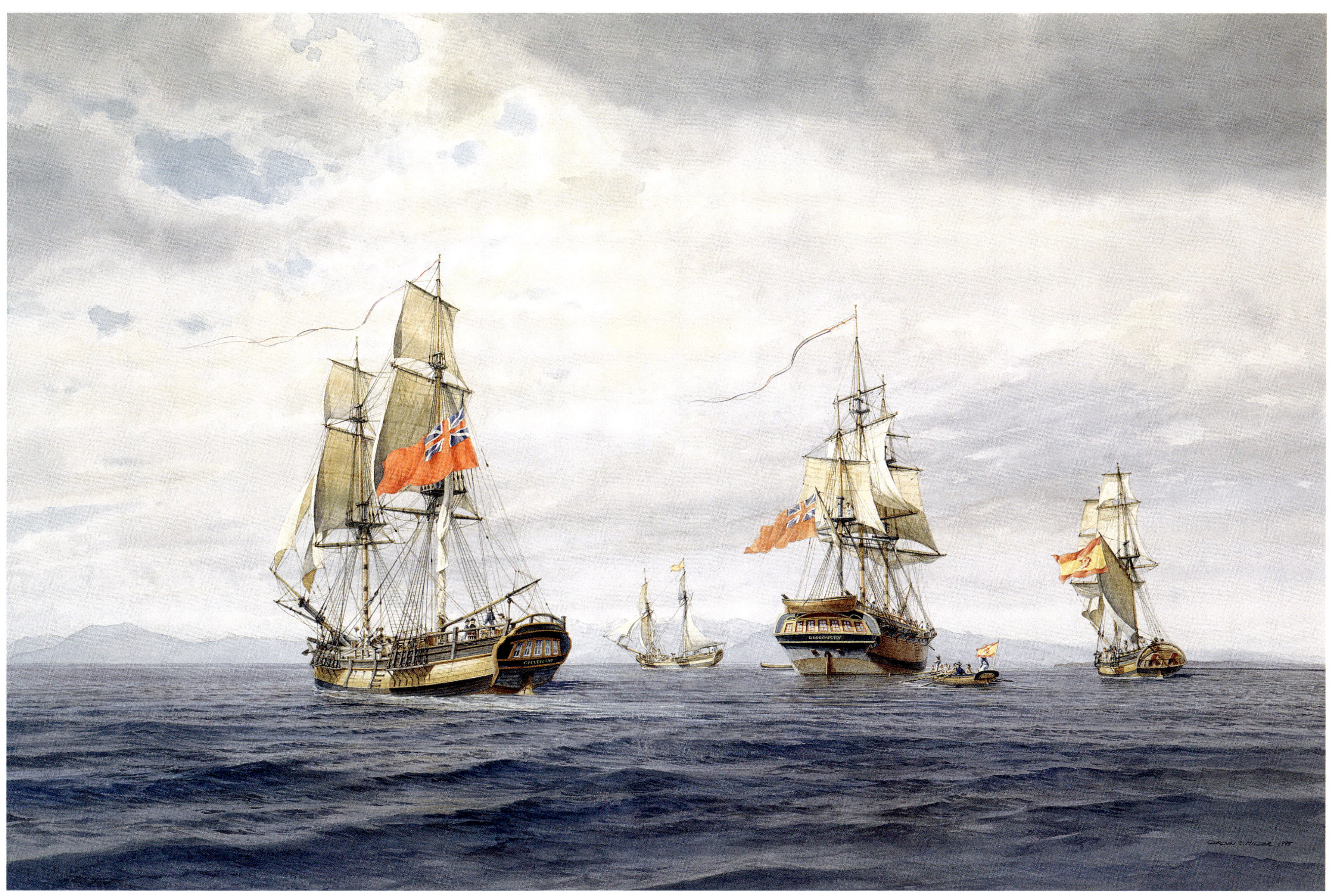
CHATHAM
DISCOVERY
GORDON T. MILLER 1995

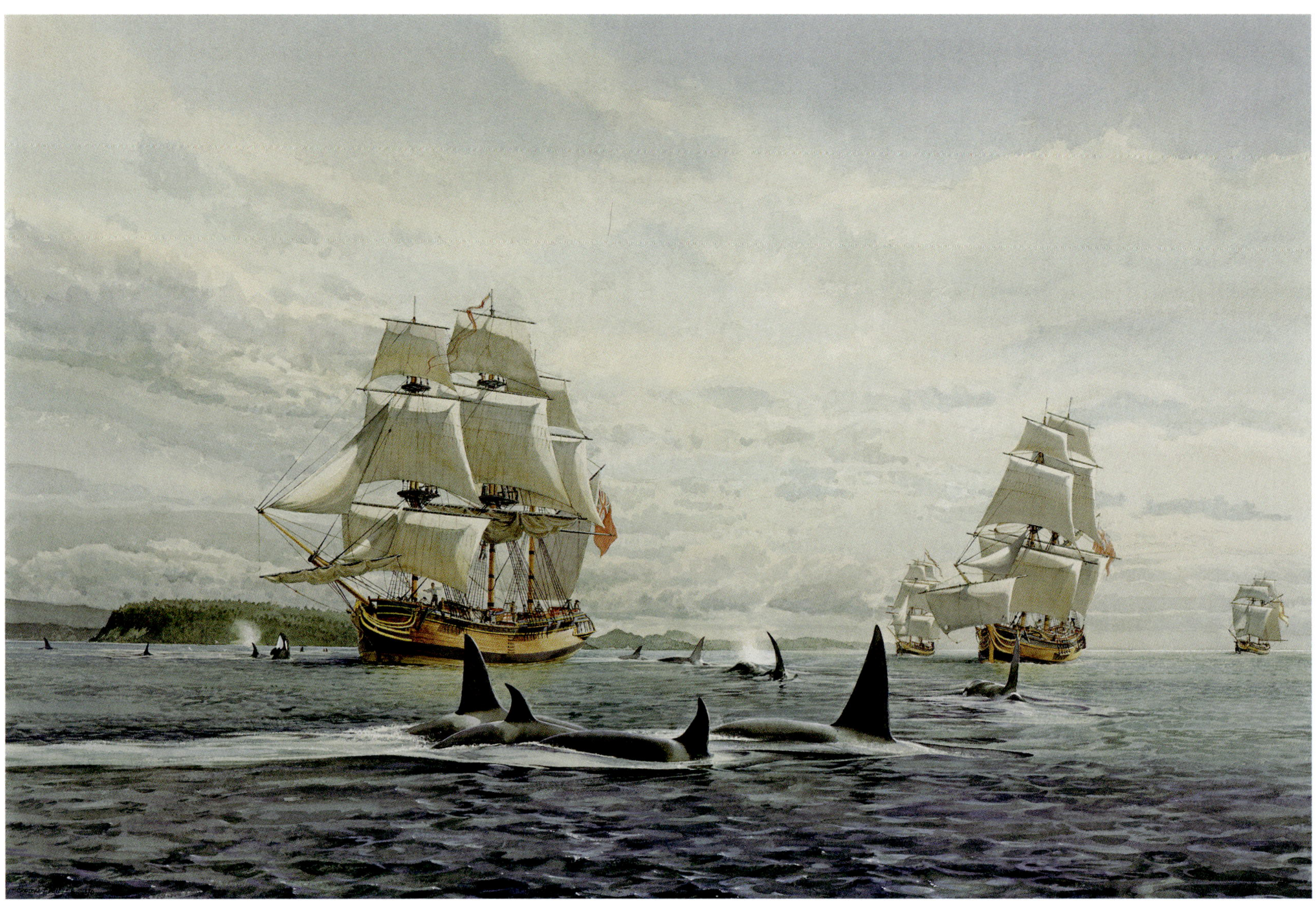

▲ **Off Thormanby Island, June 25, 1792** (WC, 30″ × 40″)
On June 25, 1792, the British ships Discovery *and* Chatham *and the Spanish ships* Sutil *and* Mexicana *made their way in company up the Strait of Georgia. In his journal George Vancouver wrote, "Until noon, the winds were light and baffling. In the course of the forenoon a great number of whales were playing about in every direction."*

➤ **Desolation Sound** (WC, 22″ × 30″)
On June 26, 1792, "At break of day… we found ourselves about half a mile from the shores of a high rocky island, whose general appearance was very inhospitable. Stupendous rocky mountains rising almost perpendicularly from the sea." Vancouver's ship had anchored in the dark behind Kinghorn Island, a very poor and unprotected anchorage.

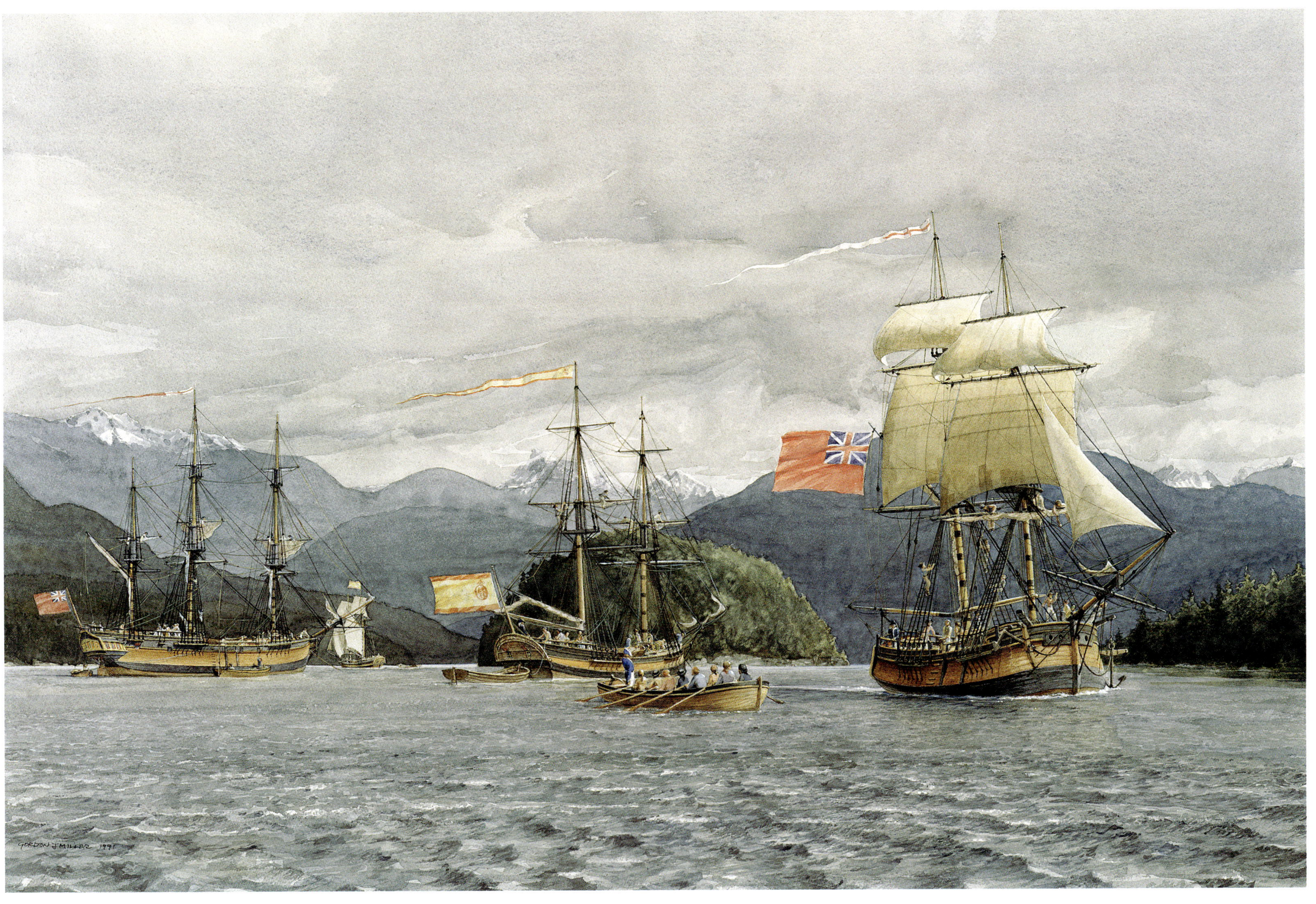
GORDON J MILLER 1991

Discovery off Cape Mudge (WC, 22″ × 30″)
George Vancouver noted in his journal: "Soon after mid-day we anchored to the northward of Point Mudge, in 37 fathoms water, on a bottom of black sand and mud. A very strong tide came from the northward . . ." His ships were visited by natives from the village, who exchanged fish and wild fruit for European articles. After dinner, Vancouver and some of the officers went ashore to visit the village and take a stroll on the beach.

Chatham entering Friendly Cove, August 28, 1792 (WC, 22″ × 30″)
The British ships Discovery *and* Chatham *arrived off Nootka on the morning of August 28, 1792. Fog in the sound prevented* Discovery *from entering, but it cleared earlier for* Chatham *and she sailed first into the anchorage. A Spanish launch escorted her in, and the fort and ship exchanged a volley of salutes. The process was repeated in the afternoon when the fog lifted, and* Discovery *was guided to the anchorage by a Spanish pilot. Another thirteen-gun salute was exchanged between the ship and the fort. So began more than six agreeable weeks of wining and dining.*

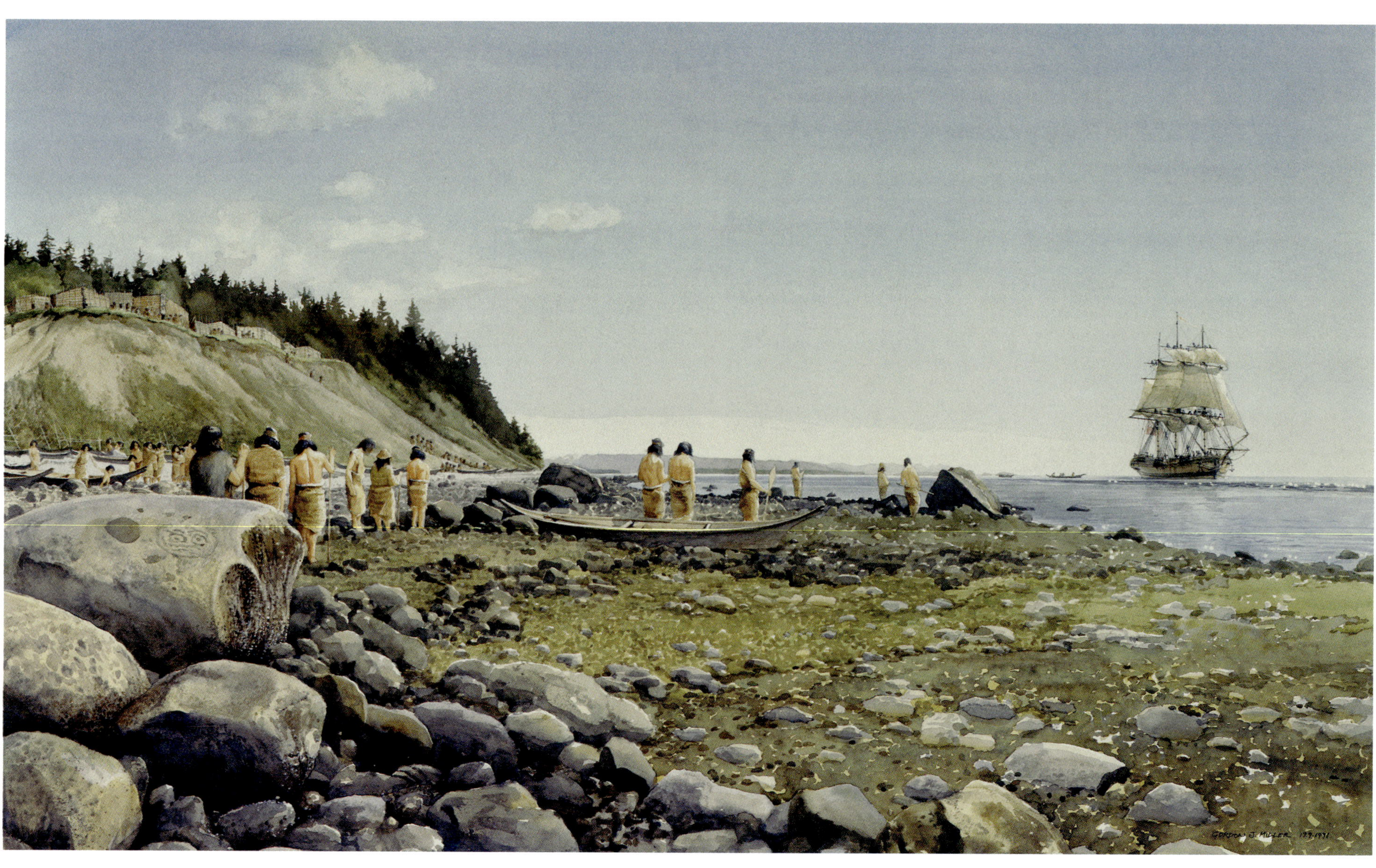

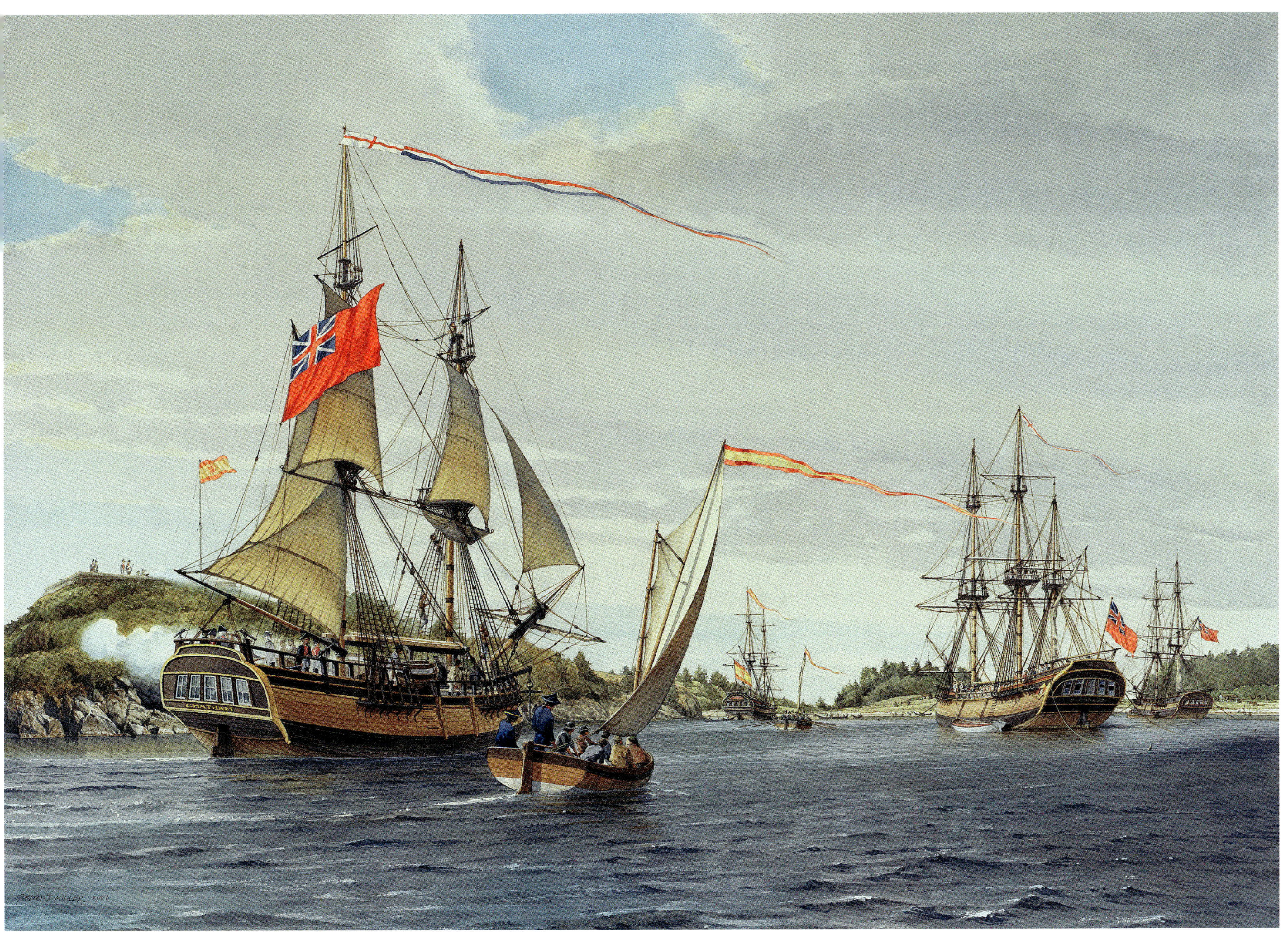
CHATHAM
GORDON T MILLER 2001

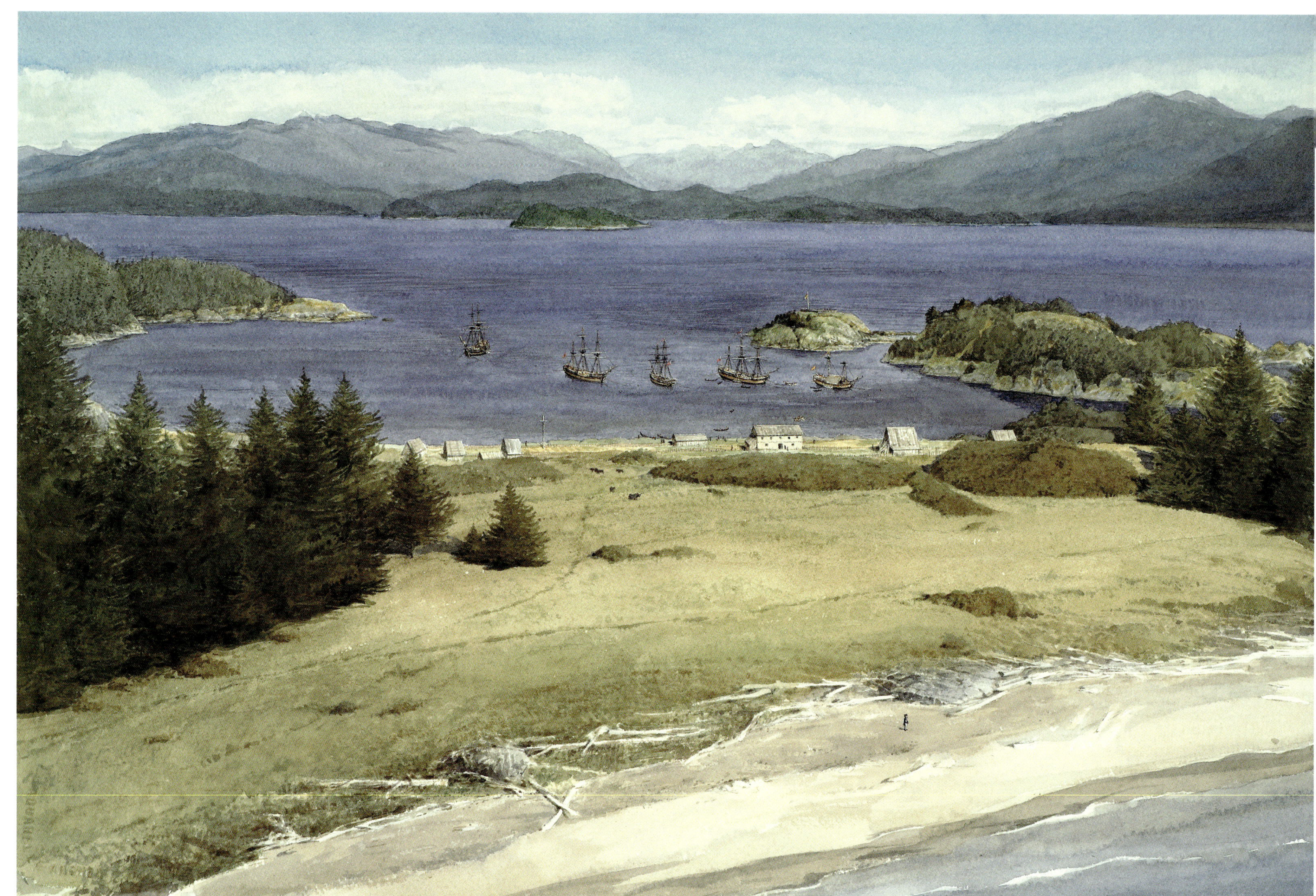

Dionisio Álcala Galiano and Cayetano Valdés from *Sutil* and *Mexicana*, the Spanish schooners that had been sent to finish the survey of the gulf begun the year before. The Spaniards anchored that night inside Point Roberts, and next day met up with *Chatham* out in the Strait of Georgia.

At the same time, Vancouver was about to embark on one of the most significant phases of the expedition. On the morning of June 11 he left Birch Bay in the pinnace, with Peter Puget in the launch. They examined Boundary Bay, rounded Point Roberts, sounded the extensive shoals at the mouth of the Fraser River and slept in the boats that night somewhere on the east side of Valdes Island. Next day the boats crossed the strait to Point Grey, entered the wide bay Vancouver named Burrard's Channel, passed through the first narrows and entered for the first time what was to become Vancouver Harbour. Accompanied by native canoes from a village on the north shore, they continued through the second narrows.

The next day they sailed out with a favorable breeze and continued for the following week to chart the coast from Howe Sound to the head of Jervis Inlet. The morning of June 22 was momentous. Returning to Birch Bay they came upon the two Spanish vessels under command of Álcala Galiano and Valdés. The cordial relations between Vancouver and the Spaniards at this meeting continued for all the time they remained in contact. Vancouver expressed privately in his journal his mortification at finding that they had preceded him in the gulf, but he also remarked at the unsuitability of their two vessels for the purpose in which they were employed.

The exhausting thirty-mile row back to Point Roberts took until after midnight, against two flood tides and a light southerly breeze, and it was eleven in the morning of June 23 before they rejoined the ships. They had covered some 330 miles in eleven and a half days, mostly by rowing. That day the observatory was struck and the ships unmoored, and at four the next morning *Discovery* and *Chatham* weighed and made sail.

By mid-afternoon, off Point Grey, they were joined by *Sutil* and *Mexicana*, and together the four ships proceeded up the gulf. On the night of June 24 they anchored behind Kinghorn Island in Desolation Sound, and next day shifted to a more secure anchorage in Teakerne Arm, where they embarked on the next extensive survey in the boats.

This was the last time the four ships would be together. On July 13 Vancouver weighed and took *Discovery* and *Chatham* around Cape Mudge (which Vancouver called Point Mudge) and up Johnson Strait, while the Spanish vessels took the mainland passages to the north. Vancouver meticulously charted the intricate coast to about 52°20′ north, where late in August they decided to terminate the work of the first season and turned south for Nootka. Vancouver arrived off Friendly Cove on August 28 and was guided in by a Spanish officer sent out to meet him. Fog had delayed their entrance, and *Chatham* had preceded *Discovery* by a few hours into the anchorage.

‹ **The Spanish establishment in Friendly Cove, 1792** (WC, 15″ × 22″)
Spain occupied Friendly Cove from 1790 to 1795, building a crude fortification on San Miguel Island at the entrance and a headquarters, barracks, blacksmith shop and gardens on the site that had been occupied by the Mowachaht village. At anchor in 1792 are Three Brothers, Daedalus, Chatham, Discovery *and* Activa.

➤ ***Jenny* off Vancouver Island** (WC, 11″ × 15″) *Summer was the foggy season on the Northwest Coast, weather that is often referred to in ships' logs as "thick." Fog restricted movement, but very few ships were lost in this period because of it.* Jenny *was an oddly rigged vessel from Bristol that was looking for furs on the coast in 1792 and again in 1794. In October 1792 she spent some time in the Columbia River at the same time that* Chatham *was surveying the river, and the two ships sailed together on November 10 from the anchorage in Baker Bay.*

Both ships exchanged salutes with the Spanish fort. Already anchored in the cove were the British store ship *Daedalus*, the trader *Three Brothers* and Quadra's *Activa*. *Sutil* and *Mexicana* arrived a few days later, but stayed only a day before departing for San Blas.

Daedalus was supposed to have carried instructions to Vancouver for the resolution of the land dispute, but they were no help. The difficult negotiations did not prevent establishment of cordial personal relations between Vancouver and Bodega y Quadra, and a great deal of visiting, dining and mutual firing of salutes typified the time of their stay. The natives complained about the constant noise, and Vancouver nearly ran out of powder.

Discovery and *Chatham* left Friendly Cove on October 12. On their way south, *Chatham* entered the Columbia River, formally took possession for Great Britain and charted the river's lower reaches. *Discovery* charted the coast south of Point Cabrillo on her way to San Francisco and Monterey, where she was the first non-Spanish vessel to call. Both vessels wintered in Hawaii. In the first summer's survey, Vancouver had accomplished much: he had accurately charted the west coast of North America between latitudes 39° and 52° north, proven the insularity of Vancouver Island, established friendly and useful relations with the Spaniards and proved conclusively that Juan de Fuca Strait was not the entry to the Northwest Passage.

The next year *Discovery* and *Chatham* continued where they had left off the year before, surveying the coast up to 56° north, including the Queen Charlotte Islands. This area of coast is so intricate and full of islands that although in four months the two ships charted hundreds of miles of shoreline, they advanced the survey northward only a little over three hundred miles. They completed the year's work on September 20 and sailed two days later, passing down the west side of the Queen Charlotte Islands on the way to Nootka. The return to Hawaii for the winter again involved a running survey of the California coast, this time down to 30° north on the Baja Peninsula.

The 1794 surveys began in April off Kodiak Island and in "Cook's River," which Vancouver followed to its head, proving the last likely entrance to a northwest passage to be a dead end. *Discovery* and *Chatham*, often separately, charted the coast, islands and inside waters from Cook Inlet down to Cape Decision, the 1793 point of departure. It was another difficult year surveying an intricate maze of channels and inlets, often in poor weather and despite the presence of hostile Tlingit. On August 19 all the work was done. Their final anchorage, on the southeast side of Baranof Island, Vancouver named Port Conclusion. On his return Vancouver stopped at Nootka, sailed to Monterey for supplies, and on December 2 left the Northwest Coast for the last time. *Discovery* anchored in the Thames on October 20, 1795, almost four and a half years after leaving Falmouth.

Vancouver had the misfortune of having aboard *Discovery* midshipman Thomas Pitt, later to become Lord

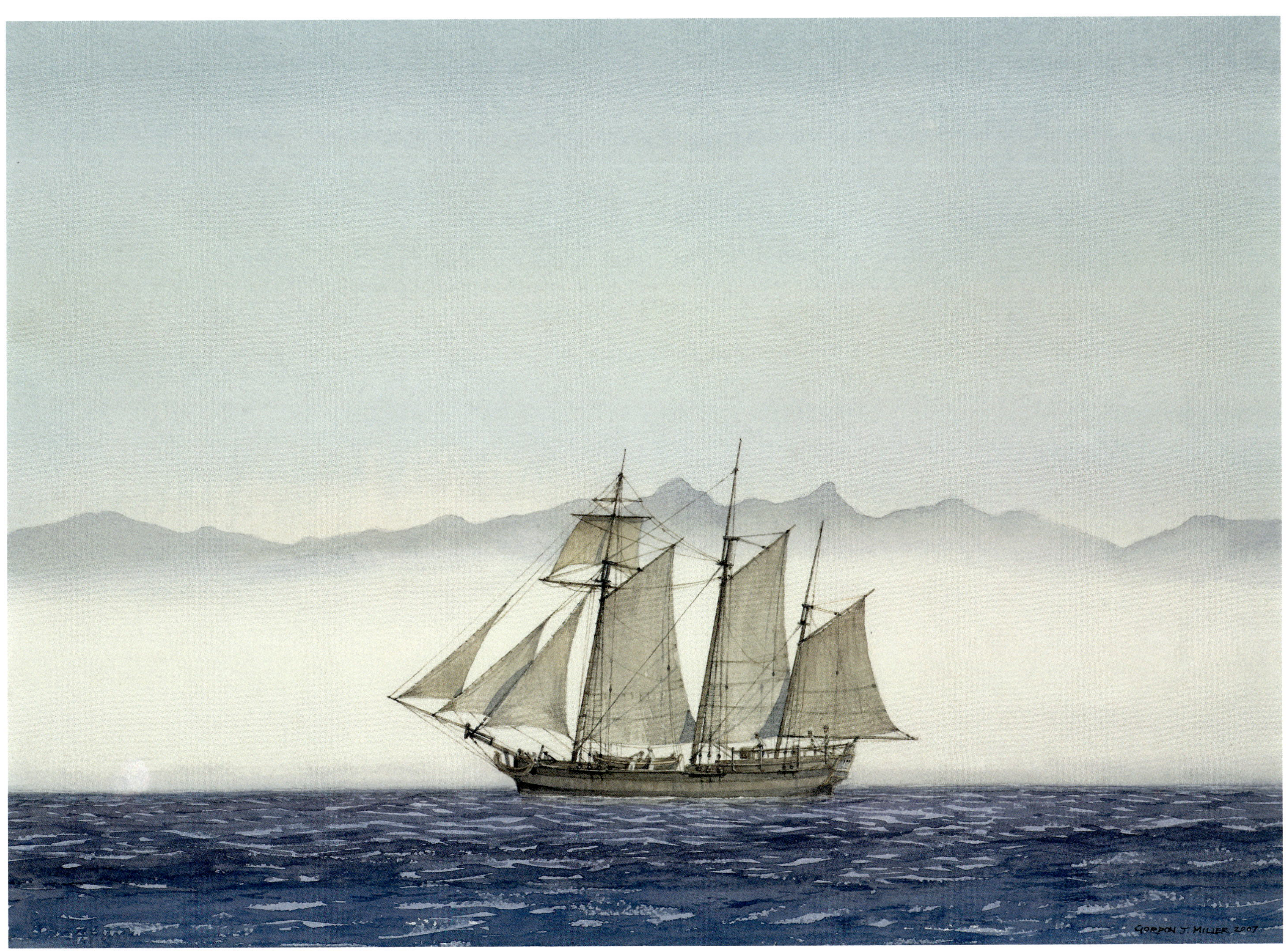
GORDON J. MILLER 2007

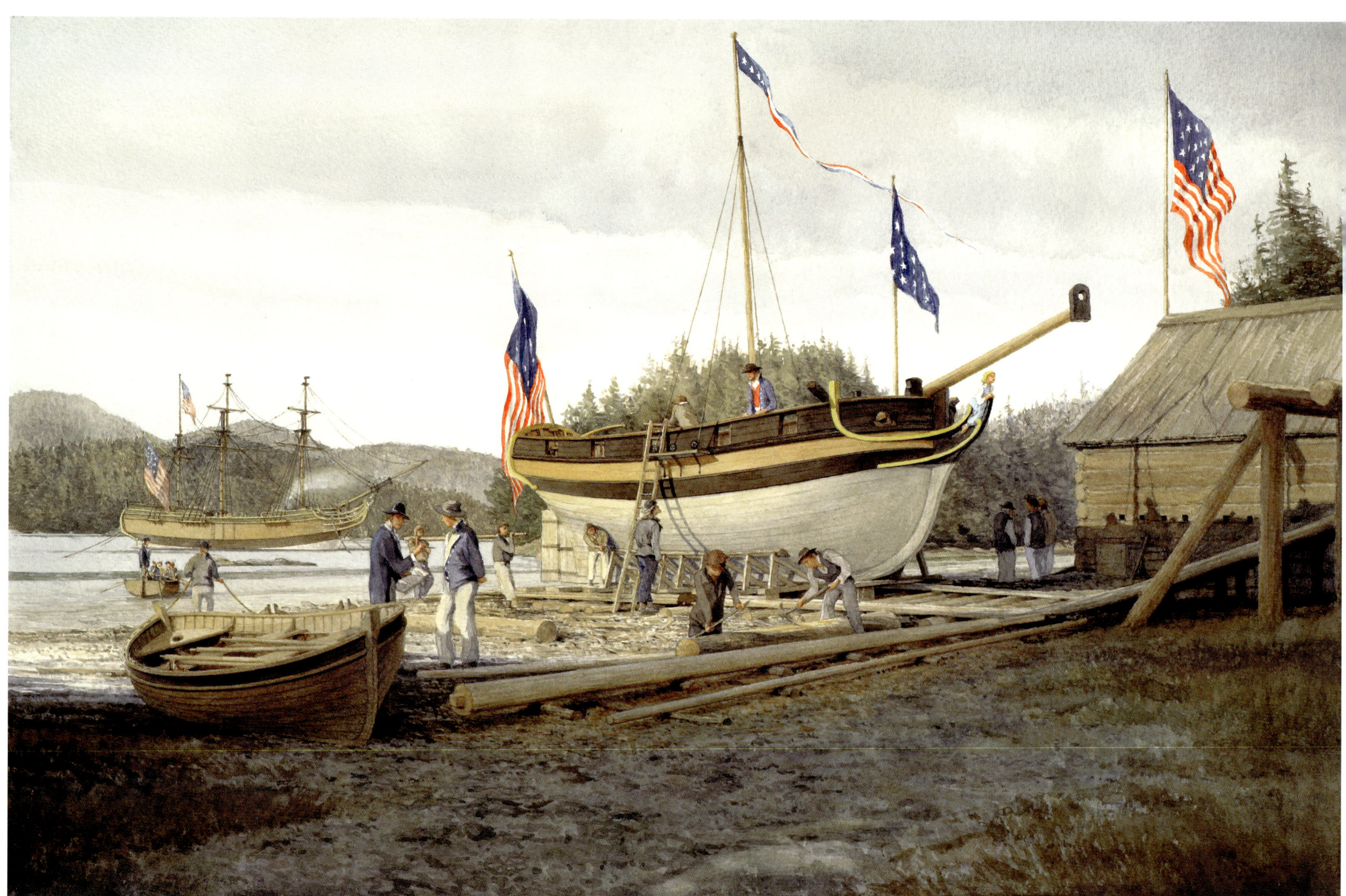

Camelford. Young Pitt took unkindly to taking orders from anyone, especially a captain he believed to be inferior by birth. A troublemaker on the voyage, he waged a bitter and public battle against Vancouver on their return to England, where he had powerful connections. One cousin of Pitt's was the prime minister of Great Britain, another the lord of the Admiralty, and a brother-in-law was minister of foreign affairs. Unfortunately, Pitt's repeated demeaning attacks focused attention away from Vancouver's real accomplishments and the acclaim he was entitled to.

Vancouver's was one of the last and one of the greatest Pacific voyages. He surveyed the last uncharted section of Australia's south coast, charted parts of the Hawaiian Islands and was instrumental in negotiating the islands' accession to Great Britain. When his voyage was finished, there was no longer hope of finding a navigable passage through North America, and the entire coast from Baja California to Cook Inlet was shown, in exquisite detail, on charts that were not improved upon for a century. Although Vancouver's achievements were largely dismissed at the time, he is finally now beginning to receive the recognition he deserves as a great navigator.

Sea Change: The End of an Era

The 1792 expeditions of Álcala Galiano and Valdés, and the Malaspina visit in 1791, marked the end of 250 years of Spanish exploration by sea of North America's west coast. Except for the many Spanish names left on coastal landmarks, Spain's withdrawal from Nootka in 1794 was also the end of any Spanish presence on the Northwest Coast. After George Vancouver sailed for home in 1794, the only government still actively interested in the area was Russia's. The British, French and Spanish navies all became engaged elsewhere—dealing with Napoleon, with revolution in France and with rebellion in the British colonies in America. The Northwest Coast was left to the fur traders.

The maritime fur trade continued much as before for another twenty years, with American vessels gradually taking over from the British until after 1805 when only ships flying the Stars and Stripes were on the coast. It was a brief period of fluorescence of native art and culture. Before the decline of the sea otter population ended that trade and whole villages were decimated by smallpox, some well-positioned Haida chiefs became very wealthy, and European tools and material caused an explosion of ceremonial artifacts, pole raising and house building. By 1810 the slaughter by the fleets of many nations had reduced sea otters to near extinction, and land animals began to replace them as an item of trade. The nature of the activity also gradually changed. Ships began to overwinter and trade all year, and some began to supply the poorly provisioned Russian posts in Alaska with food and trade goods.

Events on the other side of the continent were soon to drastically change the character of life and trade on the west coast. In the century after the granting of its charter,

‹ **Launch of *Adventure*, Clayoquot Sound, February 1792** (WC, 15″ × 22″)
Captain Robert Gray spent the winter of 1791 in Clayoquot Sound, where he fortified a base and built the sloop Adventure, *the third ship to be launched in the Pacific Northwest, in February 1792. After spending the 1792 season trading up and down the coast,* Adventure *was sold later that year to the Spanish at Nootka.*

▾ *Union* and Nuu-chah-nulth canoes off Vancouver Island (WC, 22″ × 30″)
The Nuu-chah-nulth occupied the outer coast of Vancouver Island from Cape Cook to the south coast of Juan de Fuca Strait. Union *was a small New England sloop of about ninety tons, setting a single square topsail for downwind work. She spent the summer of 1795 on the Northwest Coast, returning to Boston via China on July 8, 1796, and becoming the first American sloop to sail around the world. Remarkably, her captain, John Boit, was just nineteen years old when* Union *set sail for the Northwest Coast.*

▸ Arrival of New Bedford whaler *Pacific*, Lahaina Roads, 1837 (WC, 22″ × 30″)
The first whaling voyage to the Pacific was made by the British ship Amelia *in 1788. It was so successful that the world whaling fleets soon followed, reaching a peak in 1846, when the American fleet alone numbered 736 vessels. Just as they had been for the early explorers and traders, the Hawaiian Islands became the favored winter destination for the Pacific whaling fleets. Honolulu attracted the greatest number of whalers, but Lahaina was equally important, and in 1846 five hundred ships were counted in Lahaina Roads alone. The Pacific whale fishery collapsed in the 1860s, partly due to the discovery of gold in California.*

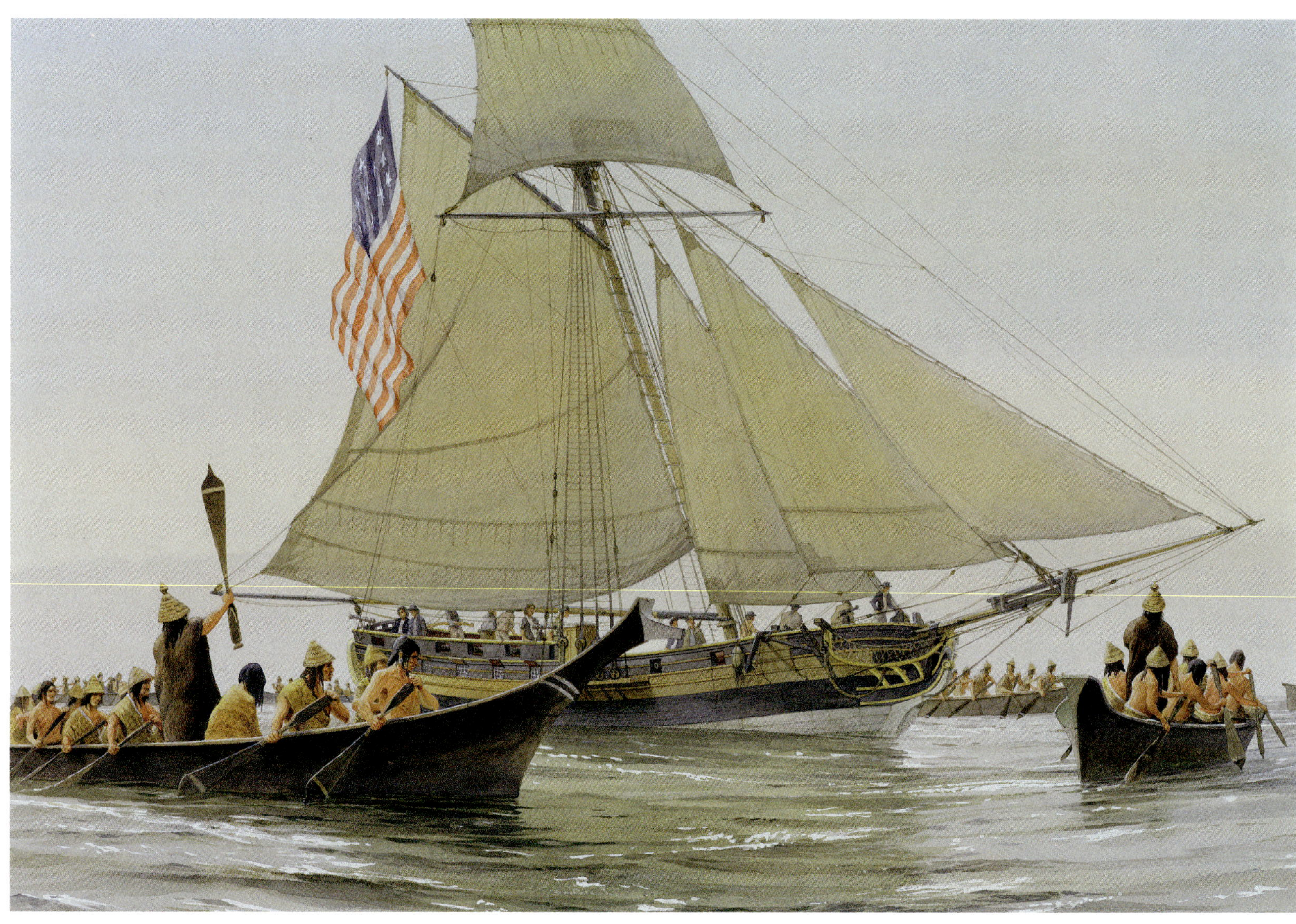

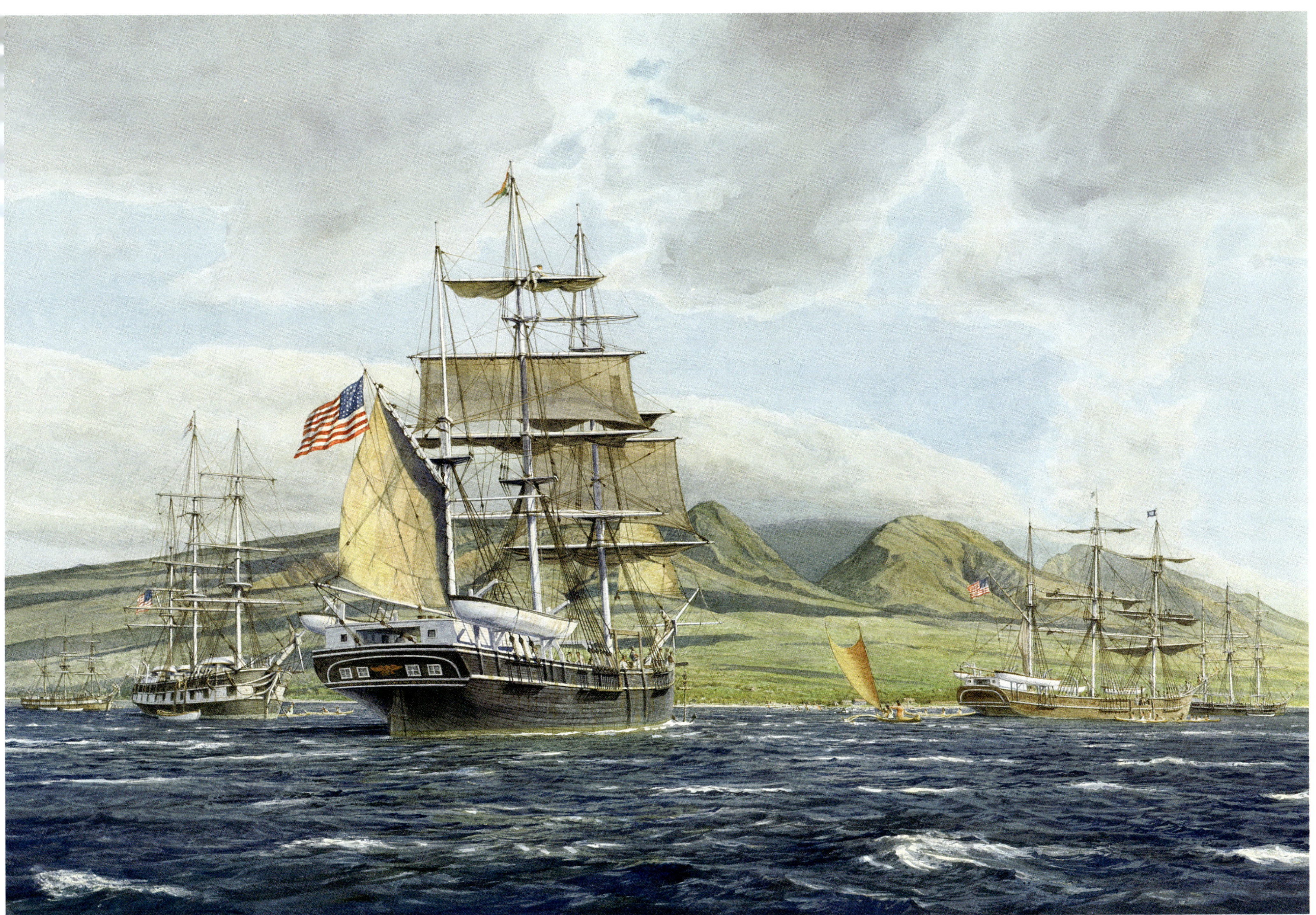

› Beaver *as she would have looked the first year on the Northwest Coast.*

›› ***Beaver* crossing the Columbia River bar, June 26, 1836** (WC, 15″ × 22″)
Beaver, *rigged as a brigantine, made her voyage to the Columbia River under canvas alone. Her engines, boiler and paddle wheels were reassembled at Fort Vancouver, and on May 16, 1836, the engineers got the steam up and tried the engines, which were found to work very well. In the following days they made several trial runs on the river, and being satisfied that all was well, anchored in Baker Bay to wait for favorable conditions to cross the bar. From* Beaver*'s log: "June 26th at 1 p.m. weighed anchor and ran towards the bar. At 2 crossed the bar."*

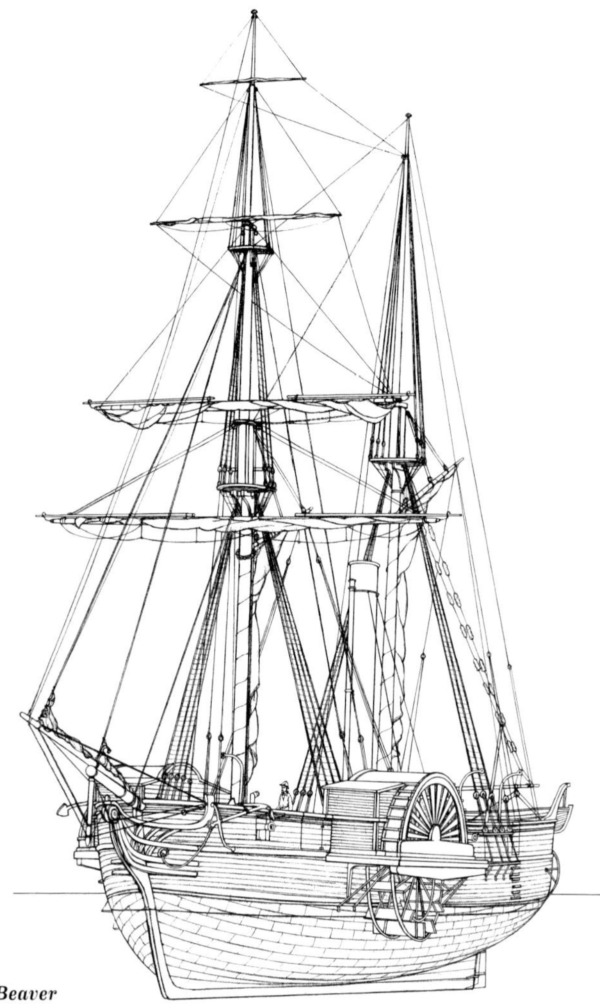

Beaver

the Hudson's Bay Company rose to dominate the fur trade over vast areas of the continent. The North West Company, with headquarters in Montreal, was formed in 1779 to compete, and these energetic and ambitious Scotsmen expanded to the west and north, creating permanent trading posts as they went. Wishing to ship furs directly to China, they began to seriously look for overland routes to the Pacific. In 1793 Alexander Mackenzie reached tidewater at Bella Coola, becoming the first European to reach the west coast by land. He was followed in 1808 by Simon Fraser, who paddled to the mouth of what he hoped was the Columbia, but was in fact the river that would be named after him.

For a short time the Columbia River was the center of intense international rivalry. The young and spirited United States was beginning to flex its muscles. By what it considered its "manifest destiny," the new nation intended to extend its territories to the Pacific. Meriwether Lewis and William Clark were sent to find the mouth of the Columbia River, reached it in 1805, built a small post they called Fort Clatsop and spent a miserable winter there before returning to the east. John Jacob Astor's newly formed American Fur Trade Company briefly occupied the site and named it Fort Astoria, but was unable to support it. Fearing abandonment or attack by the British, the Americans sold the site and all the furs collected to the North West Company in 1813. Renamed Fort George, this became the first permanent British settlement on the west coast south of Alaska and north of San Francisco.

Fur would continue to be an item of commerce until the 1850s, but dramatic changes were on the way. In 1821 the Hudson's Bay Company absorbed the rival North West Company. "The Bay" became the dominant commercial force and de facto British authority from the St. Lawrence

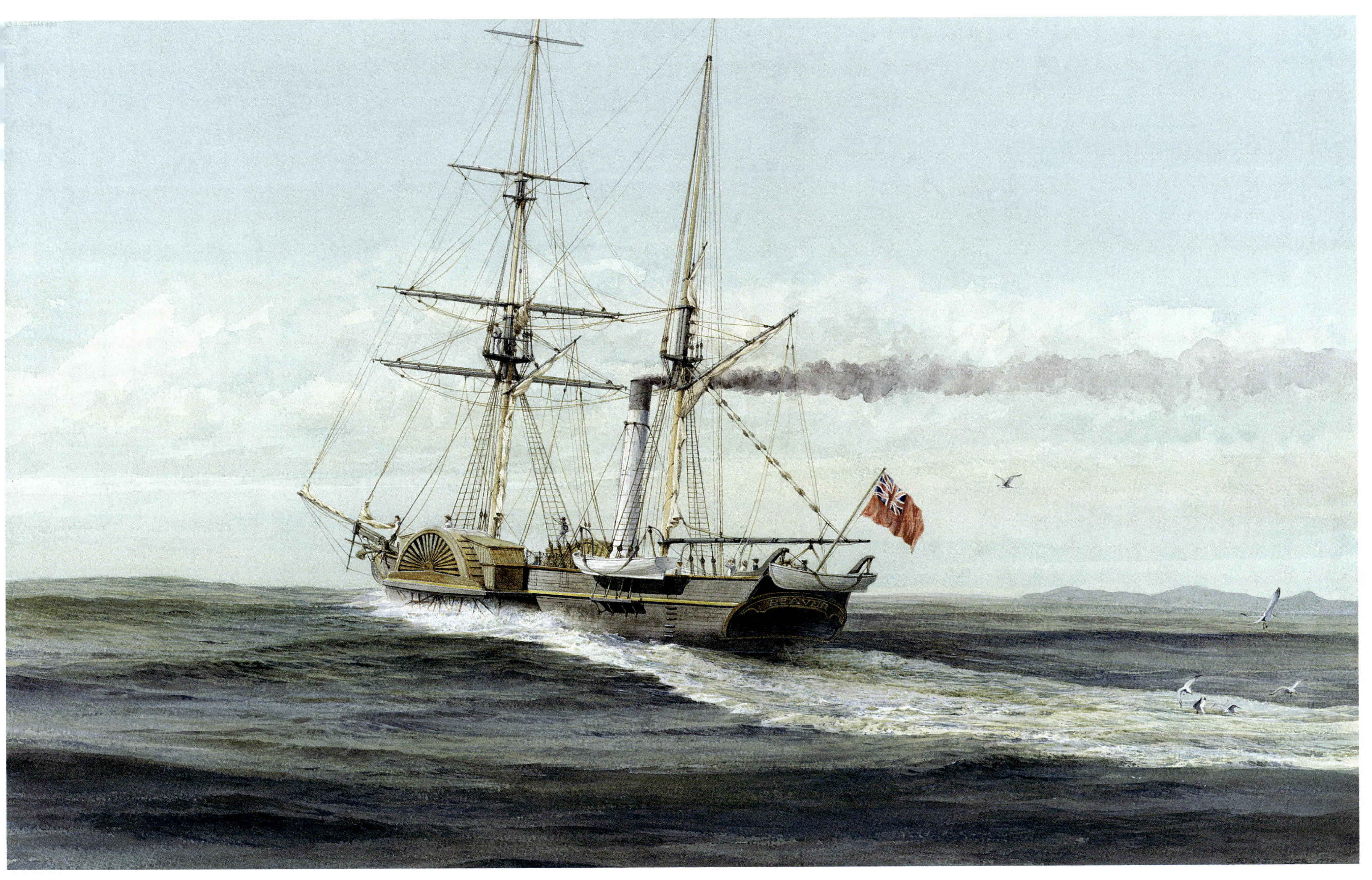

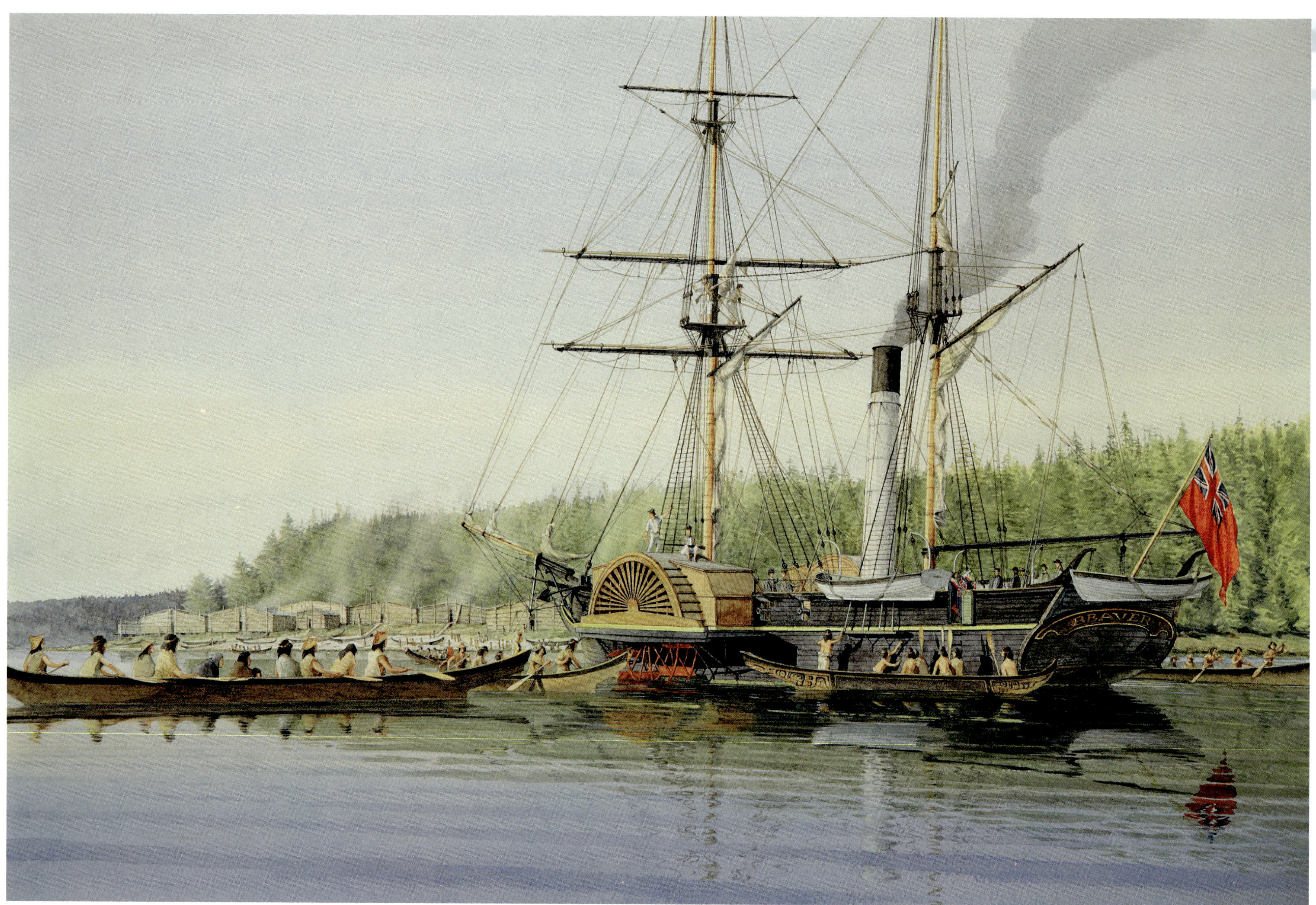
BEAVER

River to the Pacific Ocean and from the Columbia River to the Arctic. Governor George Simpson completely reorganized operations on the west coast. "Factories" were built at Fort Vancouver on the Columbia, Fort Nisqually on Puget Sound, Fort Langley on the Fraser River, Fort Victoria on Vancouver Island and Forts McLoughlin and Simpson farther up the coast. The company presence effectively ended American domination of the maritime fur trade and altered the pattern of native life. Its forts attracted natives who congregated there for trade and protection from their enemies and who became accustomed to the idea of the permanent presence of foreigners. The company relied on native labor, especially in the extensive gardens at Fort Langley, which supplied produce for northern posts.

The Hudson's Bay Company operated a Marine Department with a fleet of sailing vessels. The ships regularly supplied the forts and engaged in trade with the natives but were hostage to the winds and currents of the intricate coastline. The first vessel, the brig *William & Ann,* arrived at Fort Vancouver in April 1825, traded on the coast until September, then sailed for London. She returned, but in 1829 was lost with all hands and most of her cargo on the Columbia River bar. Her replacement, the brig *Isabella,* was lost on the bar as well on her maiden voyage in 1830. At Simpson's request, the directors in London in 1834 came to the sensible conclusion that a powered vessel would be more practical. This led to the ordering of *Beaver,* the first steamship on America's Pacific coast.

Meanwhile, American settlers had been moving southwest into Spanish territories and were beginning to flood into the Columbia River valley. The Hudson's Bay Company, realizing its posts on the Columbia would become American, moved its coastal headquarters to Fort Victoria in 1843. At this time, until it was ceded to the United States in 1848, California was largely a Spanish-Mexican territory of large haciendas. In 1849 Americans found gold at Sutter's Mill, and the stampede was on. Three hundred thousand miners flooded into the territory, half by sea, and San Francisco Bay was choked with ships, abandoned by crews desperate to reach the gold fields. This huge pool of armed labor was poised to descend on the next gold discovery.

Fearing the Americans might come north and claim more territory, Britain moved to send settlers to Vancouver Island and in 1849 declared the island a British colony. The Hudson's Bay Company was still the effective government but promised to bring out settlers and pay them to get established. When gold was discovered on the Fraser River in 1858, James Douglas, the company's chief factor at Fort Victoria, faced a tidal wave of Californians landing by the shipload at the little post and attempting to get to the gold deposits on the river. Alarmed, Britain quickly established a new colony on the mainland, and

◂ *Beaver* in Beaver Cove, northeast Vancouver Island (WC, 15″ × 22″)
On her first year in service Beaver *steamed from Puget Sound to Alaska, quickly demonstrating her least desirable characteristic: she consumed forty cords of wood a day. Hudson's Bay Company Governor George Simpson commented that it "takes about the same time to cut the wood as to burn it, she is at least as much at anchor as she is underway."* Beaver's *coastal career began in earnest in 1837, when she probed the deep mainland inlets to their ends to contact the natives as close to the interior as possible. This would be the first contact most of them had with a steamship, and no doubt it made a powerful impression.*

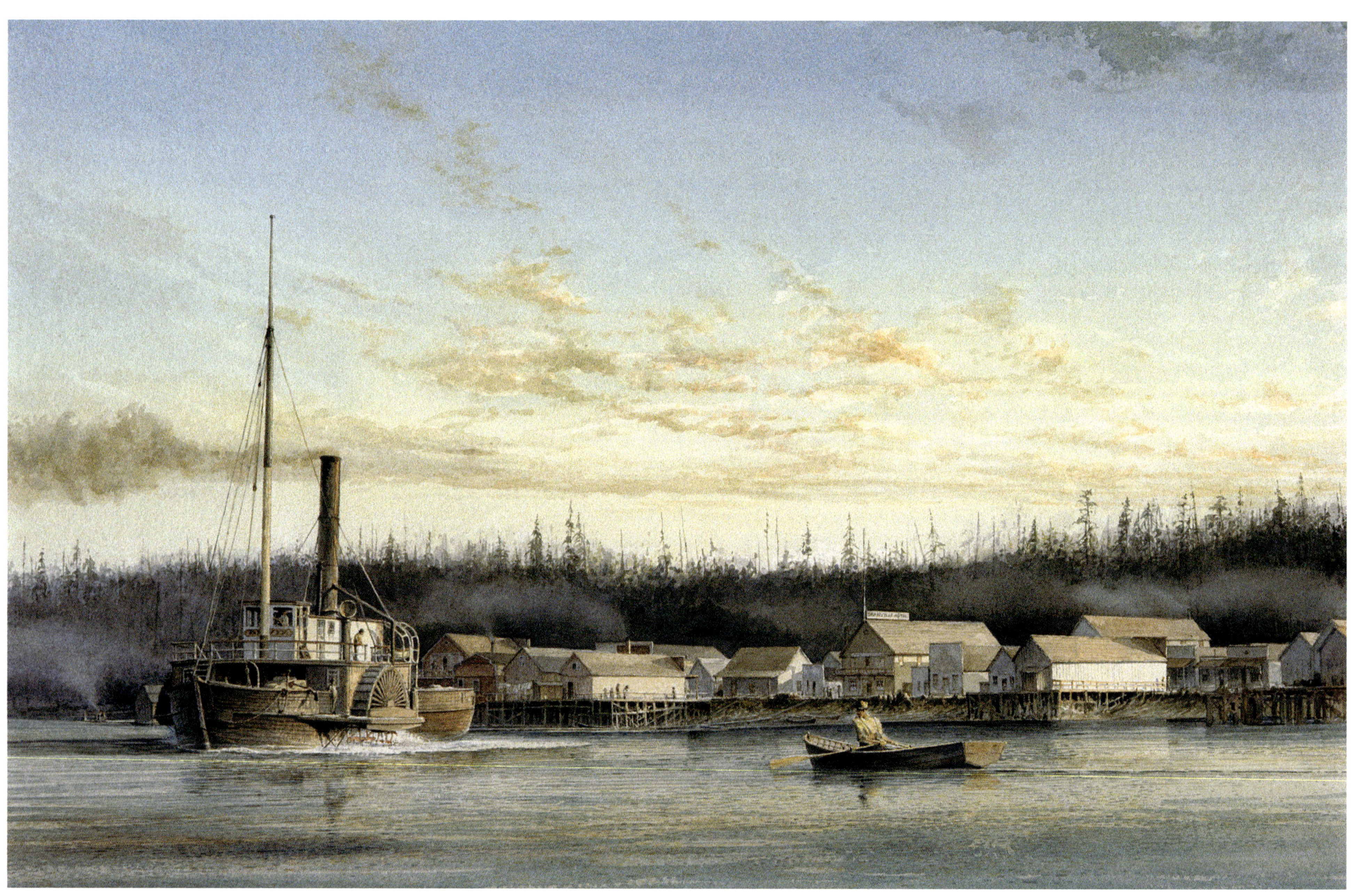

James Douglas resigned from the Hudson's Bay Company to become governor of the new colony of British Columbia.

Gold fever drew thousands of miners, miners drew entrepreneurs to supply them, the Royal Navy began to keep a permanent presence on the Pacific Station and the Royal Engineers arrived to keep order, survey townsites and build roads. In a single year, life on the coast changed dramatically and forever.

Fur had brought the first outsiders to the Pacific coast, and gold began the first invasion, but timber brought the settlers. In the bays of Puget Sound and the Inside Passage, the slopes were covered with magnificent old-growth trees, easily reached from the beaches, and there was a ready local market for lumber in New Westminster, Victoria and the gold mines in the interior. The first mill on Vancouver's Burrard Inlet was built on the north shore in 1862. Until well into the twentieth century, lumber was shipped from British Columbia in mostly square-rigged, engineless sailing vessels. As production increased and the mills in Burrard Inlet began exporting lumber to the Pacific Rim, there was an early and obvious need for tugs to tow the ships out to sea. *Beaver,* her rig cut back, was sometimes available and continued to make the occasional tow, but there was an increasing need for tugs built for the trade.

The first tug built in British Columbia, a huge side-wheel steamer named *Isabel,* went into service in 1866.

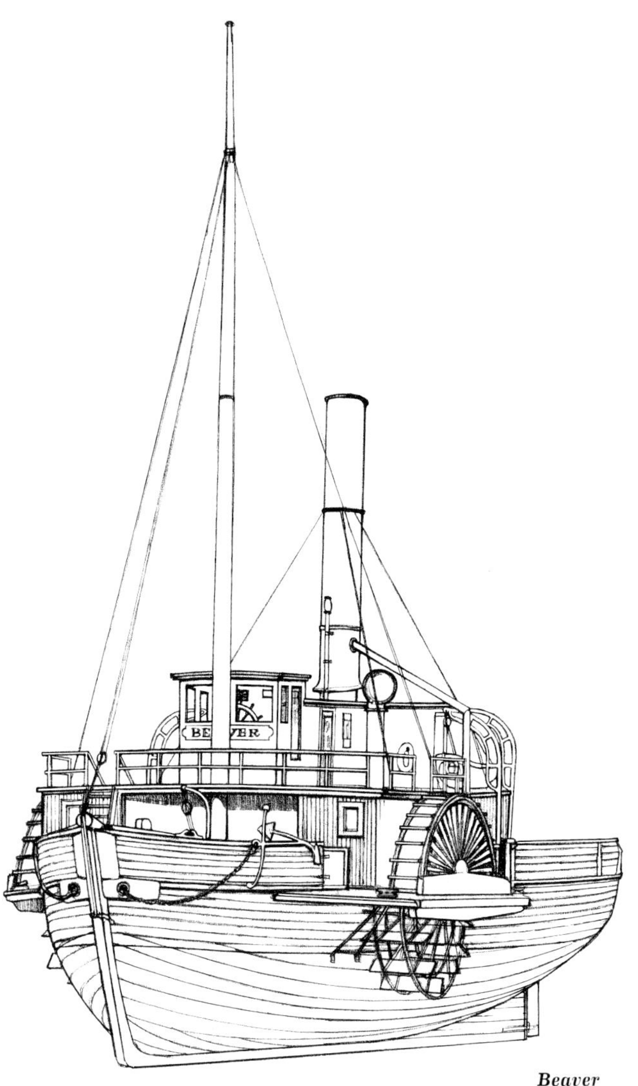

Beaver

One of the first propeller-driven tugs, *Etta White,* was purchased in 1876 by the Moodyville mill. These two handled most of the towing during the 1870s. Steamers, both passenger and freight, gradually replaced sail, until a true commercial sailing ship was a rarity.

<< ***Beaver* off Gastown, early Vancouver City** (WC, 15″ × 22″)
At the end of Beaver's *long career, there would have been almost no hint left of the graceful brigantine that had slid off the ways fifty-three years earlier; her rig was cut back and deck houses were added. She was finally sold by the Hudson's Bay Company in 1874 and converted to a tug. Under various owners she remained in this capacity until she went aground in fog at the entrance to Vancouver Harbour on July 25, 1888. Some say the fog may not have all been external.* Beaver's *entire crew had just left one of Gastown's saloons.*

< Beaver *as she would have looked in her last years as a tug.*

***Thermopylae* in Juan de Fuca Strait, June 24, 1891** (WC, 11″ × 15″)
Thermopylae *was the only true clipper to call British Columbia home. Designed for the China tea trade, she was launched in Aberdeen, Scotland, in 1868. She was nearly identical in size to her more famous rival,* Cutty Sark, *which was launched the year after. Victoria, British Columbia, was her port of registry from 1891 to 1896, when she was sold to the Portuguese navy for use as a sail training ship and renamed* Pedro Nuñes. *Hard use had worn her out, and in 1897 she was paid off from the navy, stripped of her gear and converted to a coal hulk. At the end of her useful life the Portuguese, in honor of her illustrious history, gave her a royal burial at sea. On October 13, 1907, she was towed out of the Tagus River by two warships and torpedoed while the Queen of Portugal looked on.*

***Gjøa* and *Charles Hansson* in the Northwest Passage** (WC, 15″ × 22″)
The Northwest Passage was finally conquered by a ship in 1906, when Norwegian explorer Roald Amundsen arrived at Bering Strait after a three-year westward passage from Lancaster Sound. On August 27, 1905, just after turning in at eight in the morning, Amundsen was awakened by a commotion on deck. An officer rushed into the cabin and called out: "Vessel in sight, sir!" Amundsen recalled, "The words were magical . . . It was a wonderfully fine day . . . with the wind abaft, and all sails set, we made excellent headway. It seemed as if the Gjøa *had understood that the hardest part of the struggle was over, she seemed wonderfully light in her movements."* Gjøa *had encountered* Charles Hansson, *a whaler out of San Francisco that had entered the strait from the west. The meeting of the two vessels, coming from opposite directions, marked the conquering of the Northwest Passage.*

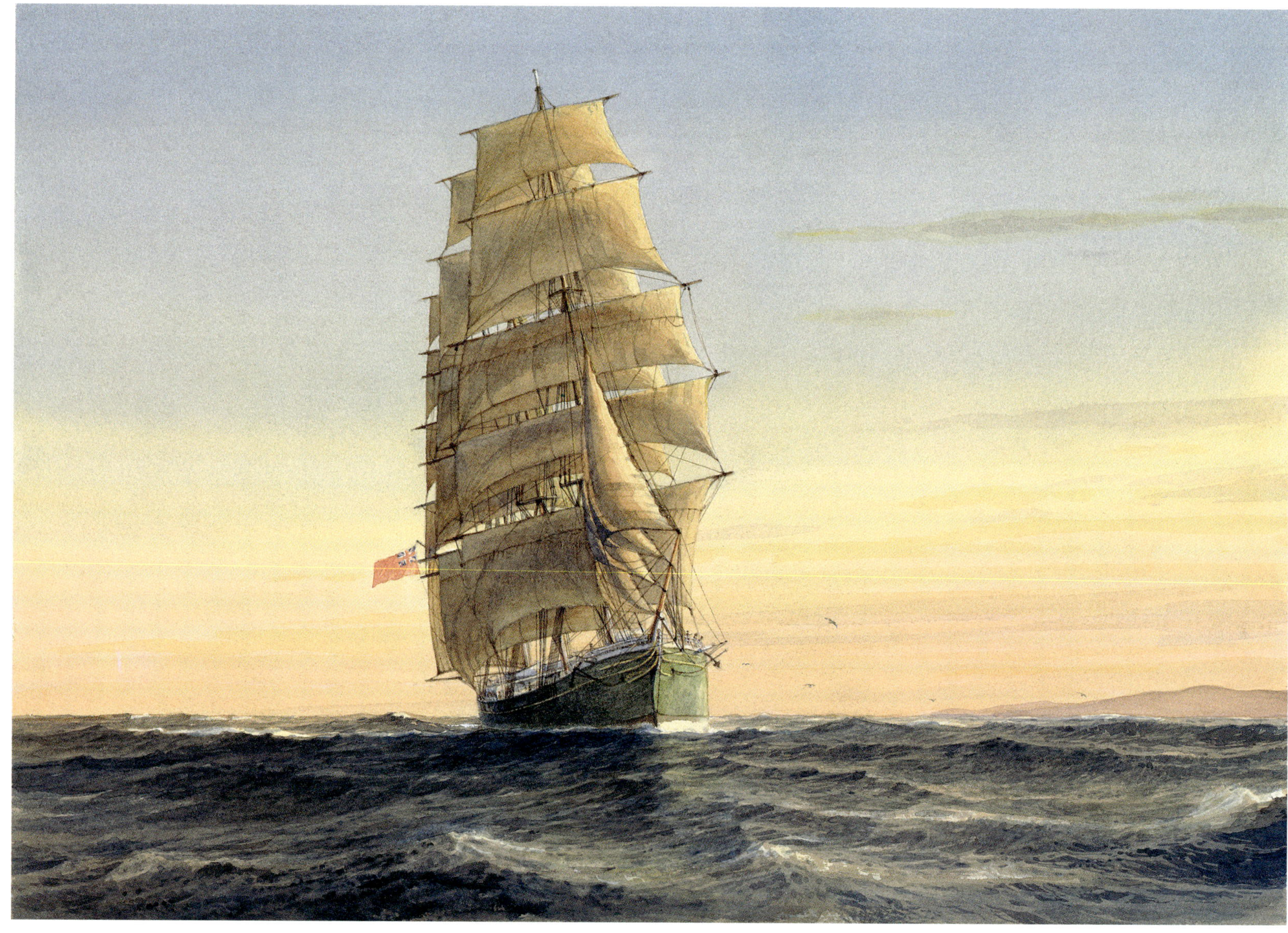

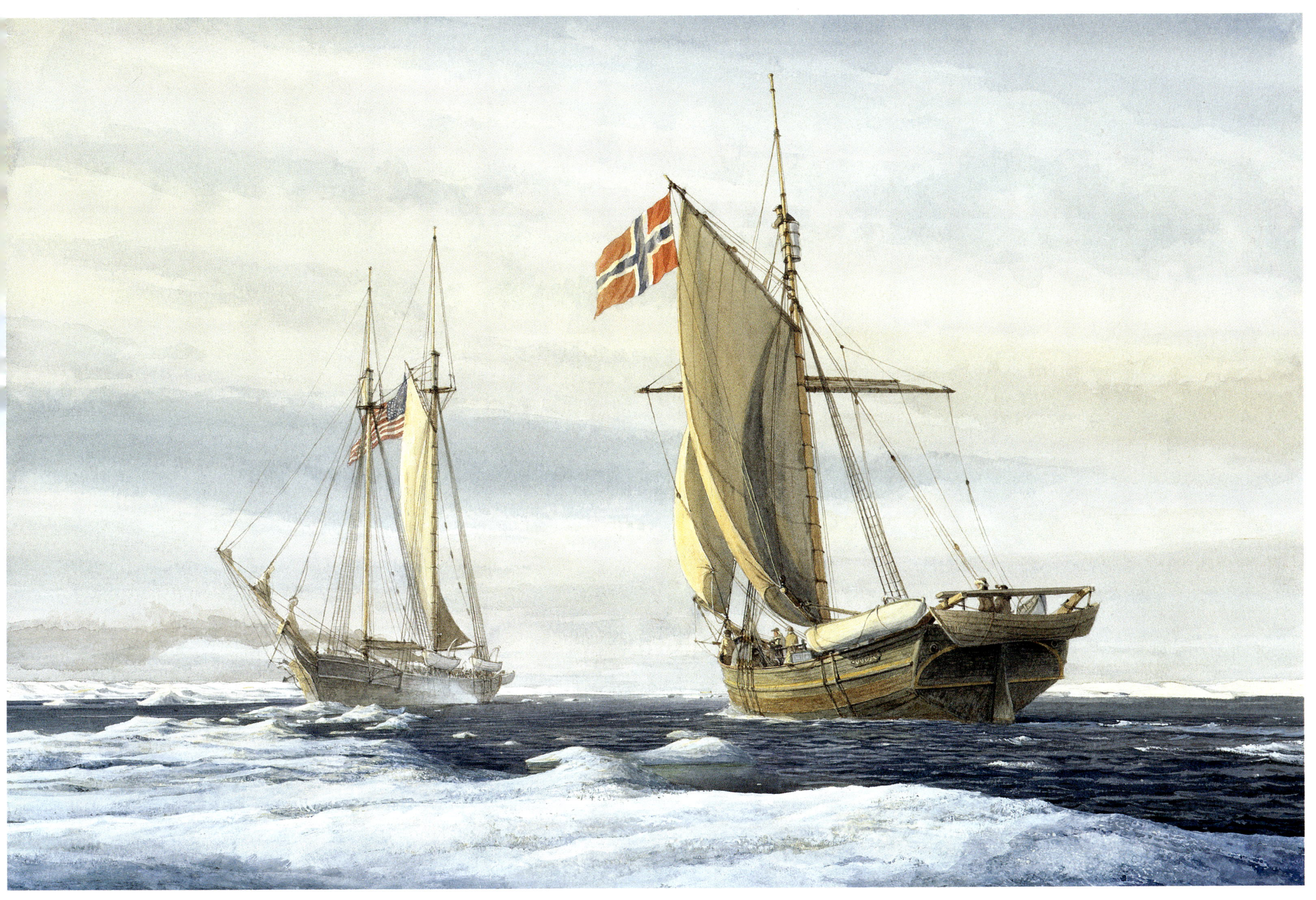

EPILOGUE:
SAILING INTO HISTORY

WHEN SS *BEAVER*'S boiler was fired and her paddles stirred the waters of the Columbia River on the morning of May 11, 1836, it was the first time a steam-powered vessel operated in the Pacific Northwest. Although the event signaled the beginning of the end of sail on this coast, it would take another 110 years for steam to completely replace wind-driven ships.

On August 5, 1946, when *Snohomish* towed *Pamir* out of Juan de Fuca Strait, she was taking part in another significant event. *Pamir* was the last ship to make a commercial voyage to those waters under sail alone. She was one of the last Cape Horners—big, strong bulk carriers designed to survive the storms of the southern ocean and compete with the steamers that were taking over the high-value commodity routes.

Pamir carried three cargoes from British Columbia after the war. After she left the last time her profitability continually declined, and she passed through several owners. Her last owners fitted *Pamir* with an engine, which old-timers predicted would be the death of her. They may have been right. In September 1957, homeward bound for Germany from the Rio de la Plata, she went down in an Atlantic hurricane with the loss of all but six of her eighty-six crew. New openings made in her deck for the engines may have been one of the factors contributing to her foundering.

Pamir's last visit to the Northwest Coast was in 1946. When she dropped her tow off the state of Washington's Cape Flattery on August 5 it was the last time she would be seen in those waters, and it marked the end of the true commercial sailing ship era on British Columbia's coast. Sailing ships still visit, but they are almost all training ships or replicas; all have auxiliary engines for propulsion and are sad reminders of another era.

Until well into the twentieth century commercial sail struggled in the losing battle to compete against steamships. The world fleets were reduced to a few barques carrying softwood from the Baltic to England and the West Indies, and the big bulk carriers in the Australian grain trade. All that are left are rusting hulks or museum exhibits; none go to sea. When *Pamir* left British Columbia's waters for the last time, she was truly sailing into history.

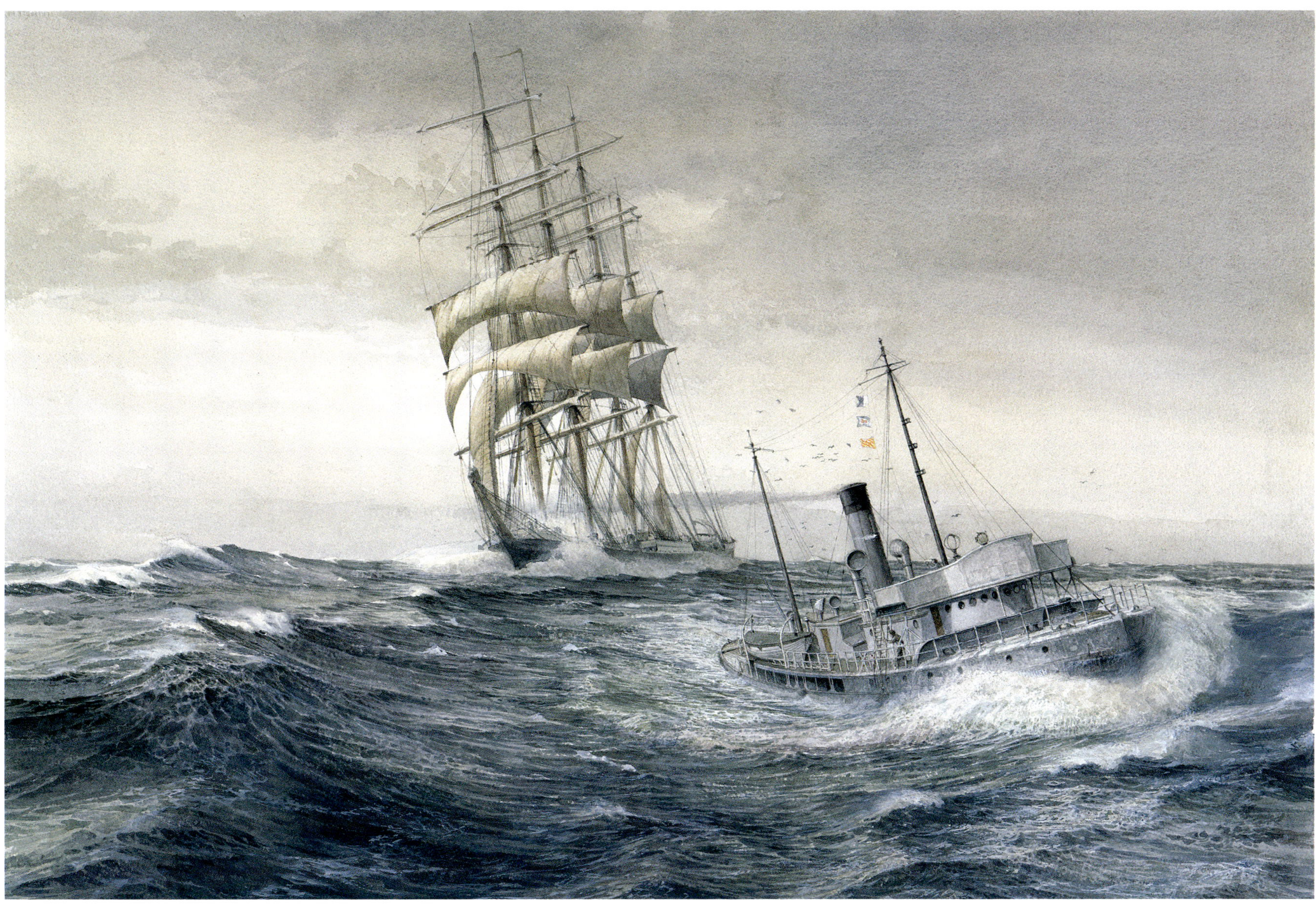

Pamir and _Snohomish_ (WC, 22″ × 30″) *On January 5, 1946, at eight in the morning,* Pamir *took a line from the tug* Snohomish *for the tow out to Cape Flattery. They entered Juan de Fuca Strait in fine weather, but shortly after midnight the glass began to fall, and by daylight a strong gale was blowing from the east. To be safe they decided to set some sail to help prevent being blown onto a lee shore. With sail on her* Pamir *began overtaking the tug, and as the wire was still attached there was a real danger of pulling* Snohomish *under. The big ship was well up to the tug's quarter by the time they let the line go.* Pamir *charged up, heeled over in huge seas, gradually adding sail as she swept by.* Snohomish *tried to signal, but in the extreme conditions the three-flag hoist which should have been "*WAY*" for "Bon Voyage," instead went up as "*AWY*." She was rolling heavily in the big seas, taking water over the wheel house. On board* Pamir, *observers described their last view of* Snohomish *"steaming away for Juan de Fuca—a fuss of white at his whistle and the international code signal streaming in the gale."*

APPENDIX: PLANS OF HISTORICAL VESSELS

THERE HAVE BEEN a lot of excellent references published recently on ship design from the seventeenth century onwards, but before that period it is not possible to be absolutely certain of the accuracy of any representation. The earliest ships were built without plans by master shipwrights, based on their years of practice and experience. The only visual reference often appears as decorations on old maps or journals, on crests or town seals, or in fanciful illustrations.

For the sake of accuracy I prefer to work from plans when developing the paintings. Reproduced here are a few of the significant vessels illustrated in this book. Where they exist they are copied from actual plans or from recent research by historians and naval architects. The rest I developed from known dimensions using the formulas followed by shipwrights of the period.

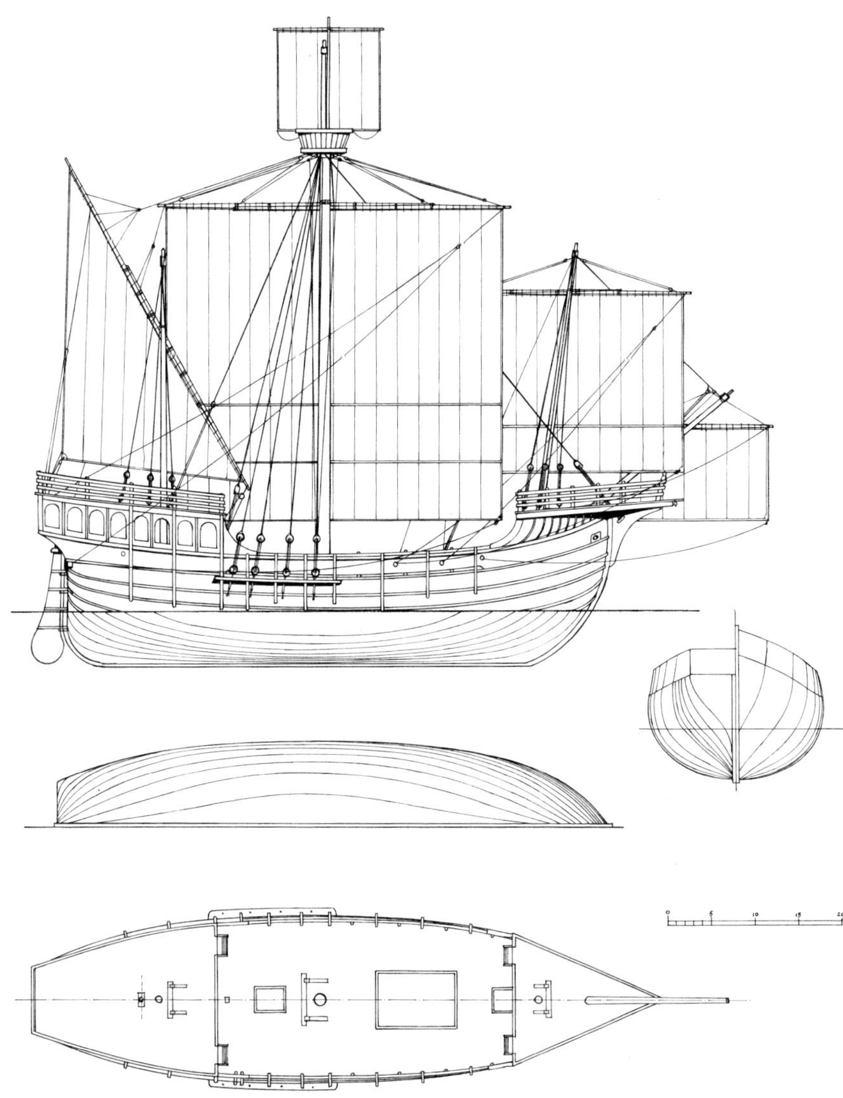

John Cabot's *Matthew*
Based on plans for a replica by Colin Mudie

Sparred length	83 ft., 0 in.
Structural length	73 ft., 0 in.
Hull length	63 ft., 0 in.
Beam	20 ft., 6 in.
Draft	6 ft., 0 in.

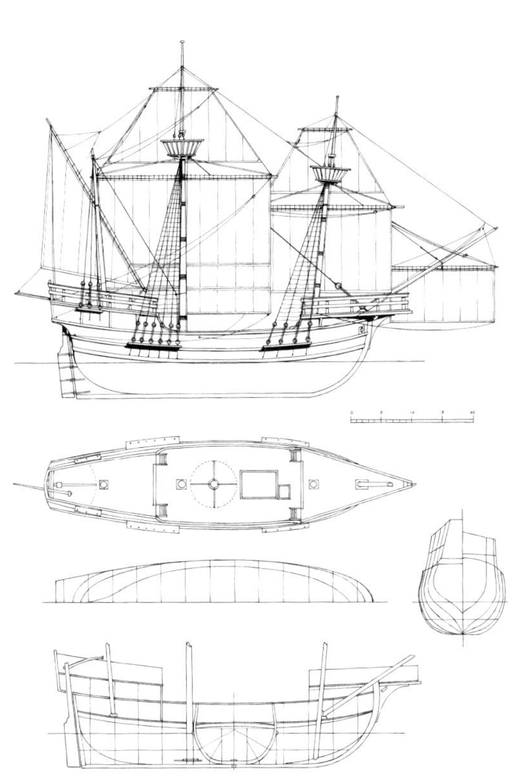

Gabriel
Frobisher expedition, 1576, 1577 and 1578

Length	49 ft., 0 in.
Beam	13 ft., 6 in.
Depth of hold	6 ft., 0 in.
Length of keel	37 ft., 0 in.
Displacement	29.97 tons

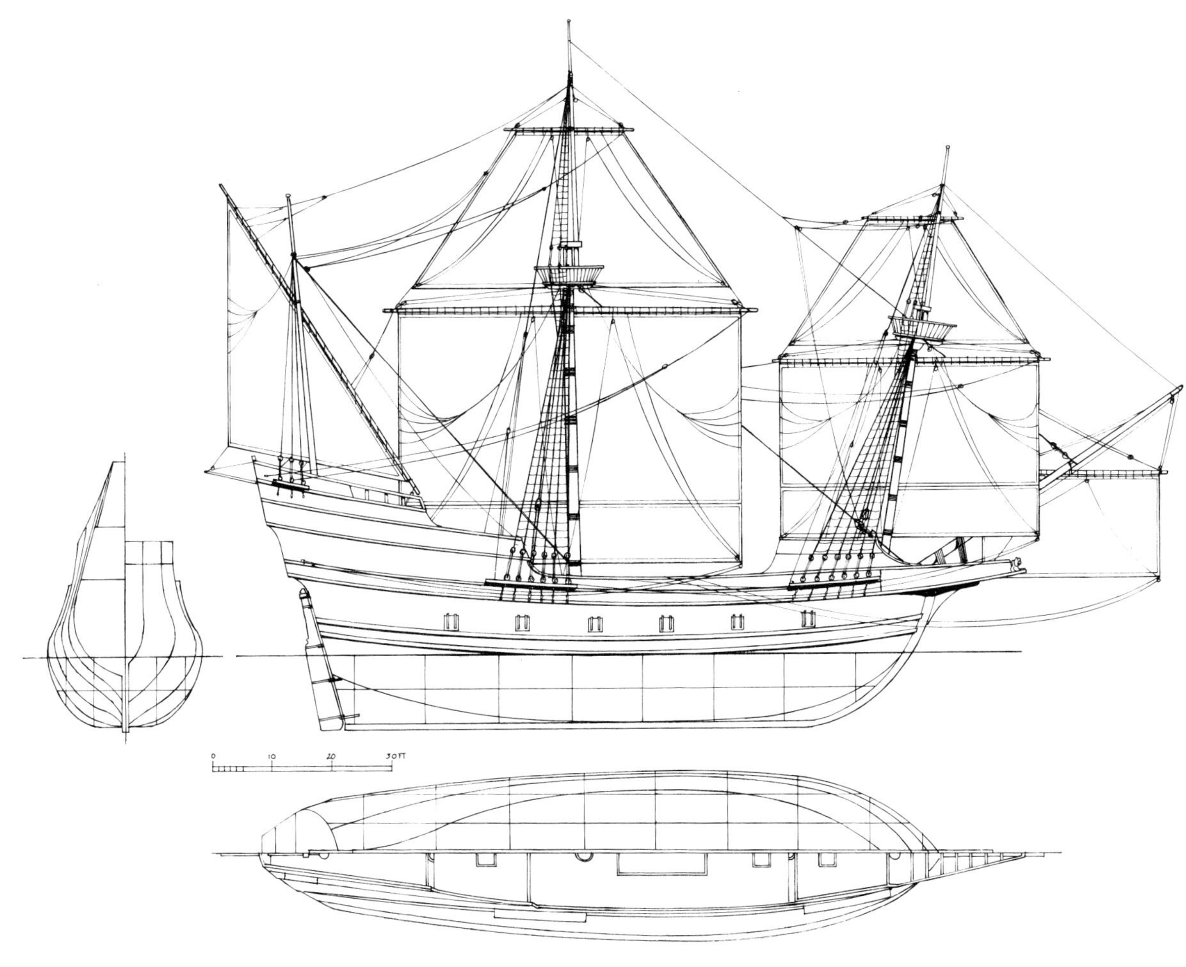

Ayde
Frobisher expedition, 1577 and 1578

Length	104 ft., 0 in.
Beam	25 ft., 6 in.
Depth of hold	12 ft., 0 in.
Length of keel	73 ft., 0 in.
Displacement	223.38 tons

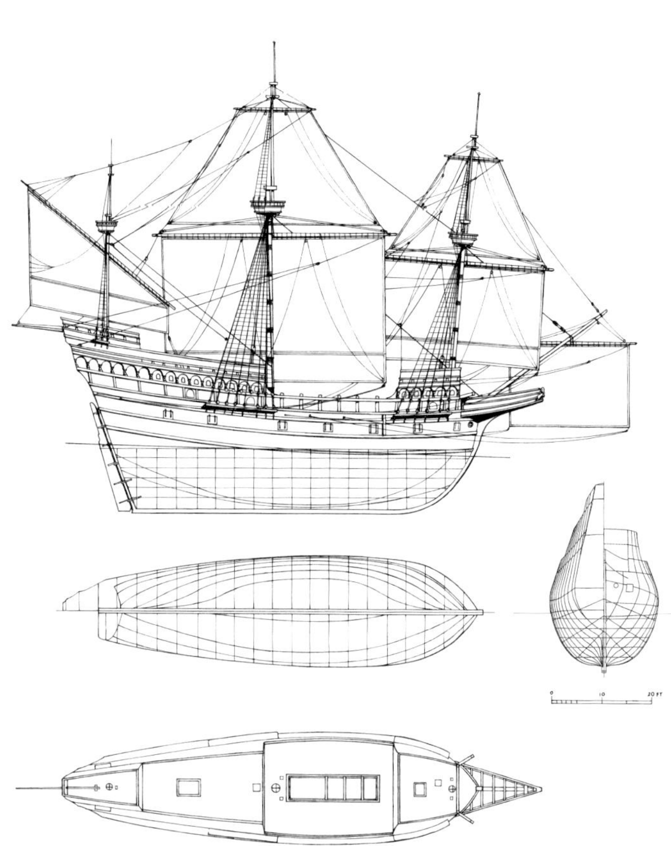

Francis Drake's *Golden Hind*
From drawings by Raymond Aker

Length of hull	85 ft., 0 in.
Beam	23 ft., 0 in.
Length of keel	56 ft., 0 in.
Depth of hold	10 ft., 0 in.
Draft	12 ft., 6 in.

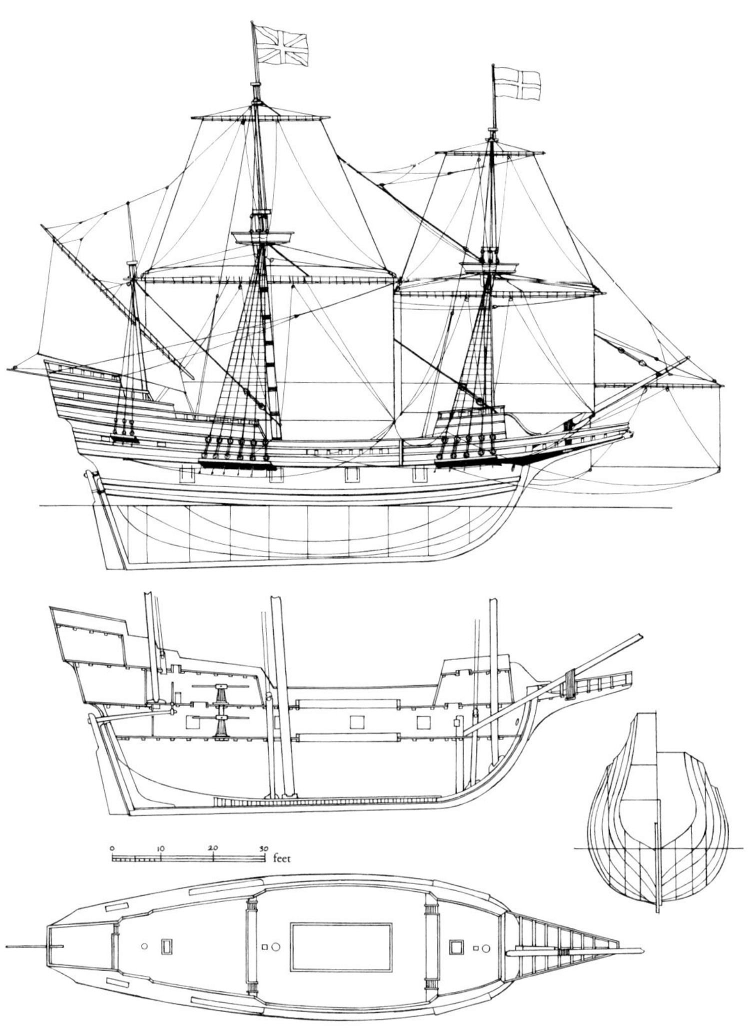

***Mayflower* of London**
Vessel charted to transport Pilgrims to North America in 1620

Length between perpendiculars	82 ft., 0 in.
Beam	28 ft., 0 in.
Length of keel	64 ft., 0 in.
Depth of hold	11 ft., 0 in.
Draft	12 ft., 0 in.

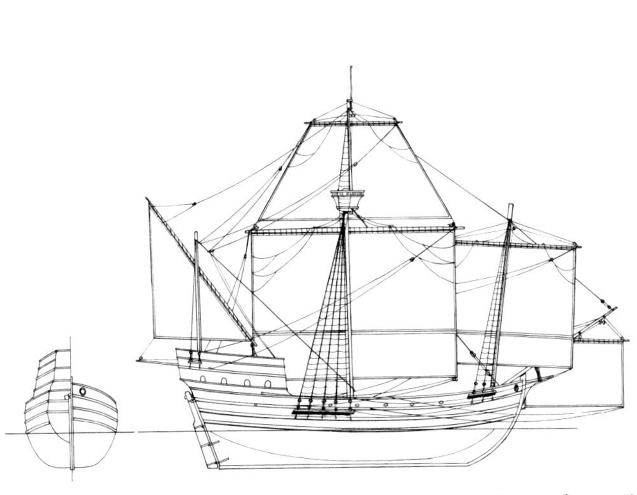

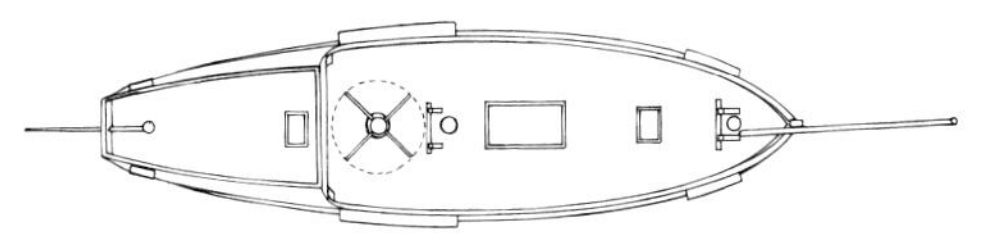

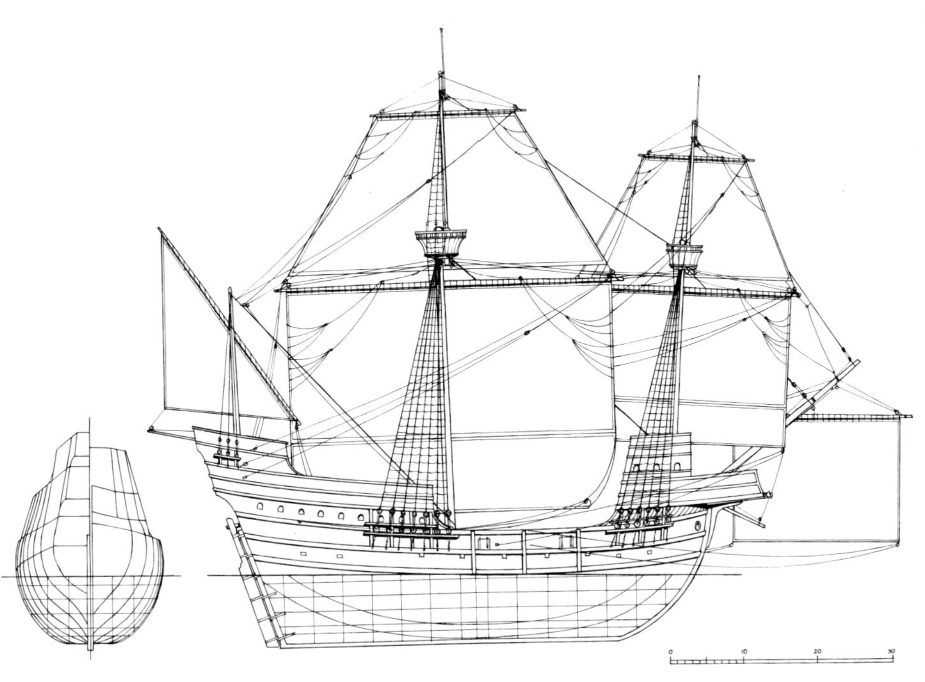

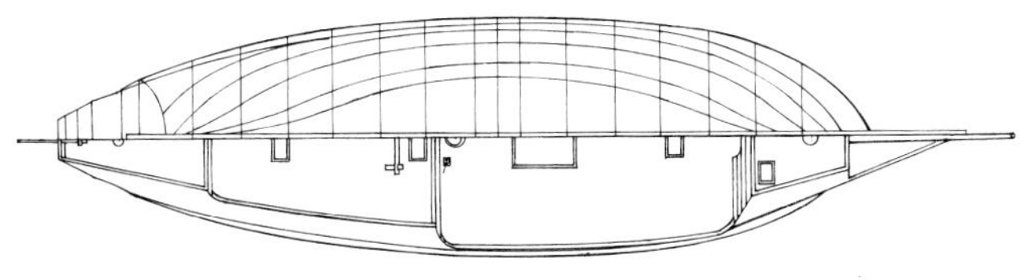

Ships of Cabrillo's 1542 voyage of exploration
From plans drawn by Raymond Aker

Victoria

Length on deck	48 ft., 11 in.
Beam	14 ft., 1.5 in.
Depth of hold	6 ft., 1.5 in.
Displacement	32.6 tons

San Salvador

Length on deck	62 ft., 1.5 in.
Beam	20 ft., 8.5 in.
Depth of hold	10 ft., 4.2 in.
Displacement	118.5 tons

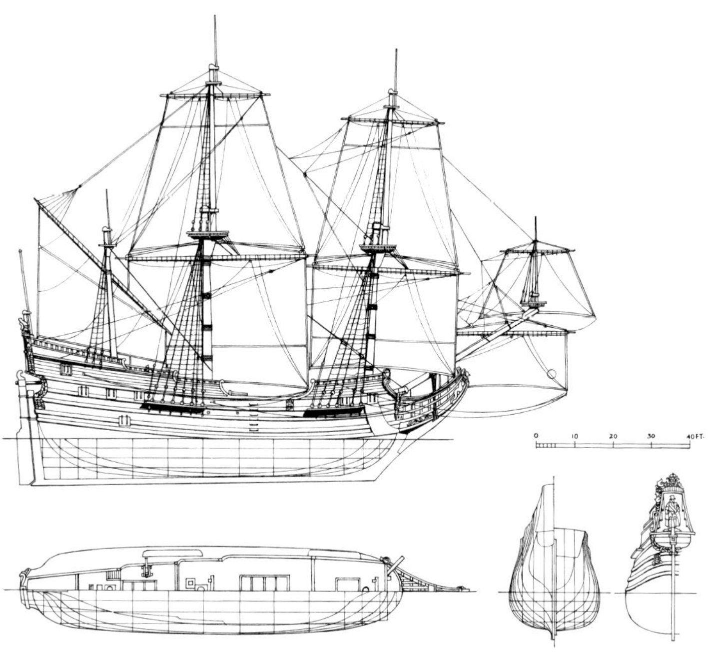

17th century flute

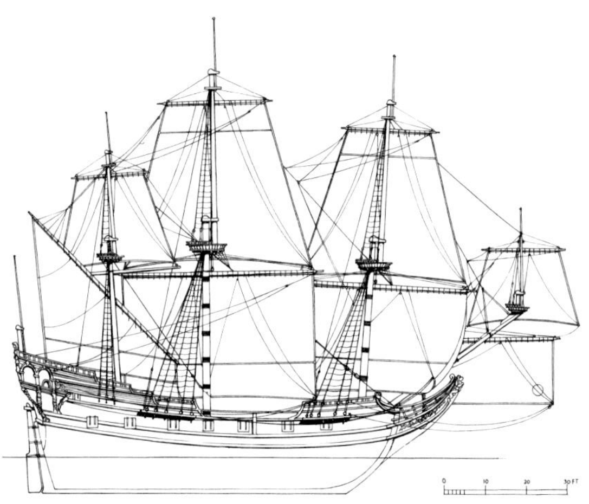

17th century Dutch pinnace

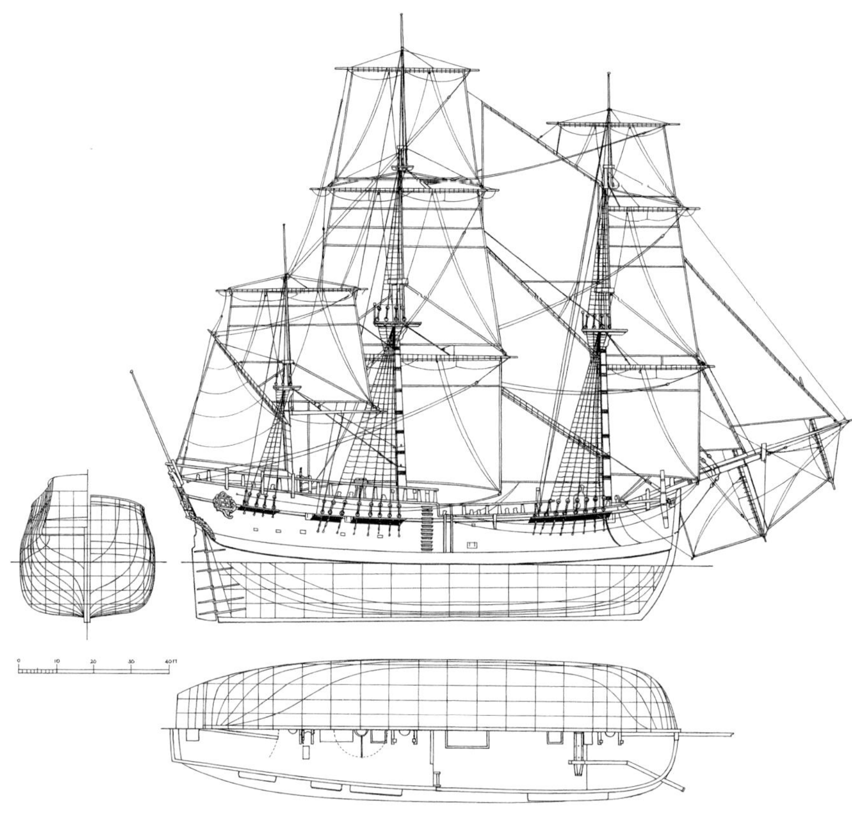

HMS *Endeavour*

Cook's ship on the 1768–71 voyage

Length overall	106 ft., 0 in.
Beam	29 ft., 3 in.
Length of keel	81 ft., 0 in.
Depth of hold	11 ft., 4 in.
Draft	14 ft., 0 in.
Displacement	368 tons

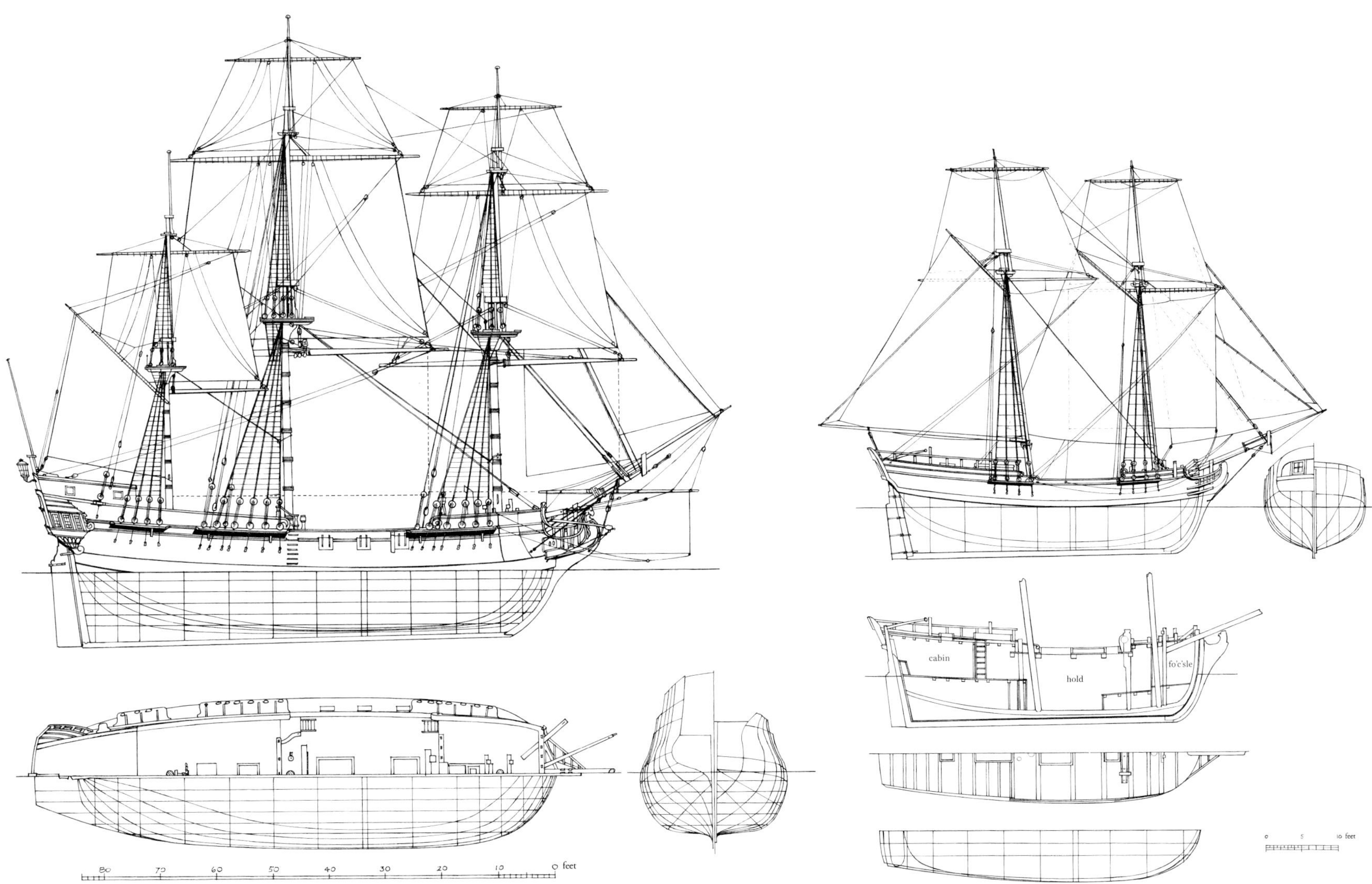

Spanish exploration and mission supply vessels built at San Blas

Santiago

Based on drawings by Hewitt R. Jackson

Length on deck 84 ft., 10 in.
Length of keel 77 ft., 2 in.
Depth of hold 11 ft., 7 in.
Beam 26 ft., 11 in.
Displacement 120.5 tons

Sonora II

Length on deck 45 ft., 9 in.
Length of keel 37 ft., 0 in.
Depth of hold 7 ft., 6 in.
Beam 14 ft., 0 in.
Displacement 59 tons

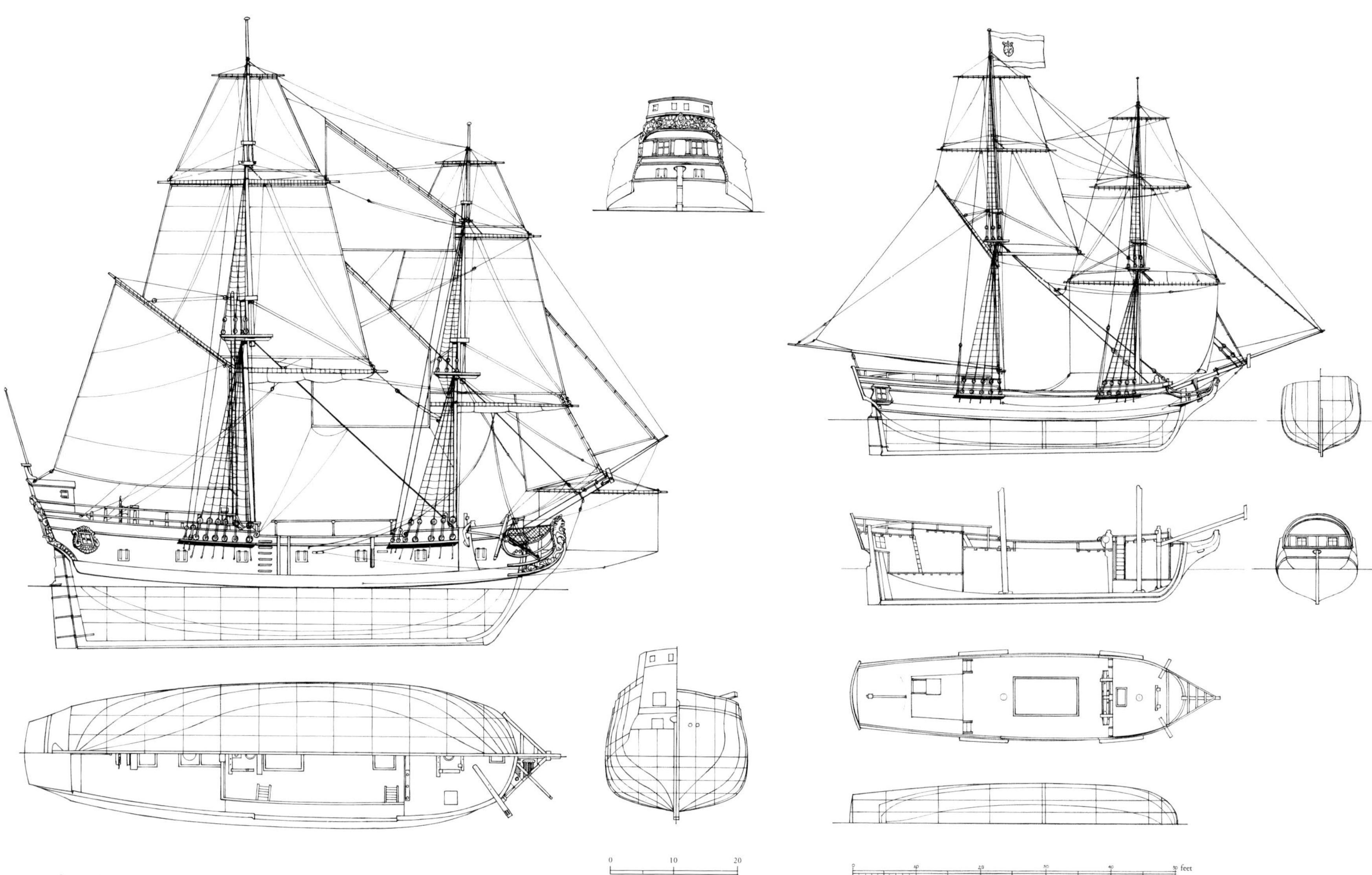

Spanish exploration vessels

San Carlos

Based on drawings by Raymond Aker

Length	79 ft., 2.25 in.
Beam	22 ft., 7.5 in.
Length of keel	64 ft., 1.25 in.
Depth of hold	10 ft., 4.375 in.
Displacement	190 tons

Sutil* and *Mexicana

(Sail plan of *Sutil*)

Length between perpendiculars	46 ft., 2 in.
Beam	12 ft., 8 in.
Length of keel	43 ft., 0 in.
Depth of hold	7 ft., 10 in.
Displacement	46.6 tons

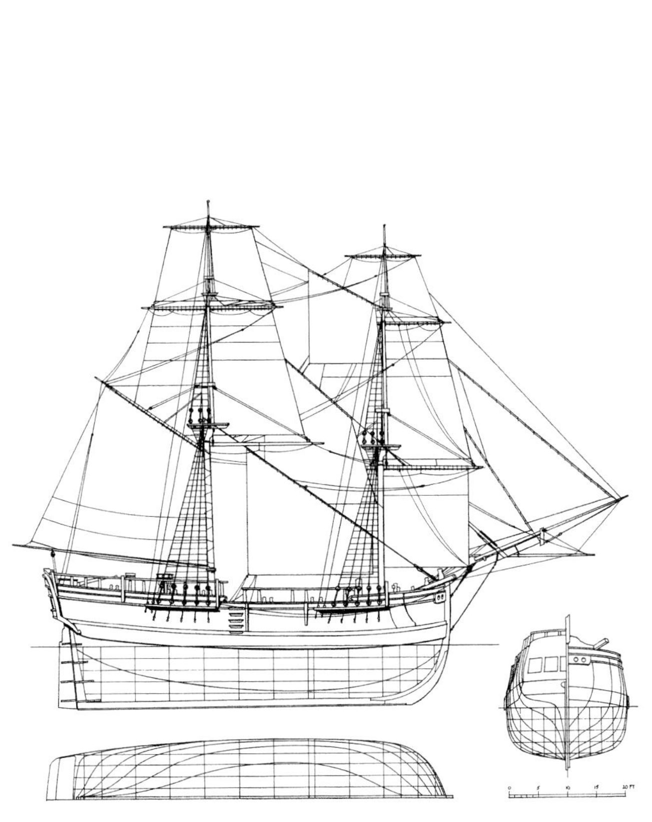

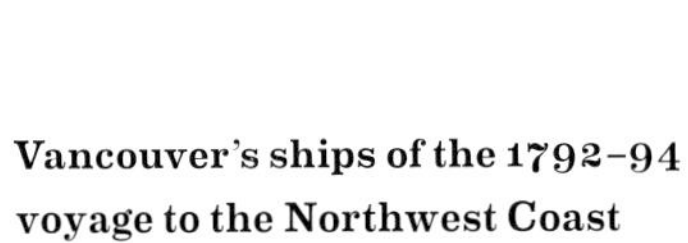

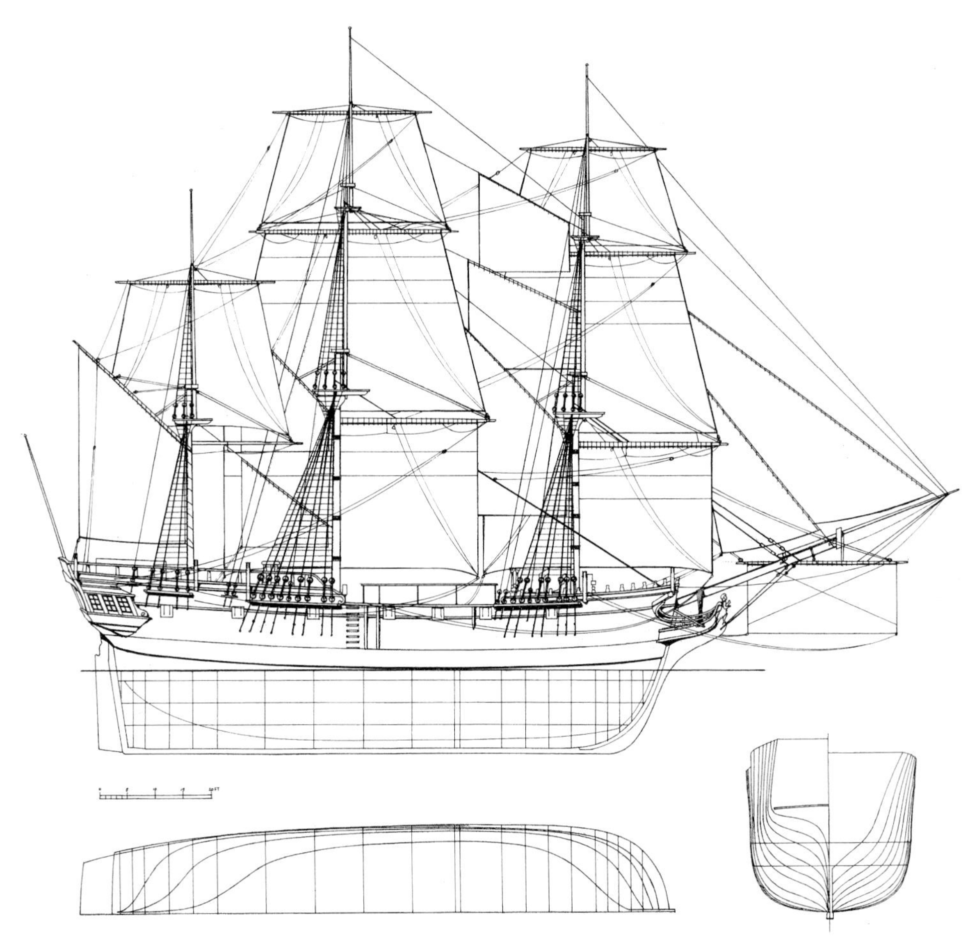

Vancouver's ships of the 1792–94 voyage to the Northwest Coast

HMS *Chatham*

Length between perpendiculars	67 ft., 5 in.
Beam	21 ft., 2 in.
Depth of hold	10 ft., 2 in.
Draft	12 ft., 3 in.
Displacement	117 tons

HMS *Discovery*

Extreme length	99 ft., 2 in.
Length of keel	77 ft., 8.625 in.
Beam	28 ft., 3.25 in.
Depth of hold	12 ft., 4 in.
Displacement	330.691 tons

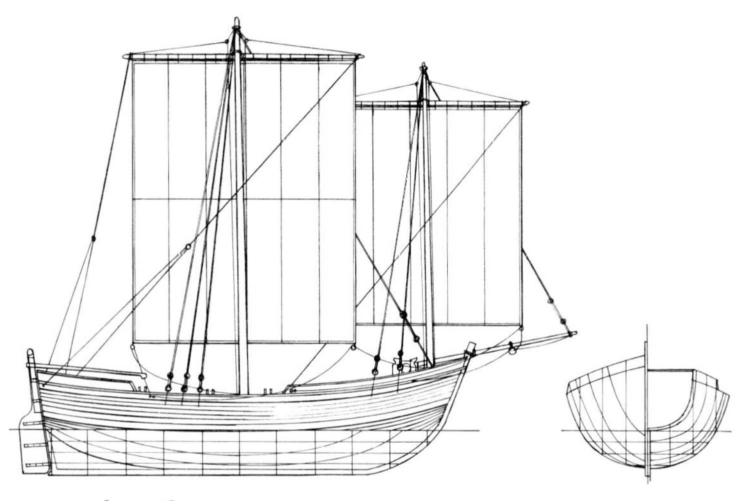

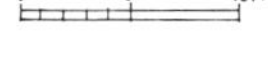

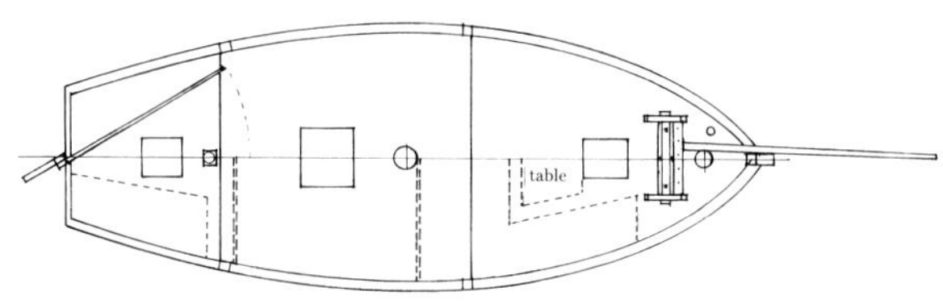

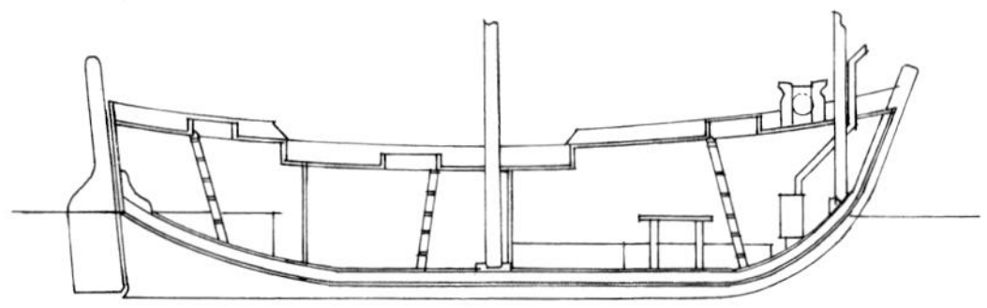

18th century Pomor *kotch*
Vessel of Russian sea mammal hunters

Length	39 ft., 4 in.
Beam	14 ft., 9 in.
Draft	4 ft., 0 in.

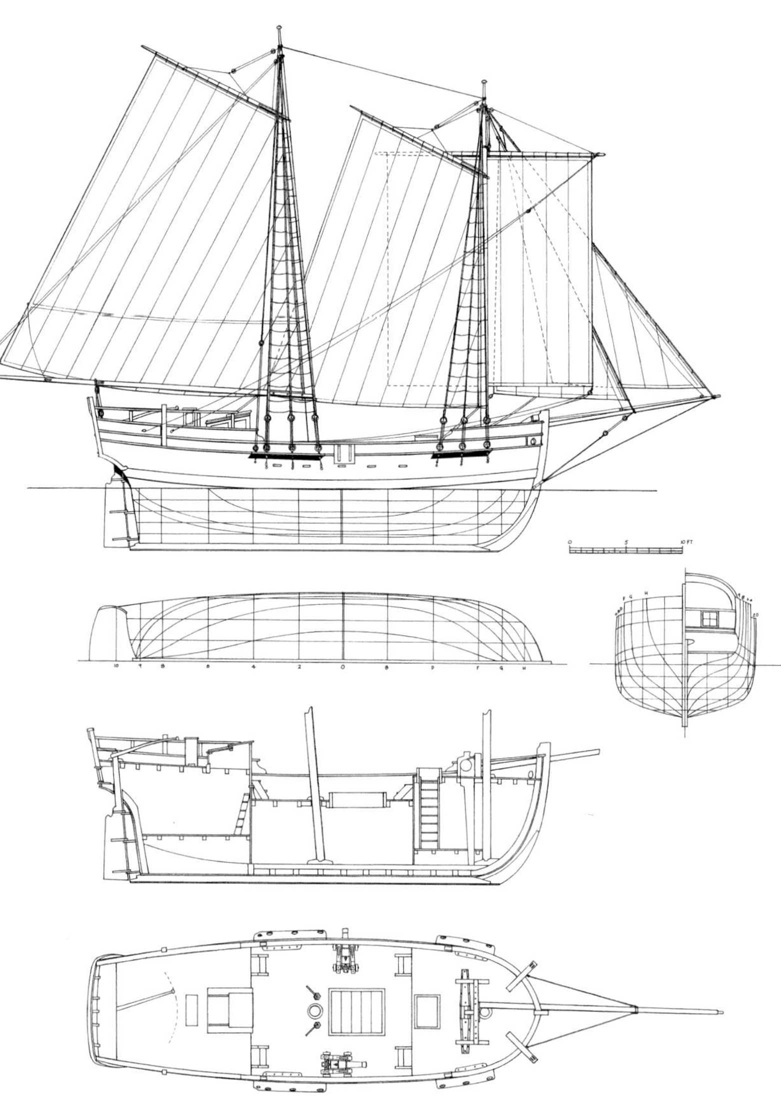

Santa Saturnina
1791 Spanish exploration vessel
Dimensions from 1793 San Blas manifest

Length between perpendiculars	35 ft., 6.75 in.
Length of keel	31 ft., 11 in.
Beam	12 ft., 4.75 in.
Depth of hold	5 ft., 9.75 in.
Draft	5 ft., 5.75 in.
Dispacement	34.75 tons

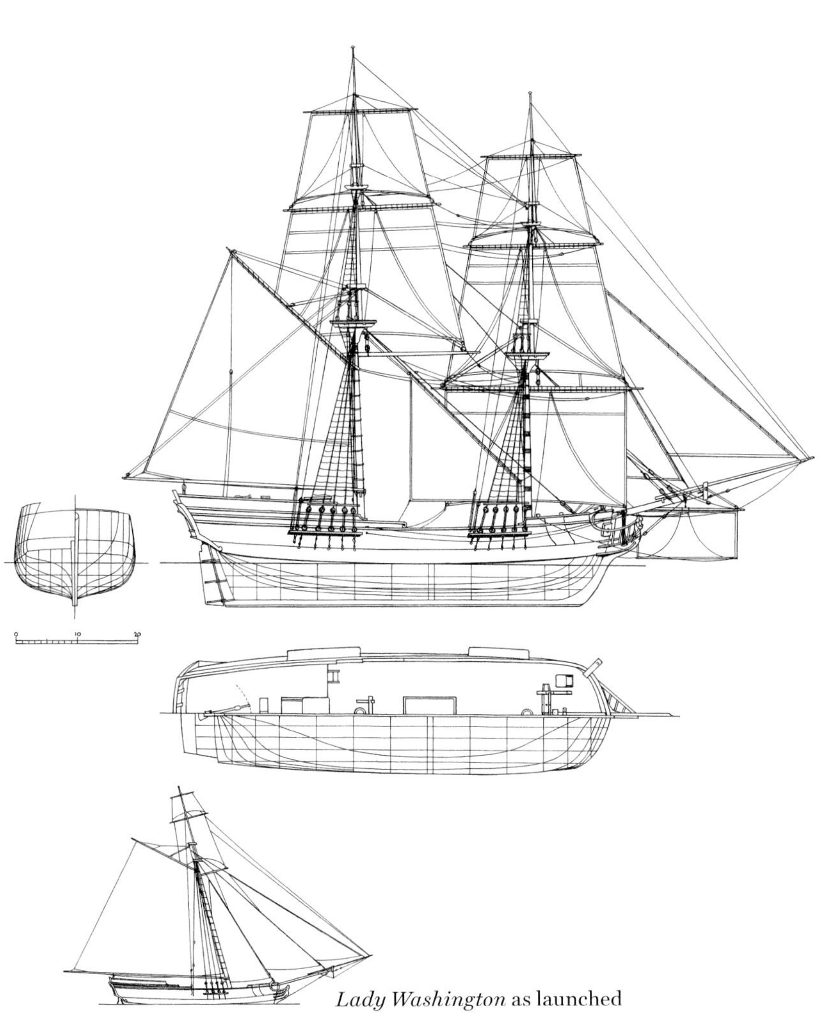

Lady Washington as launched

Ships of the first American trading venture to the Northwest Coast

***Lady Washington*, Boston**
as a brig in 1792

Length between perpendiculars	65 ft., 0 in.
Length on dock	72 ft., 6 in.
Depth of hold	9 ft., 0 in.
Beam	22 ft., 0 in.
Displacement	90 tons

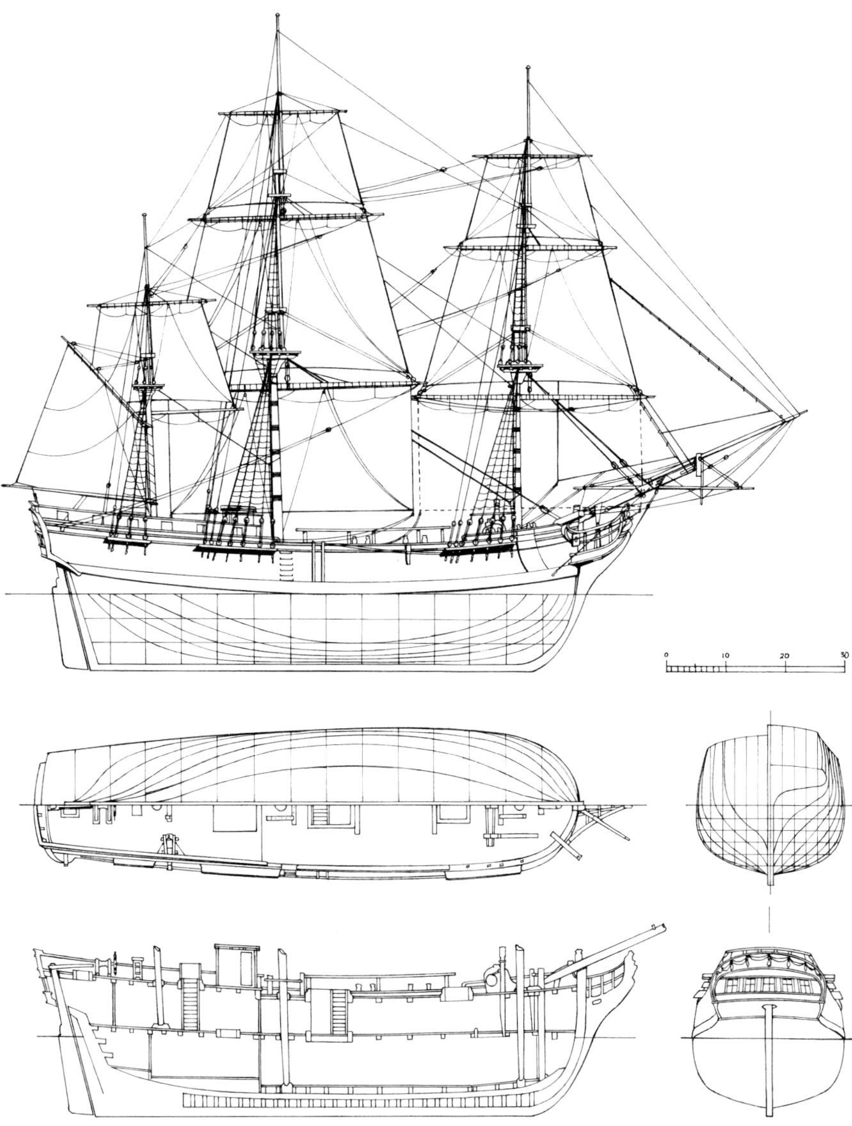

***Columbia Rediviva*, Boston**

Length between perpendiculars	85 ft., 6 in.
Length on dock	90 ft., 6 in.
Depth of hold	18 ft., 0 in.
Beam	24 ft., 6 in.
Displacement	212 tons

ACKNOWLEDGMENTS

THE INFORMATION contained in the paintings is based on the research of many scholars, most of whom I have never met, but to whom I owe a great debt of gratitude. Early in the project, when my ignorance was daunting, I was lucky to be encouraged by Hewitt Jackson, a knowledgeable and accomplished Seattle historian and maritime artist. He was very generous with the excellent and detailed plans he had produced, and diplomatic and helpful with his criticism. Later I had the good fortune to know Raymond Aker, who gave generously of his time and knowledge, and provided me with plans and copious notes of the vessels he was researching. Ray was also wonderfully tactful and helpful with his criticisms. Unfortunately, neither of these two mentors lived to see the results of their support.

For the pure enjoyment of arguing over details, I have to thank the late John Crosse, my neighbor and historian, who spent many hours in my studio challenging my assumptions, and provided even more incentive to get the facts right.

I gratefully acknowledge the generosity and support of Robin Inglis, past director of the Vancouver Maritime Museum and North Vancouver Museum and Archives; and James P. Delgado, Director of Maritime Heritage, Office of National Marine Sanctuaries, National Oceanic and Atmospheric Administration, Washington, D.C., who, as well as providing enormous assistance, suggested the idea for this book in the first place and introduced me to the publisher, and is therefore partly responsible for it. And for over thirty years, Leonard McCann, curator emeritus of the Vancouver Maritime Museum, has been the first person I have turned to for direction on local maritime history.

To the following I wish to express my thanks for help and encouragement: the librarians and volunteers of the Vancouver Maritime Museum; Robert Allen in California; Nancy Angermeyer and Richard Blagborne on Saturna Island; Captain Ron Campbell, Fisheries and Oceans Canada; Kim Davies; John Harland; Leo Hershkowitz, Professor of History, Queens College, City University of New York; Joep de Koning; Maxim Laikine; Andrei Larionov, Central Naval Museum, St.Petersburg; Michael Layland; Antonia Macarthur; Dr. George MacDonald; John McKay; Bill McLennan; Ernie Mangulins; Steve Mayo; J.E. (Ted) Roberts; Ross Shardlow; Geoff Stewart; Andrei Taberev; Richard Unger; Edward Von der Porten; and John Weir.

Finally, and most importantly, my thanks to Dale. Her contribution to this book has been immense, and her years of dedication have allowed me to have all the fun.